Nov. 1   Announcement of agreement on U.S.
          Polaris submarine base in Scotland

                                                                    of U.S.A.
                                                        ions with
                                                Cuba

1961

March 8–17   Commonwealth Prime Ministers'
             Meeting

March 24–April 12   Macmillan visits West Indies,
             U.S.A. and Canada, meeting Kennedy
             for the first time

                                          April 12   Gagarin (U.S.S.R.) first man in
                                                      space

                                          April 17–20   Unsuccessful attempt to
                                                      overthrow Castro in Cuba

April 27   Sierra Leone independent

                                          May 5   Shepard (U.S.A.) second man in space

May 31   South Africa leaves the Commonwealth

June 1   Northern Cameroons joins Federation
          of Nigeria

                                          July 1   British troops to Kuwait,
                                                    threatened by Iraq

July 25   Chancellor introduces 'Little Budget'
           and wage pause

                                          Aug. 10   U.K. applies to join E.E.C.

                                          Aug. 13   East Germany seals border with West

                                          Sept. 1   U.S.S.R. resumes nuclear bomb tests
                                                     in atmosphere

                                          Sept. 13–21   U.N. forces invade Katanga

                                          Sept. 15   U.S.A. resumes underground
                                                      nuclear bomb tests

Sept. 19   Jamaica votes to leave Federation of
            West Indies

                                          Sept. 28   Syria secedes from United Arab
                                                      Republic

                                          Oct. 10   Last British troops leave Kuwait

                                          Dec. 5   U.N. launches full-scale attack on
                                                    Katanga

Dec. 9   Tanganyika independent

                                          Dec. 21   Agreement signed to end secession
                                                     of Katanga

EX LIBRIS

M. J. ANDREWS.
21.2.84.

POINTING THE WAY

WINDS OF CHANGE
1914–1939

THE BLAST OF WAR
1939–1945

TIDES OF FORTUNE
1945–1955

RIDING THE STORM
1956–1959

POINTING THE WAY
1959–1961

The General Election, 1959: re-elected at Bromley with an increased majority

POINTING THE WAY

1959–1961

HAROLD MACMILLAN

* * * * *

LONDON

MACMILLAN

MELBOURNE · TORONTO

1972

© Thomson Newspapers Limited 1972
All Rights Reserved
Index © Macmillan London Ltd 1972

First published 1972 by
MACMILLAN LONDON LTD
London and Basingstoke
Associated companies in New York Toronto
Dublin Melbourne Johannesburg and Madras

SBN 333 12411 1

Printed in Great Britain by
ROBERT MACLEHOSE AND CO LTD
The University Press, Glasgow

Contents

Appendixes

List of Illustrations

List of Cartoons

Reproduced by courtesy of the London Express News and Feature Services.

CHAPTER I

The General Election, 1959

O N 8 September, the day after my return from Balmoral,[1] the Cabinet assembled at 3 p.m. It was a short and formal meeting. I reported my request for an early dissolution and the Queen's assent. An announcement was immediately issued from No. 10, giving the date of the dissolution, 18 September, and of Polling Day, 8 October. In accordance with recent custom, I added a statement giving my reasons for having made this request of the Crown:

> The Parliament elected in May, 1955, is now in its fifth year. A General Election must therefore take place either this autumn or early next year.
> From the point of view of home affairs there is no reason why a General Election should not be held this autumn. But the date of the Election must also be considered and decided in the light of the world situation. Important international negotiations lie ahead. It is clearly right that the people should have the opportunity of deciding, as soon as practicable, who are to represent them in these negotiations.

This declaration at least made clear one of the main grounds on which my colleagues and I hoped to receive a new mandate from the electors. Knowing that Gaitskell, the Leader of the Opposition, was in Moscow, I sent a telegram immediately after the Cabinet informing him of the proposed dates, so that he could decide whether to continue or to curtail his visits to Moscow and Warsaw.

After the announcement I received many messages of good wishes from friends in every part of the world. Two gave me particular pleasure. The first was from Bob Menzies on 14 September,

---

[1] See *Riding the Storm*, p. 750.

thanking me for a long letter which I had written to him about Eisenhower's visit. He added:

> I notice from the Press that Brother Bert Evatt has publicly communicated his good wishes to Hugh Gaitskell; this should do Hugh a satisfactory degree of harm. I will not embarrass you by public communication, but you know precisely how I feel.

The second was from an old Conservative worker in Stockton-on-Tees. Apart from sending me good wishes she recalled an incident which made a curious link with the past:

> In 1923, when you first put up for Parliament, I was living at Stockton-on-Tees, my native place, and was privileged to accompany Lady Dorothy on canvassing rounds in some of the poorest parts of the town, where she was everywhere received with the greatest kindness and courtesy: it was cold at the time, I remember, and kitchen fires and cups of tea on newspaper-spread tables were most comforting. Lady Dorothy may remember that we went upstairs to see one old bedridden lady who had formerly been a housemaid at the Viceregal Lodge, Dublin, when Lord Frederick Cavendish was assassinated in Phoenix Park, and how pleased the poor old body was to see her.[1]

A few weeks earlier I was told that the Treasury were considering the issuing of two-pound notes. Although this seemed a fairly harmless proposal I had an instinctive objection to it at this time. Accordingly I sent a note to the Chancellor of the Exchequer on 1 August:

> I have thought again about the £2 notes. I do not like any messing about with the notes this side of the Election, or anything said about it. The ordinary people will think that we are fiddling with their money. It was said that the old Duke of Devonshire (Hearty Tarty), when he could not think of anything else to say at a public meeting, banged the box with his fist and cried in a loud voice: 'I will stand no tampering with the fiduciary issue.' This brought great applause from the audience who had not the faintest idea what it meant.

[1] Letter from Mrs. M. J. Stainsby, 14 September 1959.

Remember also the famous election fought on the change of the calendar. The cry was 'Give us back our eleven days.'

£2 notes will appear to be an open confession that money has lost its value. It will be a direct disincentive to saving.

One further, although minor, point is perhaps worth recalling—a circular which I sent to all Ministers on 9 September warning them of the need for careful discrimination between the proper use of facilities which, since the Government remained in power throughout the Election, continued to be at their disposal and any misuse of them which might be a subject for criticism.

Official Cars
During the period of the General Election Ministers may continue to use, for official purposes, official cars provided from the Government Car Service or otherwise; but these cars should not be used for journeys connected with the Election. It is also undesirable that a Minister should use an official car, even on official business, in his constituency, except on an occasion when he is unexpectedly called back from his constituency on urgent official business.

Aircraft
Service aircraft should not be used for journeys connected with the Election.

The cost of civil aircraft should not be charged to public funds if used for journeys connected with the Election or other Party political business; but, exceptionally, a Minister recalled unexpectedly to his Department for urgent official business may claim repayment of the cost of an air journey if no other means of transport would meet the needs of the case.

Among the dissolution honours list, I was glad to be able to include two names. The first was that of Herbert Morrison, who agreed to accept a life peerage. I had served under him in 1940 at the Ministry of Supply, and I had known and respected him for many years. It was a real satisfaction to be able to make this small return for many kindnesses and courtesies which I had received from him whether we were working in partnership or as opponents.

The other was a viscounty accepted by James Stuart. He had

served in Parliament since 1923. He had acted first as Scottish Whip and then as Chief Whip through the greater part of the War; from 1951 to 1957 he was a most successful Secretary of State for Scotland. He was universally popular on both sides of the House. The fact that we had married sisters seemed to me no insuperable bar against my making this recommendation.

One of the most difficult problems which confronts Ministers under the conditions of modern Parliaments, with the highly organised political Parties which have now been in being for nearly a century, is how to conduct official affairs, with all their strenuous and compelling pressure, with due regard to the feelings and opinions of their followers, both in the House of Commons and outside. I have sometimes observed, and this applies to both the great Parties, that Ministers, once they are 'dressed in a little brief authority,' tend to forget the means by which they have obtained office and may hope in the future to achieve a renewed tenure. In Opposition the leaders and the rank and file of a Party are closely bound together by continual meetings in Parliament and outside. Freed from care and immediate responsibility they are in constant touch with the constituencies and the Party organisation. If they suffer from the disadvantage of not having access to official information, whether on internal or external affairs, this only allows them a greater freedom. But when a Government is firmly seated in power its relations, both with the back benches and with the Party organisation, become at once more remote and more delicate. The functions of the Government machine must be scrupulously kept separate from those of Party interests. This is of special importance to preserve the traditional impartiality of the Civil Service, on which so much depends. I was always very careful to avoid any over-stepping of this line. Nevertheless, if Ministers begin to assume too detached or authoritarian an attitude, forgetting the source from which their power springs, they will pay in due course a heavy penalty. Apart from this essential dualism in the work of a Minister, and especially of a Prime Minister, the pressure of events in the modern world makes it difficult to keep a proper balance.

With these considerations in mind, I set up, in December 1957, what I called the Steering Committee. This was a body consisting of leading Ministers, with a secretariat provided by the Conservative Research Department. Its members were Butler, Home, Hailsham, Macleod and the Chief Whip, Edward Heath. The secretary was Michael Fraser aided by Peter Goldman. The main purpose of the Steering Committee was not so much to deal with day-to-day topics as to prepare the Manifesto for the General Election whenever it might come. In these two years seventeen meetings were held – the final meeting on 3 September 1959. The Committee considered thirty-six papers on a whole range of questions, some submitted by Ministers and others by the Research Department. It took over the work of an earlier body set up by Butler in February 1957 called the Policy Study Group of which Macleod was the Chairman and Maudling one of the leading members, assisted by Jack Simon, Ormsby-Gore and Enoch Powell. Altogether during this period, by the combination of the work of these two bodies, seven drafts of a proposed Manifesto were prepared and discussed. The eighth draft, the final revise, was formally approved at a meeting which Butler called on my behalf on 8 September 1959. The subjects raised in the course of these vital discussions covered a very wide field. Although I did my best to attend all the meetings it was naturally impossible for me to do so, in view of my many commitments and constant journeys overseas. I owe a great debt to the devoted work which Butler did throughout this period. Perhaps my chief contribution was to suggest the title of the Manifesto, which at least struck a confident note. It was called *The Next Five Years*, and was published on 11 September 1959.

This document was on the whole well received by the national and provincial Press. It had the advantage of being short and simple. The main issues before the country were summarised as follows:

Do you want to go ahead on the lines which have brought prosperity at home?
Do you want your present leaders to represent you abroad?

But whatever its merits or faults, it was certainly in marked contrast to the first major propaganda effort of the Labour Party. This booklet, entitled *The Tory Swindle*, was highly coloured in every sense of the term. It lampooned the Prime Minister and his colleagues in savage and almost eighteenth-century style. 'Mr. MacBlunder, the mothball Prime Minister' was by no means the most unfriendly of the criticisms of my career and personal life. Other Ministers were attacked with equal severity. Nevertheless, it seemed clear, within a few days, that this method of electioneering was—like so much of modern Socialist theory—strangely out of date. It certainly met with very little support in the Press and proved a boomerang in the constituencies. Hailsham, who with Oliver Poole as his deputy presided over the Party organisation with conspicuous skill, immediately responded with a dignified and effective protest. I was interested to see that in the General Election of 1970 the Socialist Party repeated this mistake with the same result.

The official Labour Party Manifesto was drafted in more seemly and less personal terms. It was a document in which Gaitskell's profound economic knowledge was displayed with force and persuasiveness. Its theme was developed with power and skill. It contained, however, one fatal flaw, which as the Election proceeded was turned to Gaitskell's disadvantage. The main proposal on which the Labour Party intended to fight was a very ambitious programme of social reform partly embodying schemes already published. The most conspicuous item was a dramatic increase of pensions, the cost of which, together with the rest of the programme, could, it was claimed, be met without any increase in taxation.

All General Elections are somewhat distasteful affairs. This was the tenth in which I had taken part and was to prove the last. Apart from the heavy burden imposed upon the Ministers of the day in trying to combine their ordinary work with the immense pressure of electioneering, there is a strange sense of unreality about the whole proceedings. The uncertainty of the issues, involving, not only the fate of the Party, but also the personal future of all concerned, is necessarily distracting. But I have always found the greatest difficulty is how to avoid the exaggeration and over-simplification of complicated problems which are so tempting as the contests proceed. Happily, in this country the actual period of electioneering is restricted to some three weeks. We are indeed lucky to be spared the immensely long campaigns carried out in the United States. Nevertheless, these weeks are ones of almost frantic pressure as excitement begins to mount. There is also another disadvantage which affects leading figures and from which humbler candidates are immune. In nearly all my earlier campaigns I was confined to my own constituency and spared the additional physical effort of travelling by train and car throughout practically the whole island, interlarding major speeches at night in the great cities with a number of smaller gatherings throughout the day. Moreover, as a back-bencher, one could make the same speech at three meetings a night over and over again. They were never reported, and it was not necessary to vary either the main arguments or the language in which they were clothed. Even the jokes could be repeated in the different areas of the same town. The only person who suffered constantly from this iteration was my poor wife. I remember her once being asked whether she could or would make a political speech. 'No,' she replied, 'I am not a speech-maker; but I am an almost professional listener. In all the campaigns in which I have taken part with my father, my brother and my husband, I have sat on the platform listening to their speeches. And I am bound to say,' she added reflectively, 'that they always say the same things.' However, it was now necessary for me to attempt at least some variation in form and to prepare in the course of the night or during a railway journey a rejoinder or a counter-argument to one of Gaitskell's speeches of the night before.

I tried to maintain throughout the factual and restrained tones with which I opened the campaign in Bromley on 18 September.

> The speech was very carefully prepared and had some good material, particularly about my early years in the House and the transformation both of the Party and of the Nation that has taken place.[1]

Two new forces which had already played a small part in previous Elections now began to assert themselves. The first was the opinion polls, the second was the use of television. The opinion polls were then dominated by the memorable name of Dr. Gallup; those conducted by the *Daily Mail* and the *Daily Express* were not

[1] 18 September 1959. Quotations from my private journals and other personal memoranda are indicated by the date of the entry.

generally regarded as quite so authoritative. Now there are some half-a-dozen of these systems highly developed and all equally influential. Yet today these psephologists cannot claim a very high mathematical accuracy, however carefully those questioned are chosen from different regions and categories. Indeed their activities seem closer to the medieval art of astrology than to the science of astronomy. At the same time their findings are very influential and may even tend to lead opinion as well as reflect it—hence they are watched with the greatest attention by the rival political machines.

All our people were depressed yesterday by the *Daily Mail* 'Gallup Poll' which showed our lead reduced from seven per cent to three and a half per cent. But today the rival *Daily Express* poll shows our seven per cent lead maintained. So there is a tremendous battle among the experts. Lord Poole, who came yesterday afternoon, was calm—but thought we should have to stiffen up the attack pretty soon.[1]

On the television we were certainly inferior to our opponents at the beginning of the contest.

The Socialists had a very successful TV last night—much better than ours. Gaitskell is becoming very expert. All their campaign so far is concentrated on dirt (against Tories and business men) with bribes to the Old. They are trying to make it a Pension Election. While we must defend this flank, we must not let ourselves be diverted from the main theme—Peace and Prosperity.[1]

Our first television broadcast was a composite affair, a film produced with five of my colleagues and myself at my Sussex home. It was meant to be an intimate and useful discussion revealing to the public the thoughts of Ministers about affairs and ending with a 'live' discussion between the Foreign Secretary and myself on recent developments in the international scene. But, in spite of all our efforts, it was a failure and seemed stilted and ineffective. Much therefore would depend on later appearances.

On 26 September, I delivered a radio broadcast devoted entirely to an exposition of the Manifesto. This was reasonably effective.

[1] 22 September 1959.

But the radio reached then, and I suppose now, a smaller audience and was less dramatic than the television.

Hailsham, as Chairman of the Party, and Poole, as Deputy Chairman, were both towers of strength. Hailsham with his splendid public speeches gave inspiration to the whole Party, while Poole, calm and efficient, spent the whole time at our Headquarters, from which he directed the areas and constituencies with the skill of a supreme chief of staff.

I now began my travels, returning to London at the end of the week.

A very exhausting week has just ended. I have made full speeches (which have to be prepared and circulated to the Press) at Manchester, Birmingham and Swansea. I have made in addition quarter-of-an-hour 'whistle-stop' speeches in Bury, Heywood, Middleton, Oldham, Hyde, Stockport, Shifnal, Tettenhall, and Walsall (first day); Bromsgrove, Worcester, Tewkesbury, Stroud, Chipping Sodbury (second day). I have also made (yesterday) a sound broadcast and had two meetings at Bromley (Friday).

Unfortunately, at one of the open-air meetings, the loud-speaker either broke down or was sabotaged. So I overstrained my voice. Dr. Richardson (who has come back from his holiday to look after me) has given me some good stuff. I am to stay in bed all day today [Sunday].

In addition, I have had to prepare eight or ten newspaper articles. All this would have been quite impossible without George Christ. This man has real genius. He is also a most agreeable friend and companion. He travels with me; sits up late dictating and re-dictating with me ; and is full of ideas and phrases. . . .

There is no doubt that we have lost some ground in the first ten days. But our vedettes were out well beyond any tenable line and were bound to be driven in.

The Labour Party have—so far as policy goes—one immense bribe—10s. at once for the Old Age Pensioners. Considering their numbers, this is a dangerous 'pressure group'. If they win, it will be on this bribe and nothing else. I have taken the only possible line and declared that I will not enter into a public auction. All the same, this is our weak point.

The fact that their television performances are better than

ours, and that they are stirring up a lot of mud over some
shady characters who have done a disreputable 'property' deal,
does not matter so much. The latter may even recoil—for these
particular men are all the particular friends and supporters of
Labour. . . . But the Press has up to now been leaning to them—
chiefly because they are getting livelier views from Transport
House than from our Central Office. We are trying to put this
right.

My impression is, up to now, that we have lost ground in the
first ten days. How much, we cannot tell. The Gallup and allied
Polls will certainly reflect this during the coming week. If
everyone keeps calm, it will be all right. If our people begin to
panic, the result might be serious.

It is rather a strange feeling to lie in bed in this room at No. 10
(which I have occupied for nearly three years) and wonder
whether I shall be here in ten days' time.[1]

In the evening Poole and the Chief Whip came to see me. 'We
are going to "step up" the campaign a little, but we shall still keep
it on the same general note.'[1] The *Daily Mail* poll published on 28
September reduced our lead to two per cent, but I still felt fairly
confident.

Gaitskell now began, as is so easy for an Opposition Leader, to
fall into some obvious traps by arguing that the increased expenditure for pensions and other social reforms could be obtained by a
stricter control of the income tax allowance for 'business expenses'.
This gave me a good opportunity for counter-attack without any
breach of the standard which we had tried to enforce throughout.
In the course of a tour with quarter-hour speeches at Acton,
Uxbridge, Ealing and Chiswick—with three or four calls at other
constituencies—I was able to answer

Gaitskell's absurd idea about getting all this money out of
'business expenses'. If so, why didn't he do this in 1951, instead
of putting on nearly £400m. more in taxation.[2]

On 28 September, speaking at Newcastle, Gaitskell gave a firm
pledge that

[1] 27 September 1959.   [2] 28 September 1959.

there will be no increase in the standard or other rates of income tax under the Labour Government so long as normal peacetime conditions continue.[1]

This gave me an opening for a mocking retort:

Mr. Gaitskell . . . introduced only one Budget, fortunately for you. . . . He was faced with having to raise something like £400m. in extra taxation. . . . What did he do? . . . He put 6d. on the income tax . . . and for good measure he put a charge on spectacles and teeth under the health service.[1]

Undeterred by the obvious dangers Gaitskell and his followers continued these perilous tactics. Promises of further bounties to come followed daily without any clear picture of where the money would come from. These presented a target equally open to serious economic comment and to political chaff. Butler developed both themes in the course of some fine speeches with notable skill. After a passage of careful dissection of this irresponsible Labour programme he ended with a phrase that was taken up all over the country. 'The Labour slogan,' he declared, 'seems to be this—"a bribe a day keeps the Tories away".' For myself, as the bids rose, I adopted a line of righteous indignation—'If this is to be an auction I am not in it'.

And so the ding-dong battle continued. From 29 September to 5 October, when I got back to London, I covered an immense area. On 30 September I spoke in Glasgow and made a tour of the neighbouring constituencies. The next two days I was in Yorkshire and the East Midlands, and on 3 October in the Home Counties and the South-East and on 5 October in the Eastern area.

By the end of an effort of this kind one is completely exhausted.

I made major speeches in Glasgow, Bradford, Halifax and Nottingham—and some ten or eleven speeches every day as well—of fifteen minutes each. The weather was fine the whole time, and the crowds in each place ranged from 3,000 to 6,000. It was an extraordinary experience.[2]

On 6 October I was to make my final television appearance. I

[1] *Annual Register*, 1959, p. 35.   [2] 9 October 1959.

knew that much would depend upon its success or failure. I therefore decided to devote the whole day to its preparation.

In the last week our performances had improved and notable success was scored by Selwyn Lloyd and Lennox-Boyd interviewed by Christopher Chataway. Nevertheless, on reflection I decided to dispense with any interviewer and to content myself with a simple appeal on my own lines. I was encouraged in this decision by Gaitskell's last television broadcast, which, although admirably delivered, was spoilt by a somewhat irrelevant piece of film with which it began (about unemployment in the thirties) and by his mistake in adopting a constrained position, anchored to a large and ornate chair behind a big desk.

I decided to put myself in the hands of a consummate expert in this field, Norman Collins. On the morning of 6 October I went along with John Wyndham to his studio. We roughed out a draft, and I made two rehearsals before lunch. The plan was to keep on my feet; use as accessories only a globe, a map of Britain and some letters on a table to pick up and read at random. I hoped by this plan to bring a certain life and ease into the performance. But at lunchtime I was depressed. It was an ambitious idea, but could I make it successful? If it did not come off it would be a crashing failure; and the stakes were high. After lunch we did two or three more rehearsals changing the scheme from time to time. At 6 o'clock Norman Collins said to me, 'I think that will do. I should stand on that.' 'But,' I protested, 'I have got to go and deliver it at 8 o'clock at the B.B.C.' 'Oh, no,' he said, 'I have got the film—we will send it along.' Without telling me he had taken film records of each performance and I was thereby saved the strain of doing it 'live' with all the risks involved. The B.B.C. authorities seemed rather surprised and even pained. But there appeared to be no valid reason, legal or technical, against my supplying my own film. At any rate John Wyndham, with his usual resourcefulness, was able to convince the officials concerned and any objection was dropped. Fear of a breakdown or even sabotage induced me to go along to the television studio; if anything should go wrong with the film I was, of course, ready at hand. However, everything went well, and the programme was duly shown. In those days it was not so usual to record television programmes, and indeed there was almost the suggestion that it was not playing fair. However it seemed to me a very sensible plan, and it certainly spared me a trying ordeal. My last appeal ran as follows:

> Well, I've just got one final word that I would like to say to you—one last thought. I have been reading the Socialist Manifesto. I think a lot of it is exaggerated. But I like the title, *Britain Belongs to You*. All the same, it is not the whole truth. Britain does not belong to any of us, not a single generation. In a famous phrase, 'a nation is a partnership between the living, the dead and those yet to be born'. We are trustees, not owners. And this is far too big a trust to be played with or gambled with.
>
> I read a few days ago a speech by the wisest and the greatest of Englishmen alive today—perhaps the greatest of all time—and this is what he said: 'To build,' said Sir Winston Churchill, 'is the laborious task of years. To destroy can be the foolish act of a single day.' I would like you to think that over between now and next Thursday. Think over the trust which you hold for yourselves, your children and your grandchildren, and then I believe you will decide that ours is the best way for the next five years.

After the television broadcast on 6 October the strain of the contest was over. The next day I spent in my constituency, parading the streets and calling upon old friends. My organisation was in fine fettle and generously agreed to be content with two major speeches—the first to open the campaign and the second to close it. I accordingly held a boisterous 'wind-up' meeting where I was greatly heckled by an organisation called 'Empire Loyalists'—a contemporary manifestation of a disease of violence which although it has disappeared in this particular form has, alas, returned in other shapes.

On Polling Day Dorothy and I toured the constituency in the usual way, and spent the evening at No. 10, quietly watching the television.

> At first, it was rather anxious, especially when the two Salfords swung against us. David and Sylvia Kilmuir came in about midnight. By 1 a.m. it was clear that we would win and Gaitskell (interviewed by TV) 'conceded' the election.[1]

[1] 9 October 1959.

We thought it right to go to the Central Office at about 2 a.m. on Friday morning, where we found a very happy and excited crowd. One of our greatest satisfactions was that both my son Maurice and my son-in-law Julian Amery held their seats with increased majorities. The next day I went to Bromley where the poll was not announced until noon. My majority rose by 2,000, polling 27,055 against the Labour 11,603.

So it was all over, with a new House of Commons containing 365 Conservative, 258 Labour and 6 Liberal members. Since on the morning of Polling Day *The Times* had forecast a majority of twenty-two I felt more than satisfied—but it was impossible not to feel, with all the excitement and gratification, a sense of humility and even awe. At a Press Conference at the Central Office I tried to express this. 'We must try,' I said, 'to emphasise the fundamental unity of our people and not exaggerate the differences which divide us, important as they may be.' Nevertheless, it was a staggering result. No Party has been victorious three times running increasing its majority each time.

One more duty I was able to perform the next day. I had advised Her Majesty the Queen not to break her holiday and leave Balmoral because of the General Election. Accordingly I was glad to be able to write to her formally on 10 October:

> Madam,
> Mr. Macmillan with his humble duty to The Queen.
> I was glad that in the course of the night of 8/9 October it became clear that it would not be necessary to trouble Your Majesty to return to .London. I must admit that this situation caused me some anxiety at an earlier stage, but no point was made about this in the Press either before or after the Election. The new Americanised habit of one of the Leaders 'conceding' the Election in the early hours of the morning was an advantage from this point of view.
> I propose to think over the situation of the Government generally during the week-end and I have not yet made any definite decisions as to possible changes of Ministers. I do not anticipate that these will be on a very substantial scale and I do not see any reason why it should be necessary to ask Your

Majesty to return to London prematurely. Ministers can go from London to Balmoral as well as Sovereigns from Balmoral to London, and the former has to my mind a far better and longer tradition behind it. At any rate, perhaps I may be allowed to communicate with Your Majesty on this point, or ask my Private Secretary to discuss it with Sir Michael Adeane.

With regard to the general result of the Election, naturally my colleagues and I, and those who think with us, are more than satisfied. But we realise the heavy work that lies ahead, both at home and abroad. The people at home have become accustomed to a very high and stable economic situation. The slightest change in the barometer, although it might be due to factors quite outside our control, would correspondingly depress them. Abroad, although hopeful, they are a little more realistic.

The most encouraging feature of the Election however, from Your Majesty's point of view, is the strong impression that I have formed that Your Majesty's subjects do not wish to allow themselves to be divided into warring classes or tribes filled with hereditary animosity against each other. There was a very significant breakdown of this structure of society which, in spite of its many material advantages, was one of the chief spiritual disadvantages of the first industrial revolution. It will be curious if the second industrial revolution, through the wide spread of its amenities of life to almost every home in the country, succeeds in destroying this unfortunate product of the first. At any rate, anything that makes Your Majesty's subjects more conscious of their unity and of their duty to each other seems to me to be a real gain.

> With my humble duty,
> I remain,
> Your Majesty's faithful
> and devoted servant.

To this the Queen returned a gracious reply which while maintaining the full impartiality of the Crown encouraged me to continue to do my best to serve her as her First Minister.

Naturally, the Press and the political commentators gave full and varying reasons for this unexpected Conservative victory. *The Times*, somewhat strangely, called it 'a triumph of the middle classes', and was followed in this view by other important papers. I did not myself feel able to draw any precise conclusions. 'Victory finds many parents, but defeat is an orphan.'

> It is hard, without some thought and study, to analyse the Election result. The Liberal vote (with twice the number of candidates) nearly doubled. Much is made of this in the Press and it is perhaps exaggerated. What I think happened is that the Liberals (for the first time) took more from the Socialists, in many places, than from us. This may prove important. The great thing is to keep the Tory party on *modern* and *progressive* lines.[1]

The fact that the Liberal vote had doubled without any corresponding increase in the number of Liberal Members elected to Parliament, gave rise to some renewed talk about proportional representation. To the academic maker of constitutions such a device presents clear attractions. It is logical and seems fair. But the dangers are not to be disregarded. It is quite hard enough to govern a country with two main parties alternating in power. It is almost impossible to do so with a large number of parties all with their separate interests and all intriguing against each other. I remember a telegram from our ambassador in Paris which had amused me at the time. It was in the last period before the final collapse of the French Parliamentary system. There was, as usual, a political crisis and the ambassador reported a conversation with one of the Ministers as follows:

> 'He did not seem at all confident of the Government's prospects and seemed to think that the chances were about fifty–fifty. If they did fall,' he said sardonically, 'the best system for France might be to have no Government at all, but only a well organised Opposition which would command the unswerving allegiance of all parties.'[2]

I have always felt that with all its disadvantages we had better stick to the well-tried system of electing candidates which Churchill used to describe as 'the first past the post'.

It was now necessary to set about the task of creating what was virtually my second Administration. The three most important positions in any Government after that of the Prime Minister are

[1] 11 October 1959.   [2] 19 May 1957.

those of the Foreign Secretary, the Chancellor of the Exchequer and the Home Secretary. For the first I was determined to maintain Selwyn Lloyd, with whom I had worked so long and through such grave crises in complete harmony. That he was tired, not only with the burden of office but by the long and wearisome foreign negotiations in which he had been involved, I was well aware; and I had it in mind that I might be able to make a change in the following summer. The opportunity for this was all the more probable because Heathcoat Amory came to see me on 10 October asking to be relieved of his post in the near future, and I told Sir Norman Brook:

> He is very anxious that it should be generally known that he has no ambition to remain permanently in a high position in politics. He would be ready to serve in a sinecure post or even in a minor post but he feels unable to continue indefinitely the strain of the Treasury, which he has found a very heavy burden. The problem is (*a*) how to keep him, which is essential, and (*b*) how to meet his demands.

Fortunately, after discussion, I was able to persuade him to remain at least until the middle of the following year. I urged upon him the argument that it was vital that there should be no public or private intimation of his desire to be relieved. Nothing could be more dangerous than a feeling that a Chancellor of the Exchequer was operating on a short-term basis. Heathcoat Amory, with his usual helpfulness, accepted this view. At a later stage he proved himself ready to serve the government again when he accepted the position of High Commissioner to Canada.

With regard to the Home Office there could be no doubt. Butler was an excellent Minister and in addition led the House with conspicuous talents. We had worked most successfully and loyally together during these troubled years. Indeed, I was anxious to add to, rather than diminish, his position and strength in the Party. Accordingly, with the agreement of Hailsham, Butler took on the additional post of Chairman of the Party, the former being ready and anxious to devote himself to the new Ministry of Science where he would be responsible 'for the promotion of scientific and technological development'. It was a forward-looking appointment which was subsequently developed into an important department with an increasing range of authority. For this purpose he was given the sinecure post of Lord Privy Seal. Butler's acceptance of the Chairmanship had considerable significance, since he had been the head of the Research Department during our years in Opposition, and was regarded as the promoter of the new thought in modern Conservatism. It was very good 'symbolically. It shows the world that, after our great victory, we intend to remain progressive and not slide back into reaction.'[1]

But there was one loss which, although I had been forewarned, was especially grievous to me—Alan Lennox-Boyd. His reasons were purely personal, since he felt under a deep obligation to his wife's family, to take over the post, at least temporarily, of head of the great Guinness concern. I was forced to accept his decision but with real regret.

> He has been an outstanding Colonial Secretary, for five years of growth and development in all the Overseas Territories. If he has had bad luck over Kenya (the Hola Camp) and Nyasaland, these are very small affairs in comparison to the wonderful work which he has done.[1]

The usual public letters were exchanged, but I felt bound to write him a private note on 14 October:

> An exchange of public letters is necessary but you know that it cannot express the full measure of my regret at your going or my gratitude for what you have done. In energy unflagging, in imagination fertile, in sympathy super-abundant, in attack merciful, in defence a rock, in debate a rapier, in stature Homeric —if I said all this, which I feel, in a public letter I should be accused of hyperbole. And in no public letter could I ever add a reference to that quality of laughter which has brought you so many friends.

This left a most important post to be filled. I knew that during the next few years we must face the steady development of independence to be granted to the emerging colonial governments.

[1] 18 October 1959.

Alan Lennox-Boyd had presided over the earliest of these advances with conspicuous success. It would need a Minister of great imagination, even genius, to follow. Moreover the later stages would be even more controversial and difficult. There was one man who seemed to me to possess the obvious qualities. He had been very successful in the Ministry of Health for which he was picked out by Churchill. He had shown equal talent as Minister of Labour. It was without hesitation therefore that I selected Iain Macleod. To my great satisfaction, he accepted with enthusiasm. To fill his place was easy. The Chief Whip, Edward Heath, wanted it, and it was only right, in view of all his services, that he should now step into independent ministerial command.

The Ministry of Supply was one of those departments about which I had long been worried. Again I needed a man of determination and courage.

> I have, with some difficulty, persuaded Duncan Sandys to take over the Ministry of Supply—break it up—and form a new Ministry of Aviation. The present position of the aircraft industry is very bad. . . . If anyone can tackle the job, Duncan Sandys is the man.[1]

The Ministry of Transport and Civil Aviation was now divided into two. Harold Watkinson, the present Minister, became Minister of Defence in place of Duncan Sandys, and the remaining part of the Ministry of Transport was entrusted to my old friend and colleague Ernest Marples.

> Defence I have given to Watkinson and Transport to Marples. These are both 'self-made' men (*novi homines*) and will both do well.[1]

I brought Reggie Maudling, one of the younger successes, into the Board of Trade, and David Eccles generously agreed to return to his former position as Minister of Education. Lord Mills was anxious to give up the Ministry of Power, but I was equally determined to retain his wise advice, much valued by all his colleagues. It was, therefore, arranged that he should become Paymaster

[1] 18 October 1959.

General and remain in the Cabinet. This completed the Cabinet which was announced on Thursday, 15 October.

There now arose a difficult problem which must be resolved before the full list of the Administration could be completed. It was necessary to elect a new Speaker in the place of W. S. Morrison, who had retired from his post amid general regret at the end of the last Parliament. Had he stood he would, of course, have been re-elected to the position, but his resignation left open this vital post. It was suggested by some of the Press that since there had never been a Speaker from the Labour Party it would be a generous, even chivalrous, act if the Conservatives should waive their claim and elect a member of the Labour Party. I rather liked this idea, and accordingly on 16 October I sent a note to Butler on whose advice I chiefly relied.

I think perhaps it would be fair if I were to put my views shortly in writing.

1. I personally feel after thirty-five years' experience in the House of Commons that it would be a good thing if the cards so fell that a Party which has been either Government or Opposition during the whole of the Parliamentary life of even the oldest Member provided a Speaker at one time or another.

2. The cards have not so fallen because of the sound tradition that a Speaker of this century (not quite so true of the nineteenth century) once elected should be continued even when there was a change of Government, if he had the general confidence of the House. This is what happened in each period of Labour Government even with their great victory in 1945.

3. At the same time the interests of the House of Commons demand and the dignity of the State requires that a Speaker should be of a high calibre. It is difficult to define but I think one knows it when one sees it. Of the Labour candidates I have heard mentioned it seems to me that only Frank Soskice is in this sense of Speaker quality.

4. I therefore feel that we might indicate to Mr. Gaitskell the considerations set out in (1), (2) and (3) above, and make it clear that if Sir Frank Soskice is put forward you and I would consult our supporters with a view to securing his nomination without a vote. It would be quite an effort for us, but we would

do our best. . . . In that case we would of course expect to hold the Chairman and Deputy Chairman.

Conversations accordingly took place between Butler and Gaitskell.

> But Mr. Gaitskell would not part with him, and then tried to turn this act of generosity into a grievance, accusing us of trying to 'dictate' a Labour choice. However, this proved very thin. The Press gave it no support.[1]

He then suggested other names, none of which either Butler or I felt we could persuade our supporters to accept. As a result we decided to put forward the name of Hylton-Foster, who was then Solicitor-General and a popular figure in the House.

> We have got over the Speakership problem, with the unanimous election of Hylton-Foster, the Solicitor General. . . . [his] speech of acceptance was so good that everyone realised that he was far the best choice.

This was rather an unhappy episode, since I had hoped that our gesture would be regarded as a pleasant example of Parliamentary courtesy. Instead it turned out at the best a 'comedy of errors'.

Uncertainty about the Speaker being removed, it was now possible to complete the list of junior Ministers.

> The Service Ministers have presented no problem. I have made no change except to substitute Lord Carrington for Lord Selkirk as First Lord (Lord Selkirk is, very patriotically, going to Singapore as High Commissioner).[2]

I was very content about the general reception of the complete list from the Press and the public.

> We have managed to get eight *new* Ministers, ranging from Tony Barber (as Economic Secretary to Treasury) to Miss Pike (Assistant P.M.G.).[3]

I was particularly happy to be able to give Barber his first important appointment. He had acted as my Parliamentary Private Secretary for several years, and I had formed a high opinion of his qualities. I felt that he was a man with a career before him.

[1] 22 October 1959.   [2] 18 October 1959.   [3] 23 October 1959.

There was one name which I was forced to omit, however reluctantly. It was that of my son, Maurice. He had won Halifax for the second time and had already made a certain reputation in the House of Commons. He would normally have been in the running for at least a minor post; but I felt unwilling to be accused of partiality. I was confident that when I had left the scene he would make his own way from his own inherent qualities.

The question of the size and composition of a Cabinet is one which has been much discussed by historians and political commentators. It has to be faced by each succeeding Prime Minister. It can certainly be argued that efficiency would be promoted and overall unity on policy assisted by a smaller Cabinet—eight or nine—such as the Cabinets which were common .in the nineteenth century, incidentally mostly composed of noblemen of high rank. In war it was found possible both by Lloyd George and Churchill to work out a system of a small War Cabinet with a perfectly clear demarcation of responsibility. But war is, after all, confined to one single purpose, simple in formulation if complex in execution. Accordingly, under peace conditions both Churchill and Attlee were forced to return to the large Cabinet of the pre-war type. I thought seriously over this question before deciding; but it seemed impossible, having regard to those Ministers who must be in any Cabinet—the holders of the great posts, the Leader of the House of Lords, the Lord Chancellor and so forth—to bring down the number to anything like a working committee of eight or ten. It was politically impossible to exclude Scotland, Wales, Education. But if a Cabinet must be at least of fourteen or fifteen, the concept of a small and intimate group breaks down. I thought it wiser to let it remain at nineteen, the size it had been before the Election. Even this was only achieved with a little juggling, by appointing Lord Home Lord President of the Council as well as Commonwealth Secretary. The Cabinet must continue as it had always been, collectively responsible for all great decisions. This practice I was scrupulous in observing, as, for example, in the Middle East crisis over Lebanon and Jordan.[1] In addition we must continue to work partly through a small inner group of Ministers, meeting occasion-

[1] See *Riding the Storm*, pp. 518–19.

ally, but chiefly through committees of Ministers dealing with particular groups of subjects. That it was possible to operate the system and yet retain the confidence of the Cabinet as a whole was due partly to the generosity of my colleagues and partly to the skill of Sir Norman Brook and my private secretaries in gaining their confidence.

Thus, the Election won, the Cabinet reformed, the full Administration announced, we were ready to set out on a new adventure. The difficulties ahead of us were indeed many and complicated, especially in the international field. But the prizes were great, the theme clear—Prosperity at Home and Peace Abroad.

CHAPTER II

A Prime Minister's Life

IT may be convenient at this point to give some account of my life and work as Prime Minister—an office which I was fated to enjoy or endure for a period of nearly seven years.

I must first describe the physical background, the framework, which surrounded us. For many years No. 10 Downing Street has been famous throughout the whole world as the hub or centre of British rule and influence. Originally presented by George II to Sir Robert Walpole, it has been used by his successors without interruption until 1960, except for a period in the war when Churchill's headquarters were transferred to a safer building. It is true that many Prime Ministers in the eighteenth and nineteenth centuries—including Gladstone, Rosebery and Salisbury—did not use the House as a residence, but preferred to retain their own larger and more commodious homes. But it was occupied both by Lord John Russell and Disraeli, and during the twentieth century all Prime Ministers have both lived and worked in this historic building.

During many years No. 11 has served as a residence for the Chancellor of the Exchequer, and No. 12 as an office for the Government Whips. This set of buildings which has gone through many adaptations and changes, including the destruction of the top half of No. 12 by fire, has formed, therefore, an intimate part of history for two and a half centuries.

No. 10, though by no means a pretentious house, has a capacity for entertaining on a large scale. The addition of the great Soane dining-room, for instance, makes it possible to seat some seventy guests; and the drawing-rooms, although not magnificent saloons comparable with those of the great London mansions (now alas destroyed), have a dignity of their own. Nevertheless one of the

Return to Downing Street

Removal to Admiralty House, 2 August 1960

The Reconstruction of Downing Street

charms of the house lies in the number of small rooms which give a
sense of intimacy. The little dining-room formed out of a passage
between the pillared drawing-room and the main dining-room has
been used by many Prime Ministers for ordinary daily purposes.
But almost all the occupants have made their own changes and
adaptations. My wife, for instance, abandoned the bedroom on the
first floor for a smaller room upstairs, thereby making available an
additional sitting-room and allowing me to occupy the dressing-
room as a study for my own use. The Cabinet room on the ground
floor is not large, but seems so replete with the story of Britain that
it has a peculiar atmosphere of its own. Above the chimney-piece
hangs the portrait of the first, and one of the greatest of Prime
Ministers, Walpole.

I have already described something of the special contribution
which my wife made to our life at No. 10 from the very moment
that we moved in.[1] She filled it with children and all their paraphernalia; she also filled it with flowers. But above all she made it
seem like a family gathering in a country house with guests continually coming and going, with a large number of children's
parties and with a sense of friendliness among all the staff and
servants who worked long hours with cheerful willingness. Of
course, the great day for guests of every age was that of the Troop-
ing the Colour. I too enjoyed this annual ceremony, although
the preliminary rehearsals, with cavalry and infantry drills in the
early hours of the morning and the daily repetition of the Figaro
March, were sometimes rather trying.

Unhappily, shortly after my appointment as Prime Minister
grave apprehensions were expressed by the Office of Works about
the state of the Downing Street buildings; they had suffered partly
from age, partly from somewhat skimped work in certain parts,
but more still from German bombing. Yet to touch so hallowed an
edifice seemed to me a great responsibility. I therefore, with a
politician's natural instinct, used the device of 'passing the buck'
into other hands. In July 1957, I appointed a committee under
Lord Crawford to give their advice as to what should be done.
In the spring of 1958 they definitely recommended—greatly to my

[1] See *Riding the Storm*, page 208.

B

disappointment–that 'a major structural overhaul' of No. 10 was necessary. At the same time they proposed that the other Downing Street buildings should be repaired. In particular No. 12 should be rebuilt to its original height. While the main rooms of No. 10 and features of historic importance should be carefully preserved, the remainder of the interior should be replanned. They also proposed the reconstruction of the Treasury Buildings originally built by the great architect, William Kent. These too had suffered in the Second War. The Cabinet, after some discussion, approved this plan. Accordingly, in the autumn of the same year, after first informing Gaitskell of our intentions, I obtained the consent of Parliament. I was sorry indeed at the prospect of leaving No. 10, nor was it easy to find anywhere to go. It was not until August 1960 that the move was made–the last Cabinet meeting in the old building being held on 29 July. By a miracle of organisation the operation was completed in a week, and by 10 August we were duly installed in Admiralty House, a noble structure in the best style of the late eighteenth century, with magnificent reception rooms and dining-rooms, and embellished throughout by fine cornices, doors, and chimney-pieces.

Admiralty House was bigger and more handsome than Downing Street, but it was not quite the same thing. The Cabinet now met in the great downstairs reception room, and it seemed at first intolerably big compared with the old cosy room in Downing Street. I tried to overcome this by having a new top made for the table in the shape of a lozenge. This 'much improves the facility of those at the ends to take part–to hear and to talk and to see.'[1] Some of my colleagues thought it looked too much like a coffin. My own sitting-room looked on Whitehall, and commanded a splendid view of the dome of St. Paul's.

I hesitated to ask the Board of Admiralty to surrender this historic house even temporarily. But there was no possible alternative. All I could do was ensure that the famous Dolphin furniture should be carefully stored and thereby preserved from any misuse either by adults or children. When we had all got used to the change, so suitable seemed Admiralty House for all the modern needs of a

[1] 27 January 1961.

Prime Minister that many people felt that the large sums that would necessarily be spent on the reconstruction of Downing Street could well be saved and the change become permanent. But, apart from the feelings of the Navy, I am sure this would have been a mistake. Even today No. 10 Downing Street has a meaning and a significance which must be preserved.

As usual the work took much longer than had been expected, and it was not until the summer of 1963, a few weeks before my final illness and resignation, that we were able to move back to No. 10. There were many changes, but the essential character of the house was retained, including the hat-pegs in the waiting-room labelled with the names of the various Ministers.

The generosity of Lord and Lady Lee of Fareham had made available to Lloyd George and his successors the fine Elizabethan house of Chequers. I used it for entertaining, for which it is admirably adapted, and also for working quietly either alone or with one or two colleagues. My wife seldom went there except on duty. She preferred our own home in Sussex, where she could follow her normal avocations and escape from official duties.[1] I too spent any spare time at Birch Grove House; and I often lent Chequers to any colleagues to whom it might be convenient. Selwyn Lloyd occupied it for many months, both as Foreign Secretary and as Chancellor of the Exchequer, and found in it a source both of pleasure and relaxation.

The management of all these homes threw a heavy burden on my wife which she carried out with characteristic ease and charm. She never altered her approach to any problem whether human or material. Life was to be enjoyed and made happy for everyone. Even the troublesome things like formal entertaining, she somehow made agreeable. She carried out all these duties with a combination of dignity and simplicity which is difficult to describe but which many will still remember. Perhaps the clue to her success was that she treated everybody exactly the same; whatever their rank or station, they were all to be regarded as friends and as people in whom she took a deep personal interest. Of course, it would have been better if they had all been children, for it was with children

[1] See *Riding the Storm*, p. 207.

of all ages that she was supremely at her ease. If they must be adults it was just too bad; and the best thing to do was to treat them also more or less as children. Nor did she ever show the slightest change of spirit, whether in good times or in bad. When our popularity stood high she thought it odd, but pleasant. When it was at a low ebb she thought it odder, but still to be endured.

For these high qualities she received a full reward from the public. I remember a particular occasion in the summer of 1962, when things were not going well and I had to make a speech to the huge rally of Conservative women at the Albert Hall. She was greeted, when she rose to say a few words of acknowledgmeent, with far the greatest volume of applause that I can remember. It was meant particularly to encourage her, and it was a spontaneous tribute.

> She has not spared herself since I became Prime Minister. She has been *all over* the country, to simple and friendly meetings of women of all types. Now (when they come together at their conference) very many of them know her personally.[1]

Nor did she abandon the charitable work on which she had been employed for many years, such as the N.S.P.C.C. This took her to gatherings in every part of the country. To all her other qualities she added an almost Royal memory for names and faces.

If my seven years as Prime Minister were only made possible by the care and sustenance which my wife gave me, I owe almost as much to the devotion of my son Maurice. Although, as already stated, I did not feel it right to give him any office in the Administration, he was constantly at my side. He knew all that was going on in the Party and the House of Commons and reported it faithfully to me even when the news was unpalatable. I must also pay tribute to the loyalty and devotion of some of our staff who had been with us and remained with us for many years, both before and after my retirement. Of these the chief were Mrs. Bell, our cook, and Miss Baker, our housekeeper. I made it a practice, apart from the formal entertaining, to have food and drink available for any of my colleagues during the long hours of work. We also invited many

[1] 23 May 1962.

junior Ministers and young Members of the House of Commons and their wives. In all these strains and stresses, which under modern conditions could be very severe, both these admirable friends, rather than servants, remained unmoved. Nothing surprised them, and there was no demand, either in London or in Sussex, which they did not cheerfully meet.

I have already described the services which I received from my personal staff.[1] To these I ought to add the two Chief Whips who served me—Edward Heath and Martin Redmayne. Asquith observed that a Chief Whip should have a 'large capacity for self-assertion and self-effacement'. But in addition to these qualities, to which both my Chief Whips could lay claim, there is one even more important—absolute and undivided loyalty. Both of them gave me this without reserve.

Thus armed and equipped I was able to face, if not always to overcome, the troubles of the exciting and often turbulent years in which I bore the responsibilities of a Prime Minister. These are indeed manifold.

First and foremost is his duty to the Crown—not merely as representative of the Nation and Commonwealth, but because the smooth and efficient working of monarchy is a vital part of the working of a free constitution. He must never forget that he is the Queen's First Minister. He has to help her to the best of his ability in a varied number of matters where the interests of the Crown and of the Royal Family are concerned. I was fortunate in receiving from the Queen the most complete co-operation and confidence, and I look back with gratitude to the many kindnesses which I enjoyed at her hand. She is the Head of the Royal Family, and this fact throws upon her many duties, and sometimes problems. The Prime Minister must also protect the rights of the monarchy. Although as centuries and generations have passed, the effective power of the monarch has been considerably reduced, in many ways the royal influence has grown. Apart from the example that the Head of the Royal Family gives to her people, the Queen has a right as well as a duty to be fully informed of all the affairs not only of the United Kingdom but also of all the countries of the Common-

[1] See *Riding the Storm*, p. 192.

wealth, as well as of foreign countries. This duty was always conscientiously performed. All Cabinet papers, all departmental papers, all foreign telegrams are sent to her, and carefully studied by her. All the Cabinet's decisions, which under the Cabinet secretarial system are rapidly and accurately circulated, are available to her immediately. All great appointments under the Crown must never be a matter for formal approval. In these, as in matters of policy, it is true that the monarch must in the end yield to the formal advice given by Ministers. But the Queen has the absolute right to know, to criticise, to advise—or, as a great authority has put it, 'to advise, to encourage, and to warn'.[1] We are fortunate that these duties, which are always so important, and may well in a critical situation become vital, are so scrupulously performed. Moreover, as the years pass, the Queen will necessarily accumulate more political experience and knowledge than most of her advisers. I shall have occasion to recount later in this volume the incident of the Queen's visit to Ghana in 1961, which showed her to be at once courageous and determined.

Since her accession the Queen has made it a practice to receive her Prime Ministers at a weekly audience, generally on Tuesday afternoons. I found these at first somewhat difficult, for when making my report I could not help remembering Queen Victoria's description of Mr. Gladstone addressing her as if she were a public meeting. I, therefore, adopted the plan of sending her, whenever possible, before the audience a note about the main points which it would be my duty to raise. This made discussion easier and avoided preliminary explanations. Throughout she adopted the practice of allowing her Prime Ministers to sit rather than to stand, which made for ease of conversation. At the risk of impertinence I must pay tribute to the width and depth of the Queen's knowledge and the assiduity with which she read and absorbed the vast mass of documents circulated. I must also record with gratitude her invariable graciousness and understanding.

Apart from these formal audiences, there were periodic visits to Windsor, Sandringham and Balmoral. The last of these was a yearly event arranged to coincide with any holiday that I might

[1] Quoted by Sir Harold Nicolson, *King George V* (London, 1952), p. 121.

have been able to take in Scotland. My wife always came with me on these occasions, and we both enjoyed, especially at Balmoral, not merely the intimacy of the Royal circle but the experience of seeing what is really a museum piece of Victorian decoration. We occupied a suite of rooms on the ground floor of the Castle, with the well-known maple furniture, Stuart tartan curtains, brass ink-stands and Winterhalter prints, which must have been used by many Prime Ministers in turn for more than a century. Happily the rigorous rules laid down by Queen Victoria were no longer enforced. Disraeli describes the horror of his icy sitting-room, without central heating of any kind, and in which no fire could be lit until the appointed day in October. He suffered dreadfully from the cold of the room, however much he might have appreciated the warmth of the Royal friendship.

The next important responsibility is the duty both to form a Cabinet and from time to time to recommend its reconstruction. Asquith observed that the difficulty about making an Administration was that 'There are always more horses than oats!' There are of course occasions when the post offered falls short of expectations and is refused on that account. I had not much sympathy for this attitude. When one is in a team one should take the place in the field that the captain has decided. Moreover, I remembered the famous saying of Halifax (the Great Trimmer), 'When a man thinks his place below him he will be below his place.' In my first Government, after Eden's resignation, though I tried to restrict the changes to a minimum, I found the experience exhausting and sometimes painful.

The forming of the whole Administration took about ten days. On the whole, it has been well received. It was a *most* difficult and exhausting task. Without the help of Edward Heath, who was quite admirable, we couldn't have done it. Norman Brook was also most valuable. The letters which I wrote to retiring colleagues were regarded as out of the ordinary. I took a great deal of trouble with each one, and tried to introduce a personal note into each. The most awkward and difficult job was, naturally, parting with old friends. All of them took it very well.[1]

[1] 3 February 1957.

But Cabinets, especially over a period of years, are necessarily subject to changes. These can take various forms. Naturally, in the course of a long Administration or a series of Governments of the same Party, there are a number of resignations for private and personal reasons. There are others that take place on public grounds. In the first few months I had an example of the latter in the resignation of Lord Salisbury, from the office of Lord President of the Council. This was a great grief to me, since he was an old friend from school and university days. We were also closely connected by marriage. The occasion was the decision of the Government to liberate Archbishop Makarios from prison. A year later I was faced with the resignation of the Chancellor of the Exchequer, Peter Thorneycroft, on the question of public expenditure. Other resignations had to be accepted not on any public issue, but for private reasons, such as those of Alan Lennox-Boyd after the election of 1959, and of Derick Heathcoat Amory in 1960. But these events, sad as they are, seldom leave any lasting wound behind them. A much more disagreeable task, but one which cannot be avoided, is when either a particular Minister needs to be replaced, or the situation demands a larger Government reshuffle. In the first instance, although others may have seen signs of loss of grip and authority, the individual concerned is seldom conscious of any deterioration. After long years of office, under the tremendous burden which falls on Ministers today, it is almost impossible for any man to hold any of the most responsible posts year after year without the risk of becoming a victim to overstrain. Then there is the continual pressure of the Press, the Party machine and the Party in the House of Commons, for changes. While this can be resisted in a Government only running a single Parliament, it becomes much more difficult to do so if a Government of the same political complexion lasts for three Parliaments, twelve or thirteen years in all. Moreover, as a Parliament draws to its close, it is very important to ensure that a proper proportion of the Ministers, both of Cabinet rank and outside the Cabinet, if they are in the Lower House, should be willing to stand for election again. Otherwise a defeated Party may face a period of Opposition with no experienced men available for the front bench. A Prime Minister, both in that position and in his capacity as Leader of a Party, must give great weight to this consideration. I remembered how frequently in the past following long periods of consecutive office, a Party has drifted slowly into decay and left behind it hardly a leading figure. It was naturally very distasteful for me to have to make these decisions. Sometimes I was accused of being too loyal to my Ministers and standing by them too obstinately. Sometimes I was accused of ruthlessness in my changes. Often a colleague would come to me month after month or week after week, assuring me that his place was available any time I wanted it. If I took him at his word, he might show an unexpected indignation, which he was not anxious to disguise from the world. Nor does the public quite realise another problem which confronts a Prime Minister, and is wholly different from that, let us say, of a Chairman of a great company. The precise date of the resignation of an important official in a company, even the General Manager or Managing Director, can be discussed in detail and fixed for some period ahead. It may be announced, for instance, in the summer that the General Manager is to retire at Christmas. But this is quite impossible in the case of a Minister. You cannot have a Chancellor of the Exchequer dealing with a crisis in July, who is known to be about to retire in December. You cannot have a Foreign Secretary playing out the last few months of a long tenure of office like an employee (or even a Civil Servant) working for his pension. This means that changes have to be made quickly, without hesitation, and apparently brutally.

A careful reading of histories and memoirs makes me feel that the power of a Prime Minister has steadily grown. Although he is only *primus inter pares*, the very complexity of affairs leads to the concentration of authority in his hands. The Cabinet is so burdened with business that the collective responsibility of Ministers, although essential to our constitution, tends to be reserved for the larger issues of national importance or political significance. Naturally the closest and most intimate co-operation must exist between the Prime Minister and both the Foreign Secretary and Chancellor of the Exchequer. Almost every Cabinet begins with a statement of urgent foreign problems by the former, followed by a report of the general state of the economy and urgent individual

B2

economic questions by the latter. The time has gone since a dispatch was criticised and redrafted at a full Cabinet meeting. Alas, the dispatch, in these days of telegrams and telephones, has lost its old significance. But hardly a day passes in which the Foreign Secretary does not find a few moments to call upon the Prime Minister, probably with a proposed reply to some message from abroad, or the Chancellor of the Exchequer to speak about some crucial internal difficulty.

As regards the Cabinet I have read in some histories and text-books accounts of decisions being taken by vote. This has not been my experience, either in Cabinets in which I have sat or over which I have presided. Indeed, I cannot recall a single instance. If there was a clear difference of view between two or more sections of the Cabinet, it was my practice, after a kind of Second Reading debate, to postpone decision for a further meeting. If the matter was pressing the meeting would be held the same afternoon or evening; if not, at the next meeting of the Cabinet or at one specially called. Agreement was invariably reached.

In addition to the Foreign Secretary and the Chancellor of the Exchequer, the Prime Minister should encourage individual Ministers to come to him with their problems and discuss them informally. With the members of the Administration outside the Cabinet, whether Ministers or Under Secretaries, he should try to keep in as close touch as possible. It is a useful tradition that when the principal of a Department is away the Under Secretary comes in his place to the Cabinet, as of course do other Ministers not in the Cabinet when their particular subject is on the agenda.

Finally, Cabinet meetings should not be too solemn. A little humour can often act as a lubricant or even a solvent at tense moments. While I could not, of course, hope to rival Churchill, I had his example always in my mind.

Next, the House of Commons. No team of Ministers, however well selected, can stand except by its support. Every Prime Minister therefore must keep in close touch with the opinions and moods of Members. Churchill at the height of his power during the wartime coalition was extremely sensitive to Parliamentary humours and was anxious to show to the world, even at the most critical moments, that he governed not by personal power but by the continuous and willing confidence of a democratically elected assembly. At the same time a most valuable exercise for encouraging humility, good for the political souls of all Ministers, is that provided by our system of Parliamentary Questions. Certainly neither Hitler nor Mussolini would have found it convenient to submit themselves to such a discipline. Perhaps even the atmosphere in Paris might have been different if de Gaulle had been forced to go down to the Chamber on Tuesdays and Thursdays and face a running fire of questions. One hour is allowed each day for Questions, from 2.30 to 3.30. In 1957 it was the practice for the Prime Minister's questions to begin at number forty-five. It was thought that this would normally provide sufficient time for the questions to be reached and answered. But owing to the growing loquacity of Members and the increase in the number of supplementaries it often happened that my questions were not reached or were interrupted by the clock at 3.30. On one occasion the Labour Opposition laid a trap for me. Normally with forty-four questions to be dealt with ahead of mine I would not arrive in the Chamber until some minutes after 3.00. On 18 February none of the Labour Members, whose questions occupied the greater part of the order paper, were in their places. They hoped, of course, to catch me absent from duty. Altogether some thirty questions addressed to various Ministers were not asked. However, my ever watchful Parliamentary Private Secretary, Knox Cunningham, had heard some rumour of this tactical exercise. I was therefore in my place when the Speaker took the chair, and answered some thirty questions in succession until the hour ended. Even the Parliamentary correspondent of the *Manchester Guardian*, not always a friendly critic, was impressed:

> Mr. Macmillan's question-time yesterday made history of a kind. The self-sacrifice of the Opposition in clearing the arena for him and giving him the lion's share of the golden hour all to himself will not soon be forgotten. . . .
> There is not a veteran here who can remember when a Prime Minister last stood at the dispatch box being cross-examined for forty minutes on end . . . there was the elegant Mr. Macmillan

—slightly bronzed from his travels and dedicated to as much silence as possible in these troubled times—stalking into the arena a good half-hour before his usual cue. His ringcraft, it has to be reported, was superb.[1]

Later in the year the system was changed, and my questions came on at 3.15 p.m., whatever the number previously answered. This was a great convenience as it made it unnecessary for me to arrive until just before this time.

Apart from answering Parliamentary Questions twice a week, always an anxious and sometimes a dangerous labour, there was the need for fairly frequent speeches. Except on more or less formal occasions, such as the opening of a new session, these were nearly always when the Government was under serious attack, either by a vote of censure or a challenge on large questions of policy. I always found it much easier to end a debate than to begin it. In an opening speech, especially on an important issue, one is confined to a more or less prepared text. But in closing a debate I used only brief notes and accordingly spoke with greater freedom and usually with greater effect.

In addition to these two means available for Ministers to present their case—questions and speeches—there has grown up an additional device known as a 'Ministerial Statement' made after the end of the Question hour. Sometimes it is unavoidable; but it is always a dangerous method. Departmental officials are fond of it and even experienced Ministers are apt to fall for such easy publicity. On one occasion I wrote to a Minister who wanted to persuade me to this course:

I have thought carefully over your suggestion for a statement, but I shall do my best to avoid it at present. Of all Parliamentary techniques I have always thought the Ministerial Statement the worst. A debate is one thing : you can put forward your own arguments and answer those of your opponents; the Parliamentary Question is another: you can always call it off after two or three supplementaries. But in a statement you have all the disadvantages of exposing every flank at the same time without the power to cover any of them effectively. Supplementary

[1] *Manchester Guardian*, 19 February 1960.

Questions go on indefinitely and are not stopped by the Speaker and yet you have no right to wind up the debate.

I believe that Ministers would do well to avoid statements wherever possible, or to confine them to formal matters. I have always tried to do this where my own affairs are concerned. The inspired Question for written reply is a very good method of making a statement without being knocked about at the end.[1]

But the House of Commons does not consist merely of the Chamber. The lobbies, the dining-rooms and above all the smoking-room are of equal importance. For the first sixteen years of my Parliamentary life I had been a back-bencher; and I had learnt to love the life and the sense of comradeship which bound us all together. In the smoking-room particularly one could make many friends among all Parties, and conversations were free and un-inhibited, stimulated or soothed by drink and tobacco. In some ways it was rather like the atmosphere of a college or regiment. Perhaps it was this that kept us all so young at heart and in spirit in spite of the passing years. Certainly I can say with truth that in the course of the forty years during which I was a member of the House of Commons I made many friends and few enemies, even in my own Party.

For the management of the Party outside Parliament I relied upon the succession of Chairmen who served me and the Party so well—Poole, Hailsham, Butler and Macleod. The continued strength of a Government depends upon the maintenance of its authority with the Party and with the public. There are of course times when Party unity must be risked in a wider interest. Such a decision had to be taken when the Cabinet resolved to apply for membership of the European Economic Community and throughout the period that followed. But the Conservative Party, in or out of Parliament, must in general aim at catholicity—there must be no heresy hunts. Remembering the long years between the wars, when I was no doubt regarded as a dangerous nuisance, I always had a sneaking sympathy with a rebel, so long as he was sincere. As Leader of the Party, I had now to be more respectable and more circumspect. But I had also to be more diligent, for my position involved the

[1] Note to Minister of Supply, 22 June 1957.

preparation and delivery of innumerable speeches, on big and small occasions. Even for those on formal occasions, such as the Guildhall banquet in November, great care was necessary, for the speech might have repercussions throughout the world. Every word must be watched.

In addition to public meetings at home, to explain Government policy, and to rally Party support, I found it necessary to deliver lectures or speeches in foreign countries. These could have great significance, and required much thought and labour. In addition, abroad, but happily not at home (except for some reason at airports), there was the ordeal of the Press Conference.

Sometimes I could not help grudging all the time and effort devoted to that most ephemeral thing—a speech. A politician, as I once reminded a famous actor of my acquaintance, is in this respect most unhappily placed. An actor in a successful play can repeat the same part night after night, and in the end, almost play it in his sleep. We have to write the play, act the play, and it only runs one night!

Speeches, however well prepared, are an occasion for dangerous traps; sometimes of minor importance and sometimes involving major trouble. As an example of the first I remember a pitfall into which I fell headlong at Leicester in March 1962:

> Here we had a splendid meeting—4,000 in hall, with many standing. A good amount of opposition—some quiet, some vocal. The speech proved very successful and was very much applauded at the end. The jokes went well. But beware of oratorical questions! I was caught out by one. 'What is the obstacle to progress?' 'You are'—this floored me.[1]

More troublesome were the consequences of a remark made in Bedford on 20 July 1957.[2] In pointing out the advances in standard of life in recent years I made what seemed to me a harmless observation—'most of our people have never had it so good'. But I went on to refer to those sections of the community who had not enjoyed their full share in the growing prosperity. Moreover, my words were intended rather as a warning than a boast. For I continued to speak of the dangers of inflation:

[1] 5 March 1962.   [2] See *Riding the Storm*, pp. 350–1.

What is beginning to worry some of us is: 'Is it too good to be true?' or perhaps I should say: 'Is it too good to last?' For, amidst all this prosperity, there is one problem that has troubled us—in one way or another—ever since the war. It's the problem of rising prices.

For some reason it was not until several years later that this phrase was taken out of its context and turned into a serious charge against me, of being too materialistic and showing too little of a spiritual approach to life. The Archbishop of Canterbury made this the subject of a sermon. In 1962 my friend Lord Salisbury made it the text of a speech. To both of them I wrote privately in protest. Lord Salisbury sent a frank and friendly apology; the Archbishop's reply was less satisfactory. Curiously enough these are the inevitable hazards to which all politicians are prone. One of my great predecessors, Asquith, was for many years pursued by an answer which he had made to a Supplementary Question from a persistent and troublesome inquirer. 'You had better wait and see,' he replied, firmly and even fiercely. Yet these words, used not with a dilatory but a minatory intention, were distorted into an example of the Prime Minister's alleged sloth and lethargy. No explanation was of any use. '*Nescit vox missa reverti.*'

Finally, and most formidably, in the field of what are now called 'public relations', there were the Press and the television. As regards the Press I cannot pay too high a tribute to my adviser, Sir Harold Evans. He made no mistakes, though I made plenty. I have generally got on well with proprietors, editors and individual journalists. There have been periods when I have been overpraised; and as a corollary to this, periods when I have perhaps been too severely criticised. One must get used to being lauded one day and defamed the next. Perhaps the most trying experience is being preached at. But all this is part of the game. Now, in addition to the Press, new vehicles have come into being of vast potential influence, the sound radio and the television systems, metropolitan and provincial. It takes a long time to learn to speak tolerably well either in the House of Commons or the hustings. But in order to appear even adequately on the radio or still more on the television one must acquire a completely different and altogether new technique. Almost everything that one has learnt for public speaking has to be forgotten for a television performance. One has to remind oneself all the time that it is not a speech but a conversation; and that the audience, however large in the aggregate, in fact consists of two or three persons sitting quietly in a room, not subject to any of the emotions which can be stirred in a great public gathering.

I should mention two other matters which must be a source of continual concern to every Prime Minister. The first regards 'Security Services' for which in the broad sense he is responsible. I shall later describe in detail some of the troubles which arose under this head. The second concerns Patronage. Disraeli wrote, over a hundred years ago, in a letter to Lord Derby, these words: 'Patronage is the outward and visible sign of an inward and spiritual grace, that is power.' Although the whole field of appointments is now restricted compared with the large volume of offices, great and small, which were in the gift of Governments in old days, yet Patronage is still, in its various forms, a matter which needs great care and infinite pains. On the political side, there are the questions of honours and other distinctions, as well as appointments inside and outside the Administration in which Members of Parliament are deeply interested. As regards minor honours, there is now a convention which has been operating smoothly for many years. In these cases the Whips and the Departments have a special right to put forward their own recommendations within fairly well defined rules. These are all sifted by an elaborate procedure, and the results put before the Prime Minister for his approval. As regards peerages and major honours, these are matters in which the Prime Minister must take special care in his recommendations to the Queen. Since the Act of 1958 a new order of peerage has been created, Life Peers. In making these submissions, I consulted the Leader of the Opposition as to his wishes where members of his Party were concerned. The Conservative selections and the non-political choices were, of course, in a different category; for these I took sole responsibility. There are other equally important appointments which necessarily cause much labour and trouble. For many of these, such as the Chiefs of Staff, Governors of Colonies,

Ambassadors, High Commissioners, heads of nationalised industries, and so forth, the duty of recommendation to the Crown
rests with the Minister concerned. Nevertheless, it is the custom
that the Prime Minister's approval be secured before any submission
is made. This applies to many of the legal appointments for which
the Lord Chancellor is primarily responsible. Then there are other
places, legal and lay, for which the Prime Minister must make
recommendations himself. The Lord Chief Justice is one in the
first category and the Regius Professorships and the like in the
second. Finally, there is the ecclesiastical Patronage—the selection
of Bishops and Deans, to which should be added the filling of
those incumbencies which are, for historical reasons, in the hands
of the Crown. Some of these fall to the Prime Minister to fill;
others are the gift of the Lord Chancellor. I arranged towards the
end of my time a close co-operation between our advisers—reaching
something which in a more vulgar sphere might be called a merger.

Normally, the appointment of Bishops and Deans is a matter
which can be handled successfully by careful consultation both
within the Diocese and with the Archbishop of the Province, or
perhaps with both Archbishops. It fell to my lot to have to make a
submission to the Queen for the appointment of an Archbishop
of Canterbury, subsequent to the resignation of Archbishop Fisher.
Indeed, since the choice fell upon the then Archbishop of York,
this involved making two Archbishops. Here my responsibility
was particularly onerous, since to obtain advice was more difficult
and more delicate. But I was admirably served in all these difficult
decisions first by David Stephens and secondly by John Hewitt.

A new burden which falls to a Prime Minister today is the
number of visits which it is necessary to pay overseas. I was perhaps
unique in undertaking two long tours—the Commonwealth tour
in 1958 and the African tour in 1960. But in addition during my
term of office there were visits to Bermuda or to Nassau to meet the
President of the United States as well as six visits to Washington.
The last almost always involved a call at Ottawa. There were many
journeys to Paris and to Bonn as well as visits to Moscow, Rome,
Norway, Sweden and to Finland. In search of peace in the eastern
Mediterranean, I went to Ankara, Athens and Cyprus itself. Many,

if not all, of these involved return visits with appropriate conferences and entertainments. How different from the last century. One of Mr. Gladstone's latest biographers has calculated that during the fourteen years of his life as Prime Minister he spent on an average five months in each year at Hawarden Castle—working no doubt, but quietly in his own library.

There were of course many lighter moments in all this volume of work. Two honours gave me special pleasure—my election to the Chancellorship of Oxford in March 1960, and my appointment as a Freeman of the City of London in December 1961.

The physical as well as the intellectual strain involved was certainly heavy. Although I had inherited a strong constitution it had undoubtedly been impaired by serious wounds in the First War and by subsequent illnesses and operations. I was in my sixty-third year when I became Prime Minister, and in my seventieth when I resigned. During all this period I found it only possible to carry out my duties by taking great care and resting as much as possible—doing a great deal of my work in bed. One rule I kept to—to read for at least an hour before going to sleep and usually old favourites—Jane Austen, Dickens, Thackeray and Trollope.

However responsible the position of the Minister in charge of one of the great Departments of State—the Foreign Office, the Treasury, the Ministry of Defence and the rest—to become Prime Minister makes a complete change in one's life. In a Department, the burdens, however onerous, are to some extent limited. As Prime Minister one is answerable for everything. In a Department, the ordinary life with one's colleagues and with the outside world goes on in a normal atmosphere and follows a more or less normal pattern. The Prime Minister's position is unique. Strangely enough it is also very lonely. I imagine a captain of a ship to have something of the same feeling. For example, I had soon noticed that people do not come and see you unasked—at least not the people that you want to see. Yet with this loneliness there is a complete lack of privacy. I had grown accustomed to being guarded by detectives when I was Foreign Secretary, but one could sometimes elude them. As Prime Minister this was quite impossible. Every moment of the day and night is planned out, recorded, watched. Indeed, during the summer of 1963 when the most fantastic charges were being thrown about in the Lobbies of the House of Commons and in the less reputable by-ways of Fleet Street, I remember saying laughingly to one of my colleagues, that I alone could rebut any accusations against my private life because I had none !

There is no respite and in effect no holiday. You go away for a few days. The staff goes with you and the Press photographers too. These seemed to take a special interest in my few relaxations—golf and shooting. But the telegrams and papers followed day by day, often hour by hour; even to the golf links or the grouse moor, and by some perverse arrangement there was always a crisis in August. The only method of getting a complete holiday was to hand over the Government, with the Queen's permission, to a colleague. But this was equally to deprive a hard-worked Minister of his hard-earned rest. This was an expedient to which I never had recourse, except during a long tour—for instance, a Commonwealth tour. Then I was fortunate in being able to entrust the management of affairs to Butler. Even so the messages came—and the crises— coupled with requests for advice and decision. Nevertheless, if it was hard work, it was great fun. No one has any sympathy with the self-pitying statesman, going about, like poor Ramsay MacDonald, complaining that he felt like 'a weary Titan'. After all, the answer is easy. Nobody asked you to hold up the world. If your shoulders are tired, there are others ready and anxious to sustain the burden.

CHAPTER III

Sixes and Sevens

THE Treaty of Rome, which constituted the European Economic Community—soon to be known as the Common Market—was signed on 25 March 1957. If ratified by all the countries concerned, it was due to come into force on 1 January 1959. I have described in an earlier volume the plan which the British Government put forward with the hope of bridging the gap which threatened to develop between two groups of European powers, and thus preserving, in a vital field, the concept of European unity.[1] All through the long and often disappointing story of the European movement there has loomed the danger of still further division. Already cruelly partitioned by a line from Stettin to Trieste, was Europe now to be sub-divided by the creation of a central *bloc*— inward- rather than outward-looking—whose development might well encourage all the fissiparous tendencies of the old but fragmented continent? Already in the sphere of defence Europe was deprived of the help of the neutralist countries, like Sweden, Switzerland and, under the Treaty of 1955, Austria. Was this now to be repeated in the economic field, where it could not be balanced by the North American Alliance? Moreover, what were the political implications, as the community increased in power and authority? On the narrower issue, no doubt, the commitments accepted by the Six under the General Agreement on Tariffs and Trade (GATT) would act as a restraint. Yet those who cared deeply about the European vision felt that some action should be taken to promote the unity and expansion of European trade and commerce. Hence, under Eden's premiership, the British Government had worked out, by October 1956, a comprehensive plan. This, technically known as Plan G, was put forward for the consideration of all the mem-

[1] See *Riding the Storm*, chap. xiv.

bers of the Organisation for European Economic Co-operation (O.E.E.C.). Broadly it was a proposal for the creation of an area of complete freedom from tariffs throughout all non-Communist Europe to be reached by stages and to cover all goods other than foodstuffs—in a word, an Industrial Free Trade Area. Negotiations continued for nearly two years. At first the French Government, with whose members we had formed close ties through the dangers and trials of the Middle Eastern crisis, proved both sympathetic and favourable. All the other leading members of O.E.E.C. welcomed or professed to welcome the plan in principle. After the inevitable tendency to delay, which is endemic in democratic governments and international organisations, we were told that no final steps could be taken until the hurdles both of signature and ratification of the Treaty of Rome had been safely surmounted. Once that was accomplished, our wider scheme, as regards European industry, would surely prove acceptable. To this argument we had to yield. But the situation in France was radically changed by de Gaulle's return to power in the summer of 1958. In November, with many graceful protestations of sympathy, the French Government finally declined to participate. Our plan was dead.

This long and frustrating negotiation had, at least, brought the various nations outside the Six to sense the danger. When the Cabinet met to discuss the effect of the French veto of November 1958, we all knew that we must now face the situation both with imagination and resolution. The implementation of the Treaty of Rome was now only six weeks ahead. We must try at all costs to forestall the dangers inherent in the creation of this powerful and perhaps discriminatory bloc. The first step was a formal representation to the Six, through O.E.E.C., asking for the extension to all members of GATT of the tariff concessions they were due to make to each other on 1 January 1959, as well as for the benefits from the relaxation of quotas also envisaged for the same date. If France would agree, we should avoid the emergence of a new area of discrimination, have some hope of preventing the other European powers from being drawn into the orbit of the Common Market, and at least gain time for a consideration of a means of harmonising all European interests. If France refused, she would be in breach of the O.E.E.C. convention, as well as of the GATT treaty. On the other members of the Six, or Common Market, powers we could rely at least in principle. In practice, it would all turn on France, or rather, on de Gaulle.

The situation was complicated by the fact that we were still living in a world not merely of tariffs and quotas, but also of restrictions upon the convertibility both of the franc and of sterling. At the time I took a gloomy view of the prospects. Although in the event the Six were to pursue a far more liberal policy than we feared, this was the result of powerful and steady pressure.

> The European Trade picture is darkening. We had hoped that the suggestions of the Six for 1 January would be fairly reasonable, and might avoid *all* discrimination. But I fear this will turn out not to be true and the results of the French proposals (which they have persuaded the Germans to adopt) will be very serious indeed.[1]

At the beginning of December 1958 I received a curious appeal from the German side obviously at French instigation. Dr. Erhard came to see me accompanied by

> a lot of 'tough' Germans. He came on a hurried mission from the Six Powers, asking that *no* further meetings either of the Maudling Committee *or* of O.E.E.C. should be held till the end of January! The offer of the Six was not a negotiation; it was a statement of what they would do on 1 January. Dr. Erhard seemed rather embarrassed (as well he might be). I rejected this plea altogether.[2]

Nevertheless, I liked Erhard personally, with his large face and small mouth, recalling the pictures of Henry VIII. But he was not sufficiently persuaded of the justice of his case to make his advocacy convincing.

Since Vice-President Nixon was paying us a short visit I took the opportunity of impressing upon him our deep concern about a further sub-division of Europe. After he left I thought it worth writing on 28 November to George Humphrey, the American

[1] 28 November 1958.   [2] 4 December 1958.

Secretary for the Treasury, whom I had by now got to know pretty well.

> We are just finishing the Vice-President's visit. It has been a great success, and he has done very well. In particular his speeches have been excellent and very favourably received. I was only sorry that he could not stay longer and see as much of the modernity and industry of Britain as he has of our ancient institutions and pageantry.
> I am still preoccupied about the economic position, which I do not think at all good. As you know, I am an expansionist, and I do not believe the Free World will ultimately stand up against Communism unless the overall level of our trade keeps going up. Nor shall we attract the underdeveloped countries if we pay them wretched prices for their raw materials, and occasionally give them loans.
> Meanwhile, in Europe it looks as though we may be in for a trade war—at any rate we are having to take our precautions against one. However, I hope that we may nevertheless avoid the worst and . . . at least get an agreement which prevents discrimination next 1 January.

Like so many problems this was only part of a larger complex, which I tried to summarise in a note to the Foreign Secretary on 28 November as follows:

> *The Berlin issue* is, in fact, an ultimatum with six months to run. We shall not be able to avoid negotiation. How is it to be carried out? Will it necessarily lead to discussion of the future of a united Germany and possible 'Disengagement Plans'?

> *Tests and Surprise Attack*
> These negotiations at Geneva seem likely to drag on more or less indefinitely. If we can get American consent to abandon the link altogether, we may make some advance from the propaganda point of view, but I doubt whether we shall reach any nearer agreement.

> *European Free Trade*
> You will have no doubt read an excellent article in the *Financial Times* this morning. If not, pray do so. It is clear that the Germans have really sold out to the French on every count.

I do not think we can deal with these problems separately. The groups of Powers in this strange quadrille keep changing. In the first, it is Russia and the three occupying Powers, with Germany the most interested and with most to gain. In the second, France is out and Germany is out. In the third, the United States seem uninterested and the Germans and French have made an unholy alliance against the British. We must think of all these problems together, for that is what the British people will do. In April we are to celebrate a jubilee of NATO. It will be a rather hollow ceremony so far as we are concerned. £35m. of unrequited exports for the next fifty years or so. For the British are being discriminated against with increasingly disastrous effects on their European trade.

I am turning all this over in my mind. I think the most balanced and helpful of our colleagues to assist you on the foreign affairs side would be the Chancellor of the Exchequer. . . .

As regards Russia, it may be that Khrushchev is really working for a Summit Conference without the Chinese. In that case, it would certainly not be bad politics for me to take the lead in suggesting it.

Meanwhile the situation was further complicated by monetary questions. The French were planning to devalue the franc and make it convertible. The United Kingdom was planning to 'go convertible' but not to devalue. In the event both these operations were completed at the end of December 1958.[1] At this time I received a long communication from Adenauer assuring me that Germany was abiding by the policy of 'a multi-lateral European economic association'. But he begged that everyone should remain patient and understanding about France which was going through 'a process of political re-orientation'. Above all

> we should on no account link the question of the European economic association with the problem of Berlin and with the community of the member countries of the North Atlantic Treaty Organisation. The impression must not arise that the West is in disagreement over fundamental political principles.

He declared that the members of O.E.E.C. had asked its commission to

[1] See *Riding the Storm*, pp. 725–6.

submit to the Six not later than 1 March, 1959, proposals for a common stand which can be taken by the six member countries in the negotiations on the multi-lateral European economic association.

Finally, he made an appeal that we should keep calm at this critical moment. All this, though characteristic, was pretty cool. This letter was dated 13 December. I was not surprised to receive it. I had already had an intimation that he wished to see me, and persuade me to allow Britain to shoulder the burdens without sharing in the benefits of European co-operation. 'He, of course, wants to talk about Berlin. I shall talk to him about European Trade.'[1]

When the meeting of the O.E.E.C. took place on 15 December both of the two groups, the Six and the Rest, launched bitter complaints against each other in similar terms. Both declared that they were being asked to negotiate under the threat, either of discrimination or of retaliation. The meeting, which was an unpleasant one throughout, was accordingly adjourned in some confusion. We got little help, during these anxious weeks, from the Americans. But the Foreign Secretary had a useful discussion with de Gaulle on 22 December and reported that the General seemed to be impressed by the dangers, although preoccupied with his own larger plans and ambitions. De Gaulle and his friends had never been supporters of the Rome Treaty. Indeed, had he come earlier to power it is doubtful whether it would have been signed and ratified, at least in its existing form. Like the British, he had an instinctive dislike of the ambitious edifice of supra-national institutions which was to be set up under the Commission. Nor had he much use for the vast international bureaucracy which was already swarming and about to settle in Brussels. He, no doubt, felt that if Europe was ever to be made into a unity of any kind it should be led by France with its headquarters in Paris. In any event, without waiting for the adjourned meeting of O.E.E.C. the French took a sudden decision greatly to their credit. I felt at the time, and have no reason to change my view, that this was due entirely to de Gaulle's impulse. At the same time as the announcements of the new convertibility of the pound and the franc, which were wisely co-ordinated between

[1] 7 December 1958.

London and Paris and therefore could not be interpreted even by the French anglophobe Press as an act of hostility on our part, the French proclaimed, with some solemnity, that since they had accepted the O.E.E.C. rules they would obey them scrupulously. Accordingly the tariff cuts under the Treaty of Rome would be extended to all O.E.E.C. and GATT members. 'This is a great moral success for us,'[1] I noted in my diary. But it was a much greater victory for the French, and made a deep impression on all Europe. This was creating a new style—a decision by the General, without discussion or consultation.

Although there seemed some discrimination as regards global quotas where the new concessions were not extended beyond the Six, this was a matter more of principle than of real importance. The only trade seriously affected was that between Britain and France. On this point my colleagues decided at a meeting of the Cabinet held on the last day of the year that we should 'adopt an "attentiste" policy—in other words, wait for their answer to our proposal which now holds the field'.[1]

In the New Year discussions continued, and on 5 March 1959 a 'short-term' compromise was arranged with the French which would hold the situation for a time. In April a *modus vivendi* was worked out which was turned into a Treaty by the end of the month.

Although this broadly liberal policy was encouraging it only, of course, covered the immediate situation. What of the future?

> What we have to consider is what to do next. If we could make some agricultural concessions to Denmark, we might be able to organise another European grouping with the Scandinavian countries, Switzerland and Austria. But here the problem is our pledges to British farmers.[2]

I continued to brood over this uncertain and potentially dangerous disarray into which Europe seemed to have drifted.

> Can we organise another European Free Trade Area out of the European countries *not* in the Rome community? It is obviously in our interests, industrially and commercially. But there will be the Commonwealth objections (although this plan cannot in any

[1] 31 December 1958.   [2] 3 April 1959.

way injure Commonwealth interests). There will also be *some* price to be paid to Denmark—probably in bacon and/or blue cheese. But this—although very small—may arouse British farmers against us.[1]

The scheme we had in mind covering countries not included in the Six was limited to industry; it was only to the Danes that some agricultural concessions might have to be made. Meanwhile the Swedish Government came forward with just such a plan. Since there was a serious risk that each of these countries might negotiate separately with the Six, thus leaving us isolated with increasing damage to our economic strength, my colleagues agreed, on 7 May, that we should take up the Swedish proposal. Although we were reluctant to embark upon a policy which would accentuate the European division we believed that in the long run this might be the best and, indeed, the only method of achieving final unity. The countries concerned, in effect, amounted to the United Kingdom, Sweden, Norway, Denmark, Austria, Switzerland and Portugal, and were soon to be known as the Seven. Thus arose the common saying that poor Europe was now at 'Sixes and Sevens'. I undertook to keep in close touch with the Commonwealth to the extent that they might be affected. I also thought it wise as well as courteous to inform the Governments of the Common Market a little in advance of the establishment of the proposed working party for the new group. It naturally was essential to consult the representatives of our own agricultural and fishing industries. Events moved rapidly; by 10 June I was able to note that

> we had Ministerial Committee on European Trade Association (Stockholm group). This is going on all right, but we do not yet know what price we shall have to pay the Danes.[2]

There is always a price to be paid to somebody. The important thing is to be sure of the value of what you are buying.

The Swedish plan, which was ultimately accepted by seven European nations—sometimes known as the Outer Seven—was conceived of as a temporary measure pending the final unification of the economy of Europe. It followed very closely upon our original

[1] 6 May 1959.   [2] 10 June 1959.

proposals for an Industrial Free Trade Area. The Treaty, unlike the organisation of the Six, was to include no strong central institutions and no common tariff. Agricultural and fishing products were omitted. Initial tariff cuts by all the Seven on their trade with each other were to be twenty per cent, starting on 1 July 1960. Subsequent cuts designed to remove all tariffs on manufactured goods within the association would take place over a ten-year period.

Although agriculture and fishing were excluded, yet account had certainly to be taken of the Danes. Denmark was caught, like Hamlet, on the horns of a dilemma, 'to join or not to join'. She could not join the Six; yet the Danish fear of retaliation by the Six was very real if she were to join the Seven. We understood and appreciated their difficulty. The chief product about which the Danes were concerned was, naturally, bacon. At this time there was a ten per cent tariff in the United Kingdom on imported Danish bacon. On 12 June the Danish Prime Minister came to see me at No. 10.

> We had a very useful hour's talk about the proposed new European grouping—the Seven. I tried to persuade him (a) that I regarded this as a bridge, not an act of trade war against the Rome Powers; (b) that I did not think the Six would retaliate—many of our friends in the Six had expressed their pleasure at what was going on; (c) that we must not wait; and not try official negotiations with the Six until our organisation of the Seven was formed; (d) that he should send his Foreign Minister as soon as possible to negotiate with us on the agricultural problem on a *bilateral* basis.
>
> Mr. Hansen was rather cautious at first. He seemed particularly anxious about possible retaliation by Germany and Italy against Denmark's agricultural exports. But he finally seemed to agree to all these propositions, and Mr. Krag is to come about 22 June.[1]

The leaders of British agriculture now began to take alarm and to exert political pressure. Nevertheless when my colleagues discussed the Stockholm plan at the beginning of July, they fully realised the importance of the issues.

> The stakes in this affair are very high. . . . For if we cannot successfully organise the opposition group—Scandinavia, Denmark,

[1] 12 June 1959.

Switzerland, Austria, etc.—then we shall undoubtedly be eaten up, one by one, by the Six. Already I have heard of plans for American factories—which were to have been built in Scotland, Northern Ireland, or an area of unemployment in England—being cancelled. These are to be built in France or Germany, where the pull of the 'Common Market' attracts them.[1]

To achieve our purpose we knew that we had to make some concessions—unfortunately involving obvious dangers in the summer before a General Election. Many Conservative Members for agricultural constituencies were already becoming concerned.

For—although removing the ten per cent tariff on Danish *bacon*, with the same on *luncheon-meat*, amounts to nothing real—certainly no real injury to a home industry which is protected by *price* support (not by the tariff) yet the combination of (*a*) suspicion natural to farmers, (*b*) Sir James Turner (Lord Netherthorpe) . . . (*c*) Lord Beaverbrook and his Press may well lose us ten to twelve precious seats in the agricultural constituencies.[1]

Happily Ministers were in a resolute mood.

The Cabinet—with full knowledge of the risks but equal knowledge of their duty—decided to go ahead and give instructions to Maudling and Hare (our negotiators) accordingly. As for the tariff, we agreed to remove all the ten per cent in *three* successive bites starting on 1 July 1960.[1]

This decision was taken at a meeting early in the day. When I was told during the afternoon

that the Danes (who had asked for every other kind of concession —on milk, butter, cheese, etc.—which we refused) wanted (*a*) a better formula on *future* agricultural intention, (*b*) the tariff, to go in *one* swoop—1 July 1960,[1]

I thought it best to call my colleagues together for a final review. We decided to

stick to our formula on *future* intention—there must be no equivocation or misunderstanding here of any sort, especially as regards our right to fix our *price* support for pigs as we like. But

[1] 7 July 1959.

we gave our negotiators latitude to accept the abolition of the small tariff (ten per cent) in *two* bites instead of *three*.

Later in the day, I [learnt] that the Danes (after telephoning to their Cabinet) had agreed.[1]

Lord Netherthorpe, when he heard the news, came to protest, and we had a rather fierce argument. The retention of this small tariff would have little effect, and the bacon farmers knew it to be so. They relied on the price support. It was more a matter of psychological than of real warfare, accentuated by the General Election looming ahead.

On the whole, I think this rather firm (at certain points almost acrimonious) discussion has done good. He has certainly much toned down his statement.[2]

Since we were in the middle of a printers' strike, I could not help taking a grim pleasure from the thought that the farmers' journals would not be available and that even the moderated accounts of the farmers' leader, now roaring 'as gently as any sucking dove', would be lost in the general silence.

All the questions at issue had now been settled. Accordingly a draft of the proposed Convention was published. Since Continental holidays, at any rate as regards diplomatic negotiations are concerned, last even longer than in Britain, it did not prove possible to reach a final conclusion until after the General Election in October.

For there were wider issues than Danish bacon or Scandinavian fish fillets (soon to be thrown into the negotiations). Partly to clear my own mind and partly to stimulate discussion in the Foreign Office, I sent a memorandum to the Foreign Secretary, Selwyn Lloyd, on 22 October on the whole question of the organisation of Europe. In view of the later developments it is at least of interest in showing my thoughts at this stage.

Clearly one of the most important tasks of the next five years will be to organise the relations of the United Kingdom with Europe. For the first time since the Napoleonic era the major continental powers are united in a positive economic grouping, with considerable political aspects, which, although not specifi-

[1] 7 July 1959.   [2] 9 July 1959.

cally directed against the United Kingdom, may have the effect of excluding us both from European markets and from consultation in European policy.

For better or worse, the Common Market looks like being here to stay at least for the foreseeable future. Furthermore, if we tried to disrupt it we should unite against us all the Europeans who have felt humiliated during the past decade by the weakness of Europe. We should also probably upset the United States, as well as playing into the hands of the Russians. And, of course, the Common Market has certain advantages in bringing greater cohesion to Europe. The question is how to live with the Common Market economically and turn its political effects into channels harmless to us.

We are erecting a first line of defence in the economic field through the Seven. But this, for geographical and other reasons, is a rather tender plant. We must no doubt allow the Seven to come into being properly before we make any further economic moves, but it seems desirable to set in train as quickly as possible a thorough examination of (a) the probable effects of the Common Market on our economy, (b) the sort of price which it would be worth paying in order to be economically associated with it (something more in fact than just the concept of the Free Trade Area), and (c) the measures of defence which we might take. Much of this work will have to be done by industry, and much has already been done. But, for example, we should perhaps consider the effect of the large firms establishing assembly plants inside the Common Market area; does this help the United Kingdom generally or not? Then there is the question of investment in the Common Market which is becoming fashionable in the City.

All this economic work is more or less straightforward and could be put in hand. What is much more difficult is how to handle Europe politically. The core of the Common Market is the Franco-German Alliance. In the last resort it is the Governments of these two countries which we must influence.

The French protagonists of the European Economic Community may be divided into three camps. There are those who believe that the world is now too small for the nation state and that Europe's only chance of making her voice heard in the world is through a unified system. These people, such as Jean Monnet, believe that the Common Market with its economic arrangements will in time produce European political unity. Secondly there is a group of French Nationalists, to whom I suspect that M. Debré belongs, who believe that France can only play a big part in the world by becoming the spokesman for Europe in the Councils of the West. Finally there are the *patronat* who see in the Common Market an opportunity of preserving the traditional protected position of French industry [against Britain and America]. The French are not therefore united about the political and economic advantages to them of the European Economic Community; but all three groups of French supporters of the Community have an interest in excluding the United Kingdom from it.

The Germans see the advantages of the Common Market largely in political terms. Dr. Adenauer, in particular, fears the effect of Soviet political pressure on an isolated Western Germany, and also believes that only a Franco-German political alliance can prevent the Anglo-Saxons from doing a deal with the Russians over Eastern Europe at Germany's expense. He is, therefore, prepared to pay an economic price for French political help. German industry, on the other hand, is divided; the heavy industries probably welcome arrangements such as the Coal and Steel Community, which permit the traditional cartels to extend their influence, but the exporting industries are frightened lest by being involved in a comparatively high tariff area, they lose their markets outside the Six in return for a comparatively small gain inside the Six; this seems to be the argument which appeals particularly to Dr. Erhard and his friends. It is, however, an argument which will probably get less strong as the years go by, since it may be argued that the large 'home market' which German industry would gain inside the Six will, in time, so reduce their costs as to enable German industry to compete successfully overseas, even against retaliatory tariff barriers.

At this time the situation was still, to some extent, fluid. Neither the Common Market countries nor those of the Outer Seven were altogether satisfied. There seemed still some hope of a bridge being made between the two.

On the narrower front there was one more hurdle to be overcome before EFTA—the league of the Seven—could be finally agreed.

The Foreign Ministers' Conference in Geneva, May 1959
Left to right: Selwyn Lloyd, Couve de Murville, Herter, Petitpierre (Swiss Foreign Minister), Gromyko.
'Largely owing to Selwyn's initial efforts, the Conference has at least got started.'

The Western Summit, December 1959
Macmillan, de Gaulle, Adenauer, Eisenhower.
'A lot of good talks have taken place, and a very good atmosphere of confidence and friendship created.'

Towards the end of the summer there had been some murmurings from the Norwegians about fish, and in the few weeks before the final initialling of the Convention those slippery if succulent delicacies almost brought the negotiation to an end. On 29 October 1959, flushed with electoral success, my colleagues met to discuss and if possible resolve this last difficulty.

A long and very good discussion on the Stockholm negotiation –the F.T.A. of the Seven–which is trembling in the balance. The Norwegians are being very truculent over fish. We decided to give them a concession on canned or frozen fish. Whether they will be satisfied or not we cannot tell. But we might try to work out a compromise through the Swedes. Of course, the home fishing industry will be indignant–but the stakes are *very* high.[1]

In the end a settlement was reached. We agreed to renounce the tariff on imports of fish from the three Scandinavian countries and allow the total imports to rise to the figure of twenty-four thousand tons annually. But we retained the right to revert to the ten per cent tariff if serious damage to our own industry took place. In addition frozen fish fillets were to be free as if they were industrial products. All this was to lead naturally to trouble with our British fishermen and increased need for help in various forms. But it was nothing to the controversies which were soon to follow the progressive decision of various countries to extend their fishing limits. This was to become a minor but nevertheless continual and painful headache in the next few years.

Finally, on 20 November 1959, the agreement for a European Free Trade Association was initialled in Stockholm. The Chancellor of the Exchequer, Heathcoat Amory, and Maudling, President of the Board of Trade, represented the United Kingdom. They had indeed both done admirable work. Maudling in particular had been through a long and frustrating period of negotiation. I had charged him with the task of trying to obtain European agreement upon an Industrial Free Trade Area to cover all the countries. He had pursued his course with admirable skill, devotion and patience and almost achieved success, only to be met at the end of his long

[1] 29 October 1959.

journey by the French veto. Nevertheless he never showed a sense either of strain or undue disappointment. His equable temper was almost as useful to him as his brilliant and fertile brain.

The Convention was well received by the Press, although there was some confusion as to how it should be interpreted. Was EFTA to be presented as a bridge to lead to ultimate agreement with E.E.C., or was it to be defended on its own merits? When it came to debate I told my colleagues I felt somewhat in the position of Lord Melbourne. We must at least all say the same thing.

Meanwhile on 23 November the Chancellor of the Exchequer made a statement regarding the initialling of the Convention which seemed generally acceptable. Mr. Douglas Jay's contribution was of special interest:

> While we on this side of the House welcome this Convention, which we have supported throughout these negotiations, I ask . . . whether it would not be wise now for the members of this new Association positively and publicly to invite the members of the European Economic Community to discuss an early association between the two groups.

Heathcoat Amory had already emphasised that we had kept in close touch with the Commonwealth and that the purpose of the new association was not merely to reduce obstacles within its own membership but to look outwards beyond the confines of the member states.

At this point we became aware of the increasing anxiety shown by the American Administration over these developments in Europe. In the United States, as in other countries, there has always been a certain dualism of approach to the question of removing trade barriers. Freer trade was accepted in principle as a proper aim of policy, but in practice the forces of protectionism were powerful. Moreover, while an Administration, whether Republican or Democrat, might be swayed by liberalising views, Congress, subject to local and industrial pressure groups, tended to yield to demands for greater protection in one form or another. The United States were especially suspicious of European trading arrangements which might discriminate against American interests. But they were prepared to accept them where they saw substantial political and military advantage. At this time, with the Berlin question unresolved and the Cold War at its height, American statesmen favoured the Six against the Seven. Indeed, unconscious of the immense difficulties of different languages, traditions and world obligations of the various countries of Europe, many American critics were impatient of their inability to arrive at the same happy conclusion as the old British colonies had reached after the War of Independence, by the formation of a Federal Union. It was, therefore, with some anxiety that we prepared for the visit of Mr. Douglas Dillon, Under Secretary of State, at the beginning of December. He made it quite clear that his Government did not favour the formation of the Seven or look with anything except alarm at the prospect of ultimate negotiations between the two groups. In conversation with Dillon neither Heathcoat Amory nor Maudling was able to make much progress. The recent 'slump', or at least 'recession', in America naturally increased their alarm.

> The Americans, with their financial crisis, are being rather 'touchy' about 'non-discrimination'. But, of course, the Six, the Seven and the European Free Trade Area are and must be to some extent 'discriminatory'. The Americans, in their desire to see Europe 'integrated', were prepared (a few years ago and until recently) to abandon the strict economic line for the political advantages. Now they are not so sure.[1]

I realised, of course, that the President did not himself claim to understand these economic problems, and I could only hope that when I met him in Paris at the end of the year I would be able to relieve his anxieties. In this I was partly successful, although far the greater part of the Paris meeting was concerned with the East–West situation. At any rate I felt satisfied that the Americans would not try to bring undue pressure upon the members of the Seven during the anxious months that must pass before ratification and imple-mentation of the Stockholm Convention could be secured.

In our own House of Commons we had little difficulty, and on 14 December we carried by 183 votes to 3 a resolution welcoming

[1] 13 December 1959.

the European Free Trade Association. The Opposition were uncertain what course to follow and therefore abstained. Three Liberals voted against, and a number of Conservatives as well as Labour Members expressed their anxiety. This discussion, although somewhat confused, made me realise how in our country too, there is a wide division between approving policies in principle and accepting their practical application.

Since I left England on 5 January 1960 for an African tour and did not reach home until the middle of February I took no part in the concluding stages of this project. The necessary Bill was admirably handled by my colleagues primarily in charge—the Chancellor of the Exchequer and the President of the Board of Trade—and was passed, on its Second Reading, without a division, on 15 February, the very day of my return. The Royal Assent was given on 22 March 1960; the Convention was ratified by all the seven nations by 3 May, and on 1 July, in accordance with the agreement, there were cuts in tariffs within the group of twenty per cent and import quotas were expanded by the same proportion. Although efforts continued to be made throughout the year to bridge the gap between the two groups, the Common Market and EFTA, in spite of much good will little progress was made. If ever European unity was to be achieved, a bolder initiative would be needed. Here, at any rate, was the end of the first round in a long struggle.

CHAPTER IV

The Road to the Summit

THE General Election of 1959, like all those since the beginning of the twentieth century, was largely, but not exclusively, dominated by economic and social issues. As usual, each of the great Parties tried to adorn their traditional images with new and attractive trimmings. Yet over these conventional contests on internal policies there loomed all the time the grim shadow of the international struggle between the Communist and the Free World. Indeed it is difficult for a younger reader to realise how great a part foreign affairs, in their broadest sense, played in the political scene throughout this period. In spite of the superior military strength of the two protagonists, Russia and the United States, in terms of resources, population and armaments, the position of Britain and her influence in world affairs was of real and sometimes decisive importance. Successive Governments, whether under Attlee and Bevin or Churchill and Eden, had not hesitated to assume a commanding role. I tried to follow their example; and the value of recent initiatives of the British Government was recognised, with varying degrees of approval, both by the Western Alliance and the Soviet Government.

On my return from Moscow in March 1959, I felt that something had been gained. The immediate threat of a Russian peace treaty with Eastern Germany, involving a direct menace to the position of the Western Allies in Berlin, was at any rate postponed. The Russians had proposed a conference of Heads of Governments, commonly known as a Summit meeting. But they had declared themselves willing, if the Western Allies were not yet ready for such an ambitious enterprise, with all its hopes but all its danger, to begin with a meeting of Foreign Ministers. This plan was accepted; and the Foreign Ministers' Conference was formally opened on 11 May in Geneva. I was under no illusions. I realised that the Russians would avoid any real negotiations but try to treat the Conference as a mere preliminary to fix the procedure and date of a Summit meeting.

President Eisenhower had made it clear that he would not agree to a Summit unless some 'progress' could be made to 'justify' his acceptance of such an adventure in the eyes of the American people. Before the Foreign Ministers' Conference opened I got some indication of the nervousness prevailing in Washington from a message expressing Eisenhower's deep anxiety about our forth-coming trade talks with the Russians. These had been agreed between Khrushchev and me in Moscow.[1] Any large extension of credit, the President argued, would spare the Soviet Government the necessity of switching resources from the military programme and correspondingly increase the possibility of economic penetration in the outside world. I did my best to reassure him on 12 May 1959 by explaining in some detail our normal practice of supplementing commercial credits, extended by individual firms, through a Govern-ment agency established many years before for this purpose. As for a five-year credit, about which he seemed alarmed, this would only be applied to major projects for capital goods. I could not help adding:

> I am sure you will understand that for a country which lives upon its exports such facilities are absolutely vital, and a sub-stantial amount of our world export trade in capital goods is covered by a combination of these methods. I understand that many if not most other countries have similar arrangements. In any extension of trade with the Russians, we shall adhere to this established commercial practice.

While we could not and would not grant very large loans we were anxious to extend this form of commercial credit. Finally, I observed :

> We know that the Russians are trying to increase the consumer goods which they make available to their people. I hope that we can provide them with some of the plant and machinery they need for this purpose. On the whole, the more they do this, the better it will be, for if the people become more comfortable and their living standards rise they may become in the long run more agreeable.

[1] See *Riding the Storm*, p. 631.

The Foreign Ministers' Conference in Geneva was immediately bogged down by the question of the shape of the table. Behind this somewhat futile discussion there lurked a real issue—the degree of recognition to be afforded to the representatives of West and East Germany. The first meeting had to be cancelled, for the carpenters were still awaiting the necessary instructions. Finally, by Selwyn Lloyd's skilful efforts, agreement was reached. There would be a round table. Two inches from it there would be two tables seating the German delegations, and at a distance of two metres there would be a table seating the secretariat. On the question as to whether any of the German delegations would be allowed to intervene in the discussion an ingenious compromise was agreed after long debate. An intimation should be given to the Chairman of a request for an intervention by one of the German groups. (The Chairmanship, of course, rotated among the Foreign Ministers.) The Chairman should then ask if there were any objections. If none were raised the German representative would be allowed to speak. In addition it was generally understood that objections would not be raised so long as provocative interventions were not made; but if any of the Foreign Ministers felt it necessary he would have a right to demand an immediate private session of the four principal participants alone. All this did not seem a very helpful start; but since at one time a complete deadlock had appeared likely regarding the question of whether the table should be square, as the Americans wished; round, as the Russians demanded; or oval, as the British proposed, I felt not altogether discouraged.

For the next fortnight the Conference lumbered on.

Actually, largely owing to Selwyn's initial efforts, the Conference has at least got started. On my advice, we decided to 'lie back' and let the rest get into a muddle. The French and Germans (out of jealousy) are only too ready to accuse us of weakness and Chamberlainism. '*Nous sommes trahis*' and all that. So the Foreign Secretary has ranged himself (without undue fervour but with complete loyalty) behind the others. When the Americans began to realise that the Conference might rapidly come to an end, and the Russians revert to the old 'ultimatum' policy, they got alarmed. The French and the Germans (who only want to *seem* strong and have no real desire for trouble) have also changed their tune. It seems that the dinner party (Herter, Couve, Gromyko, Lloyd) made some progress on Friday night. The Foreign Secretary now thinks that the Conference will last another fortnight or three weeks. He hopes that it will begin to adopt a more sensible procedure and abandon speech-making in favour of discussion.[1]

On 27 May the Conference adjourned to allow the Foreign Ministers to attend the funeral of Foster Dulles in Washington. On their return, Selwyn Lloyd reported the progress, or lack of progress, to the Cabinet. I noted:

> The German Government is in a curious situation: Adenauer is still Chancellor, though he is soon to become President. He has become—like many very old men—vain, suspicious, and grasping. . . . [He] has been carrying on a great campaign of vilification of Her Majesty's Government and especially of me. I am Neville Chamberlain reincarnate, and so on. I think the German Foreign Office are rather ashamed of all this, and it is best to ignore it.[2]

Meanwhile, the Nuclear Test Conference at Geneva was also in trouble:

> I presided at a meeting of 'experts' this evening. All we could do was to try to find out what the American experts now think of the risks involved in a comprehensive agreement. We would, of course (U.K. and U.S.), honour it. But we cannot police it with absolute certainty, if the Russians decided to cheat. The real danger would be if (by underground tests which cannot really be detected) they could develop an anti-missile missile and we were not able to do so.[2]

By the end of the month the Foreign Ministers were still at work arguing about Berlin, without progress but without rupture. Meanwhile, the President of the Board of Trade reported to me that the trade talks in Moscow were going on pretty well, and a five-year agreement on satisfactory terms was signed on 24 May 1959.

Eisenhower was still pressing me for 'the production by the Foreign Ministers of a reasonable paper for us to work on at a

[1] 24 May 1959.   [2] 28 May 1959.

Summit Conference'. This together with an assurance that our rights in Berlin would not be interfered with constituted, in his view, the minimum that would 'justify' a Summit meeting.

Now a ridiculous, but tiresome, incident occurred. On 1 June *The Times* published a long and somewhat patronising article from its political correspondent, suggesting that there would be an early change at the Foreign Office. In view of the fact that the whole British and much of the Foreign Press were paying tribute to the authority which Selwyn Lloyd had now begun to exercise, especially with his Western colleagues, this article was particularly aggravating. Although it was tempered by the statement that 'no change will be made until after the General Election' the effect in Geneva was deplorable. I did my best to reassure the Foreign Secretary, who was naturally disturbed. Inevitably the Leader of the Opposition asked whether I could say who was responsible for the inspired statement that the Foreign Secretary was to be replaced. On 2 June I sent the Foreign Secretary the text of the following interchanges.

> *Prime Minister* : There was no inspired statement of any kind. But this perhaps gives me the opportunity to say that I have been reading the newspapers, as no doubt the right honourable Gentleman has been reading them, and the Foreign Secretary and I hope to carry on our work together for a very long time to come. I noticed that the assumption of these articles was that there was bound to be another five years of Conservative Government. Whether we shall complete the full stint ourselves remains to be seen.
>
> *Mr. Bevan* : Is the right honourable Gentleman aware that if statements of this sort had been made by the Opposition we should have been accused of unpatriotically stabbing the Foreign Secretary in the back in the course of international negotiations?
>
> *Prime Minister* : The Opposition do quite enough of that anyway.

Happily, Selwyn Lloyd's 'messages from Geneva show that he has taken it stoutheartedly. All the Press attack *The Times*.'[1]

A few days later Adenauer unexpectedly announced his decision not to stand for the Presidency, which he had already agreed to do, but to remain as Chancellor.

[1] 2 June 1959.

C2

He represents this as due to 'international danger' and hints darkly that it is all due to British weakness towards Russia. . . .

It is an extraordinary drama . . . in the suddenness and excited glamour in which everything is done. Our Embassy, I need hardly say, were taken completely by surprise.[1]

This decision, however, was not well received.

Adenauer seems to have a bad Press, all over the world. Even the French seem rather shocked. The Americans—whose darling Adenauer has always been—seem taken aback. But I have no doubt that the old man will get his way—at least for the moment. But I think he will have weakened his authority, and that even Germans will be less prone to believe all the rather malicious stories which he has been spreading about British statesmen and their policy of 'appeasement'.[2]

At the Foreign Ministers' Conference little progress was made. The Russians now seemed to revert to the ultimatum about Berlin, although a year's grace, subsequently extended to eighteen months, was to be accorded. This concession was part of a somewhat complex plan with some unattractive features so far as the West was concerned. Telegrams continued to pour in from Geneva.

I do my best to keep up—but often my replies are too late for another change in events. I feel that the excessive legalism of the West has (as I always foresaw) got us into a jam. I only hope that we shall not now lose the Summit. If all else fails, I may issue an invitation to Eisenhower, de Gaulle and Khrushchev myself.[3]

I was myself relieved at the extension of time. If in subsequent years it has appeared that a week is a long time in politics, twelve months is a very long time in a foreign crisis. The Russian plan was, in some respects, unacceptable as it stood. 'But I would have thought it wise to see what the public reaction is before we all take too definite a line.'[4] Our allies seemed to be more concerned about the details than relieved by the postponement of the threatened ultimatum over Berlin and the Peace Treaty.

[1] 6 June 1959.   [2] 8 June 1959.
[3] 10 June 1959.   [4] 9 June 1959.

I am afraid the last proposal by Gromyko at Geneva has upset the French and the Americans—and, of course, the Germans. Actually, stripped of its rather offensive form, it has the germ of an idea—a year's delay. The President has been made to take it too seriously—so the Summit is in danger.[1]

A very friendly, if non-committal, message from de Gaulle gave me encouragement to persevere.

There was now considerable pressure to adjourn the Foreign Ministers' Conference for a month or more. When the Foreign Secretary, whom I had not seen for some weeks, came over to London, we discussed the situation at length. He had certainly enhanced his personal position; and although there was some suspicion of us both from the French and German side, the Western team had worked well together under his leadership.

> Unfortunately, it would seem that little or no progress has been made with the Russians. Nobody knows what to do next. One plan (a very bad one) is to adjourn the Foreign Ministers' meeting for one, two or three months. Nothing, to my mind, could be worse. The Soviet Government would preserve its monolithic front—with its controlled Press and Radio. The West would be thrown into a Babel of confusion. Debates in our Parliament would be unavoidable and damaging. Another idea is to break off *sine die*, *without* plans for a Summit. That is, to the British, utterly unacceptable.[2]

It was clear to me that no real decision could be reached except at a Summit. The only purpose of a Foreign Ministers' Conference was to achieve sufficient apparent progress to make such a meeting acceptable to the Americans. Herter, whose attitude was helpful and constructive throughout, now put forward some new proposals. He even suggested that if the Foreign Ministers' Conference was to break down

> I (as Prime Minister) should issue an invitation to Eisenhower, de Gaulle and Khrushchev to meet in London (or any other acceptable place) to 'discuss the situation'. This would be a sort of 'informal' Summit. I like this plan very much.[2]

[1] 11 June 1959.   [2] 13 June 1959.

On the next day, Sunday, 14 June, I went to Chequers, where
Bob Menzies came to stay. We were alone and had a splendid talk.
Menzies had just come from Washington and gave me a useful
account of the President's general attitude. He seemed hardly to
know what to do. But we soon learnt that the Americans did not like
Herter's plan and after a meeting of the Cabinet it was decided that I
should prepare a further appeal to the President. His position had
been set out in a message to me on 4 June, and it would not be easy
to shake him. His decision seemed firm:

> As you know, I adhere to my position that a Summit meeting
> based on nothing more than wishful thinking would be a disaster.
> The world would interpret such a move as being a virtual
> surrender, while Soviet prestige would be enhanced.
>
> On the other hand, we agreed in our conversations at Camp
> David that we could afford to make a rather liberal definition of
> progress. While I agree that a document formulating our two
> positions would be a useful document, I do think we must also
> have something recognizable as a specific accomplishment. For
> example there might be included as a prerequisite in your formula
> something of this sort: 'Since the Geneva Conference is partially a
> result of the crisis of Berlin, created by the Soviet Union, there
> must be an agreement confirming the continuing status of Berlin
> pending the reunification of Germany.' I do not see how any of us
> can with self-respect go to a Summit meeting unless such a
> statement has been issued by the Soviets or an agreement to this
> effect has been consummated.

I had, of course, to accept this, but how far a postponement of any
ultimatum for twelve months or more could be considered as
'progress' in the President's mind it was difficult to tell. Eisenhower
had just sent a personal appeal to Khrushchev asking him to reconsider the position which his representatives were taking at
Geneva and to adopt a more helpful attitude. Of course, it was
possible that Khrushchev would respond favourably. But it was
more likely that he would take some dramatic action that would put
the Western Allies in a position of difficulty.

In my message to the President of 16 June I urged that we should
be prepared for such a situation. In any event we surely must get the

Conference to end in such a way that it could be followed by the Summit meeting for which the world was waiting. We should not discount the possibility that

> Mr. Khrushchev may at once make a public declaration that, as the Foreign Ministers have failed to reach any agreement, the Summit meeting should be held without delay. Indeed, it is likely that he will publicly propose a date and place for such a meeting. We shall then find that we are, in effect, summoned publicly to a Summit by Mr. Khrushchev—in circumstances in which we shall find it equally difficult to justify to public opinion either an acceptance or a refusal. This will present us with a very embarrassing dilemma.

I went on to argue that we ought to forestall this danger by ourselves proposing

> that the Heads of the four Governments should meet to consider the situation arising from the deadlock in the Foreign Ministers' meeting. What I have in mind is, not that we should have the formal Summit meeting which has been envisaged, with a throng of official advisers, and assessors from the two Germanys, and arguments about the Poles, the Czechs and the Italians, or even with an elaborate agenda; but that the Heads of the four Governments should meet informally (with their Foreign Ministers and a minimum of advisers) to talk over the situation and try to find a way through the difficulties. If we want an agreement—and surely we do—this, I am convinced, is the way to do business with Mr. Khrushchev.

(This, in fact, was the Herter plan which the Americans had previously turned down. Nevertheless, there seemed no harm in reviving it. I had sent the text of my message for the Foreign Secretary to show Herter in Geneva, who saw no objection.) Since it was clear that the Foreign Ministers' Conference could not be prolonged indefinitely, I appealed to Eisenhower to take the bold initiative. If he were not prepared to do so I would be willing to take the risk, although this might involve a rebuff. I would hope, of course, that this would not be the American reaction. Finally, I added:

I feel that this may be an important turning-point in this long struggle, and I want to be sure that the Free World by its clear demonstration of nobility and idealism is recognised as acting rightly thus bringing the greatest influence on the uncommitted nations and on moderate opinion generally.

Eisenhower, contrary to his usual usage, made special arrangements to receive Harold Caccia to discuss my message. It seems that this interview was unprecedented, for he had never received either the British Ambassador or any other Head of Mission for such a discussion. Eisenhower repeated his keen desire to find himself in agreement with me since he had a sincere regard for my views. Nevertheless, he reminded Caccia of the formula we had agreed to in the spring at Camp David. There must not be any threat to one side by the other and there must be reasonable hope arising from the preparatory work of the Foreign Ministers that a Summit meeting would be fruitful.

In the course of his long and friendly reply to me on 17 June the President threw out another suggestion which was ultimately to prove of great importance:

If Khrushchev should decide to replace Kozlov in visiting the Soviet Exhibit in New York later this month, I would be ready, assuming no objection on the part of our allies, to meet with him in an effort to get the Foreign Ministers meeting back on the tracks. While such an occurrence would seem most unlikely, yet it is the kind of thing that could be done without presenting the picture of a 'Summit' meeting. It would indeed represent only a fortuitous circumstance of which advantage could be taken.

At the same time he agreed that the Foreign Ministers' Conference must not be allowed to break up; if necessary, a short recess should be arranged.

On 16 June, the Western Ministers took an important step by putting forward a practical and conciliatory document for discussion. The decision of the Soviet Government to withdraw its troops from Berlin should be 'noted' as well as that of the Western Governments to maintain their forces at no greater than the present figure and armed only with conventional weapons. (These numbers would be further reduced if justified by later developments.) At the same time the Allies were ready for the necessary procedures governing access to be carried out if desired by German personnel. In other words this meant that we were ready to accept East Germany as agents for Soviet Russia. The same document proposed the setting up of a Quadripartite Commission to make the necessary arrangements and to consult, as required, East as well as West German officials. Much would depend on the Russian response.

Meanwhile, as might have been expected, President Eisenhower received a polite but discouraging reply from Khrushchev. The text of these exchanges was shown to me by the American Ambassador in confidence.

On 22 June the Foreign Secretary was in London for a day or two and we discussed the position at length. I summarised it as follows:

> After Geneva, what? More Geneva, for a week or two. But, if nothing is accomplished, it is either a break or the Summit. If the former, Khrushchev can do one of two things. He can invite us to a Summit. It will be equally embarrassing to refuse or to accept. If we refuse, then Khrushchev has every moral justification for immediately making his peace treaty with the Eastern Germans and handing over all Russian obligations. Or–Khrushchev can not bother to invite us to the Summit–but proceed at once to his unilateral action. Selwyn Lloyd sees all this. But we are at a loss as to how to make the Americans understand. Herter has been very helpful–but . . . he has not the authority that Dulles had, either with State Department or with the President.[1]

The difficulty remained, and neither Adenauer nor de Gaulle seemed in favour of a Summit except on similar terms to those which Eisenhower demanded. But none of them seemed to appreciate the dangers of merely drifting on. I therefore, in agreement with Selwyn Lloyd, worked out the opening shots of

> a campaign which is of capital importance if we are (*a*) to avoid risk of a *serious* catastrophe (perhaps leading through some folly to war), (*b*) to avoid a grave diplomatic defeat, with corresponding injury to our side–the Free World, (*c*) to satisfy British public opinion.[2]

[1] 22 June 1959.   [2] 23 June 1959.

Lloyd would work upon Herter, and I would continue my pressure on Eisenhower. I had so far merely acknowledged his reply agreeing with his proposal for a short adjournment of the Conference. On 23 June I sent a considered answer, after a full discussion in the Cabinet.

I observed that it seemed to me that Khrushchev was not altogether unaffected by the points which the President had made. It was true that the situation had been worsened by a somewhat hostile speech which Khrushchev had delivered before the Russians had been able to reply to the Western proposals of 16 June. It had, therefore, been decided to adjourn the Foreign Ministers' Conference until 13 July. The position could now be summed up as follows. The latest Russian proposal gave us every hope that we could get a delay of a year or a year and a half. Would it not be wise to secure this respite? If we were to insist upon a final settlement now we might have to pay a heavy price for it. Of course we could not be sure what lay behind the latest Russian moves. They had taken two forms—a somewhat ambivalent reply by Gromyko to the Western paper of 16 June and Khrushchev's truculent speech.

> We shall never know for certain why on 10 June Khrushchev appeared to revert to the method of ultimatum and repeated it in his speech of the 19th. Gromyko's latest paper of 19 June is obscure. Read in conjunction with Khrushchev's speech it could still contain a concealed ultimatum insofar as it implies that the Western presence in Berlin is only tolerated on sufferance, and by reason of an interim agreement, and might cease to have any justification at the end of the interim period or when a Peace Treaty had been signed with East Germany. I think, however, that it is meant to be slightly more accommodating towards us. This may well be a sort of clumsy response to your initiative with Khrushchev. I believe he was, in fact, impressed by what you said and made an effort at least to appear to meet your conditions for a Summit. His intemperate speech may, on this hypothesis, have been a tactical move to cover his retreat.

I then elaborated the arguments for and against an interim rather than a final solution. It was, of course, important that the Russians should not be able to point to any phrases in an interim agreement which imply that at the end of the period we should have less justification for keeping our troops in Berlin than we had at the beginning. We must not expressly or impliedly seem to set a term to our position in Berlin. The interim settlement must be a pause—though a prolonged pause—in the negotiations.

However, behind all this complicated and somewhat pedantic argument there lay a grim reality. We must not be caught in the trap of pure legalism. The important thing was access to Berlin, not the precise machinery by which it was secured. Since so much of these talks had gone on in a somewhat unreal atmosphere I thought it right to add a warning.

Perhaps I can add some general thoughts. We must maintain a public posture in which we can rally our people to resist a Russian attempt to impose their will by force. All the same, it would not be easy to persuade the British people that it was their duty to go to war in defence of West Berlin. After all, in my lifetime we have been dealt two nearly mortal blows by the Germans. People in this country will think it paradoxical, to use a mild term, to have to prepare for an even more horrible war in order to defend the liberties of people who have tried to destroy us twice in this century. Nevertheless, there is a double strain of idealism and realism in these islands to which I believe I could successfully appeal if we had first demonstrated that we have made every endeavour to put forward practical solutions and that the Russians were unwilling to accept any fair proposition. The corollary to this is that we and our allies should do and should be seen to do what ordinary people would think reasonable. For instance, it would not seem reasonable to ordinary people that West Germans who profess to desire closer contacts and reunification with the East Germans should refuse absolutely to discuss these matters in any forum with the East Germans.

All this time the Conference of Experts on the discontinuance of nuclear tests—also held at Geneva—had been proceeding at a slow tempo. It was almost deadlocked by the problem of the kind of inspection which would be required and by the new evidence produced by the Americans concerning the difficulty of effective control. Nevertheless, tests had been suspended temporarily. The Labour Party had announced plans for a Non-Nuclear Club to comprise all countries except Russia and America in default of a general disarmament agreement; but this proposal excited little public interest since it evaded the real issue. Nor did it really succeed in reconciling the two sections of the Labour Party. In general, Gaitskell showed considerable courage in standing up to the extreme pacifists, and his position was really very close to ours. Resting on our firm agreement with the Americans, the British Government was ready to accept suspension, temporary or indefinite, until the Americans could make up their minds. This they seemed unable or unwilling to do.

> The Americans (inspired by the Pentagon) seem now to be turning *against* a comprehensive agreement (to include underground tests). This, if true, is tragic.[1]

I felt almost in despair, for if nothing could be achieved in a broader sphere, the end of these tests would be at least a dramatic step forward, and give comfort to millions of people all over the world. It was a depressing prospect—the situation was drifting on without any success in either of the Geneva Conferences and without any approach to a Summit.

As a result of my visit in March the Russian ultimatum on Berlin had at least been postponed, but we had not taken up seriously their new proposal for a moratorium. We were therefore in danger that at any moment the Russians might confront us with a *fait accompli*. Although we had had some preliminary talks with our allies, I began to be more and more worried about the situation. Accordingly on 26 June I wrote to the Foreign Secretary calling his attention to the dangers:

> I have been reading a good deal lately about the beginnings of the 1914 war. Every politician who has given his account, whether it be Asquith, Samuel, Grey or Churchill, gives quite a conflicting picture of the obligations which we are supposed to have entered into with the French in 1912. On the one side it is said that we had a moral obligation (because we allowed the

[1] 7 July 1959.

military discussions to take place although only a few members of the Cabinet knew what was going on), which the Cabinet was bound to honour. On the other side, writers like Sir Herbert Samuel say that we had no moral obligations of any kind. It was always made clear that our final decision would be taken in the circumstances when they arose.

History has not settled this point yet.

I wish to be quite certain that we are in no danger of drifting into something very similar over the various military and diplomatic [plans about] Berlin. We must not allow ourselves to get into any kind of equivocal or doubtful position.

I then set out all the possibilities of Russian action and the various Allied responses; but in view of a great deal of loose talk that was going on, it was vital that we should make it clear to our allies

that we could never agree to [any military] or . . . non-military measures without at least a meeting of Heads of Government, and that we are bound neither in honour nor in law to any kind of commitment.

These are still delicate matters, although not so sensitive now as they were then. Moreover the new turn of policy in Western Germany has eased the situation. But at the time I was deeply concerned about the perils involved in a train of events which might be set off by what might start as bluff and end in irretrievable disaster. A bluff is only a bluff until someone calls it.

Although the President sent no direct reply to my appeal, that he was still seriously thinking about a Summit meeting was shown by a pleasant message which I had from him towards the end of June on other matters, and which ended up by saying:

Yesterday Mamie and I spent the day with the Queen and Prince Philip. The Prime Minister of Canada was of course present. I noted with some interest that he repeated what I believe has been an earlier suggestion of his—that Quebec might be a nice place to hold a Summit meeting if one should ever become practical. I merely replied that the place would be most convenient from my viewpoint, but the location and time made very little difference to me.

On 7 July there was a debate on Foreign Affairs in the House of Commons, which we could no longer avoid. However, it did little harm to the Government and exposed the grave differences of view in the Opposition.

> Foreign Affairs debate. Over ninety degrees outside the Chamber; much cooler inside. Foreign Secretary began with a factual speech—our hopes and fears for Geneva. Bevan answered, with a very good speech—witty and well argued, quite his old form. He only spoilt it by being too long. Gaitskell wound up with rather a 'governessy' speech. I replied, with an adequate but by no means impressive effort. So far as we were concerned, we wanted the debate to be quiet. Our opponents hardly referred to us, but concentrated on the great issue which is splitting the Socialists in two—Hydrogen Bomb or *no* Hydrogen Bomb; unilateral disarmament or Non-Nuclear Club. (I could not help reminding the House that the Non-Nuclear Club means that British foreign policy must be still more dependent on America. Yet, for years, the Socialists have urged us to be more independent of America.) Nevertheless, Gaitskell is showing considerable courage in handling this affair. He will gain by this in public estimation. There was *no* vote.[1]

On 13 July the Foreign Ministers' Conference was reconvened. On the next day the Foreign Secretary reported to me Herter's account of the President's plans in their latest form. He had apparently decided that a Summit must be held whether or not the Foreign Ministers made any progress at Geneva. In view of the dangers of the Berlin situation he had become convinced that the West must not allow the risk of war without trying to negotiate at the highest level. He intended therefore to work for a meeting of the Heads of Western Governments in Paris on about 20 August, to be followed on 1 September by a Summit meeting at Quebec with the possibility that Khrushchev might visit the United States at the same time. This indeed was a staggering change of plan; but, since it followed precisely the arguments and the appeals which I had made to him of our responsibility before the world not to let things drift to disaster, I received this message with relief and delight.

[1] 8 July 1959.

The three Western Foreign Ministers seemed now to be working well together, and the recent tendency to accuse the British Government of 'appeasement' because we wished to take a realistic approach to the Berlin problem seemed to be modified if not altogether withdrawn. If any confirmation was needed of the wisdom of the course which the President now proposed, it was to be found in a communication from Khrushchev which was given to Selwyn Lloyd by Gromyko privately on 16 July. Although couched in courteous and even friendly terms, disclaiming all idea of threat or ultimatum, it repeated the determination of the Soviet Government, if either the Conference in Geneva or a subsequent Summit failed to reach some agreement, to conclude a separate treaty with the D.D.R. (Eastern Germany). With regard to discussion of the interim arrangements for West Berlin 'the Soviet Government had water behind them'. This phrase apparently referred to the Battle of Stalingrad and the situation of an army defending a position with the river behind it —that is, with no room for manœuvre or withdrawal.

My relief at the change of heart in Washington was short-lived, for as the matters in Geneva made no progress the Americans began to shift their ground. The President was now reverting to the old formula and declaring that there was insufficient 'progress' by the Foreign Ministers to justify a Summit meeting. I hesitated whether to send any further messages, but it was clear that the Russians were meditating a new move. Khrushchev cancelled a visit to Scandinavia, and we felt almost certain that he was preparing either to sign a treaty with Eastern Germany or to issue invitations to a Summit on his own terms.

Vice-President Nixon's visit to Russia, to open an exhibition and to make a number of speeches, was a useful diversion. It also gave me an opening. The Vice-President had apparently asked for some observations about the Russians and about Khrushchev for his own information. I sent them

> through the President, and this gave an opportunity for saying something about getting on with the plan for finishing Geneva and moving to the Summit. To my great regret, the President has replied with a very odd message—which seems to be going back on everything that Herter promised to Selwyn. . . . He reverts to

the old theme that the Summit is a sort of post-graduate course, which the boys can only take if they first graduate with honours (at Geneva).[1]

Deeply disturbed by the change of position by the President I prepared a message of protest which I sent to Selwyn Lloyd. 'I asked him to show it to Herter, before I sent it off–not for comment, but for information.'[1] It was for me a truly baffling situation. Some decision must be reached which would remove the threat to Berlin and the danger of drifting into something like war. On the other hand what mattered was not the precise date of the Summit but the agreement that it should be held.

Eisenhower now took a sudden decision, without consulting his allies. He issued an invitation to Khrushchev to visit America. This invitation proposed no specific date, and it was not linked with the plan for a Summit meeting. Khrushchev at once accepted, suggesting a time 'after the hot weather'. All this made it clear that the President had altogether abandoned his plan for a Summit in September. Indeed he was now proposing to visit a number of countries in October and early November. Therefore any plan for a Summit meeting must be postponed until December, or more probably the New Year. However, there was this compensation. The Russians could hardly take a fatal decision while Khrushchev was visiting America or even while the President was in Europe.

The confusion both in Geneva and in Washington was now complete. In the event Eisenhower's invitation to Khrushchev was acclaimed by the British Press and public as a great step forward in the reduction of international tension, although this was not at all the reaction which I had anticipated.

A serious crisis has developed in the field of foreign affairs. It has caused me great annoyance–alarm—and even anger. It is not (as some of my colleagues seem to feel) the result of American bad faith, but rather of their stupidity, naïveté and incompetence. What has happened is this. The President (some days ago) sent a message through Kozlov (who is a deputy Prime Minister of the U.S.S.R. and was visiting Washington) inviting Khrushchev to go to U.S. in September, to come to Washington for two days;

[1] 23 July 1959.

and then, if there is a Summit at Quebec, to return to U.S. for a fortnight's trip. He also said that he (the President) would be glad to pay a return visit in October. . . .

Mr. Khrushchev—with great skill—replied that he would be delighted to visit America in September. Of course, if there was a Summit, he would attend it. But Summit or no Summit, he accepted the invitation and would be delighted to have President in Russia later on. As for Geneva, he had never attached much importance to these negotiations.

This has put the President into a great difficulty. His invitation was (or was intended to be) linked with a Summit and he hoped to make the Russians less intransigent at Geneva. Mr. Khrushchev has taken the bait, but avoided the hook.

Herter has confessed all this to Selwyn. He is himself distressed and hurt. (Bob Murphy actually gave the President's message *verbally* to Kozlov and did *not* give him any written *aide-memoire*.)

Herter has not dared tell the French or the Germans. The Russians may leak the news at any time. The President does not now see how he can get out of the invitation, especially as he has no written document to appeal to. So, this foolish and incredibly naïve piece of amateur diplomacy has the following results:

(*a*) He has made any further 'progress' at Geneva less likely. The Russian position will harden.

(*b*) He will have a very difficult task in explaining to the American people that there is *no* progress at Geneva and yet he has asked Khrushchev to have a jolly visit to America.

(*c*) There will be no Summit.

(*d*) The French and German Governments and people will be suspicious and angry.

(*e*) My own position here will be greatly weakened. Everyone will assume that the two Great Powers—Russia and U.S.A.—are going to fix up a deal over our heads and behind our backs. My whole policy—pursued for many years and especially during my Premiership—of close alliance and co-operation with America will be undermined. People will ask, 'Why should U.K. try to stay in the big game? Why should she be a nuclear power? You told us that this would give you power and authority in the world. But you and we have been made fools of. This shows that Gaitskell and Crossman and Co. are right. U.K. had better give up the struggle and accept, as gracefully as possible, the position of a second-rate power.'

All this trouble stems from one act of well-meant but incredibly naïve diplomacy.

Ministers were very angry indeed when I unfolded this story to them. I purposely did not try to underestimate the dangers or excuse the failure of my diplomacy.

I showed them the draft telegram which Foreign Secretary and I had prepared to go to the President, pointing out all these dangers and asking for a ruling in favour of an immediate Summit. However, I am sure he will not agree, and we must try to turn the situation somehow to our advantage.[1]

My prognostications were proved to be false and my alarm unnecessary. On 30 July I had a message from the President reiterating his view about the lack of progress at Geneva and also making it clear that in any case no Summit could take place until after Khrushchev's visit. But he now declared that this visit might, in itself, constitute 'a new situation'. In other words he was 'preparing the way'. The President also proposed a meeting of the Western Heads in Paris at the end of August. But de Gaulle characteristically—and wisely—would not consider any such idea until Khrushchev's American trip was safely over.

It is difficult even in reading through old papers and telegrams to recall the atmosphere of confusion which all this manœuvring and vacillation had brought about. I naturally was anxious for a Summit. But we had now reached the stage that from the electioneering point of view it would be better as a prospect in the future than a modified success or even failure in the past.

Meanwhile, much anxious work went into securing the best possible reception for the new plan. The President's announcement was made at 3.30 p.m. our time on Sunday, 3 August.

I had prepared a statement welcoming the President's initiative and making some slight reference to my visit to Russia earlier in the year. This was issued for 6 p.m. B.B.C. news, etc., as from Birch Grove.[2]

[1] 26 July 1959.   [2] 3 August 1959.

The Press on the next day was remarkably good. Eisenhower's gesture was widely attributed to my pioneering efforts.

There were, of course, disadvantages. The Foreign Secretary, in reporting to his colleagues about the Geneva Conference, did not disguise his view that in spite of all the difficulties real progress might have been made. But

> from the moment Mr. Khrushchev had secured *both* the invitation and the promise of the return visit, Gromyko made no step forward and several steps back.[1]

It had been a hard time for the Foreign Secretary but he had done a fine piece of work.

> Nine weeks or so in that daily round of talk, argument, lunching, dining—without any chance for relaxation—with people who are not even your friends ! And in a terrible climate, hot and humid.[1]

Nevertheless, from the political point of view this strange incident had turned out pretty well.

> No one here has suggested that the Eisenhower–Khrushchev visits are 'negotiating with Russia behind our backs' or a 'sinister deal between the two Great Powers, at the expense of smaller powers'. On the contrary, in U.K., as indeed throughout the whole world, this is said to be the result of the Macmillan initiative earlier this year. The British broke the ice. In some countries, this is welcomed; in others, deplored. But I am relieved that this is the interpretation of history which is universally accepted. It was the danger of the other interpretation which so alarmed and angered the Cabinet.[1]

Moreover the President's European tour was generally regarded as a further step towards an eventual Summit meeting.

During the summer I had received an account from Menzies of recent visits he had paid to Paris and Bonn. I always found his descriptions of his talks with the various European statesmen amusing as well as informative. Most of them spoke freely to him. I sent him a message on 1 August thanking him for his valuable report.

[1] 6 August 1959.

I think your visits to Paris and Bonn have done good. I am told that the old gentleman at Bonn has now begun to fail a little. Like all old men, he wavers between suspicion and sentimentality. He has sent me a number of very nice messages from time to time, and a few days ago delivered through the Ambassador what amounted to an apology for his bad behaviour. I have always taken the line that he is a great world figure; and being much older than me, I should treat him with respect. Nor have I any sense of personal feeling about all that he has said. I am only anxious that all the Western Allies should do the right and sensible thing in each other's interests.

I was very interested to get the account of your talk with General de Gaulle. Of course I know him well and like him. But he is not too easy to deal with; for although he has great wit, he has no sense of humour.

About the latest developments I observed :

the President, having got himself embroiled in the doctrine of 'no Summit without progress at the Foreign Ministers' meeting', is now trying to disengage. The only way that he has thought of is to substitute jollification for discussion. So he is asking Khrushchev to stay with him in America and promising a return visit to Russia. All this seems rather odd diplomacy. But if it definitely comes off I will give this plan a warm and hearty welcome as a follow-up to my visit to Moscow last February. I hope you may be able to take the same line. The result will probably be some delay in getting to the Summit. But at the same time it means a continued decrease in tension, for it is clear that the Russians can hardly take any unilateral action at Berlin while Mr. K. is surf-bathing in Florida or Mr. E. is duck-shooting in Siberia. Meanwhile we may hope that everything will go on without incident and in these affairs to waste time is to gain time.

Things now began to move more rapidly. The President was clearly determined to organise a Western Summit in some form. Meanwhile in addition to any visit he might make to Paris he would also come to London.

At the same time Selwyn Lloyd thought it right to make our position clear to Herter in Geneva. He reported to me on 3 August that he had spoken to Herter on the following lines :

I said that it was essential that the Americans did not again put themselves on the hook with regard to progress at the Foreign Ministers' meeting being a condition precedent for a Summit. Although I had not agreed with the American position on this point at this conference, it had at least been comprehensible. In fact I myself thought we had made sufficient progress and there would have been no objection to an early Summit. The President's invitation to Khrushchev had, however, altered that matter. We accepted this invitation and in fact we had welcomed it. We welcomed the fact that the President should pay a return visit to the Soviet Union. What would, however, be utterly incomprehensible to British opinion would be the fact that the President could invite Khrushchev to the United States and himself go to the Soviet Union and yet say the time was not ripe for a Summit meeting.

On receiving this message I could not refrain from sending the following reply: 'If you were an Ambassador, I would say "you spoke well". To a colleague I can only once again express my admiration and confidence.' Everything now began to move into place and this curious diplomatic quadrille led by the President of the United States began to take a useful shape.

In an attempt to meet German feelings I asked Adenauer to come to London for a talk and to stay on in such a way as to overlap with the President's visit. However, since Adenauer had apparently expressed some disappointment at not receiving one of the Presidential visits, Eisenhower, with his usual kindness, agreed to extend his tour to include Bonn.

The next development was the delivery, on 13 August, by the Soviet Ambassador, of a formal communication from the Head of the Soviet Government. This was a formidable document running to some three thousand words, twelve foolscap pages, including a two-page appendix upon his recent discussions with Vice-President Nixon and Ambassador Llewellyn Thompson. The whole was couched in very correct language and referred to all the talks we had had in Moscow and to the friendly mood in which my visit had ended. He recalled that I had said in the course of some discussion what a good thing it would be if he, Khrushchev, would meet President Eisenhower and have a frank talk with him on all these problems. It was for this reason and remembering my advice that he had accepted President Eisenhower's suggestion for a meeting with him with pleasure. After these preliminary courtesies the letter went on in effect to say this. 'There may one day be a reunified Germany, but at present there are two Germanys so we may as well conclude peace treaties with both. This does not conflict at all with everyone's desire for a free independent Berlin; but if the West persists in finding difficulties over Berlin the U.S.S.R. will have to go ahead alone and make its peace treaty with Eastern Germany. It is quite definite that on Berlin the U.S.S.R. will not agree to indefinite prolongation of the "occupation" status; but will examine proposals for safeguarding the social system of West Berlin and its communications. The stumbling-block is really Adenauer, who will not treat with the East Germans—can you and the other Western allies put pressure on him?'

A significant part of the message was an extract from the Nixon–Khrushchev talks on 26 July. Ambassador Thompson had observed, 'I simply wanted to say that if it is intended to force the development of a crisis over the Berlin question, that would not be a step towards peace.' To this Khrushchev had replied:

How is it possible to speak about 'the forcing of a crisis' by our side? Are we really doing anything which could threaten your interests? What is West Berlin to you, if you do not want to fight against us? If you merely come out in favour of the preservation in West Berlin of the social system which exists there at the moment, then we, as I have already said, are prepared to enter into negotiations, prepared to furnish any sort of guarantee. There is no difference of opinion here. It is another matter if you wish to perpetuate the occupation of West Berlin. Here there is nothing to discuss. We are against this.

We can come to an agreement about the time when a Peace Treaty should be signed. But you must bear in mind that this signature of a Peace Treaty would mean that you would lose your right to occupy West Berlin. This you must clearly understand. This is not an ultimatum—logical common sense leads to this conclusion.

The receipt of Khrushchev's communication put me in some

difficulty. In a note to the Foreign Secretary asking for his advice I gave my own view:

> If this method of diplomacy by personal messages between Heads of Government is to continue and even be extended, my instinct is that the ordinary rules of honourable behaviour should be applied.
>
> The letter is confidential and must not be published by the writer or the recipient; nor should the fact of its despatch or receipt be 'leaked' by either.

Lloyd concurred. Accordingly in acknowledging receipt of his communication I asked Khrushchev's permission to show it to the President, and only to the President, during his visit to London. To this he agreed. He also agreed that the message should be regarded as confidential and not given to the Press in any form. There was a further problem as regards de Gaulle and Adenauer. To Adenauer I sent the following communication on 20 August:

> Dear Friend, I have just returned from a short holiday during which I received a communication from Mr. Khrushchev about Germany and Berlin. This did not say anything new, although the familiar Soviet arguments were presented. I understand that General de Gaulle has received a somewhat similar communication.
>
> As you know, I have always taken the view that one should preserve the proprieties about personal messages even with the Russians, and I should not think it right to send the text of Khrushchev's message to the Heads of the Allied Governments without his permission. As his note contained no new point of substance, I do not propose in this instance to ask his agreement. I hope that you will feel that I am right in taking this decision.
>
> Although I was sorry not to have the pleasure of welcoming you to London at the beginning of September, I am very glad that President Eisenhower is visiting Bonn. I hope we shall have the pleasure of seeing you in London later in the year.
>
> With warm regards,
Harold Macmillan.

My message to de Gaulle was on similar lines. In a friendly reply, he added that he himself favoured a meeting of the Western Heads of Government to be held at the end of 1959 or early in 1960.

The perpetual question of nuclear tests was now becoming serious for us, especially in view of our General Election. We must have a policy, and since the Conference of Experts had reached no useful conclusions, it must rest with the Governments. On 26 August the United States Government announced that the suspension of tests, already decided for one year from 31 October 1958, would be extended by two months—that is, to the end of 1959. But this did not seem to me very satisfactory. I had heard from many sources of the intense emotional preoccupation, especially among young people, with the fall-out effects from nuclear tests. Since the Russian Government had announced that they would not resume tests unless the Americans did so, the matter was becoming urgent. During my talks with the President, when he was in London, I did my best to urge upon him the necessity for a comprehensive agreement banning all nuclear tests, whether underground or atmospheric. Knowing that the State Department sympathised with the British view, and it was only the Pentagon that were pressing for the continued underground tests,

> partly for the small 'tactical' weapon, to be used at one thousand yards' range; partly for the 'anti-missile' missile—which seems anyway almost a fantasy. . . . I confined myself to expressing my own views very strongly. I told President that we ought to take risks for so great a prize. We might be blessed by future ages as saviours of mankind, or we might be cursed like the man who made 'il gran rifutto'.[1]

Alas, final agreement was destined not to be reached until 1963.

Eisenhower came to Britain at the end of August.[2] His visit to London certainly afforded the British people an opportunity to express their feelings of gratitude to a man whose character they deeply admired. When he left, his own message of thanks of 1 September was generous but sincere.

> Dear Harold, You and I have had many memorable meetings but none, so far as I am concerned, has been more fruitful or

[1] 30 August 1959.   [2] This visit is described in *Riding the Storm*, p. 747.

more enjoyable than this one I am now reluctantly concluding. By virtue of your American mother, you can rightfully claim a kind of dual citizenship; but I sometimes feel a right to be an adopted son of Great Britain. Certainly I feel completely at home here, and the welcome given to me by you—and by so many of the wonderful people of this island—has warmed and touched my heart beyond any words at my command.

It seems inadequate to say 'thank you' for the courtesies, the kindnesses, and the attention to details to assure my comfort and pleasure. I know that essentially all of the direction for the trip emanated from you; I can only say that everything has been perfect.

My reply to these warm words was more than a formality.

I am sure that you cannot fail to have been impressed by the genuine warmth and friendship of the welcome which you had in this country from so many millions of the people. Of course in a way this was a tribute to you as President of the United States, our great ally and friend and the firm rock of the alliance; yet it was a real personal triumph for you. I rejoice at it with all my heart. The British people have long ago adopted you, and your visit here was just the occasion for them to show this.

Eisenhower then went on to France. On 11 September he sent me a very full report of his talks with de Gaulle. The latter was naturally preoccupied with the Algerian problem. He said frankly that it was inevitable that all the African countries should be allowed to make the choice of their own future. On the important question, which had been already raised, of the best method of keeping close contact between the American, British and French leaders,[1] the President seemed clear as to de Gaulle's wishes.

Our discussions regarding tripartite consultations were relatively brief, ending in clear agreement on the idea of conferring informally among ourselves regarding matters that lie beyond NATO. I mentioned that *ad hoc* staff committees could be established, but that I thought it unwise to establish institutions of a formal or permanent character, and he agreed.

On NATO de Gaulle seemed to put forward very moderate views.

[1] See *Riding the Storm*, pp. 452–4.

He expressed himself as heartily in favor of the North Atlantic Alliance, which he felt should be maintained and developed. He raised several questions, all well known, in a very restrained fashion. He questioned the integration of forces as taking from the people a sense of responsibility for their defence, and losing the impetus of patriotism. On this I simply pointed out the necessity of integrated control for effective military operations in the present era, and some of the difficulties that would be inescapable in a coalition of purely national forces—not only for effective combat, but also in failing to provide a basis for the presence of U.S. Forces in Europe. Both with him, and in my brief remarks at NATO and SHAPE, I stressed the need to develop a dedication to Western ideas, extending beyond the traditional national patriotism of the past.

All this seemed satisfactory, and I was relieved to feel that, at this time at any rate, the General had controlled or even overcome his natural distrust of American policy.

A message from de Gaulle on 11 September seemed to confirm this happy conclusion. After stating that he had just replied to Khrushchev setting out his view of the situation and particularly exhorting him to abandon the method of ultimatum he went on :

I have asked Monsieur Debré to inform you fully about our conversations with President Eisenhower. They have, I think, been very useful. I hope in particular that the dangers which were hanging over the Atlantic Alliance as a result of the Algerian situation have now been overcome.

> Very cordially yours,
> Charles de Gaulle.[1]

I was interested to see the President's readiness to meet de Gaulle's wishes in every way. This was shown by the concluding passages of a letter to me of 24 September.

On the subject of tripartite consultations, we will probably be moving ahead shortly, since you indicate in your letter of 16

[1]J'ai prie Monsieur Debré de vous faire informer de nos conversations avec le Président Eisenhower. Elles ont été, je crois, trés utiles. J'espère, en particulier, que le risque qui pesait sur l'Alliance Atlantique du fait de l'Algérie est maintenant dépassé.
> Bien cordialement a vous,
> Charles de Gaulle.

September that you are willing to participate in informal talks on matters of interest outside the NATO area, on the understanding of course that no new institutions are created. It is our understanding that the French wish talks to begin, perhaps in the first instance on Moroccan and Tunisian subjects, and our people will be in touch with yours on this subject.

Everything now depended upon Khrushchev's visit to the United States which began on 15 September. I thought it would amuse and perhaps assist Eisenhower to have a short character-sketch of his remarkable visitor, and on 4 September I sent the following:

In the first place, while Khrushchev is undoubtedly a clever and calculating politician whose intellectual formation has been entirely in a Communist form, he is more like a human being than Stalin ever was. While, therefore, the general trend of his policy will be more or less dictated by Communist ideas, there is a good deal of room for personal prejudices and ideas to influence things from day to day. For example, Khrushchev's 'toothache' during [my] visit to Moscow was probably partly a calculated attempt to influence [me], based on a false estimate of Western reactions to his tactics, but also partly genuine pique at some remarks made by [me]. Khrushchev may have interpreted [my] remarks about [his] creating a 'dangerous situation' in Berlin as being a sort of threat.

Secondly, Khrushchev's basic philosophy is being influenced both by the increasing development of the Soviet Union and by the dangers of nuclear war. He does not want to give up the long-term aims of the Communist Party, but he is being forced to realise that the means by which they can be achieved are altering and that the character of the struggle with Capitalism must be quite different from what Marx, Lenin and even Stalin believed.

Finally, as the memories of revolution and civil war die away Khrushchev is anxious less to be regarded as the odd man out in international affairs and more as the responsible leader of a great bloc of countries. This means that he must be more law-abiding and must try to make his policy more consistent, and at least apparently more responsible. Here the idea of 'peace' to which the Russians pay so much attention in their propaganda has had a deep effect not only on the masses to whom it was directed, but also on their leaders.

D

Khrushchev's trip was not only a political event of great importance, but it also gave unusual opportunities to the Press who
gloried in the more picturesque aspects of their visitor. Undoubtedly
the President had taken a certain risk in issuing this invitation.
Although European anxieties had been largely assuaged by his
recent round of visits, America was bitterly anti-Communist, and
there were widespread murmurings about another 'Yalta'. On the
whole the three weeks' trip, in spite of some very tense moments
caused by the outspoken speeches and Press interviews given by the
Soviet leader, proved a success. At the private talks at Camp David,
Khrushchev showed himself a pleasant guest, and it was understood that both statesmen had agreed that, whatever problems still
remained to be settled between their countries, the use of force must
be ruled out. Indeed Khrushchev himself, on his return to Moscow,
made an unusually friendly reference to the peaceful intentions of
the President of the United States. During his visit to Peking at the
end of September he went out of his way to urge the merits of 'co-
existence' and issued a warning against any attempt to test the
stability of the 'imperialist' system by force. Thus were revealed
tensions between him and his hosts which were later to develop into
open divergence.

Khrushchev took the opportunity, in his address to the Assembly
of the United Nations, to put forward a plea for comprehensive
disarmament. It was a dramatic demand for complete disarmament
to be achieved over a period of four years.

> Mr. K. has made a speech about disarmament in the U.N.
> 'Scrap the lot' is his policy. The passages about 'control' are
> vague. But as a 'propaganda' effort it seems pretty good. We must,
> however, follow it up (on the lines of the Foreign Secretary on
> Thursday at U.N.) and *not* seem to oppose K. but rather pin him
> down to concrete plans.[1]

Fortunately, we had put forward our own disarmament plan to the
Assembly on the previous day, and the Foreign Secretary's speech
had been very well received. Although our plan was less sensational
it was more practical.

[1] 19 September 1959.

It was a fortunate thing that we launched our new ideas on disarmament ahead of Mr. Khrushchev. K.'s speech yesterday was a great propaganda performance. It sets us quite a problem. We must not be cynical about it; but we must not be naïve. His plan really evades the vital question of efficient international inspection and control.[1]

Naturally many worthy men and women, actuated by the highest motives, fell ready victims into the carefully extended Russian trap. But I was surprised to learn that the Archbishop of Canterbury, normally by no means an ingenuous prelate, had given an ecstatic welcome to Khrushchev's disarmament plan without any reserve and without any reference to the British initiative. He appeared to swallow the bait, hook, line and sinker. I could not help sending him a remonstrance on 22 October:

I was interested to see in today's Press the report of your observations on Mr. Khrushchev's disarmament plan.

In welcoming it you are stated to have said that 'no Christian could possibly have put forward a better plan than this'. You are reported as going on to say 'at last somebody has said what every Christian has been praying for for years—total disarmament and full control'. Full control is of course, as you doubtless know, the hub of the whole question, especially when we are dealing with a product at once so deadly and so easily concealed as nuclear material.

The British Government welcomed the plan and at once said it should be studied by the new Disarmament Sub-Committee of ten nations which has been set up—largely at our suggestion. I think the Opposition leaders in this country took the same line. I am glad you recognised this.

But I must remind you that some days before this—indeed at the very beginning of the United Nations session—the British Government, through the Foreign Secretary, set out a plan which was detailed, progressive and in my view likely to be effective, to achieve exactly the same purposes. I am sorry that you did not feel it possible to welcome this historic move forward, made by your own countrymen. Perhaps you had not heard of it.

Equally you may not have observed the use which Communist

[1] 19 September 1959.

newspapers are making of your statement. I do not mind that so much in this country but throughout the Commonwealth and in every uncommitted country it will be used as the basis of unscrupulous propaganda.

We were now embarked on the stormy and perilous seas of a General Election. It was therefore a considerable relief to me when, on 28 September, the President stated publicly that the result of his talks with Khrushchev had been to remove many of the objections for a Summit meeting which he had hitherto felt. This was confirmed privately by the very full account of the Camp David talks which Eisenhower sent to me and which reached me while I was campaigning. Although the President still felt that a formal invitation must be issued from the three Western Powers, he made it clear to me, as indeed to the Press of the world, that the arrangements for a Summit meeting between the Heads of the three Western Governments and the Chairman of the Soviet Union were now only a question of procedure.

CHAPTER V

The Western Summit

O N 9 October I received a long message from Eisenhower. Having dragged his feet for so long he was now in something of a hurry. He proposed a Summit meeting of the four Heads of Governments, in the course of December, with a preliminary meeting of the three Western participants to which Adenauer should also be invited. (This was to become generally known as 'The Western Summit'.) But it was not only in Washington that due care had to be taken about 'prestige—the shadow cast by power'. Paris proved equally sensitive, and de Gaulle was by no means in a hurry to accept the President's change of mind as in itself decisive. Indeed, with a certain objectivity, he failed to detect any specific progress on any important questions which had resulted from the conversations between Eisenhower and Khrushchev. Consequently he thought the programme was unduly precipitate; the time had not yet come for a Summit meeting. In any event he, himself, would like to pay a visit to the United States in the spring before any meeting with the Russians took place. Consequently April would be soon enough for the meeting of the Western statesmen, with a full Summit in May or June if the prospects seemed reasonably hopeful.

For my part, I was ready to conform to any plan as to time or place that proved generally agreeable. Quebec or Geneva would be good for a Summit, with a Western preliminary in Washington or Paris.

Meanwhile, I was amused to see that the German Chancellor had immediately accepted Eisenhower's proposal.

> Poor Adenauer, who usually 'sucks up' to de Gaulle, accepted the American invitation to the Western Summit in October, before he heard that de Gaulle was going to refuse.[1]

[1] 22 October 1959.

I was not merely concerned about the date but also about the subjects to be dealt with and purpose of the full Summit meeting. I protested, therefore, against the American view that 'a Summit should confine itself to laying down guide lines'. In my view we ought at least to reach agreement on Berlin. One success would lead to another; each meeting, one might hope, proving more productive than the last. It was on these two points—that the discussions with Khrushchev should be real and not mere diplomatic courtesies and that the Summit itself should be considered as the first of a series—that I was determined to insist. This was clearly the most important contribution which I could make to the state of the world, distracted by the pressures and dangers of its fatal partition into two groups, each rapidly increasing both their demands and their arms.

At this point my friend and colleague, Walter Nash, the much respected Prime Minister of New Zealand, made a suggestion which, however well meant, was rather disturbing. He now wanted a conference of Commonwealth Prime Ministers to take place before any Summit meeting. Menzies, who had heard privately of his idea, clearly did not see great advantage in this plan; it might even lead to considerable confusion. As he wisely observed, there would be no agreed opinion and I should find myself handicapped by divided counsels. It would be much better to encourage the leading Prime Ministers of the Commonwealth to send me their views separately. Nash was not easily put off, for he was both persistent and high-minded; but eventually he was led, somewhat unwillingly, to recognise the difficulties involved.

I was now beginning to think that only Khrushchev and I were genuine supporters of an effective Summit meeting. At any rate he sent a friendly message on 14 October, immediately after the Election.

> Please accept my congratulations on the occasion of your recent election to the post of Prime Minister of Great Britain. I wish to express the hope, Mr. Macmillan, that having received the support of the majority of your people you, together with us and with the Governments of other countries, will direct your efforts in the immediate future to resolving questions of dis-

armament and other international problems so as to contribute to the ending of the 'Cold War', the reduction of international tension and to peaceful co-existence between states.

I take advantage of this opportunity to thank you for your recent dealings with me in connection with my meeting with the President of the United States Eisenhower, and to express my agreement with the opinion which you expressed in this connection that in the course of the assembly of a general Summit it would be possible to find agreement on urgent international problems. Like you I hope that the day is not far distant when we will meet round a table for discussions so as to fulfil this noble task. Allow me also to express the warm hope that the happy development in the relations between the Soviet Union and Great Britain, manifesting itself as the result of the efforts of both our Governments, and in which no small role was played by our meetings and talks in Moscow, will be successfully continued.

I could not help being rather tickled by these flatteries so pleasantly and perhaps genuinely extended from the great Communist chief to a Conservative leader.

For a few days all seemed to hang fire.

No more news about the Summit. De Gaulle is mysterious; Adenauer changes his position every day; and I fear the President may be losing heart.[1]

However, on 29 October, de Gaulle

has proposed a 'Western Summit' (with Adenauer 'to come along later') on 19 December. President Eisenhower is disgusted at the delay, but not disposed to argue any more. To this I have agreed.[2]

The French President at the same time suggested April for the actual Summit meeting. This caused me some concern and I agreed with Eisenhower that we must leave this over for discussion in Paris.

What Mr. K. will now do is obscure. He may well turn nasty and start sending ultimatums again about Berlin. Then—through

[1] 24 October 1959.   [2] 29 October 1959.

the folly, first of the Americans and then of the French, we shall have lost all the ground which I gained by the Moscow visit.[1]

In my desire not to miss this opportunity I was no doubt too anxious. Khrushchev seemed to be in a friendly mood and keen to extend his experience of foreign travel. My concern was put at rest by the announcement that Khrushchev was to visit Paris on 15 March of the following year.

> This delays the Summit somewhat, but at any rate seems to keep up the momentum and looks as if Mr. K. has not yet turned sour.[2]

Another troublesome situation now arose over an atomic explosion of a modest size, which the French proposed to make in the Sahara.

> A grave dilemma is presented to us. The Moroccans have put down a resolution in the United Nations Assembly calling on the French to abandon the Bomb Test (atomic, we think) which they have planned to set off in the Sahara. The Nigerians, Ghana and other Africans are terribly upset. It is an emotional reaction, for it is very unlikely that the Test will do any harm—certainly no more in Africa than elsewhere. They even talk about 'leaving the Commonwealth' if we do not vote *for* the resolution.
> On the other hand, if we do, the French (who always supported us and the U.S.A. on similar resolutions in the past) will be deeply affronted.[3]

In the end, after many compromise proposals had been put forward and turned down, the British and American Governments voted against the Afro-Asian resolution calling on the French to abandon their plan. However, to my regret, Canada and New Zealand and the Scandinavian countries took the other side. One of the most ludicrous aspects of the discussion was that the area where the test was to take place was described by M. Moch, the French delegate, as 'virtually uninhabited' and referred to by the Moroccan delegate as 'one of the most fertile in the Sahara'. Although in a sense it was a storm in a teacup—or rather a sand-dune—it caused me much concern.

[1] 29 October 1959.   [2] 10 November 1959.   [3] 30 October 1959.

The whole thing is all the more tiresome—and ridiculous—because everyone knows that the test will in fact take place, resolution or no resolution. But just as we have (*a*) trouble with Nigeria and Ghana and (*b*) are desperately trying to 'mend our fences' with France, it is most vexing to have this problem.[1]

Our action at the United Nations, together with some useful discussions that the Foreign Secretary had in Paris with the French Ministers, served to improve Anglo-French relations. We were anxious, and the French seemed agreeable, to use the Western European Union more effectively and thus to emphasise the essential unity of Europe in defence, in spite of what we hoped would prove only a temporary division in the economic field. It was clear, as Selwyn Lloyd wrote on 11 November, that the French thinking

> was completely governed by the need to tie Germany as tightly as possible to a Western association. They were not so frightened of a German military threat, but they did believe there was a very serious danger of Germany going neutralist. That would mean, in due course, her throwing in her lot with the Soviet bloc. The French had no confidence in the Opposition in Germany, nor did they think that Adenauer commanded the support of the majority of his own party for his policy of close association with the West.

There also seemed to be some good prospect of co-operation in the field of weapons production. Selwyn Lloyd's visit to de Gaulle was equally successful, and he reported on 12 November that

> He was very affable and relaxed. He thanked us for all the work we had done in trying to arrange a Summit meeting and explained his reasons for insisting on having Khrushchev's visit to France before the Summit. I explained our reasons for pushing on. He agreed that it should be held as soon as practicable and said that the second meeting between Western heads of Governments should take place just before the real Summit. He felt he must have an opportunity of telling his Western colleagues what had transpired between Khrushchev and himself.

It was clear also that the French were 'genuinely grateful for what

[1] 30 October 1959.

D2

we have tried to do to help them over the Sahara tests'. In thanking
the Foreign Secretary for his messages I said:

> What you have said is encouraging and I am very glad that
> you did see President de Gaulle. With all his faults he has great
> qualities, and I feel we must attune ourselves to the new situation
> in France. He is the man that matters.

A few days later Adenauer made a visit to London. At this time
I felt some concern about the growing hostility among many
people in this country to Germany and German rearmament, and
communicated my thoughts to the Foreign Secretary:

Anti-German Feeling in Britain

Apart from the papers which specialise in working up anti-
German feeling (chiefly Beaverbrook, etc.) there is I think a
genuine apprehension. I am quite sure that we are on good
ground as regards what we have agreed so far in the arming of
German troops with nuclear weapons, so long as the key of the
cupboard is in American hands. The concessions that we have
made about air-to-air and ground-to-air missiles can also be
defended, and the confusion about the warhead can be cleared
up.

But behind all this there is a feeling that the Germans pursue
a rather ambivalent policy. Nobody knows for instance how
many ex-Nazis are in fact employed either in the Army, Civil
Service or judiciary. The revival of Krupp is not very popular
here, and the Mixed Commission is likely to give in in the end.

Perhaps we could have a word about this and how to deal
with it.

In our talks before the Chancellor's arrival we agreed that the
ultimate answer to all these sources of jealousy and alarm in Western
Europe could only be the successful promotion of all possible
means of European unity. We must persuade the British people
that isolation was the least practical of all courses. We could not
prevent German recovery. We could only try to secure that her
new power, economic and military, should be used for the common
purpose.

Adenauer arrived on 17 November. The first conversation took place at four o'clock in the old Treasury Building. The room in which Queen Anne presided over meetings of her Ministers—the last monarch to do so—had been restored to its old beauty. I was struck by the way in which the Chancellor retained his extraordinary vitality in spite of his age.

We did not get beyond a general review of the world situation. But it was clear that Dr. A. had been told by his advisers to make an effort to be polite. I think they are ashamed of the foolish things which he has said about me and about H. M. G.'s policy during the last year. We covered most of the ground—the Summit, disarmament, the economic and political consequences of the Common Market, and so on. No very definite conclusions.[1]

On the next day, after luncheon at the German Embassy, we all went off to Chequers:

Meeting after dinner, where we got down to 'brass tacks'. I reproached Dr. A. for his attacks on H. M. G. and spoke very strongly. He seemed startled and angry. But his staff and especially von Brentano were clearly pleased that there was plain speaking. At first, I thought he would break off the conversation. But all ended well in a sort of reconciliation.[2]

Next day it became evident that

last night's row clearly produced a salutary effect. The talk this morning—9.30 to 12 noon—was sensible and constructive. Dr. A. agreed the text of his Press Conference address, which was moderate and sensible. He agreed to East–West Summit at the end of April, if all the others will conform.[3]

This was a less exhausting visit than some, for apart from a large dinner at No. 10 on the 17th we were able to avoid the usual flood of entertainments. I found Chequers, with its informality and comfort, admirably suited to this form of conference.

After the departure of the Chancellor I summed up my impressions as follows:

[1] 17 November 1959.   [2] 18 November 1959.   [3] 19 November 1959.

on the whole, the visit has done good. The Germans are pleased—although they fear that the old man will probably have another relapse into his suspicions and fears. The trouble is that they are all afraid of him.[1]

In this leisurely but not disagreeable approach to the major international problems there was a disturbing feature. The Geneva Conference on the discontinuance of nuclear tests was completely 'bogged down' in November, and any progress seemed to depend upon whether the Americans would accept a further moratorium on underground tests, and on what terms.

In preparation for the Paris meeting I organised a conference at Chequers at which were present Selwyn Lloyd, Heathcoat Amory, Sir Norman Brook, Sir Roger Makins, and Sir Frederick Hoyer Millar. More than six hours were spent in discussing

Europe and the world. A most useful talk, such as one can never have in London, with all the interruptions of each working day. It was agreed (among other things) that I must try to have a *private* talk in Paris both with President E. and de Gaulle *separately*. With the President, I must try to win him over to the view that we cannot afford to let the Geneva Test Conference go wrong. We *must* agree with the Russians on any reasonable terms which would give us the beginning of control and inspection. If a moratorium is the best that can be got for 'underground' tests, let us go for the moratorium. With de Gaulle, I must *ask* questions, and try to find out what he really wants—about NATO; about the Six—politically and economically; about the Germans after Adenauer; above all about the Russians. (There is much talk in diplomatic circles of a recent de G.–Khrushchev understanding, with Germany and Berlin bargained against Russian support in Algeria. I do not, myself, believe it.)[2]

We were, therefore, well prepared when we met in Paris on 19 December. Apart from the urgent matters of nuclear tests and the need to explore de Gaulle's intentions, I had set myself, during 1959, one major task. The year had opened under the shadow of the Soviet ultimatum on Berlin—it was certainly ending in a more relaxed atmosphere. Although the Summit meeting which I had

[1] 19 November 1959.   [2] 29 November 1959.

worked so hard to arrange was not to take place for several months, the delay caused me no serious anxiety. If all the Heads of State were swanning around each other's territories, one could hardly believe that there would be a sudden and fatal explosion. In a sense therefore my first objective had been attained. But I was equally anxious that the Summit should not be considered, as both the President and de Gaulle seemed to regard it, as a unique occasion. I was anxious to promote the concept of a series of meetings moving steadily forward from point to point in which 'peaceful co-existence' (to use the jargon of the day)—if not peace—could reign unchallenged in the world.

I was also anxious to persuade Eisenhower to develop more actively tripartite discussion and co-operation between Britain, France and America on a wide range of policy. Some progress had been made since de Gaulle had first started the idea, and, although difficulties had been caused by his clumsy handling,[1] I wanted this partnership to develop effectively—especially since the man now in charge of France clearly attached importance to his plan. All this would facilitate the discussion of other matters such as the economic future of Europe.

It was in this mood and with these hopes that my colleagues and I set out for Paris on the evening of 18 December.

Before the formal meeting of the Heads of Government there had been a number of discussions in Paris, between Chris Herter and Selwyn Lloyd, aided by a number of officials. As usual, these discussions covered a very wide range and a satisfactory measure of agreement was reached between the deputies. There were also quadripartite meetings on this level with Couve de Murville and von Brentano, who represented Germany. These continued throughout the main conference, partly to prepare further discussions and partly to execute the decisions made by the Heads of Government. All this machinery worked, as far as I was concerned, with its usual well-oiled precision. Having attended many conferences of this kind I have always thought it must be a source of great disillusionment and irritation to the officials, who have

---

[1] See *Riding the Storm*, pp. 452–4.

prepared the agenda so admirably and indicated so clearly the proper conclusions, to find that their principals are apt to behave in an unpredictable and sometimes irresponsible mood.

We met at the Elysée, at 9.30 a.m. on 19 December. After the usual ceremonies—guards of honour, colours, bands—all very smart and impressive—we gathered in a moderate-sized room upstairs.

There were present the four heads of Government and four interpreters. Everyone else was rigidly excluded.[1]

Since I could rely on the President's interpreter, Colonel Walters, for the translation from Dr. Adenauer and on my own knowledge of French, Philip de Zulueta was able to occupy himself by taking a record.

It was an extraordinary performance, conducted by de Gaulle with great skill and grace, with periods both of high comedy and of farce. The President's American slang contrasted strangely with de Gaulle's stately, old-fashioned French. However, the translator did his best. 'I guess I'll just have to clear my "skedool"' became '*Le calendrier diplomatique est très chargé—mais je ferai de mon mieux . . .'*.

The two highlights of the talk were as follows. De Gaulle explained that he—and he would assume all of us agreed—felt that it was now impossible to avoid a Summit meeting of some kind with Mr. Khrushchev. '*Tout le monde accepte la thèse du Premier Ministre Britannique*', etc., etc. [But] when, and where?

After some discussion, it appeared that I was the only person who had been provided with a list of international events next year. President Eisenhower suggested 20 or 21 April (the date he had been told by his people). De Gaulle said that he would much like to visit U.S.A. *before* the Summit. K. was coming to France on 15 March. He (de G.) was having the great honour of a State visit to Her Majesty in the first week in April. Then came Holy Week. Perhaps he might go to Washington on Easter Tuesday (19 April). He would stay three days in America, one in Canada—perhaps 25 April or 26 would do?

President Eisenhower gave the invitation to de Gaulle for the 19th (he could do very little else) but his 'skedool' was

[1] 19 December 1959.

beginning to look bad. There was the King of Nepal—or Siam was it? Anyway, there was a King 'due' in Washington about that time. Perhaps we could 'ring him up' and alter or adjust the date? Anyway, about 26 or 27 April was agreed. I objected that K. would probably want to be in Moscow on 'May Day' (1 May). But de Gaulle and Adenauer were rather incredulous. So much for the date.[1]

I was proved to be right, and Khrushchev, although accepting the invitation to the Summit in the most amiable terms, was not happy about the conflict with the 1 May celebrations. Before the end of the year 16 May was, in fact, agreed.

We next came to the question of the place of meeting.

> Geneva had been regarded as inevitable. '*Ce n'est pas très gai. Le lac. Et puis toute cette histoire de ce Monsieur Calvin. Non. Ce n'est pas très gai. Tout de même. . . .*' So General de Gaulle. I suggested that we might have Paris. Of course, this would mean definitely accepting the idea of a series of Summits—Paris must be followed by London, Washington, Moscow. If this was not acceptable, Geneva it must be, for a *single* meeting.
>
> De Gaulle was pleased by the idea of Paris and consequently accepted the *series* concept without demur. President Eisenhower agreed quite readily, and Adenauer less willingly. However, the decision was made.[1]

When we came to the agenda there was a rather rambling discussion 'but eventually it was agreed to make the letter of invitation pretty general, but to give more detailed instructions to the Ambassadors'.[1] All this was satisfactory, and the Foreign Ministers were called together at 11.30 a.m. to be given an account of what we had settled. The most interesting and revealing part of our discussion was what amounted to an attack on Adenauer by President Eisenhower over Berlin.

> This was very significant. Adenauer is trying to go back to last year's position—before the long meeting [of Foreign Ministers] at Geneva, when (after all) some loosening of the position took place. Meanwhile, the Americans have moved from their very rigid position and are ready to consider various

[1] 19 December 1959.

plans for the future of Berlin which they were unwilling even to discuss some time ago. The Chancellor no doubt was aware of this. But the President was very firm and almost rude. He was thoroughly exasperated. As a result of being 'bullied' a bit, the German Chancellor collapsed and did not speak again.[1]

There was another interesting point raised by de Gaulle in the discussion of a possible agenda. He was anxious that the question of underdeveloped countries be raised and the possibility, if something like a real *détente* could be reached with the Soviet Government, of embarking upon joint agricultural, social and other plans. This would indeed be a dramatic partnership between the Communist and the non-Communist world. If the Russians agreed it would be a real advance—if they refused it would not matter greatly. This imaginative suggestion was alas doomed to fail in the general collapse in the following year. In any case at this stage it seemed best to ask our experts to study the possibilities without too much publicity. I was particularly interested in a remark by de Gaulle about Khrushchev which seemed to me exactly right. Khrushchev had of course not renounced Communism. At the same time he was perhaps a man who felt also some responsibility for the world. That was why de Gaulle thought it important to have practical contacts with the Russians.

The greater part of our discussion, apart from the date and place of the meeting, was devoted to the agenda, and naturally this turned on the two great subjects of Berlin and Disarmament. On the latter there was general agreement that discussions should begin in the Ten-Power Committee on the basis of the British proposals. Although this decision did not constitute any marked advance it was sensible and practical. On Germany and Berlin the discussion was mainly taken up by the spirited argument between Adenauer and the President. One other interchange has remained vividly in my mind. In agreeing to Paris as the place for the first meeting, I added that I could only do so if future meetings were envisaged in other cities. Chancellor Adenauer then somewhat cynically observed that such a plan was helpful in winning elections.

[1] 19 December 1959.

I replied rather angrily that I was not thinking of elections but of our duty to God and to mankind. Eisenhower then came to my support. He declared that he had no interest in elections but thought that it would be a good plan to have a Summit meeting every year. There would then be a regular system of preparation without exciting too much anticipation of dramatic results.

The next day, 20 December, was Sunday. Selwyn Lloyd and I went to breakfast with the President at 8.00 a.m. at the American Embassy. This is an hour of the day which seems to suit American statesmen better than their British counterparts. I have never felt quite up to grilled chops and marmalade at that time. Eisenhower told us about Khrushchev's visit to the United States and the discussions at Camp David. Perhaps the most interesting point was made by Herter, who was also present. He felt that Khrushchev had many difficulties to consider in his own country. There were people whom he had to consult and inform and whose support was necessary to him. He was by no means in the undisputed and unchallengeable position enjoyed by Stalin. Unfortunately, this was not the general view of the President's advisers. Had it been so, the outcome of the Summit in May 1960 might have been happier.

Eisenhower also talked about his tour of India, Pakistan, Afghanistan and Iran. I raised the question of the nuclear test conference at Geneva and urged the necessity of reaching some agreement even if it included provisions for it to be denounced if one side or the other were dissatisfied with the system of control. Herter regarded this provision as quite sufficient to protect American security.

Although the President seemed to be enjoying the meetings,

I did *not* think [him] . . . very well. He looked terribly flushed and seemed very restless. He was as friendly as ever. Of course, he has had a gruelling tour, half round the world, with crowds, speeches, interviews and all the rest. The chief anxiety I have now with U.S.A. is about the Geneva H-Bomb Test Conference. We put in a strong plea for a 'political' settlement, whatever the scientists may say. But the President is nervous about Congress.[1]

[1] 20 December 1959.

We were now due at Rambouillet, where a tripartite meeting had been planned. We arrived at about 10.30 a.m. and began the talks immediately. There were present de Gaulle, Eisenhower and myself.

> This lasted for two hours after which Adenauer arrived for luncheon. By this rather ingenious arrangement de Gaulle in fact brought into being the 'Tripartite' system which he has been working for during the last two years.[1]

This was confirmed by a short discussion in which I have no doubt the President went a bit further than he intended. At any rate when de Gaulle suggested

> that there should be regular tripartite discussions between U.S., U.K. and France on 'matters of common interest, outside and transcending NATO', the President—to my great surprise—at once accepted. Fortunately, he suggested London as the place.... Eisenhower, of course, stipulated that the London discussions should be 'clandestine'. De Gaulle said they would be '*très prudents*'. But naturally, since de Gaulle attaches much more importance to the *fact* of the Tripartite talks than to the *substance* of them, it will soon become known—from French sources. De Gaulle clearly thought that I had persuaded the President to accept what he has consistently rejected. This will do no harm—although it is clear that the President acted more or less from impulse and not on advice.[1]

De Gaulle seemed very satisfied with the morning's work and since this was the first item raised the rest of the talk went on very amicably.

In accepting this plan President Eisenhower made it clear that the group could meet in any of the three capitals. On the whole he preferred London, since it was important that there should be no question of any contact between the tripartite machinery and that of NATO. He thought that each country should supply two or three men. This seemed to give de Gaulle all that he needed; but the fact that this group when established made very little progress confirmed my view that he was more anxious that it

[1] 20 December 1959.

should be known to exist than troubled about its work. It was the prestige of the tripartite arrangement which he valued at this period when he was trying to rebuild his own authority and that of France.

On Berlin de Gaulle observed with great truth that one should not allow Khrushchev to adopt an attitude of superiority to the West over Berlin. It would be wrong to admit that the Berlin 'situation' was abnormal: the true position was that the D.D.R. was its cause. It would be most important not to allow Khrushchev to say that the Berlin 'situation' needed changing. This was a tactic which he was employing most adroitly. The East German régime was quite artificial. When it came to the question of German frontiers and of unification the discussion continued on very realistic lines.

We then passed to Africa. There was going to be a rapid evolution in that continent, and it was important that it should be helped and guided by the West. It would not be wise for the United States to try to replace France or Britain in Africa, for if the old colonial powers were excluded the new countries would fall to Communism. After much discussion on the problems of emerging Africa and the various roles which France, Britain and the United States might play, it was decided that this matter should be taken up further in the tripartite discussions already arranged. This was followed by ominous references to NATO. The German army had not yet really come into being, and de Gaulle tried to argue that the burden of the alliance lay upon our three countries. I could not help taking him up on this issue, since there were twelve German divisions formed or forming. Was he so anxious that they should form a separate army of their own? Was it not wise to keep the system of an international command alive and thus merge the national forces? I could see that the General was not happy about all this; he was clearly contemplating the policy which he was afterwards to press more ruthlessly.

When we turned to economic questions I remarked that my British colleagues and I were worried about the economic divisions of Europe and that a solution of this problem must be found. In reply de Gaulle claimed with truth that since he had assumed power France had been able, so far, to liberalise her trading policy.

Before the end of the meeting, which M. Debré had now joined, we reverted to some NATO problems. Eisenhower had the last word. He said that he did not like to think of the breaking up of NATO; he believed profoundly in co-operative effort. If any country was able to stand on its own, at least for a time, it was the United States; yet he was not an isolationist. He was for 'interdependence' and co-operation in the good cause.

The talk between the three of us recalled many memories to which de Gaulle graciously referred at luncheon. The last time that we had talked together had been at Algiers, some sixteen years before, when both Eisenhower and I had done our best to support de Gaulle's claims to be recognised as the approved leader of all France outside German clutches. He knew well that, in our different ways, we had both worked hard to overcome the jealousy of Roosevelt and the anxiety of Churchill. It was strange that the same three men were now meeting together as Heads of their respective countries or Governments.

I had been a little anxious as to how Adenauer would accept his exclusion from the earlier conference, but when he arrived for luncheon de Gaulle managed this with his usual combination of exquisite courtesy and complete assurance. The luncheon was good but short, and at 2.30 p.m. we resumed our work. We had a long lecture from Adenauer about Communism—its origins, its implications, and its dangers. The effect was somewhat soporific, and when I woke up I found a rather confused conversation going on chiefly about the future of divided Germany. However at 4.30 p.m. the Foreign Ministers arrived, having completed their task. The letters to Khrushchev which they had prepared were quickly agreed, as well as the instructions in identical terms to the three Ambassadors in Moscow. An appropriate communiqué was also settled.

We then turned to the question of economic problems of Europe. I was glad to find that the Foreign Ministers had agreed a policy (and a communiqué) on this, which was to use the next meeting of O.E.E.C. (in January) to inaugurate discussions. There was left a certain doubt as to how far these talks would be *within* O.E.E.C. But we got substantially what London wanted. All this is symptomatic of the new mood of

French friendship towards us, which clearly reflects instructions from de Gaulle.

On the whole, a satisfactory day. I have for many weeks been puzzling about the problem of getting nearer to the French without losing the Americans. The President has really solved this for me. We found out later in the evening that the State Department were rather concerned. Since they had no proper record of the discussion, I arranged for ours to be made available to Chris Herter.[1]

The next morning Selwyn Lloyd and I breakfasted with the President and Herter at the American Embassy. Unhappily, there had been a change of mood and Eisenhower was very critical of what he called the light-hearted way in which de Gaulle approached many defence matters. The President already sensed his jealousy of NATO, an organisation for which Eisenhower had a genuine and very natural loyalty. Otherwise, he

seemed in better form, but still very flushed. I fear he may be working up for another attack. We went over all the ground, with Herter and Selwyn Lloyd. I have better hopes that the President will take the right line over the H-Bomb Tests. But with an anxious and critical Congress, he will not find it at all easy.[2]

In the event, although the President was unwilling to agree to continue the moratorium formally, he at least met us halfway. On 29 December, two days before the voluntary moratorium was due to expire, he announced that the United States Government was willing to continue the negotiations, up to now abortive, for a system of control and inspection; while considering itself free to resume tests, it would not in fact do so without prior warning. The Three-Power Conference on the discontinuance of tests therefore resumed its labours in the New Year and continued its discussion in a somewhat dilatory manner. Meanwhile there were no tests on either side.

The Summit Conference was now drawing to an end, and in a suitably Christmas spirit. On 21 December there was a

Plenary Session at 10.30 a.m.—at the Elysée. There was little to do—except confirm the decisions. Apart from the decisions

[1] 20 December 1959.   [2] 21 December 1959.

about the Summit and about O.E.E.C., it might seem that little
has been done to justify so large a gathering of important people.
I think that would not be quite fair. A lot of good talks have
taken place, and a very good atmosphere of confidence and
friendship created.[1]

There followed luncheon, after which President Eisenhower left
for Spain and Adenauer for Bonn. Our purpose was achieved, and
there was nothing more left for us to do.

The day ended with a strange but fascinating interview with
General de Gaulle. I was asked for *'une tasse de thé'* at 5.30, in
the private apartments of the Elysée. Only Madame de Gaulle
(whom I had not seen since Algiers days, but seemed better and
younger). Philip de Zulueta came with me. After a quarter of an
hour of very pleasant 'small talk', we adjourned to the General's
room. (He dislikes the Elysée very much. It is heavy and ornate
and there are no proper sitting-rooms—only saloons.) We talked
for an hour—on France, on America, largely on Germany and
its future, on Russia—indeed on everything. He spoke very
freely and in a most friendly and even affectionate mood—*'Cher
ami'* and all that. . . . This conversation at least gives me a chance
of getting some European economic compromise (the Six and
the Seven) with the only man who is capable of making it today.[1]

My relations with de Gaulle during the Algiers period had been
close and even intimate, but owing to the circumstances under
which we were both working he was often in an irritable and
frustrated mood. Now he seemed calm and relaxed. As always he
was the master of a witty or mordant phrase. But now the bitterness
had gone. One or two of his sayings I must recall.

Speaking of Germany he said that he felt it unlikely that even
in the future the West Germans would be seduced by the Russians.
(This was a danger which alarmed some of his advisers.) The only
thing that might make them desperate would be their abandonment
by the West. Thus in the economic field it was very important that
Western Germany should be tied in with France. There must be no
more economic *'Drang nach Osten'*. It was for this reason that he

[1] 21 December 1959.

had approved the Common Market, although he had no real liking for it. When we discussed the prospects of German reunification, he agreed that it could not happen for a long time; but then in fact Germany had not been united for centuries. There was Prussia, the Rhineland, the Free Cities and so on. Germany was thus quite unlike the centralised countries such as France and Britain. The really awkward thing about the division of Germany was that Eastern Germany was Communist, and this naturally made West Germans unhappy and angry.

About Khrushchev, de Gaulle admitted that he regarded his forthcoming visit with considerable distaste. The situation was simple, and required little argument. All that the West wanted from Khrushchev was not to start a war. This, of course, was said partly to tease me, and in further conversation he admitted that we must gradually work out a *modus vivendi*. But it was clear that the General thought me too much of an enthusiast. Nevertheless, he agreed that it would be possible to make a real arrangement with the Russians one day. They would become more *bourgeois*; they would have intellectuals, men of letters, doctors and students; above all they were human beings. The Poles and the Czechs and the other East Europeans and even the Russians would retain their national characteristics in spite of Bolshevism. So one day, if there was no war, there might be a real chance of peace; if so, it was vital that Western Europe should be together. While we must work with the United States in a close alliance, as Europe grew in strength and power she would rely more on her own stability.

One phrase de Gaulle threw out which particularly attracted me. Marxism, he said, was a philosophy for an underdeveloped country. It was suitable for the Chinese, or the Africans, who all liked to sing together and work together; but it was not suitable for more developed countries. It was interesting how keen the Russians were to know about the West.

M. Debré, the French Prime Minister, had been present during part of our meeting at Rambouillet on the previous day. I mentioned that I was to dine with him that evening. I understood that he managed the Parliament, which must be a great convenience to de Gaulle. He replied that clearly Parliament was disagreeable, but it was not dangerous. Now it was hard to overturn a Government. And in any case, France was calm.

The day ended with a pleasant dinner for British and French only given at the Matignon.

Debré (Prime Minister), Couve de Murville (Foreign Minister), Joxe (also an old friend from Algiers days and now Minister of State with de Gaulle), and several other of the leading French personalities, including Courcel, the General's Chef de Cabinet and confidant. Selwyn Lloyd, Hoyer Millar, Gladwyn Jebb, [Sir Anthony] Rumbold, etc. No business, just interesting and amusing talk. Joxe (who had been nearly three years in Moscow as Ambassador) gave a fascinating account of the days which followed the death of Stalin and the rise and fall of Beria.[1]

The next day, 22 December, before leaving, I dictated notes to the Foreign Secretary, the Chancellor of the Exchequer and other of my leading colleagues

about the Paris meeting and the lessons to be drawn. I feel we have now a chance to get much nearer to the French, without in any way upsetting the Americans. The economic division of Europe must somehow be avoided. This means an arrangement with de Gaulle.[2]

My note to the Foreign Secretary ran as follows:

You will have seen the record of my talk with President de Gaulle. For a long time I have been puzzled as to how to use my old friendship with de Gaulle and how to restore our old relations with the French without disloyalty to the Americans. It is this that has made me so uncertain in recent weeks, and even months.

From Bermuda I set myself to rebuild the Anglo-American Alliance to its former strength. This has been achieved and must never be abandoned. The President spoke very warmly about the Anglo-American Defence talks and it is quite clear that he wishes to preserve the special Anglo-American relationship.

At the same time de Gaulle passionately wants the tripartite discussions to elevate France out of the ruck of European countries, including Germany, and to put her in a different category. But there was no possibility of our agreeing to this at

[1] 21 December 1959.   [2] 22 December 1959.

the cost of our relations with the Americans. The President's ready acceptance of de Gaulle's proposals on Sunday morning at Rambouillet seemed at first rather astonishing. Herter may regard it as a blunder—many in the State Department will hold this view. But the President, although inexpert in negotiation, has some very firm ideas of his own. The fact that he refused to have a serious row with de Gaulle about NATO, and the fact that he so readily agreed to the tripartite and so-called 'clandestine' (this was his own word) discussions in London may well represent not a blunder but a definite decision. He may be wiser than the State Department. At any rate from our point of view he has done exactly what I wanted. He enabled me to have a conversation with de Gaulle on Monday night which would have been quite impossible without disloyalty to the Americans if the President had not taken this line on Sunday morning.

I hope therefore—and I really do regard this as of vital importance—that we shall do nothing in private talks or arrangements with the State Department to reduce the importance of the position taken at Rambouillet or to try to get out of it. If de Gaulle thought that we were trying to get out of it he would not forgive me and would change his whole opinion. When therefore the French come forward with suggestions as to how the Rambouillet agreement is to be carried out I hope we shall be forthcoming. If there is any hesitation let it be the Americans and not ourselves. I am quite entitled surely to work upon what the President said and proposed. It is not my object to pull him back because the State Department think he may have gone too far. As for the reactions in other NATO countries, I am not so much concerned about that. With good management by Roberts it can surely be explained that this tripartite relationship is largely related to areas of the world not covered by NATO, e.g. Africa, the Far East, etc.

Now I come to the vital point. My purpose now must be to support de Gaulle on the political front and his desire to join the ranks of the Great Powers, and to encourage him to get the fruits of his famous memorandum,[1] and so forth. In return he must give to me the greatest practical accommodation that he can on the economic front. The future of British trade in Europe

[1] On tripartite consultation between France, U.K. and U.S.A., see *Riding the Storm*, pp. 452–4.

is far more important than whether a few French fighters are or are not to be put under the command of SACEUR. If there is a global war the fighters will be useless anyway. As we do not believe there will be a global war, what is really important is British trade interests. I am therefore very anxious indeed about how the Rambouillet agreement is to be handled. We must carry out this agreement honourably and not allow it to be whittled away by the Americans—or, if they do the whittling, it must be clear that we stand by our undertaking.

It was therefore with a thankful heart that I went home to enjoy the Christmas festivities surrounded by my large family. So far I had every reason for hope; our relations with France appeared to be fully restored and there seemed every possibility of a forward movement towards the unity of Western Europe. As regards Russia my main purpose had been amply achieved. The Summit meeting for which I had striven for so long was now definitely agreed. If it was to be delayed until May that made little difference since the time was to be occupied with visits from East to West. It was equally clear that the Summit meeting was now to be considered as part of a series. At our first meeting President Eisenhower had actually said that it would be a good plan to think in terms of a Summit meeting every year. This would avoid the dangers of raising too many expectations of success on too wide a front, and it would become a routine. In commenting on this statement Adenauer remarked, rather grumpily, that we were trying to 'organise world government'. The idea, however fantastic, did not seem to cause any of his colleagues undue alarm. Indeed might there not be a hope that little by little if the meetings between East and West, the Communist and the Free World, became part of the accepted instrument by which peace was to be maintained and the progress of mankind ensured we might be embarking upon a practical method of making effective the ideas of the founders of the United Nations organisation? What the Security Council had failed to do in New York in the atmosphere of intrigue and confusion in that vast assembly might perhaps be gradually brought about in the quiet meetings of four statesmen held in regular sequence in one or other of their capitals.

Alas, both these hopes were to be bitterly disappointed. Yet perhaps as the years go by it may prove that my colleagues and I pointed the way at that Paris meeting along a road which others will some day follow.

CHAPTER VI

An African Journey

By the end of the Parliament of 1955–9, the former British Imperial possessions in Asia, great and small, had almost all joined the old Dominions in independence, becoming, in the words of the Balfour formula, 'autonomous communities . . . freely associated as members of the British Commonwealth of Nations'.[1] The problems of the remaining dependent colonial territories—in which various constitutional changes were already taking place marking the road towards final independence—were, with few exceptions, concentrated in Africa.

There is a common illusion that this story, begun during and after the First World War and concluded within less than twenty years of the Second, is one of weakness and decay, resulting from the loss of will to govern inherent in a democratic system. This is an undeserved libel on a people who twice in my lifetime demonstrated their courage and tenacity, as well as against its leaders. As regards what we used to call the old Commonwealth countries—Canada, Australia, New Zealand and South Africa—even the most rabid imperialist can never have seriously contemplated continuing in any form the rule of Whitehall over these buoyant and expanding territories.

Even in the second stage, whatever might be said about the methods employed and the immediate sufferings involved, the great majority both in Parliament and outside were persuaded that the evolutionary progress of India and Ceylon towards self-government could not be resisted. It is a vulgar but false jibe that the British people by a series of gestures unique in history abandoned their Empire in a fit of frivolity or impatience. They had not lost the will or even the power to rule. But they did not conceive of themselves as

[1] See *Winds of Change*, p. 22, and *Tides of Fortune*, chap. ix.

having the right to govern in perpetuity. It was rather their duty to spread to other nations those advantages which through the long course of centuries they had won for themselves. Nor indeed was this a sudden resolve arising from the final extension of the franchise to the whole British community, male and female, which followed the First War. Its basis stretched back into the nineteenth century, when, as a result of Lord Macaulay's famous Minute, an educational system was devised for India which was to open the best brains of her people from childhood onwards 'to the powerful influence of English Liberal and scientific thought'. Indeed it was in the precepts of Whig and Liberal philosophy that the students of India were inspired—or at any rate examined. By a strange if admirable impartiality the speeches of Burke and Sheridan delivered on the impeachment of Warren Hastings became a favourite choice for study by aspiring Indian undergraduates.

Moreover, the devotion of a century of British officials was deliberately directed to the work of preparation, through steadily increasing Indian participation in every field of public life. The independence of India, therefore, was not a sudden whim or act of despair by an exhausted people. It was the culmination of a set purpose of nearly four generations.

In approaching the final stages of the evolution of the remaining colonial territories into independent states, although the numbers involved were not so great, the difficulties were considerable. Just as in India there had been many races and religions, with a population ranging from a highly developed and educated minority to outcastes and primitive tribes, so we had to deal in many of the colonial territories with European minorities, with tribal forces and often with the backwardness of poverty. We had also to bear in mind, in the new division of the world which overshadowed all other considerations, the impact upon global strategy of the withdrawal of British control from certain key areas. It was for that reason that I clung with such determination and happily success to our military positions in Cyprus, in Aden and in Singapore.

It could, of course, be argued that the British Government was mistaken in even considering self-government in many of these diverse and often non-viable territories. In some of them only a generation or two divided their inhabitants from primitive and even savage conditions. The intense tribal hatreds, the thin veneer of civilisation which the missionary and the trader as well as the administrator had been able to impose, the short period of apprenticeship afforded by the incorporation of Africans into the Civil Service and later in the Governor's Council—all these were powerful arguments in favour of delay. Even if independence should be regarded as an ultimate goal, as in India, yet no practical observer could claim that in most of the colonies concerned the time was ripe. There must be a longer interval before the British Government could be justified in abandoning its responsibilities. The peoples were not ready—they had much to learn. This argument, too, Macaulay had met more than a century ago:

> Many politicians of our time are in the habit of laying it down as a self-evident proposition, that no people ought to be free till they are fit to use their freedom. The maxim is worthy of the fool in the old story, who resolved not to go into the water till he had learnt to swim. If men are to wait for liberty till they become wise and good in slavery, they may indeed wait for ever.[1]

But a better justification for the forward moves upon which both Labour and Conservative Governments were determined may perhaps be found in the advice of a practical administrator rather than a theoretical philosopher. I recall a conversation at this time with one of the men most experienced in these problems, who had spent his life in the Colonial Service. I asked him to give me his frank opinion whether the people over whose destinies he was now presiding were ready for independence. They had reached the stage of a Governor's Council, in which all the members were Africans and the Governor held only reserve rights of defence, law and order and external policies. 'Are they ready', I asked, 'for this great change for which they are shouting so vigorously with perhaps little knowledge of what will ensue? Freedom, freedom, freedom.' 'Oh no,' he replied, 'of course, they are not ready for it.' 'When will they be ready?' 'Oh,' he said, 'in perhaps fifteen or twenty years.

[1] Thomas Babington Macaulay, *Critical and Historical Essays* (London 1851), 'Essay on Milton', p. 19.

They are learning fast; but it will take at least that time before their leaders are ready to take full responsibility.' 'What then would you advise?' The Governor did not hesitate or even pause for reflection. 'I should give it to them at once—as soon as possible.' When I expressed some surprise, he developed an argument which seemed to me, as to him, unanswerable. 'If the fifteen or twenty years were to be applied in learning the job, in increasing their experience of local government, or of central administration, why then I would be all for it. But that is not what will happen. All the most intelligent men capable of government will be in rebellion. I will have to put them in prison. There they will learn nothing about administration, only about hatred and revenge. They will not be fruitful, but wasted years; so I say, give them independence now.' Nor was this judgement unique. It was shared by all his most experienced and reflective colleagues.

I had long determined that if the result of the General Election was to confirm me in office I would make, at the first convenient moment, a journey to Africa. In 1958 I had visited almost every major country in the Commonwealth outside Africa.[1] If I could snatch a few weeks of comparative calm in our external and internal affairs, I might hope to complete a tour never before undertaken by any Prime Minister in office. The rising tide of nationalism in Africa was then not so evident as it was soon to become. Yet I was conscious of dangers and storms ahead. I hoped by a personal visit not only to inform myself on some of the difficulties involved in the next stages of constitutional advance, but perhaps by focusing public opinion at home on this problem lift it to a plane above that of narrow party politics.

Accordingly, the plans were made, and my wife and I left England on 5 January 1960, reaching home on 15 February, just after my sixty-sixth birthday. In these weeks we travelled 13,360 miles by air, 5,410 by sea, and about 800 by road. If this journey was not so long in distance as my 1958 tour, it was mentally and morally more testing. In 1958 I had visited many countries which had long been given their independence and were well established in their own confidence. Here we were confronted with the last

[1] See *Riding the Storm*, chap. xii.

stages of the transformation from Empire to Commonwealth. Though the populations, white or black, were in a state, some of alarm and some of frenzied hope, regarding the future, everywhere there was a sense of uncertainty while a new order was being born. Therefore, although the outward pattern of my tour was very similar to that of 1958—informal discussions with Premiers or Governors, more formal meetings with councils or Ministers, civic luncheons, receptions, visits to places of local scenic or economic importance—yet the substance and purpose of the journey were very different. In 1958 I was concerned with cementing links between Britain and Commonwealth countries on a basis which had long been accepted and agreed. Their status was well established, and the questions which I had to discuss with them were those which we shared as partners. In Africa everything was in flux. The problem of race relations, itself one of great complexity and likely to arouse strong passions and bitter controversy, dominated all other issues. If private discussions were matters of some delicacy, public reference to these matters was even more dangerous. Almost anything I might say would give offence in some quarters; yet if I said nothing but platitudes I would be thought by public opinion, both at home and in Africa, to have failed in my duty.

I tried to steer a steady and consistent course and, without shirking the controversial issues, to concentrate on large issues of public policy in my main speeches. Of these the two most important were made at Salisbury and Cape Town. In private discussions with the various leaders I adopted the plan of treating them as partners in a joint enterprise. This led sometimes to disputation, but seldom to misunderstanding.

The personal welcome accorded to us wherever we went was spontaneous and impressive. I was made conscious of a real warmth and feeling towards Britain and to the Commonwealth. Perplexing as were the problems as a whole, not merely racial but economic and social, there was a touching confidence in the ability of British statesmen to make an effective contribution to their solution. Moreover even where there were strong differences of opinion I felt there was a respect for the policy and point of view of the British Government.

Landing at Accra, January 1960
'Surf boats manned by splendid Africans with their rhythmic wielding of their paddles.'

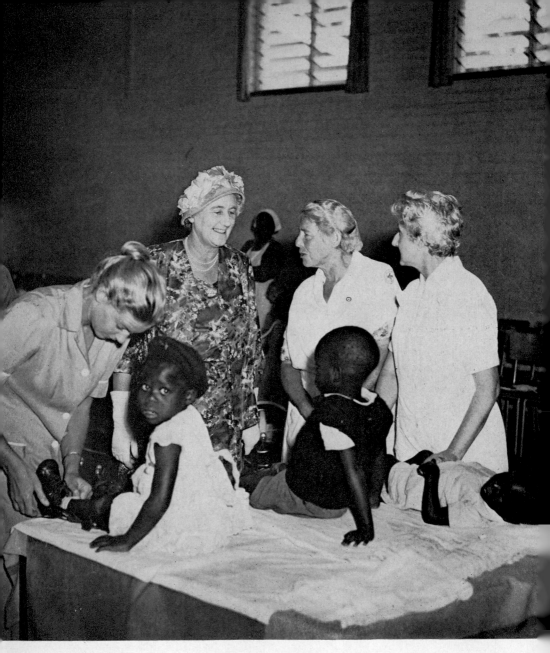

Lady Dorothy visiting a children's hospital at Lusaka

As usual the agreed programme in each place was inflated by new commitments or engagements, and there was a good deal of official business to be transacted apart from mere courtesy visits. There were early starts, long days and short night stops. Moreover, in spite of the forbearance of my colleagues in London and Butler's admirable management of day-to-day business, several hours each day, or rather night, had to be devoted to answering telegrams from home. All this would have been quite impossible had it not been for the extraordinary skill and devotion of my staff. Sir Norman Brook came with me as before—a man who was not only one of the greatest of public servants but a loyal friend and delightful companion. Tim Bligh, my principal private secretary, and John Wyndham ran the office and all the arrangements with their usual skill. Harold Evans dealt with the many delicate questions of 'public relations' with quiet efficiency. I was fortunate in having a representative from the Commonwealth Office, Mr. D. W. S. Hunt, and from the Colonial Office, Mr. J. H. Robertson. Nor should I forget the services of my valet, Sydney Beecroft, and of Dorothy's maid, Edith Baker, both devoted servants of long standing. As usual my wife threw herself into every situation with enthusiasm and undertook in addition to my engagements many visits of her own to hospitals, schools, clinics and similar institutions. Those who remember her will readily imagine the personal success that she achieved wherever she went.

Ghana had become independent in 1957, and I had first met Nkrumah, a colourful if somewhat exotic Prime Minister, at the Commonwealth Conference of that year. I also had further talks with him in 1958 when he paid a visit to England. At this time he had not yet abandoned the mechanisms of party government in order to establish the near dictatorship which he ultimately adopted. When we visited the National Assembly I was able to see the Speaker's Chair, which had been presented by the British House of Commons, as an active part of political life and not as a mere historical relic. I was even, although against some protests, able to meet members of the Opposition parties, including Dr. J. B. Danquah and Mr. J. E. Appiah, who were still at liberty. It was clear, however, that the country was drifting towards a single-party system, and that Nkrumah would soon emerge in the position of a

E

dictator. I was warned by some of the most intelligent and experienced observers of the scene, including my old friend from war days,
Sir Robert Jackson, that this tendency was inevitable. It would not
necessarily be permanent. He and others impressed upon me that
we must be patient and take a long view. We too in our long history
had passed through the stormy seas of Tudor tyranny in one
century and military government and despotism in the next before
reaching calmer waters of agreed constitutional procedures.

Nkrumah was an engaging character with much charm of manner
and courtesy when he cared to display those qualities. I liked him
then and in subsequent years when I met him. Although I cannot
claim to have foreseen at the time the extent to which he would
succumb to the temptations of power, it was already clear that he had
begun to claim and would soon exercise an authority beyond that
conferred by any parliamentary system. At this period we had few
constitutional matters to discuss. Ghana was still under the normal
constitution of Commonwealth countries as they first reach independence. Lord Listowel, who was our gracious and generous host,
was Governor-General exercising his functions in the name of the
Monarch. Nevertheless Nkrumah made it clear that he wished
Ghana to become a republic as soon as possible. A republican
constitution would soon be published and submitted to his Parliament. I explained to him that although this was not incompatible
with membership of the Commonwealth—the precedents of India
and Pakistan were there for all to see—yet this matter must follow
an orderly course. Nkrumah was very ready for the Queen to be
recognised as Head of the Commonwealth according to the formula
already in force. It was evident that he was more concerned that he
should become the President of the republic. All this was discussed
in a friendly way, for it was already clear that the republican system
would be adopted by all the African territories when the time came.

As regards the economic situation, Ghana is, or should be, a rich
country. I knew from my experience at the Colonial Office the
immense sums that we had been able to accumulate through the
West African Produce Control Board mainly from the sales of
cocoa at very high prices in war time.[1] The British authorities in

[1] See *The Blast of War*, pp. 174–5.

Ghana had therefore been able to hand on to their successors several hundreds of millions of pounds immediately available for development purposes. It was by this means that the great harbour at Tema had been financed. Although a good deal was to be squandered on less productive operations during the next few years yet there were valuable plans such as the Volta River project which now held the field. Nkrumah's talks, therefore, were concentrated not so much upon the problems of Ghana which seemed to be proceeding well from his point of view, but those of Africa as a whole. He tried to persuade me to agree to a joint statement of principles for what he called 'the freedom of Africa', but he readily accepted my argument that any statement of principles made by me would be more natural at the end rather than at the beginning of my tour. I shall always carry away a pleasant memory of Nkrumah's personal courtesy on this and on subsequent occasions. I shall not forget the little private meetings that Dorothy and I had with his wife, and the pride and pleasure which he took in his newly born son. Whatever may have been his public faults and mistakes—and they no doubt were many—he had many private virtues.

Neither my wife nor I had ever been to West Africa, and on this first visit we were both delighted with the colourful scene. In the programme which had been arranged, we saw only Accra and its immediate neighbourhood. This was partly due to shortage of time and partly, no doubt, because the Government of Ghana preferred that we should confine ourselves to those areas where their influence was supreme. In pursuance of my statement that I had come 'to see and to learn' I was taken to see not only the site of the Volta River project at Akosombo but the whole great harbour at Tema, then nearly completed, together with the growing township and developing area. I naturally visited the famous Achimota School, the nursery of many of Ghana's most prominent politicians and officials, and in addition I saw the University College. Although the Assembly was not in session, I was presented to all the Members who were in Accra, and there was the usual State Reception including a banquet on 9 January, where I delivered a long and careful speech. Since at this stage it was not necessary to deal with any of the graver issues, it was chiefly confined to matters of local importance.

In referring to the constitutional advance of the old British colonies (Nigeria would soon follow Ghana, and others in due course) I used a phrase to which the Press paid no particular attention—'the wind of change is blowing right through Africa'. When I repeated it at a later stage it was to echo through the world. Meanwhile, I made an appeal which perhaps is still valid.

I recognise frankly that on every aspect of these difficult and baffling problems we cannot always see eye to eye on every point. But as you have said—and I am grateful for it, Mr. Prime Minister—in this difficult period of change and development the most important thing for us is to keep in touch, to exchange ideas, to make sure that we understand each other's point of view. For while we may all properly question the soundness of another man's opinion, we should hesitate lightly to question his sincerity. That is true inside a single country—it is indeed the very basis of Parliamentary Government. It is still more true in external affairs. This business of getting to know each other's mind is one of the things I believe our Commonwealth association is best fitted to develop.

Apart from all these private talks and public functions, what remained most vividly in my mind was a colourful scene of old Accra harbour where the ships stood off and all the cargo for centuries was discharged by surf boats manned by splendid Africans with their rhythmic wielding of their paddles. We were taken in one of these long canoes splashing through the sea. It was an exciting experience. Now with the opening of Tema harbour all this is no doubt a thing of the past. Perhaps the other most memorable event was the visit to Accra market, where the people crowded round us and the famous 'mammies' gave us a glorious welcome. Nkrumah throughout showed an enchanting hospitality and good nature.

We left Accra Airport in the afternoon of 11 January after nearly six crowded days, arriving at Ikeja Airport, Lagos, on the same evening. Here we were met by the Governor-General, Sir James Robertson, and his wife, as well as by the Prime Minister of the Federation of Nigeria, Abubakar. Ghana had been independent for some three years. After a long painful process of constitution-making the formal date for independence of Nigeria had been fixed for 1 October 1960. To produce an agreed structure for the Federation had been the work of nearly ten years, and success was largely due to the patient efforts first of Oliver Lyttelton and then of Alan Lennox-Boyd—two great Colonial Secretaries. There had been many abortive schemes and many setbacks. It was clear from the beginning that any constitution for so large a country with such divergent elements and interests could only be upon a federal basis. But to reach agreement as to the transferred or residual powers between the regions needed a long and difficult negotiation.

Nigeria, like many parts of Africa, has suffered from the careless, some might even say criminal, methods by which the different portions of the newly discovered parts of Africa were divided during the grab for colonies by the rival European powers. One has only to look at the map to see how little account was taken of natural features or tribal groupings. There was thus imposed upon a large part of the continent an artificial system for which there was no basis of national loyalty. When steps were taken towards self-government in Nigeria, the new constitution of January 1947, in the hope of creating a centralising sentiment, linked the native authorities of the various regions with a Legislative Council at the centre through the functioning of three regional Executive Councils—Northern, Eastern and Western. By the end of 1949 there had been general agreement upon a federal form of government with regional legislatures. Although in the constitution of 1951 the British Governor-General held certain reserve powers, there was an elected majority in the central legislature. But there was naturally a fierce battle about the division of seats between the regions. A number of parties emerged which, although known as parties, in fact represented tribal and territorial interests. Chief Obafemi Awolowo's Action Group represented the Western Region where the Yoruba prevailed. The Northern People's Congress won the Northern Region where the Hausa people were predominant. The National Council of Nigeria and the Cameroons were successful in Lagos and won great support in the Eastern Region where the Ibos were the strongest, though not the only, tribe. Hence when the formal opening of the House of Representatives took place in 1952 it was clear that the political divisions were not based upon the normal conflicts which divide parties, but represented regional power. As a result of persistent conflicts the machinery of the new Federation creaked and groaned. Indeed it was almost paralysed by disagreements and disputes. At a congress held at Lagos in 1954 it was decided that Lagos itself should become the Federal capital but with its own local government. Moreover, the scope of the regional councils was enlarged by the transfer to them of residual powers.

A Constitutional Conference which met during June 1957 tried to reach an agreement on the division of functions between the federal and regional governments. It broke up on a note of discord. The regional leaders demanded independence in 1959, but Lennox-Boyd, the Colonial Secretary of State, wisely refused to set a definite date until some of the outstanding issues had been settled. At the same time Abubakar Tafawa Balewa of the Northern Region became the first Prime Minister of the Federation.

The Conference was re-convened in 1958, and although it was decided to leave some awkward questions regarding the demarcation of certain states and the protection of minorities until after 'the strains of independence had been taken', the skilful diplomacy of the Colonial Secretary seemed to have brought all the different interests to a reasonable point of concord. The date for independence was therefore fixed for 1 October 1960. In December 1959, Federal elections were held. The balance of forces remained as before, each of the three regional parties winning in its own region, with the Northern People's Congress having the largest number of seats, but not an overall majority.

An attempt was made to form a coalition between the leaders of the Western and Eastern Regions. But this failed, and just before we arrived a new negotiation had taken place in the course of which after some pretty hard bargaining agreement had been reached between Abubakar, representing the North, and Dr. Nnamdi Azikiwe, whose party was broadly based upon the East. The basis of this compact was that Dr. Azikiwe, known all over the country as 'Zik', should become President of the Senate and in due course a candidate for the post of Governor-General. All this was explained to me with great clarity but without bitterness by Abubakar at our first meeting on the morning of 12 January. He frankly conceded the dangers that lay ahead, and it was for that reason that he was anxious, if possible, to retain the services of Sir James Robertson for at least a year, since he commanded the complete confidence of everybody of every party and of every interest. He observed to me that 'all the main parties had fought the election on the basis that they had the national interest at heart'. I replied that this was true of most parliamentary elections. Yes, but here there was a difference. Although they made this claim the regional pull was very strong. The Prime Minister added that 'considerable bitterness had been aroused during the election campaign'. He had now to work hard to nurse the country into a sense of national unity. He went on to explain the complications within the regions. Each party, although primarily based on its own region, would try to gain ground in the others by exploiting tribal or religious differences. I found that neither the Prime Minister, rightly preoccupied with this funda-mental domestic problem, nor the other politicians were interested in developments elsewhere in Africa. I was, therefore, not embar-rassed as in Ghana with insistent advice about the pace of consti-tutional advance in other African territories.

All through my visit the federal and regional question was clearly dominant. The sad events that followed, beginning with the murder of Abubakar and ending in the Civil War, showed how well justified were these fears regarding the stability of a federal system. But at the time Abubakar was hopeful that as years passed the younger men would begin to think of themselves as Nigerians and develop a genuine patriotism for Nigeria as their country. In spite of the tragic history of recent years there seems no reason to doubt that in the long run his hopes will be realised.

After my talk with the Prime Minister on 12 January I was introduced to the Council Chamber where the new Council or Cabinet was meeting for the first time. In my short speech I ventured to refer to the difficulties which had come upon many other countries,

by a lack of cohesion within their Parliaments or Cabinets which had resulted in a breakdown of Parliamentary government. For Parliamentary government to be successful, there must be loyalty to the system. One of the most important aspects of the British concept of Parliamentary government was that of Cabinet responsibility. In a Cabinet composed of Ministers of one Party, there would inevitably be differences of opinion; the differences would perhaps be greater when the Cabinet was a coalition. Ministers should be free to voice their differences in discussion in the Cabinet, but once a conclusion had been reached, then all members of the Government should stand by that decision and present a united front to the country. The Press and others would try to find and exploit differences between Ministers and so they should always be on their guard. Long experience in the United Kingdom had shown the value of this principle of collective responsibility.

Sir Norman Brook had been invited by Abubakar to attend, and I made some reference to the working of the Cabinet secretariat and its important role. A long and interesting discussion followed, and at the request of the Prime Minister Sir Norman explained the working of a Cabinet and of the various departments and the role of different officials. All this was listened to with great attention. The meeting lasted for one and a half hours, after which I met the Leader of the Opposition, Chief Awolowo, and some of his supporters. Sir Frederic Metcalfe, formerly Clerk of the House of Commons, was acting as Speaker of the House of Representatives, a very remarkable tribute to a great public servant. I was struck by the fact that all the Leaders of the Opposition spoke of his work with the highest respect. On general matters, as I expected, there seemed to be no great issues between the parties, except that the Action Group, the Opposition, wanted more states to be created in order to protect some of the minorities in the Eastern and Western Regions.

I next met the Premier of the Southern Cameroons, Mr. J. N. Foncha, who had made a special journey to see me since I was unable to include the Southern Cameroons in my tour. The problem of the future of the Cameroons was then unresolved. All this day and the next was occupied by a variety of meetings, discussions, a tour of Lagos, with a special regard to the redevelopment of the slum area, as well as other local receptions. But the main event was a meeting on 13 January at the National Hall where the Senate and House of Representatives met in joint session. This was indeed a splendid and moving occasion which has long remained in my memory. The assembly was a wonderful sight with all kinds of national costumes of different designs and colours, perhaps the most striking being the splendid train of Chief Festus Okotie-Eboh, the Minister of Finance, and the imposing figure of the Sardauna of Sokoto. After the formal opening by the Governor-General, who read the Speech from the Throne, I was invited to the floor of the House. Although much of my speech was directed to this supreme occasion which marked the opening of the first Parliament of an independent Nigeria, I thought it right to refer, at some length, to the wider issues of the Commonwealth and to give some account of the various problems in Europe and the state of our negotiations with Moscow. Nevertheless the most important message that I could give them was that of the value of the Parliamentary and democratic system and the appeal to try to maintain it in spite of all the dangers to which it might be subjected. The Federation was bound to suffer many stresses and strains. So indeed as time passed, was the Commonwealth itself. Yet it was in all our interests to work hand-in-hand together.

Nigeria has come—I think we can claim this—to independence without strife or bitterness between our peoples. It has been a notable triumph of the principle of partnership in practice, and I trust that that partnership between equals will continue in the years to come. You, for your part, can be assured of the boundless goodwill of the people of Britain.

The next day we left Lagos for short visits to the three regional capitals. We were only able to devote one day to Ibadan in the west and Enugu in the east, and these, of course, were largely taken up with the usual ceremonies of meeting the Governor and Council of each region and discussions on their special problems. In the Northern Region, where I spent an additional day, I was taken to see the Emir of Zaria. It was a day of burning sunshine, but free from the humidity of the South. Two things remained chiefly in my memory—the wonderful display of horsemanship in Muslim surroundings reminiscent more of Morocco or Pakistan than of West Africa. The other was a Fives Court built on the Etonian model by

E2

the Sardauna just outside Kaduna. All the Ministers and chief officials were constant players—whether compulsorily or voluntarily I was not told. These visits to the different regions, although so short, did at least allow me to realise how difficult had been the formation of the Federation with its immense variety of peoples, religions and traditions.

When the troubles began involving assassination and attempted secession, one could not be surprised. On the other hand, that Nigeria has survived these tribulations is a tribute not only to those responsible but to those first founders who gave their loyalty and in some cases, alas, their lives for the cause that was dear to them.

We left Kaduna Airport at 7.30 a.m. on 18 January, and after a short stop at Lagos took our leave of the Governor-General and the Prime Minister at 10 o'clock to go to Salisbury in our R.A.F. Britannia. It had been a strenuous but inspiring visit. I felt then, as I still feel, that, great as may be the difficulties ahead, there was a genuine attachment of Nigeria to Great Britain and to the Common-wealth. No opportunity seemed to be lost either by the leading politicians or by the ordinary people to express their gratitude for all that Nigeria had received from Britain in the past, and their deter-mination that our association, though changed in form, would continue in substance in the future.

To pass from Ghana and Nigeria with all their hopes and fears, their tribal and personal rivalries, and to reach Salisbury, the capital of the Federation, was to enter a different world. Ghana was African-ruled and had been independent for nearly three years. Nigeria was about to reach independence and was to be ruled by Africans. Here, therefore, we were in an atmosphere of accomplish-ment and expectation. Moreover, there was a sense of fun and merriment characteristic of the ebullience of these happy folk which made even formal dinners end informally with dancing 'high life' to the music of a police band.

Salisbury was altogether different. It had still a colonial atmo-sphere. The Governor-General, Lord Dalhousie, and his wife received us with the greatest hospitality in their beautiful residence, typical of a viceregal tradition. Although the Prime Minister of Southern Rhodesia represented in effect a European Parliament responsible to a European electorate, the other two territories of the Federation were ruled by British Governors supported by advisory councils in which either the officials held a majority or the reserve powers were sufficient to enforce the Governor's will.

In the nine days which I was able to spend in the Federation I could not help being struck by the sense of uncertainty, whether among Europeans or Africans. This uneasiness spread from the political to the business world. The foundations of the Federation were already being questioned, and both in Northern Rhodesia and in Nyasaland there was unrest. Unfortunately in the latter it had been necessary for the Governor to imprison Dr. Hastings Banda, the acknowledged leader of the African people throughout the area. In order to understand what lay behind this sense of insecurity it is necessary to go back a little into the history of previous years.

Southern Rhodesia, with a small European and a large African population (but an almost entirely European electorate), had advanced almost to the point of independence. It had become a self-governing colony as long ago as 1923. In effect it enjoyed virtual autonomy. The only powers reserved to the British Government were in order to prevent constitutional amendments detrimental to African interests. The Prime Minister was given the right to attend, without being a full member, at the Conferences of Commonwealth Prime Ministers. Only the last steps were necessary before such independence would be granted by any British Government in accordance with the long tradition of the developing Commonwealth. It is true that the population of some two hundred thousand Europeans found themselves responsible for some three and a half million Africans. But this consideration had not deterred a Liberal and 'progressive' Government elected in 1906 with a vast majority from unhesitatingly handing over to the Europeans of South Africa the fate of some four million Africans, even though the South African Government must become dominated by the Dutch and the British influence be largely reduced. This step could never be reversed, and indeed until recent years had never been questioned.

Now the settlers of Southern Rhodesia found themselves brought to the brink of independence and yet precluded from obtaining their ambition because of the new sensitivity, as to the rights of the Africans, of British people of all parties. Moreover, as already one African country, Ghana, had received independence and others were on the point of reaching it, this underlined the lack of balance of the position throughout the Federation. At the very moment of my visit, the Kenya constitutional conference was sitting in London. It was certain that over the next few years East Africa would itself reach independence and upon an African basis. Furthermore, both in Northern Rhodesia and in Nyasaland, nothing could prevent the steady increase of members representing the Africans—first appointed, and then elected. Yet it was 'unthinkable' that power should be handed to the Europeans of Southern Rhodesia as it had been in 1910 to the Boers in South Africa. The best efforts would of course be made to protect European economic interests and to recognise their wonderful pioneering work in developing agriculture and trade. But the anomaly, even the dilemma, was now clear. Either the Federation must move forward to a genuinely 'multi-racial' structure by which power and responsibility would be shared between the Europeans and the Africans, or it must be dissolved; and the danger was that its dissolution would be accompanied by grave turmoil and disaster. This did not at all imply African rule on a 'one man, one vote' basis—it implied some genuine system of partnership with fair representation of the different elements in an agreed system. This, therefore, was the message with which I was entrusted by my colleagues and broadly by the people of Britain. This was the meaning of multi-racialism as we tried to promulgate this idealistic but perhaps impracticable concept. At the same time I was determined, if multi-racialism could be fairly adopted, to give every support to the maintenance of the Federation which had such clear advantages for all the peoples concerned of whatever race or class.

The Federation of the three territories had been proposed originally in the last years of the Labour Government. It was taken up in Churchill's Administration of 1951 by the Ministers concerned (Southern Rhodesia came under the Commonwealth Secretary, as did later the Federation as a whole, whereas Northern Rhodesia and Nyasaland were the responsibility of the Colonial Office). The economic advantages of making a single area of these vast territories were overwhelming and had been generally accepted. Each was dependent upon the other. Indeed without Federation the building of the great Kariba dam could scarcely have been undertaken, from which Northern Rhodesia was to draw the vital supplies of electric power for the copper belt and Southern Rhodesia was to gain equally for all its industrial and urban development.

It seemed therefore reasonable upon general grounds to suppose that the Federation would succeed. At any rate the experiment was made; and, although taking little part in these decisions, I must share in a collective responsibility. Had I then realised, or had indeed any of us realised, the almost revolutionary way in which the situation would develop and the rapid growth of African Nationalism throughout the whole African continent, I think I should have opposed the putting together of three countries so opposite in their character and so different in their history. Southern Rhodesia would be bound to be for many years, at any rate, dominated by the European community. The most one could hope for was a gradual increase in the African suffrage and in African representation. But the other two territories, where the Europeans were few in number and largely transient, not colonists but employees, would be bound to move forward on the road to independence in the same way as the other British colonies in Africa. Indeed, had we been able to foresee these rapid and radical changes, not only in British colonies, but in French territories culminating in the abandonment by the leading champion of French national pride, General de Gaulle, of over one million colonists in Algeria, then no doubt we would have hesitated. Thus both British Ministers and many others would have been spared much painful controversy and bitter recrimination. In any event, in 1953 the Federation was launched; the three legislatures accepted the constitution, although it was ominous that in Northern Rhodesia and in Nyasaland members representing the Africans opposed the project. In Southern Rhodesia it was approved by a referendum of the predominantly European electorate.

In 1957 as the result of discussions in London the powers of the Federal Government, especially in regard to external affairs, were enlarged. More doubtfully the British Government agreed to a category of 'special' voters, such as those Africans who lacked the normal financial or educational qualifications. The Labour party criticised the proposals as negative in respect of African interests. However, it was at the same time agreed that there should be a review of the constitution in 1960. At the end of 1957 the African National Congresses of the three territories reaffirmed their opposition to Federation and declared their intention to boycott the elections. This they did when they took place in November 1958. The elections were won by the existing Government, the Federal Party, led by Sir Roy Welensky; but there had already emerged on the European side a demand for full independence and the Dominion Party was threatening a unilateral declaration of independence. By 1958, therefore, the dilemma was beginning to be inescapable. If the Federation remained, how could there be real African progress in the two territories in which they were unquestionably predominant? If it collapsed, the European controlled Southern Rhodesia would either declare its independence if it felt itself to be viable, or perhaps seek to join South Africa.

In November 1958, Welensky came to Britain to negotiate about the new constitution for Northern Rhodesia.

> A great row is brewing in Rhodesia, partly because of Welensky's character, partly because the Colonial Office and the Commonwealth Office are at daggers drawn.[1]

On 21 November I had my first talk with Sir Roy since his election as Federal Prime Minister and, indeed, the first in a long series of conferences and discussions both in person and in writing which were to last until the end of my Premiership. At this first meeting he seemed both relaxed and confident. A few days later, when he came to lunch,

> he seemed in excellent form having won his election so easily. He still objects to two points in the proposed constitution for Northern Rhodesia. Over one of these—approval of candidates by tribal chiefs—I feel we should meet his views. On the other, nomination by Governor of two African members of Council, I think he is perhaps right theoretically. He says such a statutory

[1] 25 October 1958.

provision is contrary to the whole concept of a multi-racial or partnership state. In practice, however, I think it necessary in the early stages of constitutional progress.[1]

Agreement was finally reached on this issue; but during the latter part of 1958 and all 1959 there was trouble in the northern territories. A state of emergency had to be declared both in Northern Rhodesia and in Nyasaland with large-scale arrests, and the same step had to be taken even in Southern Rhodesia where a state of emergency lasted from 26 February 1959 until 20 May 1960. It was clear that African unrest, although spasmodic, was widespread. Sometimes it was avowedly political and sometimes it was associated with industrial or agricultural grievances. Although our policy was to make every effort to maintain the Federation on the multi-racial basis, which was at least formally accepted by the Europeans, I began to doubt how this delicate balance could be maintained.

A most troublesome situation is developing in Northern Rhodesia and Nyasaland. A sort of reign of terror has been brought about through the 'extremist' native leaders, supported by the Socialist Party and papers like *Manchester Guardian* and *Observer*. There is a most regrettable division of responsibility between the various Governments concerned.

It looks as if the Federation plan, although economically correct (since Nyasaland is not 'viable') is regarded with such great suspicion by 'advanced' native opinion as to be politically unacceptable.[2]

The whole question came before the Cabinet on 17 March. In view of the constitutional review promised for 1960 we decided to set up a Royal Commission as soon as possible—'to advise upon the future of the Federation'. We had not only to persuade the Government of the Federation to take part in what would, in fact, be a Commission representing all five Governments—the United Kingdom, the Federal and the three territories—but we had also, if possible, to obtain the support and representation of the Labour Opposition. There followed a long negotiation carried on with outstanding tact and skill by Lord Home, who was then Commonwealth Secretary.

[1] 24 November 1958.   [2] 5 March 1959.

Alec Home got back yesterday from Salisbury. He gave rather a bad account of Welensky. He is clearly in a very excitable and nervous state (as everyone is in Africa) but he has got him to agree a programme, in general terms, for the period preceding the 'review' laid down by the Act. There would be (1) work by officials, (2) a Commission representing the five Governments, with U.K. Privy Councillors, and some other experts—economic, constitutional, etc. If we can only get (a) the Governor of Northern Rhodesia and Nyasaland to agree, (b) the Socialist leaders to agree, we may be able to gain a little time for serious thinking. Otherwise there is danger of a real bust-up.[1]

On 17 April I was able to send Welensky an outline of the proposed plan, and discussions continued in a long series of telegrams.

Another telegram from Welensky. After a talk with Commonwealth and Colonial Secretaries, I got off a reply. The plan for a Commission to report on Central Africa is going ahead slowly. But since it depends—to some extent—on the Opposition appointing their Privy Councillors, I fear they may try to wreck it by boycotting it.[2]

On 7 May I asked Gaitskell, Griffiths and Callaghan to meet me in the hope of obtaining their co-operation, but I could not help feeling that the approaching General Election at home was beginning to cast its sinister shadow.

Africa is in a dangerous condition, fanned by the Left here for purely political advantage. I see that Gaitskell has been in Ghana and making inflammatory speeches there. The Scottish Kirk Assembly is more responsible but has some dangerous and subtle agitators. . . .

So long as the Conservatives are in power here, Roy Welensky can be held back from anything very foolish. If the Socialists get in, 1960 may be a fatal year in Central Africa. Unhappily, African opinion is all the time being inflamed, so that even if we get in again and can influence the European settlers, we may find the natives quite out of hand.[3]

It was difficult in the circumstances to blame Labour politicians. They had tried everything else—the Rent Act, cost of living,

[1] 6 April 1959.   [2] 4 May 1959.   [3] 24 May 1959.

unemployment, Russia. All these hares had failed to run at all or had been rapidly killed. So it was a little tempting to concentrate upon Africa and Tory reaction. I was confirmed in this view on 4 June when I met the Opposition leaders again.

> We have been in negotiation for a 'bi-partisan approach' to African problems. This was the third meeting. As I expected, their position had hardened. Seeing nothing else to clutch at— full employment has been restored and the economy is stable— they cannot resist trying to exploit the African situation.[1]

I therefore felt that we had to consult again with Welensky, for if the Liberal and Labour Oppositions in the United Kingdom refused to take part in the Commission it must fail in one of its prime purposes which was to lift the Central African problems out of the arena of British party politics. Accordingly Welensky came to London at the beginning of July.

> Two hours and a half with Sir Roy Welensky. It was very hot, and we sat in the garden at No. 10. Alec and Alan (Commonwealth and Colonial Secretaries) were there. We had only general talk, in which we made progress. He is, I think, sincere. . . . But he is very sensitive and liable to outbursts of angry indignation.[2]

Points to which we wanted to bring him were

> (a) A reasonable Commission—with five or six Africans on it.
> (b) A declaration of policy in favour of the multi-racial concept and giving Nyasaland a prospect of self-government.[2]

Agreement was finally reached on 8 July.

> Welensky at 12.15 p.m. and to luncheon. He and his team came to three. We had our three Ministers—to luncheon also came Butler. I have got full agreement now on the terms of reference and the composition of the proposed Commission. Of course, we know that the Socialists—who want a purely Parliamentary commission—will be against it. We shall have to judge whether or not to *withdraw* the plan, or let it stand.[3]

In my letter to the Queen on 19 July I reported as follows:

[1] 4 June 1959.   [2] 6 July 1959.   [3] 8 July 1959.

Sir Roy Welensky has now returned to Salisbury. I think he found his visit most useful. We had some good talks with him, and were able to reach complete agreement on the Preparatory Advisory Commission to help with the work leading up to the 1960 Review and with how this should be presented. I am hoping to see the Leader of the Opposition on Monday 20 July, to tell him the Government's latest proposals, and I will do my best to induce him not to make too critical a position. But I am not confident of my powers of persuasion. I intend to make a statement in the House after Questions the following afternoon. This will help to clear away the ground for the debate on the Central African Federation for which the Opposition have asked on Wednesday 22 July.

The membership of the Commission has now been agreed as follows:

The Chairman—from the United Kingdom

Six Privy Councillors—Members of the United Kingdom Parliament

Six independent members, of whom four will be chosen from the United Kingdom and two, we hope, from other Commonwealth countries having experience of Federation

Four proposed by the Federal Government

Three each proposed by the three Territorial Governments.

The thirteen members drawn from Central Africa will include five Africans. None will be members of their respective Governments or legislatures. This seems to Your Majesty's advisers a fair and sensible plan.

Accordingly I made the announcement on 21 July and a debate followed the next day.

Gaitskell opened—one hour—rather academic, waspish rather than rude—quite effective. I answered forty minutes. My speech was rather heavy and except in the last five minutes little life or colour. But I think it succeeded in the main object—to damp down the general temperature. After this, the House was almost completely empty till the wind-up. Callaghan . . . violent, and most helpful in driving back our doubters into the fold. Colonial Secretary ended with the best speech I have ever heard him make and one of the best speeches I have ever heard in the House of

Commons. Majority fifty. Grimond and his few Liberals praised my plan and voted against us ![1]

The Parliamentary position was secure, and the public, on the whole, satisfied; but there was one point which Gaitskell and his colleagues made which worried me. Would the Africans on the Commission really represent African opinion? After all their most powerful spokesmen were, unhappily, in detention camps.

All this, of course, took place in the middle of many other preoccupations at home and abroad. Fortunately I was able to persuade my old and loyal friend, Walter Monckton, to become the Chairman. It was not an easy thing for him to accept, for his health was already beginning to cause anxiety. That he finally agreed was due entirely to his high sense of duty. His name would command universal support, and I was accordingly delighted when, by the beginning of September, he made it clear to me that he would be ready to serve.

The General Election now intervened, and it would not be possible to select the whole Commission until after the election. Discussions, however, continued at the official level. After the election, while Lord Home remained as Commonwealth Secretary, a change became necessary at the Colonial Office and Alan Lennox-Boyd was succeeded by Iain Macleod.[2]

On 31 October Welensky had a change of mind. The truth about this man, whom I liked and respected, was that under a bluff and burly exterior he concealed an impulsive and often suspicious temperament. Yet his heart was in the right place. Welensky now suggested that, since agreement on the membership of the Commission could not be reached, the whole idea should be abandoned. He pointed out that, in any case, his Government had never been keen on the plan. I replied immediately that in my view the Commission would be of the greatest value. Even if Opposition support was not forthcoming, we must go ahead. To this he finally acquiesced; but I did not abandon my attempt to persuade Gaitskell to co-operate. However, it was impossible to delay indefinitely. Accordingly on 24 November I made a statement in the House of

[1] 22 July 1959. [2] See above pp. 18–19.

Commons giving the terms of reference and the composition of the Commission. The composition was certainly impressive. In addition to Lord Monckton, whose appointment would command universal approval, there were other notable members, including, as Vice-Chairman, Sir Donald MacGillivray, who had had a distinguished career in Colonial administration and especially as High Commissioner for Malaya. The United Kingdom independent members included Mrs. Elspeth Huxley, Professor D. T. Jack and Dr. R. H. W. Shepherd, the well-known missionary of the Church of Scotland.[1] Since the matter was to become one of some controversy it is right to record the terms of reference which I read to the House on 24 November:

> In the light of the information provided by the Committee of Officials and of any additional information the Commission may require, to advise the five Governments, in preparation for the 1960 review, on the constitutional programme and framework best suited to the achievement of the objects contained in the Constitution of 1953, including the Preamble.

I went on to say

> The House will note that these make special reference to the Constitution of 1953, including the Preamble, with all its safeguards.

Gaitskell pressed very hard that the terms of reference should be altered to include freedom to consider not only changes in the Federation but its liquidation. While I was not prepared to go so far as that, I repeated the undertaking that I had given in July:

> I regard the Commission as free, in practice, to hear all points of view from whatever quarter and on whatever subject. It will, of course, be for the Commission to decide what use to make of the material which reaches them. I am sure that the House will have full confidence in my noble Friend Lord Monckton's ability to deal with this.
>
> In these cases, I do not think that it is ever wise to be too specific or rigid in interpretation. But the House will see that

[1] *Report of the Advisory Commission on the Review of the Constitution of Rhodesia and Nyasaland*, Cmnd. 1148 (H.M.S.O., 1960).

these terms will permit the Commission to consider the whole field of the redistribution of powers in either direction between the Federation and the territories and to advise on the timing of any programme and the character of any changes in the framework that it may suggest.

Being further pressed in supplementary questions, both by Gaitskell and Bevan, I could only repeat what I had said. It was clear that the Commission was appointed to try to make Federation work in some form or other and find a solution acceptable to all the races in all the territories concerned. 'If the Commission thinks that it could not fulfil its task to its satisfaction within the terms of reference no doubt it would say so.' It seemed to me, and still seems, that this question was somewhat pedantic. In my last reply I summarised it as follows:

Of course, it may be—pray God it will not be—that the problems of Central Africa are insoluble, or it may be that within what we are trying to do they are insoluble. In that case, I have no doubt that a Commission of this kind will find a way of expressing its opinion. We are trying to see whether there is a way along what everybody believes to be the best lines. If it can be found, and if we can get the confidence of all concerned who seek to advise us how to do it along those lines we will do it. We should not give up the job as hopeless from the start.

But I persevered in my attempt to persuade the Opposition Leader.

I saw Mr. Gaitskell after Questions and told him I could not make any change in the terms of reference for the Central African Commission or in the explanatory statement which I had made about them in Parliament. Would he now appoint his three representatives? He seemed rather taken aback and tried to 'negotiate'—but I would not allow this. He said he would let me know his decision after consulting the Shadow Cabinet *and* the Parliamentary Party.[1]

I could not help feeling that

the Labour Party are trying to use the problems of Africa to reunite their divided party. They have put down what amounts to

[1] 1 December 1959.

a vote of censure, especially with regard to my visit to the Union of South Africa.[1]

The next day I received the Opposition decision.

> Mr. Gaitskell has now at last made up his mind. The Opposition refuse to join the Central African Commission. This is disappointing, but it is perhaps better that they should stay out than join with merely wrecking tactics.[2]

However, I was determined to try to get at least some cross-bench members to complete the Parliamentary element in the Commission.

> On the whole, I think the best course is just to appoint the three Conservatives and leave it at that. I saw both Herbert Morrison (of Lambeth) today and Hartley Shawcross. Lord M. was very helpful and sympathetic. He thinks the Labour leaders have behaved foolishly. But he doesn't want to join himself— partly not to quarrel openly with his Party (in spite of his contempt for them) and partly on health grounds. I think Lord S. will help us if we wish it.[3]

Very generously and much to my delight Lord Shawcross, with characteristic patriotism, agreed to serve.

It was not to be expected that the Opposition would resist a final fling, and a short debate was staged on 7 December as a demonstration against my African tour and especially my proposed visit to the Union of South Africa. However, it rather petered out. At any rate, this concentration on the iniquities of South Africa rather relieved the pressure on the Federation.

The next week

> I was led into a row with Gaitskell at Question Time—which is rather a mistake for me. Nor did I come off better—it was drawn, rather in his favour.[4]

This arose from an alleged statement of Sir Roy Welensky giving a somewhat narrower interpretation to the terms of reference of the Commission than that which I had put forward. However, since I

[1] 2 December 1959.   [2] 3 December 1959.
[3] 4 December 1959.   [4] 17 December 1959.

left for Paris on the next day for the so-called Western Summit there was at least an interval for reflection before my African tour began.

It was clear from my first private talk with Welensky in Salisbury and afterwards with some of his colleagues, that there were two points which were causing the Ministers of the Federation acute anxiety. The first was the almost metaphysical argument about the terms of reference of the Commission. I thought this had been satisfactorily settled before leaving London on 5 January, but two events had taken place which caused Welensky grave concern. Shawcross, as a member of the Commission, had used words during a television interview which were taken somewhat out of context, but could certainly be interpreted to mean that if he became convinced that Federation was impossible he would certainly say so. Moreover, at a Press Conference at Lagos I was reported as saying that before the ultimate British responsibility was removed the people of Nyasaland and Northern Rhodesia would be given their opportunity to decide. Actually these words were altogether misreported and I was able to deal with the matter in some detail in my speech in Salisbury on the 19th. Meanwhile these two unlucky incidents did not help to calm the tensions which were already beginning to mount.

A second point to which a tremendous amount of talk was devoted, during my visit as well as in my telegrams later on, was the question of the evidence to be given before the Commission. A disagreement soon became manifest between the British Government's pledge that witnesses would be protected and the Federal Government's desire to prevent the Commission hearing being used for African Nationalist propaganda. This was, of course, of vital importance, involving both the immunity of witnesses and the availability of certain important evidence which could only be given if those detained under the 'Emergency' were set free. This question was to lead to a long and bitter dispute about the release of Dr. Banda.

But at my private talks with both Welensky and Sir Edgar Whitehead, the Prime Minister of Southern Rhodesia, I felt that these troubles, although painful, were of a minor character. The fundamental question was the continuance of the Federation, or, in the event of its dissolution, what should follow. Thus a great dispute upon the terms of reference seemed irrelevant. The real issue lay deeper. Nor were the interests of the different parties and personalities the same. In the few days that I was in Salisbury this became abundantly clear. Sir Roy Welensky and the Federal Ministers had an interest as well as a genuine belief in preserving the Federation. Whitehead, Prime Minister of Southern Rhodesia, whom I saw alone and afterwards with his Cabinet, was more concerned about the urgent problem of Southern Rhodesia which had become impatient and restive at the idea of remaining in the Federation if this proved likely to impede the path to independence. Whitehead, who was a cultivated and broadminded man with sound political instincts, was frank about the dangers ahead. He feared that, unless rapid progress towards independence could be achieved, the Dominion Party or even more extreme forces would make his position intolerable. Indeed when I saw the representatives of the Dominion Party they proposed immediate independence for Southern Rhodesia to whose territory they wished to add Kariba and the copper belt. Whitehead also encouraged me to see, at his house, African representatives of different parties and views, whom he entertained with great good feeling and among whom he was clearly respected. These were chiefly interested in asking the British Government not to give up 'the reserved rights' over legislation affecting Africans. Without this they had no confidence that the Europeans in Rhodesia would behave fairly towards them.

All these discussions and interviews together with the formalities and social entertainments left little time to prepare the important speech by which I hoped to allay some of the anxieties and to answer some of the questions. This took place on the afternoon of 19 January. It was addressed to the Rhodesian National Fairs Association. The audience filled two cinemas and overflowed into the streets outside. To prepare this address involved much late work at night and could not, in any case, have been done without the devoted help of my small staff.

My main purpose was to assure my listeners that I had not come for the purpose of constitutional negotiations, but to learn something of the problems and to have personal talks with the political leaders representing all shades of opinion in a friendly and informal atmosphere.

I have been greatly heartened by the very kind welcome which my wife and I have received since our arrival. Nor do I forget, nobody could forget, the loyalty and devotion of all your people to the Crown and to the Commonwealth. Both in war and in many difficult emergencies which have arisen since the war, whenever we are in need we know that we can look to the support of your forces for the defence of our common interests.

I next pointed out the post-war developments.

In all parts of this continent the tide of nationalism is flowing fast. Fifteen years ago, at the end of the war, we saw something very similar in Asia, and many countries, of very different races and civilisation, were then pressing their claim to independent national life. The British Government and Parliament of those days decided not to seek to stifle or restrain what they recognised as the legitimate national aspirations of peoples for whose destinies Britain had hitherto been responsible. As a result, India, Pakistan, Ceylon, Malaya, all stand with us today as free and equal partners in the Commonwealth. Now we are faced with a similar growth of national consciousness in Africa. This is one of the facts of the African situation today. We must accept it as a fact, and take it into account in forming our policies.

In a long speech dealing with many aspects of the economic and political problems of Africa and paying tribute to the work of the pioneers, I made a straight appeal in support of a multi-racial solution of the problem in the Federation. This gave me an opportunity to refer to the misunderstanding arising from what I had said in Lagos.

In the fullness of time we hope that the Federation—with the full consent of the peoples of its three territories—will add in the complete sense its strength and influence to our Commonwealth association. We hope that its people, European, African and Asian alike, will play their full part in forging the future of a great nation, of which all will be citizens and in all take a common pride. But this cannot come about unless confidence can be built up on all sides. I must therefore say again today in Salisbury what I and my colleagues have said in Parliament in London: that, whatever the outcome of the Monckton Commission on the form of the Federation and whatever the outcome of the 1960 Conference, Her Majesty's Government in the United Kingdom will not withdraw their protection from the people of Nyasaland or Northern Rhodesia until their people so desire. I fear that something which I said about this at a Press Conference in Lagos on 13 January has been misunderstood or misrepresented. I should like to take the opportunity to repeat the words which I actually used, and having some little experience I now go about at these conferences with a tape-recording machine, and I quote from the record as played back by the machine. I said this: 'the Government of the United Kingdom has made it clear— abundantly clear—that we will not remove the protection of the British Government to either of the Northern Territories— Northern Rhodesia or Nyasaland—until it is clear that the expressed wish of these people is to enter into a full and inde- pendent Federation . . .'. As you will see, I was speaking of the independent Federation of the future. I was repeating in other words exactly what I said and what Sir Roy knows I said in Parliament on 22 July. I said this : 'the British Government will certainly not withdraw its protection from Nysasaland and Rhodesia in the short run, and in the long run our object is to advance these territories to fully responsible government. They will then be able to dispense with our protection and stand entirely on their own feet as components of the Federation. When all the units are in a position to agree, and are agreed that British Government protection is no longer needed—then, and only then —can the whole Federation go forward to full independence and full membership . . .'. That is the negative side, and it does not rest only on my statements or those of my colleagues. It is inherent in the preamble to the Federal Constitution.

The positive side was to make a determined effort to build up a Federation on a basis of co-operation from which all could draw mutual advantages. Its purpose was to benefit all people of every race. Its success would depend upon forbearance, patience and understanding. These were high and honourable aims. I was struck by the fact that the audience applauded vigorously not only my expressions of support for the Federation, but also the numerous passages in which I reaffirmed our duty towards the Africans and praised the concept of partnership. The immediate effect on confidence was certainly marked; but European temper at Salisbury and elsewhere was volatile, and it was not long before there were signs of a reversion to the earlier state of anxiety and suspicion. Moderate opinion began to yield to extremist ambitions.

Salisbury at that time was developing with great rapidity. Yet it was certainly something of a burden to a small community to support the great structure of government which the Federation implied. In addition to the Governor-General and the Federal Parliament and Ministers, there was also the Governor of Southern Rhodesia, Sir Humphrey Gibbs, together with the Parliamentary and Ministerial structure. There was also the local government, consisting of the Mayor and councillors. For me all this implied even in a short visit a good deal of junketing, gubernatorial, Ministerial and civic, as well as serious discussion. I was glad to have an opportunity in addition to have a talk with old Lord Malvern, whose long experience made his advice particularly valuable.

Early in the morning on 21 January, we flew to Lusaka. I shall never forget the beauty of Government House with its strange garden and aviary, or the quiet charm of the Governor, Sir Evelyn Hone. Almost immediately on our arrival I attended a meeting of the Executive Council of Northern Rhodesia then operating in the accepted colonial style. It consisted largely of British officials, but included two African members. The rest of the morning was spent in seeing the representatives of different parties including the United Federal Party (Sir Roy Welensky's supporters) and the Central Africa Party of which the leading spirit was Sir John Moffat. In the afternoon I saw representatives of the Dominion Party and of the African National Congress. I also received a visit from the Paramount Chief of Barotseland and later attended a meeting of representatives of various African organisations led by Mr. Ngandu. After we had finished all these discussions, there was a dinner at Government House. As we drove about the town on this and subsequent days there were a number of demonstrations with flags and slogans, but on a very modest and even respectful basis. Our remaining days in Northern Rhodesia were taken up with a tour of the copper belt, a visit to the Kariba dam and a quiet Sunday spent at the Victoria Falls, which seemed to me even more spectacular and beautiful than Niagara.

In spite of the hurry of a visit of this kind, some impressions could be formed. In Northern Rhodesia the Governor, in his quiet way, clearly commanded respect and even affection; but naturally, since the Europeans are so small a population compared to those in Southern Rhodesia, the importance of African opinion was more clearly understood. In Southern Rhodesia I had to listen to many speeches or statements expressing a paternalistic attitude by Europeans towards Africans who took the view that it would be many years, even decades, before Africans would be sufficiently educated to take an effective part in administration and government. But in Northern Rhodesia, where the Africans felt themselves stronger, the chief discussions seemed to concentrate on the need to increase the franchise and introduce more African Ministers on to the Council rather than on hostility towards the Federation. The Africans were anxious lest Federation should hold up their own development, but they seemed to recognise its economic advantages.

When we reached Nyasaland, on 25 January, I was immediately conscious of a much greater sense of strain. The Governor, Sir Robert Armitage, met us at Chileka Airport and we went by road to Zomba. After a meeting of the Executive Council I saw representatives of all the political parties, the Malawi Congress Party, the Congress Liberation Party and the Central Africa Party. This was followed by a long and private discussion with the Governor and his chief advisers. In Nyasaland it was clear that there was extreme hostility to Federation. It is true that the state of emergency was still in force, but there was a feeling also of suspense and uncertainty. Everything was felt to depend upon the release of Dr. Banda. Indeed the prevailing impression left upon me was that in Nyasaland the cause of Federation was almost desperate because of the strength of African opinion against it. The only grounds for hope seemed to lie in so rapid an advance to self-government in all matters of territorial interests as to reconcile Dr. Banda and his supporters to continue to work within the Federal framework.

In the two short days that we were able to spend there, my wife and I were much delighted with the scenery of Nyasaland and the charm of the country. On 26 January we drove to Blantyre for a civic luncheon given by the Mayor. Here we were confronted with a considerable crowd of Africans carrying placards and shouting slogans. Naturally, much was made of this in the Press at home in an exaggerated form. To anyone who had been accustomed to election-eering in the North of England in the twenties it seemed a very tame affair, and indeed such confusion as there was might be attributed more to over-anxiety on the part of the police than to any particular animosity shown towards us by the crowd. Short as this visit was I came away saddened. It seemed to me that the officials were dispirited, and the policies embodied in the state of emergency had failed. The Federation itself could only be made tolerable if it was accepted by the local African leadership—that meant, and could only mean, Dr. Banda, now held in detention. So long as he remained in detention, the Malawi Congress Party, organised by Orton Chirwa, as Banda's lieutenant, was clearly gaining in power and strength every day.

We returned to Salisbury on the afternoon of 26 January, and I dined quietly with Welensky, Edgar Whitehead and Lord Malvern at a hotel in the town. There followed a useful talk, but it mainly dealt with generalities. I had little opportunity for any detailed discussion with Welensky even upon the urgent question of Dr. Banda's situation. The new Colonial Secretary was pressing for his immediate release, and, whereas all kinds of different views were put forward to me when I was in Nyasaland, many of which I thought impracticable, I had the advantage of a meeting with Dingle Foot, legal adviser to Dr. Banda. He felt that Banda would certainly co-operate with the Monckton Commission if the state of emergency was ended, the detainees released and the witnesses had complete freedom to submit their evidence either orally or in writing. It can well be imagined how complicated a decision on this matter became. It was necessary, if possible, to harmonise the views of the Federal Government and the Governor of Nyasaland, the two Secretaries of State responsible and a Prime Minister moving about Africa from place to place.

Accordingly I informed Welensky that I would consult further with my colleagues and would wait for communication with London. He would very shortly receive a message from Lord Home, the Commonwealth Secretary.

It was in this somewhat tense atmosphere that our visit to the Federation came to an end. We had to struggle on and do our best to carry out our undertakings with loyalty and courage. But from the nature of the problem, the character of the individuals concerned and the inevitable contrast between the rapid movement towards political freedom in some parts of Africa and the apparent determination of the European population in others to maintain its supremacy, I could not but view the future with apprehension. Indeed, even amidst the many other problems that were to face the Government during the years of my premiership, the complications, confusions and conflicts of Central Africa seemed never to be absent from our minds and were destined to absorb an immense amount of effort with little corresponding result.

I was now to set about the most difficult part of my journey. Although I knew that I should be received with the natural courtesy of the South African people, British and Dutch, it would be indeed a delicate operation to put forward my own position and that of my colleagues without impinging on the rules of hospitality or shrinking from what I felt it would be necessary to say. After a short stop in Bechuanaland, where I was met by Sir John Maud, the British High Commissioner in South Africa, we reached Johannesburg in the afternoon of 27 January. To those who know South Africa it is not necessary to describe the beauties of its climate and scenery. On the other hand it was impossible to escape from the oppressive realisation of the many unsolved and perhaps insoluble problems darkening the relations between the races.

The visit, although so short, enabled us to travel over a wide area, to the Bechuanaland Protectorate, the Northern Transvaal, the Rand, Swaziland, Durban, Bloemfontein and Basutoland. The Foreign Minister, Eric Louw, accompanied me throughout, and other Ministers joined from time to time. In addition to the Ministers I was able to meet a good many representatives of different points of view, including prominent industrialists from the Rand, many of them with experience not limited to South Africa, as well as such important figures as Mr. Harry Oppenheimer and Mr. Flather, Editor of the *Star*. This tour involved a great deal of travelling, and the daily programmes were often exacting. We spent five nights at Pretoria and four at Cape Town. The Government were very anxious to show me the various improvements that they had made for the Bantu people, especially some of the new housing estates. Everywhere we went we were received with the greatest kindness and, although the Government were unwilling for me to meet leaders of the African National Congress, I was enabled, from time to time, to meet a number of individuals, including the Archbishop of Cape Town, Dr. Joost de Blank, Mrs. Margaret Ballinger, the Parliamentary leaders of the African Representatives and Mr. Patrick Duncan of the Liberal Party. Before leaving I had a talk with Sir de Villiers Graaff, the leader of the United Party, and also with the leaders of the Progressive Party. But these, alas, had little influence against the dominant power of the Nationalists.

All this sightseeing, including visits to the many impressive memorials to the past history of South Africa, covered ground which is well-known. Perhaps the most impressive was the Rhodes Memorial and the Voortrekker Monument. The welcome I received from the population in Durban and Cape Town was strikingly different from elsewhere. But this was explained by the fact that on what were called security grounds at Johannesburg the Union authorities insisted on keeping secret our time of arrival and routing. I remarked to the Mayor that I thought the security arrangements excessive, and this led to an apology from the Foreign Minister; but it was clear to me that the Government and the Union authorities were not anxious to allow too much enthusiasm to be publicly shown. Where there were large English-speaking elements it was impossible to prevent it and indeed on occasions the demonstrations were deeply moving. Nevertheless, I felt that the Government, although doing everything to make our visit acceptable, were a little anxious about its effect. There had been talk at home of a boycott on South African exports; but this was only given a vague backing by the Labour Party and was clearly a mere demonstration.

The important business of the tour began only on 2 February when I reached Cape Town. We stayed in a delightful house called Groote Schuur where we were the Prime Minister's guests. I had long discussions with Dr. Verwoerd, at most of which Mr. Louw, as well as Norman Brook and John Maud, were present. These were most illuminating, and it was only during these days that I began to realise to the full extent the degree of obstinacy, amounting really to fanaticism, which Dr. Verwoerd brought to the consideration of his policies. Apartheid to him was more than a political philosophy, it was a religion; a religion based on the Old Testament rather than on the New, and recalling in its expression some of the attitudes and even the phrases which had become famous in the Scottish history of the seventeenth century. If Dr. Verwoerd spoke in that strange but attractive lilting voice which is characteristic of Dutch South Africans speaking English, he had all the force of argument of some of the great Calvinist leaders of our Scottish kirk. He was certainly as convinced as John Knox himself that he alone could be right, and that there was no question of argument but merely a statement of his will. He would have made a good impression on the Synod of Dort. Even in small matters he had pressed apartheid to its extreme. In a country where there is at least the advantage of being able to enlist the services of an African staff, he refused to have a single African in his house. An old and rather incompetent Dutch butler looked after us. The house, which might have been so gay, was strangely grim. Yet I have seldom met a couple with greater charm than Dr. Verwoerd and his wife. She was particularly attractive in her quiet and friendly attitude and looked after my wife with a genuine warmth which could not be mistaken for mere convention. The Prime Minister, with his quiet voice, would expound his views without any gesture or emotion. At first I almost mistook this calm and measured tone for a willingness to enter into sincere discussion and at least to try to understand the position which I was upholding. All through I had the strange feeling that, although on the South African side there was an almost pathetic desire to be understood, there was no comprehension of how the fixed policies of her Government were regarded by the outside world. There was a plaintive, almost naïve, sense of grievance. They

With Dr Verwoerd, February 1960
'He was certainly as convinced as John Knox himself that he alone could be right.'

Speaking to the Parliament of the Union of South Africa, 3 February 1960

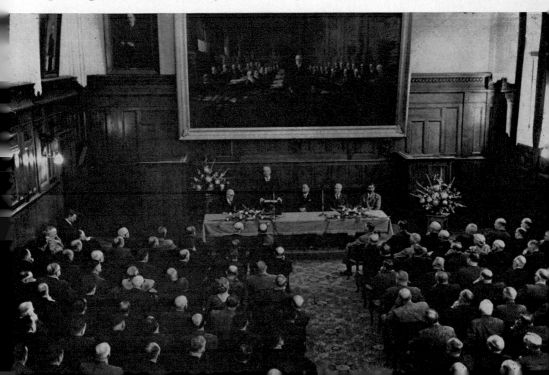

The Prime Ministers' Conference, 3 May 1960

Front row: Cooray (Minister of Justice, Ceylon), Nash, Nehru, The Queen, Diefenbaker, Menzies, Louw (Minister of

believed that their unpopularity, whether external or internal, arose not from their own policies but from the cold attitude shown to them both by the United Kingdom and the United States. The Foreign Minister seemed to be convinced that South Africa might form an effective bridge between the Western Powers and the uncommitted African states if we would only show more sympathy with South Africa's objectives.

One point at least was gained. The question of the High Commission territories was raised, and Dr. Verwoerd made it clear that he did not intend, at present, to press the question of transferring them to the Union.

Our long conferences were carried out upon a low note without acrimony or even heat. I had the unusual experience of soon noticing that nothing one could say or put forward would have the smallest effect upon the views of this determined man. Normally in politics there is a certain give and take between both sides of an argument; and even in political questions which raise deep feelings in the House of Commons or in Party controversy, at home most people at least try to understand, meet or sometimes partially accept the argument of their opponents. But here it was a blank wall. His charming smile, his courtesy, his readiness to expound his views without any concealment and at any length were in a sense impressive. But they filled me with gloom.

Dr. Verwoerd had already announced on 20 January his intention of holding a referendum to decide whether the Union should become a republic. When discussing the change-over to a republican form of government while maintaining, at least at the outset, membership of the Commonwealth, Dr. Verwoerd tried to extract from me some impression or view that he could use to advantage during the referendum campaign. I refused to lend myself to this and said nothing to suggest that public opinion in the United Kingdom was indifferent as to whether the monarchical system would be abandoned. Indeed it was clear from my reception, especially in Cape Town and Durban, that there was a strong minority determined to do everything possible to remain both under the Throne and within the Commonwealth. On the morning of 4 February we talked mostly about the republic and the Commonwealth and the

F

position of the Queen as Head of the Commonwealth. To my surprise he said that there was still a strong feeling in South Africa against recognising the Queen as Head of the Commonwealth. I replied that I was amazed by this statement. It seemed to me that if he really believed in reconciliation and co-operation it was pretty ungenerous to the people of British descent who formed nearly half the European population, to whom the end of the monarchy would be a serious blow, if he now tried to avoid recognising the Queen as Head of the Commonwealth. What India, Pakistan and many other countries were prepared to do surely South Africa could accept. His attitude seemed to me not merely illiberal but definitely shabby.

Dr. Verwoerd asked me to advise him as to whether he should raise on a hypothetical basis, at the May meeting of the Commonwealth Prime Ministers, the question of whether South Africa could remain in the Commonwealth if she became a republic. Since he pressed me to put my feelings in writing I did so in the following terms on 4 February:

> I promised to try to put into writing what I said to you this morning about the procedural questions relating to the Union's remaining within the Commonwealth if it becomes a republic.
>
> All other countries which have remained within the Commonwealth as republics have asked, before taking a formal step of constituting a republic, whether the other members would be content that they should remain thereafter in the Commonwealth. If therefore it is likely that the Union will become a republic within, say, the next two years, it would be in accordance with precedent if the matter were raised at the May meeting on a hypothetical basis. I realise that in your case there is in a sense a double hypothesis, first that the country will vote for a republic and secondly that having become a republic it will desire to remain in the Commonwealth. Nevertheless there would be advantage in raising the matter in May, when it can be done orally rather than leaving it to be settled by correspondence at a later date.
>
> I venture to repeat that this is an additional reason why I hope that you will be able to come in person. But in any event this will be an important meeting, (a) politically, because it will immediately precede the Summit meeting; and (b) constitutionally,

because it will decide whether Ghana should remain in the Commonwealth after becoming a republic and whether Nigeria should be admitted to full Commonwealth membership on attaining independence.

Moreover, as I told you, I would feel it would be a great advantage if at such a meeting you and I and, say, Menzies and Diefenbaker and Nash could have informal talks together about all these problems. I am sure we will all gain.

I shall be glad if you will regard this as a private and confidential letter. It would be a great inconvenience if what I have said were made known in any way, either directly or indirectly.

My address to the two Houses of Parliament took place at 10.30 a.m. on 3 February. It was in many ways the most important event in the whole African tour. I had approached this ordeal with much trepidation, and I had taken the greatest care in the preparation of my speech. The occasion was an important one, for it marked the Fiftieth Anniversary of the birth of the Union Parliament. It was, therefore, in a sense a jubilee celebration. Nevertheless, I knew that much of what I would be constrained to say would be disagreeable to many of my hearers.

The meeting took place in a historic building—the Chamber of the old Cape Colony Parliament. The audience amounted to some two hundred and fifty, of which ninety were members of the Senate and the rest of the House of Commons. I sat on a platform with the Prime Minister, the Opposition leaders, the Speaker and one or two other officials. On entering the door there was a polite ripple of applause. Although I had given Dr. Verwoerd an indication of what I intended to say, it was clear that, having merely seen the main outlines, the full effect of the actual text and especially of certain phrases came to him as a surprise, and perhaps a shock. I began by speaking of the pleasure that my wife and I had had in our travels through Africa and of the privilege to be visiting South Africa in 1960, the year of the 'Golden Wedding of the Union'.

In the fifty years of their nationhood the people of South Africa have built a strong economy founded upon healthy agriculture and thriving and resilient industries. . . . I have seen the great city of Durban, with its wonderful port, and the sky-scrapers of Johannesburg, standing where seventy years ago there was nothing but the open veldt.

I turned next to Britain's part in this development—nearly two-thirds of the overseas investment outstanding in the Union at the end of 1956 was British. Our economies were now largely inter-dependent, Britain supplying one-third of all South Africa's imports and buying one-third of all her exports. I spoke of the contribution that South Africa had made to our common cause during the war and of the technical assistance which she was offering to the less well-developed parts of Africa in time of peace.

I then broached the topic which has caused this speech to be regarded as something of a watershed in African affairs—the emergence of nationalism in the African continent.

> Ever since the break-up of the Roman Empire one of the constant facts of political life in Europe has been the emergence of independent nations. They have come into existence over the centuries in different forms, with different kinds of Government, but all have been inspired by a deep, keen feeling of nationalism, which has grown as the nations have grown.
>
> In the twentieth century, and especially since the end of the war, the processes which gave birth to the nation states of Europe have been repeated all over the world. We have seen the awakening of national consciousness in peoples who have for centuries lived in dependence upon some other power. Fifteen years ago this movement spread through Asia. Many countries there of different races and civilisations pressed their claim to an independent national life. Today the same thing is happening in Africa, and the most striking of all the impressions I have formed since I left London a month ago is of the strength of this African national consciousness. In different places it takes different forms, but it is happening everywhere. The wind of change is blowing through this continent, and, whether we like it or not, this growth of national consciousness is a political fact. We must all accept it as a fact, and our national policies must take account of it.

With what some of the critics regarded as a malicious deftness but which was really intended to soften the impact I continued :

Of course, you understand this better than anyone. You are sprung from Europe, the home of nationalism, and here in Africa you have yourselves created a new nation. Indeed, in the history of our times yours will be recorded as the first of the African nationalisms, and this tide of national consciousness which is now rising in Africa is a fact for which you and we and the other nations of the Western World are ultimately responsible. For its causes are to be found in the achievements of Western civilisation, in the pushing forward of the frontiers of knowledge, in the applying of science in the service of human needs, in the expanding of food production, in the speeding and multiplying of the means of communication, and perhaps, above all, the spread of education.

Where would these new emerging nations align themselves—with the West or with the Communist East? What guidance would they receive from the independent members of the Commonwealth?

It is a basic principle of our modern Commonwealth that we respect each other's sovereignty in matters of internal policy. At the same time we must recognise that in this shrinking world in which we live today the internal policies of one nation may have effects outside it. We may sometimes be tempted to say to each other 'Mind your own business,' but in these days I would myself expand the old saying so that it runs: 'Mind your own business, but mind how it affects my business, too.'

We realised, I told my audience, that what we in the United Kingdom did in the Commonwealth countries now reaching independence must inevitably have consequences for the Union. We would act with full knowledge of the responsibility we had to all our friends; but equally in our own areas we must each do what we thought right; and that must, in our view, include offering the opportunity for an increasing share in political power and responsibility.

I went on to discuss the special problems of countries inhabited by several different races, pointing out that this applied not only to Africa but also, for instance, to Malaya, inhabited by both Chinese and Malays. The United Kingdom's attitude, I said, was expressed by the Foreign Secretary, Selwyn Lloyd, when he spoke at the United Nations General Assembly on 17 September 1959.

These were his words: 'In those territories where different races or tribes live side by side the task is to ensure that all the people may enjoy security and freedom and the chance to contribute as individuals to the progress and well being of these countries. We reject the idea of any inherent superiority of one race over another. Our policy therefore is non-racial. It offers a future in which Africans, Europeans, Asians, the peoples of the Pacific and others with whom we are concerned, will all play their full part as citizens in the countries where they live, and in which feelings of race will be submerged in loyalty to new nations.'

I recognised that the members of the Union Parliament had to face problems very different from those which confronted the parliaments of countries with homogeneous populations but I added:

As a fellow member of the Commonwealth it is our earnest desire to give South Africa our support and encouragement, but I hope you won't mind my saying frankly that there are some aspects of your policies which make it impossible for us to do this without being false to our own deep convictions about the political destinies of free men to which in our own territories we are trying to give effect.

I went on to speak of the impossibility, whether for men or nations, of living in isolation.

What Dr. John Donne said of individual men three hundred years ago is true today of my country, your country, and all the countries of the world:
'Any man's death diminishes me, because I am involved in Mankind. And therefore never send to know for whom the bell tolls; it tolls for thee.'

It was in this conviction of the interdependence of nations, I told my audience, that I had made my journey to Moscow in 1959. It was in this belief that I had encouraged contacts between individuals and contacts in trade between the Western and the Communist world. 'I certainly do not believe,' I said, 'in refusing to trade with people because you may happen to dislike the way they manage their internal affairs at home.' I went on to express my disapproval of the attempts being made in Britain to boycott South African goods. It could only have serious effects on Commonwealth relations.

The independent members of the Commonwealth do not always agree on every subject. It is not a condition of their association that they should do so. On the contrary, the strength of our Commonwealth lies largely in the fact that it is a free association of independent sovereign states, each responsible for ordering its own affairs but co-operating in the pursuit of common aims and purposes in world affairs. Moreover these differences may be transitory. In time they may be resolved. Our duty is to see them in perspective against the background of our long association. Of this at any rate I am certain—those of us who by grace of the electorate are temporarily in charge of affairs in your country and in mine, we fleeting transient phantoms on the great stage of history, we have no right to sweep aside on this account the friendship that exists between our countries, for that is the legacy of history.

And I ended:

Let us resolve to build, not to destroy, and let us remember always that weakness comes from division, strength from unity.[1]

The speech lasted for nearly fifty minutes, and as soon as I sat down Dr. Verwoerd thought it necessary to include in an official vote of thanks an impromptu defence of his policies, putting the case, as he expressed it, 'for justice for the white man'. The first reactions, however, in the local Press were much less hostile than I expected, and it was not until the news came of the reception of the speech in Britain and throughout the world that criticism combined with a good deal of self-pity and resentment began to develop. It was unfortunate, although perhaps inevitable, that the British Press singled out certain phrases like 'wind of change' as headlines or accentuated certain passages which were likely to

[1] For the full text see Appendix 1.

cause the most hostile comment in South Africa, without giving some of the balancing phrases and tributes to the history of Dutch and British alike in building up such a great structure of economic strength by individual effort and devotion. Undoubtedly, however, a great number of thinking people were impressed; and I was struck in the remaining days that we spent in South Africa by the attitude even of those to whom the speech must have been something of a blow.

We dined alone that night at Groote Schuur. Dr. Verwoerd, although clearly pained by the scene in the Parliament House, made little direct reference to the speech. He preferred to initiate a discussion on the state of relations between East and West with special reference to the German problem. There was some talk about the High Commission territories. Dr. Verwoerd and Mr. Louw seemed to be affronted by the constitutional changes that we were introducing without prior consultation with the Union Government. I refused to do more than take note of his protest. Perhaps the most interesting thing which the Prime Minister said was an admission of what he called 'the strength of the prejudices held in Westminster and by world opinion at large against the internal policies of the Union Government'. Indeed both at this meeting and at a further talk the next morning I sensed not exactly resentment but genuine sorrow at their growing isolation.

Our journey was now coming to an end. The last days were spent in sightseeing and a variety of formal functions. We both attended a state banquet at the Castle in Cape Town given by the South African Government, in the course of which Dr. Verwoerd made a short and somewhat formal speech to which I replied in the same mood. There was a curious tenseness displayed by the Ministers, combined with a tremendous display of exuberant friendship when we appeared in public. This was, no doubt, because the people of British descent were determined to demonstrate their loyalties. Indeed at a luncheon at the town hall on the day of our departure the Mayor, Mrs. Newton Thompson, a woman of great character, and obvious popularity, proposed the loyal toast, and 'God Save the Queen' was played—an event unusual in the Union. I thought it appropriate to give the toast of South Africa, after which 'Die Stem' was played.

We had determined to take a short holiday and return by sea. The drive to the docks was a remarkable experience. The streets were decorated with flags and bunting and lined with immense crowds on either side. I insisted on an open car so that I could stand up and acknowledge the cheers. Dr. Verwoerd sat somewhat moodily on my right hand throughout this demonstration. A large and enthusiastic crowd had assembled on the quayside and after a guard of honour and the various formalities we said good-bye to our hosts, Dr. and Mrs. Verwoerd, Mr. and Mrs. Louw, and with a special sense of gratitude to Sir John and Lady Maud. The British High Commissioner showed throughout an extraordinary knowledge of the local situation. He was moreover a source of permanent support, combining as he did deep sincerity and an acute sense of humour. The last words were spoken, the band played the well-known songs of farewell; and the lines were cast off amid the strains of 'Auld Lang Syne'. Then the crowd spontaneously sang 'God Save the Queen'. As the ship went slowly away the crowd refused to leave. They remained waving and shouting as long as they could see us on the bridge. It was a moving and impressive scene.

We returned by sea as far as Las Palmas in the *Capetown Castle*, a most comfortable and agreeable journey. It gave me an opportunity to rest and reflect after a tour during which I had travelled over 13,000 miles. But apart from reflection there was plenty to keep us occupied.

Every night we had to deal with a considerable volume of business from home. Butler has obviously been managing very well. But my decisions have had to include an increase of one per cent (four per cent to five per cent) in Bank Rate; refusal to make any more concessions over Cyprus and (of course) the final stages of 'The Queen's Affair'. The Cabinet agreed to the plan which the Lord Chancellor managed to work out with Her Majesty—that is, the 'name' of the House, Family and Dynasty to be Windsor—the name of any 'de-royalised' grandson, etc., of the Queen and Prince Philip to be 'Mountbatten-Windsor' (like Spencer-Churchill).[1]

[1] 7 February 1960.

On the home side generally the chief matter was the concern felt by the Chancellor of the Exchequer for the economy.

> He fears a new inflation. I finally agreed to the Bank Rate increase because experience has shown that this instrument (if it is to be of any use) must be used early. Moreover, the interest rates in U.S.A. and West Germany made it necessary to protect sterling from their pressure. All the same, I would have been for letting this happen and losing reserves, if it had not been desirable to do a little bit of squeezing *internally*. So I agreed. Butler was clearly doubtful; but he also yielded to the arguments deployed by the Treasury.[1]

I had already been warned of the inevitable rise in the estimates and the possibility of new taxation.

> The problems confronting us now have been listed by Norman Brook as follows:
>
> 1. *Railway strike*: due to start on 15 February!
> 2. *Cyprus*: issue uncertain. Julian Amery has gone out to see the Archbishop.
> 3. *Nuclear Tests Conference*: under political pressure at home, the Americans are being very sticky. Ormsby-Gore has gone to Washington.
> 4. *Defence policy:* some big decisions still needed on defence of deterrent, etc.
> 5. *Government expenditure*: it is clear that we *must* try to enforce some economies.
> 6. *Summit Conference*: preparations are going ahead very slowly. . . .
> 7. *Commonwealth Prime Ministers*: Agenda.
> 8. *Policy towards Germany*: Sir A. Rumbold is said to have a new plan.

Apart from matters arising out of Africa, the final details of the Cyprus settlement caused me special anxiety.

> Cyprus goes 'on' and 'off'—like a dish at a cheap restaurant. Julian Amery was sent out to see the Governor and the Archbishop. No progress. A complete deadlock. Then, as he was getting into the aeroplane, a message from Makarios wanting to

[1] 7 February 1960.

resume. He did so—but to little effect. I think Makarios will bargain up to the last point. But will he throw it all away on the difference between an area eleven miles by eleven, or six miles by six (his own suggestion)?[1]

Here patience was to reap its reward.

> The rest of the messages were about the Railway negotiations. I heard last night that a settlement was reached. Five per cent 'interim' increase. This is one per cent more than the Cabinet hoped. But I feel sure they were right to authorise Robertson to accept. When the Guillebaud report does come out, I feel sure it will suggest at least five per cent. For although the Railways *don't* pay (and perhaps never *can* pay) railway workers are definitely low paid workers in comparison with other trades.[1]

On the tour itself I was satisfied that we had done our best. My wife in particular had made, as usual, a great impression by her charm and willingness to undergo any degree of fatigue or dis-comfort in order to give pleasure to our hosts of every rank and every type. There had been a good deal of opposition from the Labour leaders in the House of Commons at my visiting South Africa at the time when they and the T.U.C. were favouring boycott. But fortunately I was able not only to make the visit, but also to end it, in a way that gave general satisfaction to the Press and public at home and throughout the Western world. It was fortunate that the Cape Town speech was the climax of the tour, and the South African visit not a regrettable obligation but a planned culmination. Certainly I had no reason to complain of the reception, and I had kept the Queen closely informed throughout my absence and received her usual gracious support and sympathy.[2] While on the journey home I received a message, dated 15 February, from the President.

> Dear Harold:
> On your return to England, I want you to know that I have been enormously impressed with the great skill with which you carried out your tour of Africa. I am certain that in your visits

---

[1] 13 February 1960.
[2] For details of my letter to the Queen see Appendix 2.

to each of the countries and territories you have made significant contribution toward the resolution of many critical issues.

Very frankly, I was especially struck by your masterful address in Cape Town, and your analysis of the forces of nationalism in Africa.

Please accept my belated birthday greetings and best wishes.

With warm personal regard,

As ever,

Ike

Nevertheless, I felt there were many threatening clouds on the horizon. They were not long in closing in.

In Ghana things would be quiet, at any rate for the time being. Nigeria under the firm guidance of Sir James Robertson would await the date of formal independence. But in the Central African Federation, as in the Union, trouble would, I felt, soon begin. I was not mistaken. Before I left South Africa many telegrams had passed between me, the Commonwealth Secretary and the Colonial Secretary on the question of constitutional advance in Nyasaland and above all on the release of Dr. Banda. I had already warned Welensky that he might expect a communication after I had heard from London. I had also told the Queen of my anxieties about Nyasaland.[1] The Commonwealth Secretary was naturally anxious to make progress; and progress involved Banda's release. He commanded, and has continued to command, the confidence of his people. Events have proved that we were right in showing our own confidence in him. But naturally a great storm was beginning to blow up during my last days in the Union, which pursued me in the calm waters of the Atlantic.

There was some talk of inviting Welensky to London; but it was generally agreed that Lord Home should make an immediate visit to Salisbury. Meanwhile the Monckton Commission had assembled at Victoria Falls on 15 February. The Colonial Secretary was determined, and I thought rightly, to let out Banda as soon as possible. He could assist the Commission as a free man, and it would be almost a farce to discuss constitutional reforms of Nyasaland without Banda. But the Federal Government was opposed to

[1] See Appendix 2, p. 485.

this, and the Governors of Northern Rhodesia and Nyasaland were also for delay. Meanwhile, there was one bright break in the clouds after we returned to London.

> Iain Macleod came in after dinner to tell me that the Kenya conference—after many difficulties—has reached a successful conclusion, everyone (except Group-Captain Briggs) being in agreement. This is certainly a great triumph for the Colonial Secretary.[1]

There was a real clash of opinion over Banda. The Commonwealth Office not unnaturally felt that there was strong reason for accepting the views of the Federal Cabinet, who were bitterly distrustful and adamantly opposed to his release, at least while the Commission was in Nyasaland. But this view was argued against with equal vehemence by Macleod. For a few days it looked as if there could be no reconciliation and that I should be faced with the resignation of one or other of two colleagues for both of whom I felt great confidence and affection. Fortunately, nothing leaked out in the Press, and in discussion with Macleod

> I asked him if it would make a difference to his attitude if Banda were released three days *before* Monckton left Nyasaland instead of three days *after*. He was quite excited by this and said it would solve this problem.[2]

Home accepted this and with great skill persuaded the Federal Cabinet to agree. This would

> secure (if possible) Banda's release in Nyasaland *just before* the Moncktonians left. This would give him a chance (if he wished to do so) of giving evidence *in his own country* and as a *free man*.[2]

I confess that the end of this minor crisis was a great relief to me. It is difficult after so many years to realise the nervous strain which can develop over such delicate issues. The situation was aggravated by the anomaly of two Secretaries of State being in charge of the same territories in their different aspects, the Commonwealth Secretary acting in respect of the Federation as a whole, and for

[1] 21 February 1960. [2] 24 February 1960.

Southern Rhodesia, while the Colonial Secretary was equally responsible for Northern Rhodesia and Nyasaland. When questioned in the House of Commons about Banda's release, I naturally replied that the matter was primarily for the Governor to decide but I added, 'that the ultimate responsibility is on the Government'.

Banda was set free on 1 April, and Macleod, who was in Nyasaland at the time, found him by no means resentful, nor did any disorder occur as a result. I had to inform the Queen frankly of my anxieties for the future.[1] These were not relieved when, on 7 April, Dr. Banda announced on television that at the forthcoming constitutional talks in June he would demand immediate self-government and secession from the Federation. In spite of all the growing sense of tension, it was clear that we must await the report of the Monckton Commission. In the event Dr. Banda became an admirable leader and ruler of his people, by whom he is respected and loved. I formed later an intimate friendship with this attractive and courageous man, which has lasted through many years.

In the Union of South Africa, March 1960 marked the beginning of a series of events which seemed to form the turning point in the history of race relations. The Pan-African Congress (a more extreme organisation than the old-established African National Congress) had planned a number of demonstrations to protest against the pass laws. On the morning of 21 March a crowd of several thousand Africans gathered at the police station in the Sharpeville African township, near Vereeniging. Their leaders claimed that the Africans intended merely to make a peaceful protest and then offer themselves for arrest. The police, on the other hand, declared that the crowd was dangerously out of hand and that shots had been fired at the police station. Whatever the truth about the mood of the people—and this became a matter of acute controversy—the police opened fire and continued firing for some minutes with rifles and automatic weapons. Sixty-seven Africans were killed and about one hundred and eighty wounded. Disturbances continued, and all public meetings were banned by the Government and a state of emergency declared. A large number of arrests took place throughout the country.

[1] See Appendix 2, p. 487.

There has been a tragic incident in South Africa. The Union Government's policy on 'passes' and various other forms of pressure on the Africans have produced a sort of despair. So they have started something like 'passive resistance'. This resulted in two very tragic events—one in the Transvaal and one near Cape Town. Sixty to one hundred Africans have been killed and over two hundred wounded. The British Press has 'gone to town' on this—with all sorts of dreadful pictures, etc.[1]

A Private Notice question in the House of Commons was very properly refused by the Speaker, but Alport, the Minister of State, answered a number of supplementary questions very well and composedly. The reaction throughout the world was immediate.

The Canadians and Indians—with somewhat different degrees of indignation—have condemned South Africa. So has U.S.A.[2]

The Prime Minister of Malaya sent me a telegram expressing abhorrence and proposing that the matter should be discussed at the Conference of Commonwealth Prime Ministers in May. But more immediate action was now threatened.

The Afro-Asians in New York are busy, and within a few days we shall be confronted with another critical decision—what to do or say at the Security Council. We must not forget that there will now be a tremendous effort to stoke up similar riots in Rhodesia or Nyasaland or Kenya, in order to put the United Kingdom in the dock.[2]

So far as the House of Commons was concerned I did not foresee any great difficulties. My concern was how to deal with the matter in the United Nations without leading to a break up of the Commonwealth into two opposing groups. Throughout these troubles both Macleod and Home were particularly helpful, and I received strong support from Butler in trying to steer a middle course. The first question was that of the 'inscription' of the Sharpeville affair on the agenda of the Security Council. Verwoerd sent me an appeal urging me to help in opposing this, but the Foreign Secretary, who was in Washington, reported that he did not think it was possible to prevent discussion. Indeed he thought it

[1] 22 March 1960.　　　　[2] 23 March 1960.

would be a serious error to challenge inscription. We should be badly beaten and our influence for steering a later discussion in a reasonable fashion would be diminished.

He went on to argue that he found, in practice, that Article 2 (7)[1] was not any real protection in this sort of case and would not serve us in our own troubles. I felt bound to accept this view. It would clearly be wiser to try to obtain a moderate resolution for which we could count on American support. There were, nevertheless, difficulties in such a course. Australia was against inscription on well-based if somewhat obsolescent legal grounds. They regarded the matter as one of domestic jurisdiction. But obviously the Afro-Asian countries would not accept this view.

Meanwhile I had received a telephone message from the President asking me to come over to Washington immediately to discuss the whole question of nuclear tests and the possibility of reaching an agreement with the Russians. I felt it impossible to decline this invitation in view of the importance and urgency of the question. Accordingly, I spent from 26 to 31 March in Washington engaged in a long series of discussions. As regards Africa, it afforded an opportunity to discuss the whole question with the President and the Secretary of State, Chris Herter. When the Security Council met on 30 March our delegate raised no formal objection to placing the matter on the Council's agenda. However, both we and the French maintained that while Article 2(7) did not ban discussion, it did exclude intervention.

I kept Dr. Verwoerd closely informed of our tactics and the reasons for them. When I returned to London from Washington on the afternoon of 31 March, I was met by Selwyn Lloyd.

Africa still seems to dominate affairs here. We had a lot of telegrams backward and forward about the 'inscription' of this item on Security Council. The Afro-Asians are making a great deal of trouble in U.N. . . .

But we now have to decide what sort of resolution we ought to work for and what we are to do about any resolution—vote for,

[1] This article of the United Nations Charter refers to matters of domestic jurisdiction.

abstain, or vote against (which means veto). Foreign Secretary and I discussed this on way to London.[1]

Ecuador introduced a resolution deploring apartheid and requesting the Secretary-General to make 'such arrangement as would adequately help in upholding the purposes and principles of the Charter'. Fortunately, the full text was available to us when the Cabinet met.

> It is a real dilemma. The old Commonwealth countries (like Australia) think we should *veto* it. The new Commonwealth (like India and Ghana) will never forgive us if we do.
>
> I urged that we [should take] little notice of public opinion in Britain or in the House of Commons. Our main duty now was to keep the Commonwealth from splitting or disintegrating.[2]

As a result we decided on a not very noble, but very sensible, course—indeed the only one open to us. We would abstain. The French joined us, and the resolution was accordingly carried with two abstentions but without a veto.

In justifying our decision to Menzies I could only rely upon the need to keep the Commonwealth from disintegrating. As I wrote to the Queen on 3 April 'my supreme task is to try to steer the Commonwealth through this crisis and to avoid anything in the nature of disintegration'.[3] In a message to Verwoerd I explained our tactics; we could not but agree that the whole United Nations involvement was contrary to the letter and perhaps even the spirit of the Charter, but we could not prevent it. The use of the veto in the Security Council might well have precipitated the calling of a special Assembly with even worse results.

On 9 April a message was brought to me, while I was working quietly in the Cabinet Room, reporting

> that an attack has been made on Dr. Verwoerd, the Prime Minister of the Union. According to the Press, he was shot in the face and in the neck and is in danger. Also, according to the Press, he was shot by a white man. I devoutly hope this part is true.[4]

[1] 31 March 1960.   [2] 1 April 1960.
[3] See Appendix 2, p. 486.   [4] 9 April 1960.

He was proved eventually to be both a madman and a Liberal. Dr. Verwoerd made a remarkable recovery from the wound, but the attempted assassination did nothing to delay the growing pressure in the United Nations.

There was now a demand that the Secretary-General, Dr. Hammarskjöld, should visit South Africa, and we did all we could to persuade Louw, who was acting for Verwoerd, to be co-operative in the event of his visit. However, the growing crisis in the Congo led to this plan being abandoned. Meanwhile, although we had somehow managed to avoid the most dangerous pitfalls in the United Nations, I looked with considerable apprehension to what would happen when the Commonwealth Prime Ministers met in May.

This gathering lasted from 3 to 13 May. On the day before the opening a slight change was introduced, at the Queen's suggestion, in the usual ceremonies. Instead of the traditional dinner being held at Buckingham Palace it took place at Windsor.

> It was very splendid and I think they enjoyed it. (Poor Mr. Louw could never enjoy anything very much, I would think.) But it made a long day—and I felt very tired when we got home. The Queen did not leave till just midnight.
>
> Dinner was in the Waterloo Room, and after dinner we went round the State Apartments. It is sad that they do not live in these rooms, instead of having to use the rather garish George IV gilded saloons. The pictures in the State Rooms are wonderfully and beautifully displayed.[1]

At this conference a large number of important questions were discussed, including the usual review of foreign and defence policy and of the general economic situation throughout the world. Nevertheless, it was inevitable that since we met so soon after the Sharpeville tragedy the members of the Conference should be much preoccupied with problems of racial policy in South Africa. The Prime Minister of Malaya, Tunku Abdul Rahman, at the opening meeting, raised the whole question of racial discrimination in South Africa and its effects upon relations between the Union and other

[1] 2 May 1960.

members of the Commonwealth. He hoped that an opportunity would be found for discussion while the Prime Ministers were in London. Abdul Rahman, who we all knew and loved under the title of 'The Tunku', made his statement in the most moderate terms. Eric Louw, who represented the Union in the absence of Dr. Verwoerd who was recovering from his wounds, argued that the sole responsibility for domestic policies rested with the Union Government. However, with the help of Menzies, who carried more weight than any other Prime Minister,

> we got through (or over) the first hurdle without too much difficulty. . . . But I sense trouble coming all the same. It was agreed that the racial question in South Africa was, essentially, a matter of *internal* policy, though it had its reactions on the Commonwealth as a whole. It was agreed to discuss the problem with Mr. Louw 'upstairs'—and Prime Ministers alone. (There are thirty–forty people in the Cabinet room at formal or plenary sessions.) Once this was settled, the main business could go on.[1]

All this was achieved by about noon, 'giving me time to open on "world situation—Russia, etc." before luncheon'.[1]

At the afternoon session

> both Nehru (India) and Ayub (Pakistan) made admirable and impressive speeches. There was then rather a battle about the 'communiqué'. This set out the discussion and the agreement about South Africa. The Tunku talked a lot. . . . Mr. Louw (to be fair) was objective and correct. The sad thing is that he can never be gracious.[1]

At my afternoon audience with the Queen I reported progress. She

> has now been *formally* invited to visit the Republics of India, Pakistan and Malaya and is rather pleased. I think it is a very good sign.[1]

The next day

> the 'plenary' session continued—on world situation. I thought all the Prime Ministers good—especially Menzies. We adjourned at twelve noon (for the first 'informal talk' on South Africa). . . .

[1] 3 May 1960.

I heard after luncheon that the first informal session (which I did *not* attend) had gone very badly. . . . The 'plenary' went well—disarmament, Nuclear Tests, etc. Foreign Secretary spoke very well. Second informal session at 5.15 p.m.

Dorothy and I gave an immense dinner—followed by reception. Afterwards we all went to the Queen's party at Buckingham Palace. A very long, but quite interesting day. The feeling *against* South Africa is swelling to really dangerous proportions.[1]

5 May was an unlucky day and can best, perhaps, be described in my own record made at the time.

Eric Louw gave a Press Conference yesterday—bitter, unyielding—but very well done (so the Press say). It fills this morning's newspapers. The Tunku has replied by issuing an offensive (and inaccurate) attack. This appeared at lunch time. The morning session passed off well enough (on Economic situation, etc.). But at the end of the afternoon session there was a row between them. Nkrumah of Ghana, who 'joined' last year and is behaving with great restraint, is said to regard the Tunku's performances with disfavour.

He thinks that a 'new boy' ought to behave better. President and Field-Marshal Ayub of Pakistan, who is like an old Indian Army Colonel, thinks that 'none of them come out of the top drawer, anyway'. Diefenbaker—who is . . . deaf and very sensitive—joined in, very angry at some remark made by Louw in answer to a question about what Canada thought about it all. With a Johnsonian force he replied 'Nothing, Sir.' As the hour of recess was near, I appealed to everyone to think over all these problems during the weekend and adjourned the meeting. The prospects are pretty bad. If we *do nothing*, the Commonwealth will seem to have no faith and no purpose. If we *do too much* South Africa will secede and this may mean the beginning of a general break-up.[2]

I had invited a number of the Prime Ministers and my colleagues to Chequers for the weekend. They arrived in the course of the afternoon.

Nehru came for luncheon. We were alone. He seemed in good form. On South Africa his position had hardened, I thought. He

[1] 4 May 1960.   [2] 5 May 1960.

now thought that we must say something collectively, if only about the external effect of South Africa's internal policies. However, he talked almost exclusively during luncheon and afterwards about Russia, China and Communism. He has clearly been much shaken by the Chinese aggression.[1] His line is that they are fundamentally a more brutal and ruthless people than the Russians. He thinks their Communism is more theoretical and fervent. The Russians are 'backsliding' into bourgeoisie—not so the Chinese. He does not really think that the Chinese want to join U.N. They are better off with a grievance and freedom to do what they like. When Nehru reproved them for acting 'contrary to the Charter', they enquired blandly, 'What Charter?'[2]

Later in the day we were joined by

Dr. Nkrumah, the Tunku, Prime Minister Walter Nash, Prime Minister Menzies and Alec Home. We tried to hatch out some plan for next week but did not get very far. Sir Norman Brook was there too and helpful.

There are two problems—

(1) the unfinished or adjourned row between Eric Louw and the Tunku, and how to handle it, and perhaps turn it to our advantage;

(2) the South African application about becoming a republic.

My Prime Minister colleagues are very nice, and their general idea is to leave it all to me to find a way out! I thought Nkrumah very sensible. He is absolutely against trying to force South Africa out of the Commonwealth.[2]

When we met on Monday morning there was a curious scene.

Louw raised a 'point of order'—a remark made by the Tunku last week. (It was the hare which was started but not killed on Friday evening.) Louw spoke—too long—but ably. The Malayan Prime Minister replied shortly. Then everyone spoke—every single one of them—I wound up at 12.30 p.m. Poor Mr. Louw was thus hoist with his own petard with a vengeance. He complained—but only at the end of a two-and-a-half-hour discussion

[1] Border clashes between Chinese and Indian troops occurred during the autumn of 1959.
[2] 7 May 1960.

on Apartheid—all of which, according to him, is out of order. But he had bought it. The debate did good. All the Prime Ministers can now say not merely that there have been 'informal' discussions—there has been a discussion in *restricted session* (for, at Louw's own request I had asked all *except* Prime Ministers to leave the Cabinet room) lasting two and a half hours, at which every aspect—internal and external—of South African policy was fully debated. I thought *all* the Prime Ministers were pretty good.[1]

In the end 'after a little wrangling, we issued an *agreed* communiqué, saying what had happened'.[1] Just before luncheon we voted that Nigeria would, when she became independent, join the Commonwealth. The Prime Minister of Nigeria, Abubakar, was upstairs in the drawing-room waiting. We all went upstairs to drink his health, and a pleasant little ceremony took place.

During these days there were many other distractions, including the disaster which began to threaten the long awaited Summit in Paris. However, we struggled on manfully, and on the morning of 12 May finished the regular work of the Conference.

Except for the South African trouble, which seems to keep getting into everything, like King Charles's head with poor Mr. Dick, our meetings have been useful and constructive. On political, strategic and economic questions I have sensed a greater unity than at previous meetings. Nehru (thoroughly shaken by his Chinese experiences) has not been so pontifical as usual about 'non-alignment'. President Ayub has been a worthy representative of Pakistan—the first serious figure since Liaqat Ali Khan. Dr. Nkrumah has been sensible and moderate, even on African affairs. Of the Old Commonwealth countries, Menzies has been a tower of strength—and much less provocative than last time. Nash is a nice, good-natured, well-intentioned old-fashioned Liberal—a bore, but sincere and Christian gentleman.[2]

I found Diefenbaker more difficult to understand. Personally he made himself most agreeable, but he seemed to me too much absorbed in Canadian Party politics.

In the afternoon we started on the final communiqué, always the

[1] 9 May 1960.   [2] 12 May 1960.

most difficult part of any conference, and, of course, in the circumstances of this meeting especially dangerous.

> On the proposed paragraph on South Africa and racialism, a most tense situation arose. (I had seen the Queen at 2.30 p.m. to warn her of this trouble.)
>
> At 7.00 p.m. I adjourned the meeting, with nothing settled, but no actual outbursts. Everyone felt strongly, but behaved well. . . . It was agreed that we should think over the situation and meet the next day.[1]

During the evening there was much coming and going. Unfortunately I had to wind up a debate in the House of Commons on Foreign Affairs—chiefly about the Summit meeting in Paris, which meant sitting in the House from 7 p.m. until 10 o'clock. When I got back to No. 10,

> Alec and I worked out (with Brook's help) a draft clause for the communiqué which we thought might do. The *great* danger of no agreement is twofold. First, there may be two if not three groups formed (apart from South Africa). The extremists (brown or black) the less extreme (brown and white) the still less extreme (white—especially Australia) as well as (of course) South Africa.[1]

We finished our work at midnight, but there was still the ordinary routine to be completed before I could get to bed in the early hours of the morning.

The next day was indeed an anxious one. I was due to leave for Paris within a day or two, and the Conference could not be prolonged. Again it seems best to use my own record.

> One could hardly have a worse omen for the final stages of the Commonwealth Conference than Friday the thirteenth. But it has all turned out well—or, at least, far beyond our expectations or even our hopes. We actually settled—by unanimous agreement —a *text* of the vital paragraph and finished the whole Conference with an agreed communiqué by noon ! I had to break off once, to convince Louw (who has really behaved very decently) and I had some anxious moments with the Tunku (Malaya) and with Nehru. Nkrumah was most statesmanlike. . . . Nash was helpful

[1] 12 May 1960.

with Nehru and the Tunku. Menzies was excellent with Louw. But I had to pull out all the stops—personal appeal, etc., etc. But, hurrah, hurrah! In spite of all the newspapers, and the B.B.C. and the I.T.V. and the Labour Party and the Liberals—who all want a row and will be bitterly disappointed—we have saved the unity of the Commonwealth (at least for the time) *without* any sacrifice of principle.[1]

The communiqué consisted of no less than fifteen clauses. The last and vital one finally read as follows:

Whilst reaffirming the traditional practice that Commonwealth conferenc :s do not discuss the internal affairs of member countries Ministers availed themselves of Mr. Louw's presence in London to have informal discussions with him about the racial situation in South Africa. During these informal discussions Mr. Louw gave information and answered questions on the Union's policies, and other Ministers conveyed to him their views on the South African problem. The Ministers emphasised that the Commonwealth itself is a multi-racial association and expressed the need to ensure good relations between all member states and peoples of the Commonwealth.[2]

I sent an immediate report to the Queen:

The official text is weak but has the advantage of being agreed. It was accepted by the South African representative after a good deal of discussion and fortunately was agreed by those Prime Ministers and Ministers who felt most strongly about South African racial policies. It does not, of course, make any progress in the solution of the problem, but it does at least keep the Commonwealth for the time being from being broken up. I hope that Your Majesty will feel that this is the best that we can hope for in the present circumstances.

I sent, before finishing this anxious day, a letter of thanks to Sir Norman Brook in the following terms:

I want to thank you for the wonderful way in which you helped me through the difficulties of the Commonwealth

[1] 13 May 1960.
[2] For the full text see *Annual Register*, 1960, pp. 526–7.

Conference. It was certainly very rough going, but it was a great encouragement to me to be able to rely on your ceaseless and untiring efforts.

I also wrote to those of my colleagues who had been of special help—above all the Commonwealth Secretary.

Thus ended an anxious and exacting period. Alas, it was destined to be only an interval before a new and even more painful Conference which was to meet in the following year.

CHAPTER VII

The Summit that Failed

W HEN I returned from Africa in the middle of February 1960, I viewed the prospects for the Summit with mixed feelings. Khrushchev's declaration on 8 January that if the Summit produced no agreement on Berlin he would make a separate peace treaty leaving access to be controlled by the East German Government—the D.D.R.—was perhaps to be expected. Although he added a somewhat sinister threat, 'if the West then attacked, the U.S.S.R. had the bombs ready', there was no immediate need for anxiety. As regards the perennial problem of disarmament, the Ten-Power Committee at Geneva was seized with the British proposals, which had been favourably received both at home and in most foreign countries. This, together with the Five-Power Working Group at Washington, could be trusted to continue in the same decorous and protracted negotiation which had become an almost conventional and stylised exercise in diplomatic warfare. But the larger the issues and the wider the concepts put forward by the various Powers, the less hopeful became the prospects of agreement. To this the people of Britain, and, no doubt, of other countries, had become more or less reconciled. If there was no great advance to be hoped for there was no immediate danger to be feared. It was quite otherwise with the pressing question of nuclear tests.

Even by 1960 the anxiety of the public had begun to change. Its fears were no longer so directly concentrated upon the prospect of atomic warfare. Although there were the usual 'ban-the-bomb' meetings and demonstrations, the paradox that the bomb with all its horrors seemed to be the greatest guarantee against the outbreak of a third world war was now becoming gradually recognised even by the most idealistic or alarmist groups in our social or political life. If it were really true, as President Kennedy was to say a few years later, that America could wipe out Russia twice over and Russia could wipe out America once over, it did not seem likely that even the most ambitious or the most ruthless statesman would consciously enter upon so unrewarding an adventure. But if the sense of terror, which had dominated so many of our people, especially our young people, about the threat of annihilation by nuclear warfare had grown less oppressive, a new and genuine source of alarm had been created by the profusion, in recent years, of atomic tests. Each side had at varying intervals exploded a number of engines of varying but steadily increasing tonnage, which were alleged to produce the most disturbing results, lasting for many years, by polluting the atmosphere with a degree of radiation which would become painfully evident throughout succeeding generations. The most distressing pictures were drawn of the spread either of impotence and infertility among men and women, or the birth of a whole progeny of deformed children equally afflicted by mental and bodily aberrations.

Much genuine interest therefore concentrated upon the Nuclear Test Conference due to resume at the beginning of January. In spite of the usual bargaining, both sides seemed to be slowly edging closer together during the next few weeks. After a number of proposals and counter-proposals, which it would be tedious to recall in detail, on 16 February the Russians unexpectedly offered to allow a number of Western inspection teams to visit the site of virtually any earth tremor in the Soviet Union in order to ascertain whether this was due to natural or artificial causes. For it was the difficulty of being sure whether an underground test had been made surreptitiously that seemed, in American eyes, to be an insuperable bar against either a moratorium or the final abandonment of all nuclear tests. This new Soviet proposal appeared to be a complete reversal of their old position, although the Russians at the same time made clear that they would require an agreement outlawing any form of test of whatever size. I was becoming rather concerned at the slow American reaction to these undoubted advances. I was particularly anxious about their apparent refusal of a moratorium. However a new factor now came into some prominence.

The French nuclear test was approaching, and I had undertaken, at the Western Summit Conference at the end of 1959, to pay a short visit to de Gaulle timed to take place before Khrushchev's visit to France. Accordingly I arrived at Rambouillet on Saturday afternoon, 12 March, leaving after tea on Sunday 13 March. This meeting, at de Gaulle's wish, was kept completely informal. We had two and a half hours alone before dinner with no one present except Philip de Zulueta and on the French side Baron de Courcel. To dinner there came only the General's daughter and son-in-law, and after dinner general conversation followed until ten o'clock, when we went to bed. Sunday morning our talks continued; and in the afternoon Michel Debré, the Prime Minister, arrived at three o'clock.

> We all set off in cars to a spot in the middle of the forest . . . here we all got out (Dorothy, Madame de Gaulle, etc.), and de Gaulle, Debré and I walked along a ride and back—for some forty minutes, talking. Back to the Palace and a talk *à trois* till five o'clock. We then had tea and left for Paris.[1]

We were back in London at 10.30 p.m. I confess that

> I felt tired from the strain of talking nothing but French . . . and trying not to fall into any major error of judgement.[1]

Our talks were intimate, and so far as I could judge most friendly. It began, as usual, with complaints against France's allies in the war.

> I had fortunately read the last volume of his Memoirs, and I asked de Gaulle why he continually harped on the theme of the 'Anglo-Saxons'. Apart from a general feeling that he is left out of Anglo-American talks, and jealousy of my close association with this particular President, it clearly all stems from the War. He resented—rather absurdly in the setting of Vichy and all that—the Roosevelt–Churchill hegemony. He goes back too—in his retentive mind—to all the rows about Syria; about D-day; about the position of the French Army in the final stages of the war ; about Yalta . . . and all the rest.[1]

In reply I could at least remind him

[1] 13 March 1960.

of our *tripartite* discussion at Rambouillet only a few months ago, and said that I would do all I could to make such discussions periodic and fruitful. In addition, I would welcome frequent Anglo-French talks and a real renewal of Anglo-French friendship. We had no empires left—and therefore no rivalries. All those days were past.[1]

I turned next to the question of Europe and Germany. De Gaulle

does *not* want political integration. He accepted the economic integration implied in the Treaty of Rome with regret. But it was signed, and he could not go back on it. But it *has* had a useful effect in making French industry more competitive. Politically, it keeps Germany looking to the West.[1]

The question of united Germany must be presented as an ultimate ideal but at the moment it was impracticable. Meanwhile, he did not

fear Germany for at least twenty-five years—if it can be kept in the Western group. As regards Berlin, etc., his chief object is to support Adenauer, because—if he is let down—more dangerous sentiments may begin to develop in Germany. At present (though he does not like people like Herr Strauss) he is not fearful, but rather contemptuous of the Bonn regime. Moreover, since we have all helped Germany so much since the war, he does not feel that there is the material (poverty and unemployment) for a new sort of Hitler to exploit.[1]

When we turned to the actual Berlin issue soon to be discussed at the Summit, de Gaulle clearly thought that, while we must present a united front, a *modus vivendi* might be found at the last moment.

De Gaulle thinks that Khrushchev has presented himself so much as the man of Peace that he will not want an absolutely barren Summit.[1]

We next turned to the question of defence.

On the bomb, he wants nuclear disarmament. If not, France must have the bomb, by one means or another. If the Americans will not—or cannot—give France the information or the weapon,

[1] 13 March 1960.

he will have to go ahead, whatever the cost. He said he fully
realised now how great and continuous the cost would be, both
for the weapon and the means of delivery. I told him our position
and our own future problems. We were all right till the late sixties
—after that, we were not sure what to do.[1]

Although, of course, I was to give de Gaulle later on a much more
precise account of our difficulties over prolonging the life of the
bomber, this was a first intimation that we might have to turn to
some other method of delivery. We then had some discussion on
the control of the Western nuclear deterrent.

> Did he want full control, or would he consider a NATO, a
> W.E.U., or an Anglo-French control? He would reflect on this.[1]

He talked a good deal about Africa.

> He was reconciled to independence of all the former French
> colonies, with—at the best—a sort of Commonwealth system.[1]

On Algeria he was determined that there must be

> a political settlement. But the military situation was much
> improved. West Algeria was calm. Even in the East, a *de facto*
> end of the rebellion might be in sight. He would then bring the
> Army home.[1]

When this had happened he could embark on a reorganisation of
NATO.

> He believed in NATO. But its 'set-up' was absurd. Armies
> could not be divided. They must be organised into national units.
> This was particularly true of the French Army. By a NATO
> command structure, it was demoralised. When the army could be
> got back from Algeria, he would raise the whole issue. Besides,
> except for the Church, the Army was the only stable thing in
> France. The Germans should be the advanced guard; the French
> the main Defence; Britain should cover the Low Countries and
> the sea; America should be the grand reserve.[1]

As to the stationing of these troops 'there could be "elements" in
Germany—but not the main armies'.[1] As regards the command

[1] 13 March 1960.

he had no objection to an allied C.-in-C. (even an American) but it should be like Foch at the end of the First War, but not like SHAPE. I did not say much on all this, but made a mental note that [all this might be turned to our advantage].[1]

On the Saturday after dinner he spoke a good deal about France and its history.

He knows that she is not easily governed, but he thinks that the political parties are still unpopular and that he has the nation's support. He must use this position while he can.

He remarked . . . that in this very room Charles X had abdicated. He went to England—Louis Philippe went off in a *fiacre*—also to England. Napoleon III went to England, too. He paused—and said that he would no doubt be welcomed.[1]

He was very frank about the agricultural difficulties of France.

There is a row going on with the farmers—who are out-of-date and need *remembrement*, i.e. larger units, to replace the small and scattered units which result from constant partition of land under the Code Napoléon.[1]

In this situation the politicians were naturally demanding a meeting of the Assembly.

He will refuse. His plans are not yet ready. Let them wait till the proper day—end of April.[1]

I came back more than ever impressed by this figure with whom I was destined to have such strange and varying relations over many years in such different circumstances.

Now that he is old (sixty-nine) and mellowed, his charm is great. He speaks beautiful, rather old-fashioned French. He seems quite impersonal and disinterested. He said he never expected to return to power—at least not in recent years.[1]

Immediately on my return I reported my impressions to the Queen and also sent a personal message to President Eisenhower.

To the President I reported the General's anxieties and indeed suspicions.

[1] 13 March 1960.

His main themes remain unchanged. I do not know if you have read the third volume of his book; it is wonderfully written and gives a picture of his rather mystical thinking on these great matters.

I think he is disappointed that nothing much has followed from our discussions at Rambouillet about tripartite talks, but he accepts the fact that they are really going to take place because of all the meetings round and about the Summit. We shall have our meeting on the way up and, no doubt, on the way down. His own approach to things makes him prefer a talk with the heads rather than an elaborate machinery, and I think he accepted that a new piece of mechanism was undesirable. At the same time I think he would like what he called a very small continuing method of carrying further any discussions that we three might have, even if only to name the subjects for the next discussion. This could easily be done by the Ambassadors, without any special staff.

Eisenhower was genuinely puzzled by the French attitude and replied on 18 March expressing his concern.

It has been a source of amazement to me that he seems to be unable to fathom the methods by which our three governments could easily keep in close touch on main issues. I explained to him how you and ourselves used both normal diplomatic exchanges, personal communications and, in acute cases, ad hoc committees to keep together. I think that the difficulty may lie in his memory of the British–American 'Combined Chiefs of Staff' of World War II days, and his resentment that the French staffs were not integrated into that body. In any event, I have always made it clear that I was ready to do anything reasonable to maintain contacts and mutual understandings among us three; I adhere to this policy. But I think I made it also clear to him that it was impractical to have frequent 'Heads of Government' Conferences and yet, as you say, he seems to prefer this kind of approach to any on our common problems.

Indeed this whole matter continued to be a source of difficulty. As time went on and no proposals came from Paris calculated to give greater strength and vigour to the tripartite plan agreed at Rambouillet I began to suspect that either de Gaulle did not understand

The Summit that failed, May 1960

'Khrushchev came, not alone ... but in full state—Gromyko, Marshal Malinovsky and one or two others.'

'He made a speech in violent terms.'

The end of the Summit, 19 May 1960
'There was now little to be done except try to conceal as best as I could my disappointment amounting almost to despair—so much attempted, so little achieved.'

and could not operate on the lines which the President and I had found natural, or else he preferred to nurse grievances rather than to resolve a problem of organisation. I regret now that we did not press forward from London with a more definite scheme which would have tested the genuineness of French desires.

After making a long report to the Queen on 14 March on the lines of my own records I added:

General de Gaulle is much looking forward to his visit to this country. Madame de Gaulle is very shy and speaks practically no English. She is a woman of considerable character: I have even heard it said that she is the only human being of whom the General stands mildly in awe—but I can scarcely believe this.

A few days later at a meeting of the Test Ban Conference at Geneva, where the scientists argued with a certain professional urbanity, the Russians suddenly made a forward move. The Americans had previously declared their readiness to ban all explosions that could be monitored, that is to say, all those above a certain magnitude. The Russians now very unexpectedly accepted this on the condition of its being linked to a moratorium of small tests during a period of further research. Thus

they have proposed the very plan for abolition of nuclear tests which we have for months been urging on the Americans! We must now bring tremendous pressure on the Americans to agree. The President will be sympathetic; so will the State Department. But I am not sure of the Pentagon and certain of the hostility of the Atomic [Energy Commission].

There will also be complications about getting a treaty through the Senate in an election year. Nevertheless, it is a wonderful chance. If necessary, I will go off to Washington to persuade the President.[1]

This seemed to me a real opportunity for reaching the agreement for which the public were looking so anxiously. If the Russians would agree to the banning of all the large tests it seemed incredible to me that the Americans could refuse at least some moratorium on

[1] 20 March 1960.

G

the small tests while the scientists were trying to discover how these also might be made subject to detection.

> Foreign Secretary came in before luncheon and we talked over the Geneva Test situation. I decided to telephone to Eisenhower and try to stimulate his interest. I got through at 3.00 p.m. (10.00 a.m. in Washington). He seemed rather vague about it. but said he would look into it and ring me back. This he did at 7.30 p.m. He was not sure what they would do. But he would ring again on Wednesday. (. . . they have a great meeting fixed for Wednesday of all the departments and agencies concerned.) I said I would come over and talk to him. He thought that might be quite a good idea.[1]

I was determined not to miss this chance of easing the path to the Summit by creating an atmosphere of agreement on a point about which the general public in all countries were so concerned. 'It is at least hopeful that it was Herter who suggested that I should telephone to the President.'[1] I had not long to wait for my answer. On 23 March

> the President telephoned about 4.00 p.m. (our time) and made it clear that he would like me to come over to discuss the Test Agreement. He seemed very friendly. He has engagements on Sunday, but would like to set aside Monday and Tuesday for the talks. So I will go. I am sure it is worth it, but I do *not* feel very hopeful. The Americans are divided, and with an administration on the way out, the Pentagon and the Atomic groups are gaining strength.[2]

In order to allay any misunderstanding I sent telegrams to de Gaulle and Adenauer, as well as to the Commonwealth Prime Ministers to explain the purpose of my proposed visit to Washington. De Gaulle's reply of 26 March was especially friendly:

Dear Friend
    Thank you very much for your kindness in letting me know your views regarding the latest developments in the Geneva negotiations about nuclear tests. Thank you, too, for telling me

[1] 21 March 1960.   [2] 23 March 1960.

of your decision to discuss them with President Eisenhower without delay.

You know my sincere desire to see a genuine nuclear disarmament brought about, and the reasons why France cannot be associated with an agreement which does not serve this end.

We shall, I hope, soon have an opportunity to talk about this matter again. Meanwhile, all my best wishes for your journey.

Very sincerely yours

C. de Gaulle[1]

Meanwhile, I received a message, dated 19 March, from Khrushchev which, although making no specific reference to the Russians' move at Geneva, was of so friendly a character and expressed so hopeful a view of the Paris meeting that I felt correspondingly encouraged and almost elated.

Dear Mr. Prime Minister,

I am taking this opportunity to extend heartfelt greetings and best wishes to you and your colleagues through our new Ambassador.

It is always a pleasure to recall that following the exchange of views we had last year in Moscow Soviet–British relations have been developing to the mutual benefit of our two countries and there now exist all grounds to believe that these relations will continue to develop favourably.

In our opinion, the discernible rapprochement in relations between the Soviet Union and Great Britain as well as in the relations between the U.S.S.R. and the other Western Powers is creating definite opportunities for a further normalisation and expansion of ties between the countries of East and West.

[1] Cher Ami,

Merci beaucoup de l'attention que vous avez eu de me faire connaître votre position à l'égard des derniers développements de la négociation de Genève concernant les expériences nucléaires. Merci, également, de m'avoir informé de votre décision d'en entretenir sans délai le Président Eisenhower.

Vous connaissez le désir sincere que j'ai de voir réaliser un désarmement nucléaire que soit réel et les raisons pour lesquelles la France ne pourrait s'associer à un accord qui ne répondrait pas à cet objectif.

Nous aurons, je l'espère, l'occasion de parler bientôt à nouveau de cette affaire. En attendant, tous mes meilleurs vœux pour votre voyage.

Bien cordialement à vous,

C. de Gaulle

At present, due to the efforts of the Governments of our countries as well as certain other states such forms of relations between the countries of East and West as negotiations on pressing international problems, mutually beneficial economic ties and contacts in the field of culture and science are ever more actively making a way for themselves. You will, I believe, agree that today the major task is to further the already achieved positive developments in relations between the countries of East and West.

I note with great gratification that in your letter to me of 12 February you also speak of the possibility to develop such relations and on your part express readiness to promote the achievement of progress in international relations.

The Soviet Government expresses the hope that the first in the series of conferences of Heads of Governments which is to be held in Paris will already constitute an important step in the settlement of the problems to which you and I devoted no little time in the course of our talks in Moscow.

We would like to hope that all the participants in the conference will strive towards the attainment of this goal and will do their utmost to promote the creation of a favourable atmosphere for a successful meeting of the Heads of Government.

Very respectfully,

N. Khrushchev

At the same time Caccia, our Ambassador in Washington, sent a rather gloomy telegram warning me of the emotional pressure which was building up in Washington over the Soviet proposals. It was an election year, and there was already a fear that Eisenhower was too much under British influence, or might yield too easily to the persuasions of his old friends instead of resting upon the advice of the Defence Departments who felt that in any Russian proposal there must be, however artfully concealed, an inevitable trap.

I was to spend four days, 27–31 March, in America and as regards the main purpose of our visit all went well.

We had a meeting of our team (including Sir William Penney) at 11.00 a.m. The Americans have circulated a 'position paper' about the Geneva Test Conference—which is, after all, the main purpose of my visit. All sorts of other questions have been added—Sixes and Sevens (that is the economic split in Europe) Skybolt and Polaris (American nuclear devices which we need if we abandon our rocket, Blue Streak) U.N. and South Africa. The Summit. But I must keep to the first object and concentrate on that.

The American paper is unexpectedly good. It obviously represents a triumph for the State Department over the Pentagon and the Atomic Energy Commission. It is therefore the President's own decision—or so it seems to me. It accepts the principle of the moratorium for underground explosions 'below the threshold', although it says one to two years (the Russians proposed four to five) and requires (for sound reasons, owing to the nature of the U.S. Constitution) that the moratorium should result from *executive* action, and not be part of the treaty. (This, if the Russians can be made to understand, is the only practical way. For a Treaty, even if signed in May or June could not be ratified till the spring of next year by the next Congress. But the President can order the moratorium himself.)

Of course, there are a lot of difficult points . . . still to be negotiated—about the control system, about the experiments during the moratorium, about atomic explosions for peaceful purposes (e.g. building a harbour or a dam) and—most tricky of all—the number of inspections. (This is the quota idea which I started a year ago in Moscow.) But if the Russians are sincere themselves and are convinced of our sincerity, a Treaty should be negotiable.[1]

In the afternoon

Chris Herter came at 5.30 p.m. and chatted—alone—for an hour. We covered a lot a ground. He is a sincere man, and seems really proud of the line he has taken on the Tests. The President seems (as he sometimes does) to have made the final decisions himself, and by himself.[1]

The next day we drove to the White House, at 11.30 a.m., and left by helicopter for Camp David. I always enjoyed the atmosphere at this delightful spot high in the mountains, where life was both simple and comfortable. It was equally adaptable to work or rest, or

[1] 27 March 1960.

a mixture of both. On this occasion the talks began soon after luncheon and lasted almost until bedtime.

> Yesterday's talks were encouraging, and before dinner (followed by the inevitable film) we had given the Americans the text of the 'declaration' on the Nuclear Tests (which I had dictated in the Embassy) which we propose should be issued by the President and me. The situation is now pretty clear. The President has definitely decided to go along with me and accepted the moratorium on tests 'below the threshold.' This has been bitterly resented and violently opposed by two powerful groups—the Pentagon and the Atomic Energy Commission. The reason advanced is that the Russians will cheat and that scientists will *not* be able to devise a satisfactory system to distinguish the smaller *test* bangs from normal *earthquake* bangs. The real reason is that the Atomic Commission and the Pentagon are very keen to go on *indefinitely* with experiments (large and small) so as to keep refining upon and perfecting the art of nuclear weapons. This is, in a way, natural. But it means that, even when the President has reached a decision, there is a tremendous effort to hedge it around with so many 'ifs' and 'ans' as to make it ineffective.
>
> Therefore they wanted a moratorium of six months or one year to be put forward. The President supported me in merely taking the line that the Russian five or four years was too long.
>
> By lunch time today, all arguments were resolved. The President has stood very firm and the declaration has come out in a very good form. It is to be published at 4.00 p.m. (9.00 p.m. our time).[1]

The joint communiqué was generally regarded as an acceptance of the Russians' proposals. In effect this meant the signing as soon as possible of an agreement between the Three Powers banning altogether any form of tests whether atmospheric or underground above a certain minimum. In addition there would be a temporary standstill on all the smaller tests below the so-called threshold—that is of a seismic magnitude of 4.75. The length of the moratorium was still a matter for discussion. The Russians had proposed five years, while the President, since he would act not by formal treaty in this

[1] 29 March 1960.

respect but by his own executive power, wished to limit it until the
end of his term of office in January 1961. There seemed, however,
to be little danger of any serious dispute, for if the main treaty was
agreed it was clear that the moratorium on small tests would be
maintained.

There were still some outstanding points—the fixing of an annual
quota of on-site inspections, the composition of the control commission and arrangements authorising detonations for peaceful purposes. But there was a general assumption that such real progress on
the eve of the Summit meeting would lead to final agreement. All
the omens were good.

Apart from its immediate purpose, which proved very successful,
I thoroughly enjoyed this visit. My old friend was in fine form and
clearly welcomed the chance of an uninhibited talk. On 29 March,
the joint statement having now been approved, Eisenhower and I
went for a drive, first to his farm at Gettysburg and then to the
various battlefield memorials.

> He talked a great deal and very freely about himself, his
> future plans, American politics (he is *very* anxious for Nixon to
> win, so as to continue the present Anglo-American relations
> unchanged), his feelings about Monty and Brookie (both he
> admires immensely, though he resents the books as largely unfair,
> even to their authors), his hopes of the Summit (he thinks we
> *should* be able to get some settlement on *Berlin*, if only we would
> guarantee to accept for ever the present frontiers of Germany
> (Oder–Neisse)), his hopes for a Nuclear Test Agreement (he is
> *really* keen on this and—although he has not said much about it
> yet—would accept further concessions in the course of negotia-
> tion to get it) and many other matters.[1]

The experts, British and American, had now left the Camp. 'Only
the President and his aide; Philip de Zulueta and myself for
dinner—and two hours of film.'[1]
On the following morning

> after two fine days, the weather broke in the night. Camp David
> is about 1,800 feet up in the mountains, and was in cloud this

[1] 29 March 1960.

morning. So we had to motor to Washington instead of using the helicopter. We left at 8.00 a.m. and reached the Embassy at 10.15 a.m.[1]

I had a busy day in front of me including luncheon with Senator Fulbright and the Senate Committee on Foreign Relations,

fortified for the occasion by Senator Anderson and some of the members of his Atomic Committee. Senator Fulbright is a very charming and civilised man (he was a Rhodes scholar). The luncheon was *really* useful. I said a few words, and then answered questions about the British view of Russia, the Summit, Nuclear Test Agreement, etc. I thought Senator Anderson had thought again about the last. He had made rather an intemperate speech some days ago, but he had begun to change his tune.[1]

After luncheon

the Senators (ninety or more) were collected. The Vice-President came in and took the Chair. I was introduced into the Senate Chamber and made a short—extempore—speech. This seemed to go very well and was much applauded. Then each Senator in turn came up to shake hands.

It is a strange but very human little ceremony and is a great honour. How pleased my mother would have been. She regarded a Senator of the United States as almost the highest degree of dignity and felicity to which mortals could aspire. (I told them this in the speech to the Senators and they enjoyed it. I added that although as a child I had always been rather sceptical about Mother's view of the Senate, I now understood and approved.)[1]

There was still quite a programme to get through.

I went to call on Mrs. Foster Dulles (Janet). She seemed pleased.

Then the Press.
Then the Commonwealth High Commission.
Then dinner.
Then to call on Herter to say good-bye.
Then to call on the President and 'Mamie' to say good-bye.
Then to the airport ; off at 11.00 p.m.[1]

[1] 30 March 1960.

On my return I wrote at length to the Queen giving her a full account of recent events in Washington, including my unofficial talks with the President. Once again when I had my audience on 4 April I was astonished at Her Majesty's grasp of all the details set out in various messages and telegrams. I also made a report to the House of Commons which was generously received by all parties.

We had now only a few weeks to wait for the Summit meeting for which I had striven so hard. Nor was there any delay in taking steps to assist the operation of the Nuclear Test Agreement. Plans were already being made to establish a chain of seismic research stations for the purpose of monitoring any underground explosions, and I was pleased to find the ready acceptance with which this proposal was met throughout the Commonwealth.

Meanwhile we had a pleasant interlude with the official visit of General de Gaulle. He arrived on 5 April and left on the morning of 8 April. He was received with great enthusiasm by large crowds. As usual the visit consisted of a number of formal occasions interspersed with some private discussions. Since it was a State Visit everything was done in great style, and de Gaulle stayed at Buckingham Palace as the guest of the Queen.

[We] met General de Gaulle at 12.30 p.m. It was quite a ceremony. The Queen, Prince Philip and all the Royals. Field-Marshal Lord Alexander is attached to de Gaulle's [staff]; household cavalry [escort], state landaus, etc. There was quite a good crowd on the route, up Victoria Street, Whitehall, etc.[1]

In the course of the evening I went to call upon him in his apartments in Buckingham Palace for an hour's talk from 6.00 to 7.00 p.m.

The General seemed very relaxed. He gave a good account of his talks with Khrushchev. He feels that we should start the Summit with disarmament. On Berlin, he thinks that Khrushchev will agree, in the end, to something like the proposal which the Western Foreign Ministers made at Geneva last summer.

De Gaulle thinks that Khrushchev *does* want a 'détente'—*does* want disarmament, but that (except perhaps for Eisenhower) the Americans want neither.[1]

[1] 5 April 1960.

G2

The State Dinner at the Palace was carried out with its traditional magnificence and clearly gave considerable pleasure to the French. The General behaved with his usual courtesy and dignity. Since my mother-in-law, the Dowager Duchess of Devonshire, had died a few days before, my wife went to Chatsworth with the children for the funeral, and accordingly I did not go to the Guildhall ceremony. On the following day 'I was told that the audience was very enthusiastic and de Gaulle made a good speech'.[1] In the evening we had a formal dinner at the French Embassy. 'All very grand, but all the same people as last night.'[1]

7 April was a very busy day with no work accomplished but ceremonies of outstanding beauty and significance.

> 10.00 a.m. a fine military review on Horse Guards. The weather was bad. 11.30 a.m. Westminster Hall. A wonderfully impressive ceremony. De Gaulle made a most interesting, generous and moving speech. He spoke entirely without a text, in French. His tribute to Sir Winston was good. He made a most friendly reference to me. Then, drinks with the Speaker, 12.15 to 1.00 p.m.
>
> Then Dorothy and I, with the Foreign Secretary, were hosts at a luncheon at Chelsea Hospital. This too was a fine performance. (Fortunately no speeches.)[2]

The General was very much taken with the Chelsea Hospital—the British equivalent to Les Invalides. It was a noble sight to see him review all the pensioners in their red coats and medals. On this day, at any rate, his affection for Britain seemed to make him forgetful of his suspicions.

About this time I received a message from Eisenhower which showed that he intended to treat the Paris Conference as a serious enterprise. He was very anxious that the meetings should not be formal. They should be small and intimate, without the great crowd of 'advisers' which made any real discussion almost impossible. He sent me a draft of a letter which he proposed to send to Khrushchev and he was, at the same time, consulting de Gaulle. If we both agreed he would send off his message. All this was very encouraging, and I began to entertain high hopes. I had worked hard to achieve

[1] 6 April 1960.   [2] 7 April 1960.

the Summit, and in the course of a long campaign I had had to overcome the lack of interest and even the resistance of France and America, and the suspicions of Germany. I had been accused of pursuing this plan merely for political advantage at home. This I knew to be unfair and untrue. I had seen enough of two wars to feel myself dedicated to the opportunity of making at least a beginning of reasonable relations between the two worlds that had sprung into being—the Communist and the Free World. If at the same time the first stage of disarmament—the abolition of nuclear tests—could be achieved, if perhaps the immediate problem of access to Berlin could be resolved, this Summit meeting would indeed be justified. Moreover, having got agreement that it should be in Paris under the presidency of General de Gaulle I felt sure that we would have the lively support of the French Government and people. In addition, the concept of a yearly meeting of the four Heads of State in Paris, Moscow, Washington and London had been virtually accepted. We were therefore on the eve of a great step forward. Perhaps future generations would look back on this meeting as the beginning of a new era.

We were not due to leave for Paris until the middle of May and I had, as already described, some anxious moments during the Conference of Commonwealth Prime Ministers. But I was buoyed up during most of the London Conference by the even larger prospects which seemed to be in our grasp. Then, while the Commonwealth Conference was still sitting, the blow fell. I was staying at Chequers, a glorious warm and sunny day—7 May, when a message was brought to me which marked the opening stages of a drama which, in spite of periods of comedy and even farce, ended tragically. Before the third week of May had reached its close the grand edifice which I had worked so long and so painfully to build seemed totally and finally destroyed.

The story of the American U2 aeroplane began with an announcement made by Khrushchev on 5 May at a joint session of the Supreme Soviet. He stated that an American plane had been shot down over Russia on 1 May but gave no further details. These aeroplanes were used for photographic flights at very high altitudes and were, of course, a form of highly sophisticated espionage.

Realising the dangers of some mishap the American authorities had given instructions that in view of the Summit meeting this exercise should cease at the end of April. By an extraordinary piece of bad luck, the causes of which were then unknown to us, on the very last flight the plane had

> had a failure (perhaps of oxygen), lost height and been shot down ... the pilot did not go by his ejection chair (which would have automatically blown up the machine in the air) but by parachute. He did not poison himself ... but has been taken prisoner (with his poison needle in his pocket! The Russians have got the machine, the cameras, a lot of the photographs—and the pilot.[1]

On the same day the United States National Aeronautics and Space Administration announced that a U2 research plane, used 'to study meteorological conditions at high altitudes', had been missing since 1 May when its pilot reported that he was having oxygen difficulties over the Lake Van area of Turkey. President Eisenhower ordered a complete enquiry into the affair while the State Department spokesman, Mr. Lincoln White, declared that there was absolutely no deliberate attempt to violate Soviet airspace and never had been. Unhappily, on 7 May, Khrushchev made a second statement to the Supreme Soviet which made nonsense of the American disclaimer. He disclosed that the pilot of the U2, Captain Francis Gary Powers, was 'alive and well' in Soviet hands, that he had admitted he was on a spying mission over Soviet territory, that the plane's equipment was for aerial photography, that a film from the wreckage had been developed showing areas of the Soviet Union, and that Captain Powers had in his possession among other things a poison pin, a silent pistol, French gold francs, two gold watches, and 'seven gold rings for ladies'. After these disclosures the State Department the same day denied there had been any authorisation by the Administration of the flight Khrushchev had described, but said 'U2 aircraft have made flights along the frontiers of the free world for the past four years' as a precaution against surprise attack.

This was the news that was being brought to me while I was

[1] 7 May 1960.

awaiting my Commonwealth guests in the hope of finding some solution to the difficulties and dangers surrounding the Commonwealth Prime Ministers' Conference. Although I tried to keep a bold face and devote myself to the immediate work in hand it was hard to avoid a feeling almost of despair.

> The President, State Department and Pentagon have all told separate and conflicting stories, and are clearly in a state of panic.
> Khrushchev has made two very amusing and effective speeches, attacking the Americans for spying incompetently and lying incompetently too. He may declare the Summit off. Or the Americans may be stung into doing so.
> Quite a pleasant Saturday—the Commonwealth in pieces and the Summit doomed ![1]

On Sunday, 8 May, I had no direct news, but it seemed a very queer story.

> The pilot could *not* (say the experts) have parachuted from 70,000 feet and landed alive. Why did he not use the ejection seat, which would have automatically set off a mechanism to destroy the aeroplane ?[2]

That evening I was informed that an urgent letter had arrived from Khrushchev. Accordingly the Soviet Ambassador called at No. 10 the next morning. Although the letter was full of complaints I was relieved to find that there was no suggestion that the Summit would not take place. In view of the type of Cold War statements which American statesmen were still making Khrushchev doubted the sincerity with which they would go to Paris. He complained of the support for Adenauer, the provocation of the spy flights and, above all, about President Eisenhower's announcement that he would not be able to stay for more than a week in Paris and if the discussions continued his place would be taken by Vice-President Nixon. All this led him to wonder whether the Americans were really taking the Conference seriously. Nevertheless, to my immense relief the letter made no threat to cancel the Conference or to bring its proceedings prematurely to an end. Indeed the concluding passages declared that he had reached no such decision. It ended

[1] 7 May 1960.   [2] 8 May 1960.

with an appeal which, in view of the provocation of which he could reasonably complain, seemed to me to be a clear sign that he wished the Conference to proceed :

> Keeping in mind our talks together, the value of which we both recognise and ... being aware of your realistic approach to the assessment of the international situation I allow myself not only to express to you my apprehensions but I also wish to express the confidence that you will correctly understand the motives I have been guided by. If I approach you today with this letter, I am doing it solely for the sake of the success of the cause of peace and for the sake of the solution of the questions which still separate the Powers, especially due to the fact that remnants of the Second World War still exist in Europe.
>
> I hope that all the participants of the Conference will have a mutual desire to reach understanding on the questions to be considered at the Summit Conference and that we all shall act being fully aware of the responsibility which rests with our countries and with us, as the leaders of states vested with high authority.

The next day while I was engaged in the Commonwealth Conference careful study was given by the Foreign Office to the reply to Khrushchev's letter. I was not altogether satisfied with the draft and accordingly,

> Philip de Zulueta and I have composed one of our own, to which Foreign Secretary has agreed. It has been despatched.[1]

The letter ran as follows :

> I have carefully studied your letter to me of 8 May which your Ambassador delivered on the morning of 9 May.
>
> Let me say at once that I was grateful to you for so frankly setting out your apprehensions about the Summit Conference. May I reply with equal frankness ? I will not try to comment on the detailed points you mention, which caused you concern, except to say that I know that President Eisenhower is devoted to the cause of peace and really anxious for the success of the Summit meeting. When we met last year I was keen to encourage the idea of meetings between Heads of Government because I sincerely

----

[1] 10 May 1960.

believed, as I believe you did, that such meetings offered the best hope of making real progress on important international issues. Since then there has really been considerable progress and looking back on the efforts which all of us have made in the last twelve months I do not think that we need be despondent.

As you know, I have held the view that some relaxation of tension which would make possible discussions between the Heads of Government would be an advantage to all of us. I did not wish for this relaxation of tension because of some vague belief that we could evade important questions by pretending that they do not exist. On the contrary I wished to see a position reached in which the four Heads of Government could sit down together in a serious spirit to make a start in solving those questions on which unhappily there are still differences of view between us. Such discussions are the only hope which I see for progress for our peoples and for the world.

In the past year I believe that all the Heads of Government who are to meet in Paris next week have made some contribution to this atmosphere of negotiation. If I may say so I think that you yourself made a great contribution after your talks with President Eisenhower in the United States last autumn in removing what at one time seemed to be a serious obstacle to the Summit meeting being held at all. I think you would agree that President Eisenhower and President de Gaulle have also played their part. Perhaps we may now be too inclined to take this progress for granted ; but I do not believe that it has been the intention of any of us to make our work in Paris more difficult.

Of course it is an almost universal problem of politics that when situations improve new dangers often appear. If problems are acute and even dangerous, then no one thinks of anything else. But when solutions seem to be in sight, or at least the two sides begin to talk the language of discussion rather than the language of crisis, then to some extent people begin to take this happier state of affairs for granted. The balance is always difficult to strike.

It would indeed be wrong for any of us to underestimate the difficulties of the problems with which we shall deal at our meeting next week. I agree with your view that we shall only make step-by-step progress to resolve these difficulties if all of us sincerely work for mutually acceptable solutions.

Since we had the opportunity of discussion during my visit to the Soviet Union you have yourself had talks with President Eisenhower and President de Gaulle. I have myself no doubt that both of them are coming to the Summit meeting with a serious determination to do the best that they can for the peace of the world and the future of mankind. I am sure that your talks with these two statesmen must have convinced you of their sincerity. So, in spite of the difficulties I am hopeful that we shall make progress.

I was glad to learn that President de Gaulle has suggested that we should, so far as possible, conduct our deliberations in Paris in a private manner and not by means of public exchanges in a large assembly. As I ventured to say to you when I was in the Soviet Union, however desirable it may be to put on record one's own point of view before the world, diplomacy by public statement does not always help serious negotiation. I was pleased to hear from President de Gaulle that in general you agreed with this view although you expressed the opinion that in certain circumstances it might be necessary to explain our points of view to public opinion during the conference. Of course we cannot lay down in advance exactly how we should conduct our talks, but I would hope that the circumstances which you fear will not arise. Naturally, we may at some stage have to give some public indication of what our positions are. But the important thing is that we should try to avoid doing this in such a way or at such a time as to make it more difficult to make progress in the private discussions which I hope will prove so valuable.

I look forward very much to renewing in Paris on 16 May the friendly acquaintance and intimate discussions which commenced during my visit to your country last spring.

Meanwhile, on 9 May, the Secretary of State, Chris Herter, had issued another somewhat equivocal statement admitting that the 'extensive aerial surveillance' though 'normally of a peripheral character' was 'occasionally by penetration.' He stressed, however, that 'specific missions of these unarmed aircraft have not been subject to presidential authorization', though since the beginning of his Administration President Eisenhower had ordered the gathering 'by every possible means' of 'information required to protect the United States against surprise attack'. Mr. Herter also said the Government of the United States would be derelict in its responsibility . . . if it did not . . . take such measures as are possible unilaterally to lessen and overcome the danger of surprise attack. In fact the United States has not and does not shirk this responsibility.

Even now I felt the situation might be retrieved if only the Americans would make no further statements until they reached Paris. Unhappily in spite of our appeals they seemed to have become quite distracted and without any clear plan. The President should have said nothing or at the most he should have taken the line that British Prime Ministers have always taken of these security operations or complaints of espionage—that these are matters which are not discussed. Khrushchev might well have accepted either silence or some formal disclaimer. Unhappily, with characteristic honesty, Eisenhower stated, at a Press Conference, that the U2 flights had been made with his knowledge and approval. Although on the same day, 11 May, Khrushchev had stated publicly that he expected the Summit to take place and even on his arrival in Paris issued a fairly moderate statement, yet it was clear that the hardening of the Soviet line was largely due to Eisenhower's unlucky admission. Those who had studied most carefully the situation in Moscow were aware that there was considerable opposition to Khrushchev's policy of 'peaceful co-existence' and to the whole concept of a détente between the East and the West. These feelings were, of course, equally dominant in Peking. Khrushchev was not in Stalin's unique position; for by abandoning the terror as an instrument of policy he had markedly weakened the autocratic power enjoyed by his predecessor. Even if the President had made it clear that he had now ordered the abandonment of U2 flights (which he had) instead of leaving this to be dragged out of him when he got to Paris, Khrushchev might have thought it possible to continue. From his first letter to me I was convinced that he would try to find some way out, in order to allow the Summit to take place to which he was as much committed as I.

When I had to speak at the end of a debate on Foreign Affairs on 12 May, the mood of the House of Commons was helpful and even optimistic. One member said with perfect truth that in the last few days many leading men on both sides had lost wonderful opportunities to keep their mouths shut. I declared that we could still look forward to the meeting as the first of a series which might gradually achieve real progress. Such was the feeling of the whole House, which had not failed to observe the distinction which Khrushchev was so far making between the propaganda use of this incident and his personal view of the usefulness of some Summit agreement.

I sent a note to Butler on 14 May :

> I was on the point of dictating a letter to you when you rang up tonight. I am indeed grateful to you for your thought. I will keep you closely informed of what happens in Paris. I go with a good deal of anxiety—but then, one never knows : the Commonwealth Conference at one time looked hopeless but turned out not too badly.
>
> It is a wonderful help to me with all these troubles to feel that the House of Commons and the Party are in your safe hands.

I left for Paris on the morning of 15 May full of apprehension. After arriving at the Embassy I learnt that Khrushchev had asked to see me at 4.30 p.m. Before that there was a quadripartite meeting at the Elysée :

> De Gaulle, Eisenhower, Adenauer, Harold Macmillan. It was pretty formal—no one got down to brass tacks.[1]

It was clear that everything must depend upon the Russian mood.

> Khrushchev came, not alone or with only the interpreter (as I expected) but in full state—Gromyko (Foreign Affairs), Marshal Malinovsky (Defence) and one or two others. He made a speech in violent terms, attacked the U.S.A., President Eisenhower, the Pentagon, reactionary and imperialist forces generally; all (of course) in connection with the U2 aircraft shot down over Russia. He said that his *friend* (bitterly repeated again and again) his friend Eisenhower had betrayed him. He then proceeded with a formal declaration, actually read from a bit of paper, but not left as a formal *note*, in terms which we learned a little later from the French was a declaration in the same terms as he had left with de Gaulle.

[1] 15 May 1960.

[In this declaration he stated that] it would be impossible to carry on the Summit Conference, unless President Eisenhower (a) condemned what had been done by air espionage, (b) expressed his regret, (c) said he would never do it again, (d) punished the criminals.

I did my best to reason with Khrushchev (who was personally quite agreeable) but did not succeed in appeasing him. . . .

I reminded him of his letter to me delivered only a few days ago (but *after* the aircraft incident) in which he discussed . . . *how* the Summit Conference should be conducted and what might be the best lines of progress. Khrushchev did not deny this, but was obviously incensed by the statements made by Herter and Eisenhower during last week, which he thought aggravated their offence. President Eisenhower had justified the 'espionage flights' and threatened to go on with them.[1]

In spite of Khrushchev's indignation I still believed that he would not press his feelings to the point of disrupting the whole Conference. After Khrushchev had left my staff reported the conversation to the French and the Americans.

The French view was cynical, but logical. The Conference was over. The Americans were more hopeful and thought it largely bluster. The British thought the Conference might be saved if the President would take a reasonable line—especially undertake to make no more U2 flights.[1]

This incidentally involved no great sacrifice because it was clear that whatever might have been its advantages this particular method was now 'blown'—like an agent who has been caught or exposed. There was much coming and going between all the staffs of the three Western countries who seemed to be all on excellent terms. At six o'clock there was a tripartite meeting :

De Gaulle, Eisenhower, Harold Macmillan—with only translators. . . . No one quite knew what to do or how it would develop. De Gaulle was pretty sure that Khrushchev would press it to the point of rupture. Eisenhower was not convinced, and I refused to accept this conclusion. Anyway, we must work to prevent the Conference breaking down before it has even started.

[1] 15 May 1960.

Dinner quietly at Embassy. I went to bed with rather a heavy heart but not without hope.

It was a bad sign that the Russians had refused the *private* session with which the Conference had been planned to open— four Heads of Government only (with four interpreters)—and demanded a *plenary* session. It was agreed that this should be held at 11.00 a.m. at the Elysée (instead of 10.00 a.m. arranged for the *private* session).[1]

The next day was one of the most agonising as well as exhausting which I have ever been through except, perhaps, in battle.

I was called at 7.15 a.m., having slept rather badly. I got to the American Embassy, where it had been arranged that I should have breakfast with President Eisenhower, before 8 a.m. We had our meal alone, in a . . . sitting-room upstairs, with the door open, and two French footmen, in cotton gloves, serving a series of rather improbable dishes. The President, after consuming some 'cereals' and (I think) some figs, was given a steak and some jelly. I was fortunate enough to get a boiled egg.

I thought Ike depressed and uncertain. The conversation was rather strained. I made it clear that we stood absolutely together. . . . and it was just bad luck that the Americans, after a great run of successes, had suffered this set-back. Anyway, the only thing was to make the best of things together. Ike seemed to cheer up at this, but still didn't quite know what to do. He had, of course, received yesterday evening, both from the French and from ourselves, a complete account of Khrushchev's démarche.

I asked him what he was going to say at 11 a.m. He said that his people had been working late on a text. But he had not seen the last version. At 8.45 a.m. or 9 a.m. Herter came in and at last the text was produced. It was *not* very good and much too truculent. Nor did it make it at all clear whether the Americans still claimed the right to make these flights (contrary to international law) or whether they were going to abandon them.

On this, a lot of other people began to crowd into the room and argue. There was great confusion, and some bitterness. Actually, I felt that the Americans were in considerable disarray. However, the phrase was finally agreed 'in point of fact, these

[1] 15 May 1960.

flights were suspended after the recent incident *and are not* to be resumed'.[1]

The meeting at the Elysée began just after 11. It was opened in a very dignified manner by de Gaulle, as President, with a few formal remarks welcoming the commencement of the Conference. Then the expected blow fell.

> Khrushchev—who sat on [de Gaulle's] left—with Eisenhower opposite and me on his right—then claimed the right to speak.

He stood up to address us, and

> with a gesture reminiscent of Mr. Micawber ... pulled a large wad of folio typewritten papers out of his pocket and began to speak. (The interpretation was done by paragraphs.) Khrushchev tried to pulverise Ike (as Micawber did Heep) by a mixture of abuse, vitriolic and offensive, and legal argument. It must have lasted (with French and English translation) three-quarters of an hour. It was a most unpleasant performance. The President could scarcely contain himself, but he did. When Khrushchev had finished, Ike ... read his declaration very quietly and with restraint. It was short and quite effective. In addition to his demands (apology, punishment of offenders, no further over-flying) Khrushchev added two points—both intended to be as offensive as possible to Eisenhower. The two new points were (*a*) that the Summit should now be postponed for six to eight months—i.e. till the Presidency of Eisenhower had ended (*b*) that Eisenhower's proposed visit to Russia (in return for Khrushchev's to U.S.A.) must be cancelled. Both of these were couched in ironical and wounding terms.[1]

I followed President Eisenhower and contented myself with a few simple phrases.

> I deplored that after a long and painful ascent towards the Summit, it should be found to be so clouded. I understood the feelings that had been aroused, but I made this appeal. What had happened, had happened. We all knew that espionage was a fact of life, and a disagreeable one. Moreover, most espionage activities involved the violation of national sovereignties. I then went

[1] 16 May 1960.

on to say that Mr. Khrushchev's whole argument had been based on statements that over-flights were still American policy. That was not so. I then quoted the President's words 'and are not to be resumed'. Therefore, the conference would not be 'under threat'. I said I was glad that Mr. Khrushchev had not suggested the abandonment of the Summit Conference, but only its adjournment. But *ce qui est déferré est perdu*. (What is postponed, is lost.) The eyes of the world were on the Heads of Governments, and the hopes of the peoples of the world rested on them. I hoped, after these explanations, we could proceed with our work, and I appealed to them to do this.[1]

De Gaulle then made an admirable speech, clear, logical and effective. He pointed out that since the object of the Conference was to reduce internatoinal tension the events of recent days were a reason not for abandoning it but for continuing its work to a successful conclusion. The incident was an additional reason for our meeting. He went on to point out that the Russian satellites or 'sputniks' could be just as much complained about as a form of espionage as the American U2. This point was made with great skill in the following words.

> In the present world situation, the overflight of an aircraft or of any device can be considered a grave element whose nature can increase international tension. This overflight, or these overflights, by devices or aircraft, may be expected to develop in the future. What applies to aircraft on this matter applies as much to satellites.
>
> At the present time, anyway, a Soviet satellite passes each day over the sky of France. It flies over it at an altitude much higher than an airplane, but it still flies over it.[2]

He went on to say :

> As time goes on, more of these overflights will occur. They risk becoming a sort of second nature in our universe. Actually,

[1] 16 May 1960.

[2] *Documents relating to the meetings between the President of the French Republic, the President of the United States of America, the Chairman of the Council of Ministers of the Union of Soviet Socialist Republics and the Prime Minister of the United Kingdom—Paris—15–17 May 1960. Cmnd. 1052 (H.M.S.O., May 1960).*

all these devices have now the possibility, the planes and the satellites, to photograph the territories of all the nations and to carry terrible destruction. All the powers meeting today have the duty of examining this question in the framework of general disarmament, as, in fact, had been scheduled. If it is desired, France would be ready to make concrete proposals on this subject and to do this immediately.

Anyway, it is not good for the interest of the whole of humanity that a break-up taking place today, could occur on the basis of such a local incident.[1]

After these statements there was a long argument.

Khrushchev tried to make out that the President's abandonment of overflights only applied till January 1961 (when his period of office ended). This was explained as merely the only pledge which a President of U.S.A. could give constitutionally. Then Khrushchev said that the pledge was not made publicly. So I proposed an agreed communiqué of our proceedings, making this public. No. Khrushchev would publish the whole text of his offensive speech. The argument went on till nearly 2 p.m. and then we gave it up. However, it was agreed to take [time] to think it over and perhaps have private and bilateral talks, before an opening meeting of the Conference at 11 a.m. next day.[2]

I was still determined to try to save the Conference if at all possible. To do this I would see personally, and if possible alone, de Gaulle, Eisenhower and Khrushchev in that order. These meetings began at 6 p.m., and with a short interval for some food at the British Embassy, lasted until midnight.

De Gaulle was charming, but 'not amused'. He thought there was no hope of saving the Conference. Khrushchev's brutality was deliberate. They had made the decision in Moscow, before he came, for whatever reason. However, he had no objection to my efforts.

President Eisenhower was relaxed, but talked very strongly against Khrushchev. He was a real S.O.B. He did not see what more he could do. He had gone a long way in his offer. He could

[1] Ibid.   [2] 16 May 1960.

not 'condemn' the action which he had authorised. . . . The demand for punishment was absurd. What more could he do? I said I supposed he could 'say he was sorry'—or, preferably, [make] a formal diplomatic apology. But I really could not press Ike much further. His staff (including Herter) obviously thought he should have reacted more strongly or left the room himself. It was a terrible thing for their President to be insulted in this way.

Khrushchev was polite, but quite immovable. The Marshal (silent, immovable, hardly even blinking) and Gromyko (also silent) as well as others were present. (I went to the Russian Embassy.) However, at the end of a very long talk, I got the impression that he would not act . . . without seeing me again.[1]

But the next day began ominously.

My hopes were rudely and rapidly dashed. Khrushchev has given an informal Press Conference (at 9.25 a.m.) in which he reiterated *all* his demands on the Americans.

However, we all three Westerners (Heads of Governments, followed by Ministers of Foreign Affairs) met at 10 a.m. at the Elysée. It was agreed that de Gaulle should now send out a formal invitation for the Summit Conference to start the work at 3 p.m. This was done. Naturally, both the U.S. and U.K. will accept.[2]

As we were leaving the Elysée

President Eisenhower asked if he could come with me to our Embassy. He had only been in it once and would like a talk. He and I left the Elysée in Ike's *open* car and drove the short distance to our Embassy. He obviously wanted this very much and my agreement gratified him. . . . After a short talk in the garden, we went off for a drive (also in the open car) only returning for luncheon. We had some good and useful talk. But the driver and detective could overhear, which limited the scope of talk. There were large crowds everywhere, and we were much applauded. Ike's object was clear—ingenuously clear. But it suited me. If Khrushchev must break up the Summit Conference, there is no reason to let him break up the Anglo-American alliance.[2]

[1] 16 May 1960.   [2] 17 May 1960.

We duly met at the Elysée at three o'clock. Just before the meeting the consulate of the Soviet Embassy had telephoned to ask, on Khrushchev's behalf, whether his conditions had yet been fulfilled.

Then a series of most complicated messages arrived [from the Russians] one cancelling or expanding another, with almost ludicrous effect. Couve de Murville acted as the Mercury for these strange messages. [In view of their] general tenor, which was to ask whether the Russian requirements had been 'met', [both Eisenhower and de Gaulle] wanted to issue our formal declaration that the Conference was at an end. I strongly objected to this and had rather an unpleasant scene. But I said that we must not seem to be breaking up the Conference ourselves. All the world had looked forward to this day. Churches and chapels everywhere had prayed for success. We could not 'call it a day' on a telephone message. Let [Khrushchev] at least write a letter, so that we had some agreed document to reply on. He ought to write, anyway, as a matter of courtesy. Although de Gaulle thought nothing of the general argument, the last point did appeal to him.[1]

At first it appeared that Khrushchev refused to reply in writing, but after several interchanges a statement was brought at 4.15 p.m. on his behalf. It ran as follows :

I am ready to take part in the meeting with President de Gaulle, Mr. Macmillan and President Eisenhower, to have an exchange of views on the questions raised by the American spokesman, if the following conditions are fulfilled : if the United States has, in fact, decided to condemn the treacherous intrusion of American military aircraft into Soviet air space, publicly to express their regrets for this intrusion, to punish those responsible, and to give assurances that in future there will be no further intrusion. After having received such assurances, we will be ready to take part in the Summit Conference.[2]

After some discussion it was agreed that de Gaulle should send a formal reply on behalf of the three Western members of the Conference. The significant passage ran as follows :

[1] 17 May 1960.   [2] Cmnd. 1052.

In answer to the questions which you put in your letter I wish to make it clear that this meeting was intended to begin the discussion on the problems which we had agreed to examine at the Summit Conference. The meeting should thus have constituted the first session of this Conference.[1]

The general temper of my colleagues had not been improved by the news that had come in regarding Khrushchev's activities. Not content with the Press Conference, he seemed to have travelled into the countryside accompanied by Pressmen and held a series of meetings wherever he could collect a few villagers to listen to him. De Gaulle treated this with the utmost contempt. These election meetings 'in a barn' did not appeal to him.

Before we separated

after a long wrangle with the Americans on one phrase, an agreed statement was prepared, to be put out by the three Powers when there was no further hope. The statement is important because it pledges us to work for Peace and says quite clearly 'they themselves remain ready to take part in such negotiations at any suitable time in the future'. I was very pleased to get this agreed text—especially the earlier part pledging ourselves to negotiation as the means to settle 'all outstanding international questions'. But this means really 'another Summit Conference with a new President'. Can President Eisenhower and the Americans generally 'pocket their insult'? I fear it has been difficult to get agreement on the words (which in view of Khrushchev's time-table is a direct attack on Ike). But we got them.

The next question was when to issue this declaration? My colleagues pressed for [an immediate release]. I refused and asked for 10 a.m. on the eighteenth. (I intended further bilateral talks with the Russians, in a last bid for success.) After a great struggle, we got agreement to *meet* again at the Elysée at 9.30 p.m. and to make a final decision then.

My purpose in this was to make every effort possible for the Conference to start and *not* to appear to be the first to make the official break.[2]

Later in the evening

[1] Cmnd. 1052.   [2] 17 May 1960.

and on our invitation, Gromyko came for a long talk with Selwyn Lloyd at the British Embassy. Gromyko made it clear that they had fully decided to break up the Conference. But he was quite hopeful about going on with the 'Test' Conference at Geneva. (Indeed, it has made good progress yesterday and today !)[1]

At 9.30 p.m. Eisenhower, de Gaulle and I met again at the Elysée to revise the final text of our declaration. I could no longer ask for delay. It was accordingly issued at 10 p.m.

It was well worded, especially the second paragraph, which ran as follows :

'[The Three Heads of Government] regret that these discussions, so important for world peace, could not take place. For their part, they remain unshaken in their conviction that all outstanding international questions should be settled, not by the use of threat of force but by peaceful means through negotiation. They themselves remain ready to take part in such negotiations at any suitable time in the future.'

So ended—before it had ever begun—the Summit Conference.[1]

I invited Khrushchev to come and see me before he left. He arrived at 10.30 a.m. on 18 May,

but with all his followers or his 'tail', as a Highland chief would have said. . . . The conversation was stiff, but not uninteresting. He maintained his desire for 'peaceful co-existence', for another Summit Conference etc. I said all this depended on what he actually did—not what he said—during the interval. He said that I ought to have brought more pressure on President Eisenhower to accept all, instead of only one, of his terms. I said, 'Do you really think that?' It was quite a short interview, as he was on his way to the Elysée, to say goodbye to de Gaulle, his host. He did *not* make any attempt to see President Eisenhower.[2]

The President called in the afternoon and we had an hour's talk alone.

He seemed very upset at the turn of events, so I tried my best to comfort him. But I said we must now really try to get rid of divisions in the Free World—about nuclear arms, about NATO,

[1] 17 May 1960.   [2] 18 May 1960.

about economic grouping (Sixes and Sevens), etc., etc. I thought we might revive the idea floated last autumn at Rambouillet —i.e. a sort of Anglo-Franco-American informal group. He agreed, so long as it could really be informal, and the other organisations (NATO, CENTO, SEATO) not annoyed or alarmed.[1]

There was a final meeting at the Elysée at 5 p.m. :

De Gaulle and Couve de Murville, President Eisenhower and Herter, Harold Macmillan and Selwyn Lloyd—a few officials. The accounts of Khrushchev's [second] 'Press Conference' in Paris were just coming through. It was a terrible performance, reminiscent of Hitler at his worst. He threatens, rants, uses filthy words of abuse (Germans are bastards, etc. !) but—if you analyse it clearly—he does not actually commit himself to anything. He has a draft treaty with East Germany. He has the pen in his hand. But he does not say just *when* he will sign. He also—in the intervals between the play-acting and the invective—holds out hopes for another Summit meeting soon. *Qualis artifex* if he would only perish !!!!!!!!!!![1]

There was then a long discussion about what we should do in the event of Khrushchev's signing a peace treaty with East Germany. It was agreed that we could not object to the treaty itself; but the question of how best to handle the protection of the Western rights in the city of Berlin was not easy to resolve. However, I was glad to find that both Eisenhower and de Gaulle were very practical in their approach.

We passed then to the future structure of our relations. Eisenhower opened up on a 'tripartite' system, under the cover of the Summit Powers. He did not want to disturb existing machinery. De Gaulle accepted this—reminded us of the disasters which had resulted from *not* acting closely together.[1]

On returning to the Embassy I found the British journalists who had just come from Khrushchev's Press Conference at the Palais de Chaillot.

They seemed (especially the Left-Wing papers) really shocked

[1] 18 May 1960.

by Khrushchev's 'Press Conference'. They would talk of nothing but Hitler.[1]

After dinner we began to draft a statement for the House of Commons.

> I telephoned to Butler who did not think the statement necessary before Friday at 11 a.m. I was anxious to have another day in Paris—to rest, and to see both Debré (French Prime Minister) and de Gaulle. He said Gaitskell would not press the point. I also said we should not have the debate too soon. In Khrushchev's words 'let the dust settle'.[1]

The next day, 19 May, after a very useful talk with Debré, for whom I had a great regard, and a meeting of the Commonwealth Ambassadors in Paris, there was a formal luncheon at the Elysée

> in honour of the British. (Yesterday was for the Americans, who left early this morning.) Very grand, very stately, very friendly. De Gaulle seemed in a good humour. I told him we must bring about economic as well as political co-operation in Western Europe. Could we not use this set-back to do this? He agreed, in rather a pontifical way.
> He took me after luncheon to see the little 'Salon d'Argent'— the room in which Napoleon abdicated after Waterloo, and the table on which he signed the document. De Gaulle seemed to take a rather mordant pleasure in these memories![2]

There was now little to be done except try to conceal as best I could my disappointment amounting almost to despair—so much attempted so little achieved. On getting back to London I found a charming and sympathetic message from the Queen. In sending her, on 19 May, a long statement of the whole story for her information and records I could not but express my gratitude at her kindness.

> I hope I may say how heartened I was on my return to 10 Downing Street to receive the message which Sir Michael Adeane had transmitted on your behalf. It is indeed sad to have returned without anything to show for our work of the last few years, and I shall not conceal from Your Majesty the shock and disappointment which I have sustained.

[1] 18 May 1960.   [2] 19 May 1960.

The President, on his return on 18 May, sent me a pleasant enough message but the harm had been done.

> That we did not succeed in our hopes to bring to the world a little greater assurance of the peace that must somehow be achieved is the unhappy fact that we must accept. Certainly you did everything that you possibly could to bring about a degree of civilised behaviour in the arrogant and intransigent man from Moscow; no one could have tried harder. I applaud your efforts; no one could have done more.
>
> As we have said in our meetings, we shall have to make a reappraisal of the facts of today's world. I shall be in touch with you, I know, within the near future.
>
> Meantime, my thanks and warm personal regard. Always your devoted friend.

There were the usual telegrams to be sent to all the Commonwealth Prime Ministers, and a day or two later a pleasant answer from de Gaulle in reply to my letter of thanks for his hospitality and guidance.

> I am very grateful for what you say in your letter, for which I thank you.
>
> I assure you that I appreciate the community of outlook and action which we have shown during these days in Paris, which I well realise, moreover, have disappointed you in other respects. Like you I hope and believe that all in all our alliance has been strengthened, and that, to my mind, is the most important thing of all.
>
> Rest assured at all events that I was glad to see you again. I too hope that we can soon meet once more.[1]

The universal sympathy from the leaders of the Commonwealth and from the Press was reflected in the House of Commons.

[1] J'ai été très sensible aux termes de votre lettre et vous en remercie.

Croyez bien que j'ai apprécié la communauté de vues et d'action qui s'est affirmée entre nous à l'occasion de ces journées de Paris, dont je comprends fort bien, d'ailleurs, qu'elles vous aient déçu à d'autres égards. Comme vous, je souhaite et je crois qu'au total notre alliance s'en trouvera renforcée et c'est, à mon avis, ce qui est, par dessus tout, essentiel.

Soyez assuré, en tous cas, que j'ai été heureux de vous revoir. J'espère, moi aussi, que nous pourrons bientôt nous rencontrer de nouveau. (21 May 1960.)

We finished the statement last night and had some final touches this morning. Cabinet at 10 a.m. (in House of Commons). All the colleagues friendly. Some valuable additions or amendments were made. . . . The House (for a Friday) was very full — I should think 450 members. I got a good cheer.

The statement was received in silence, but with muffled applause at the end. Gaitskell behaved well. Grimond asked one polite . . . question. Shinwell made a kind remark and then it was over. (The Socialist fellow-travellers protested, but in vain.)[1]

There was one curious feature of Khrushchev's conduct of this whole affair. We had all been dreading what he would say in his mass meeting in East Berlin. While there were harsh words for Adenauer and Brandt, he made it clear that 'the time was not right for a separate Peace Treaty with East Germany. The present condition would be maintained until the next Summit Conference which he expected to take place in eight months' time.' This statement, according to all the Press reports, was not well received, but listened to in silence. In reflecting subsequently upon this strange development, I have often thought that all the experts throughout the world may have tried to read too much into what was, perhaps, a simple human reaction. It was certainly true that Khrushchev had risked much by his whole attitude of trying to achieve 'co-existence', and even some degree of co-operation, between the Communist and the non-Communist world. It was, of course, doctrinally dangerous and was especially criticised by the rigid dogmatists in China and Albania. He had rested very strongly upon his sincere admiration for Eisenhower which was shared by many of the leading soldiers of Russia and to whose straightforwardness, if his volume of reminiscences is authentic, Khrushchev paid tribute many years later. The U2 incident was a blow to the image which he had built up, and the inept American handling of the affair with all its denials, contradictions, reassessments and excuses must have given him genuine offence. Although an orthodox Communist, he was a human being — impulsive, emotional and capable of rapid changes of feeling. He may have acted partly under pressure and partly under a real sense of indignation. When he once got going on his

[1] 20 May 1960.

theme he could not easily control his words and relapsed into vulgar abuse. A greater man would have made all the capital he could by his protests, but would have seized the opportunity to rise above his feelings of injury and thus shown himself the dominant figure in world politics. By his actual handling of the affair he lost a great opportunity—but so, alas, did the whole world.

Lord Amory, after his retirement, with Lady Dorothy and Rachel Macmillan at a youth club in Ashdown Forest

'Heathcoat Amory is a sweet man—a really charming character. But...he feels his responsibilities almost too much.'

Chancellor of Oxford

'I have thoroughly enjoyed my post. . . . I have tried to carry out such duties as properly fall to the post conscientiously but not obtrusively.'

CHAPTER VIII

A Touch on the Brake

THE British economy, like the British weather, is apt to be variable. Nor do the professional forecasters show any more marked success in the prognostications of economic changes than they do in the science of meteorology. The truth is that in both cases our island is almost as exposed to rapid alterations of pressure resulting from great movements across the oceans as from disturbances within its own limited area.

I was not surprised, therefore, when there was some fall in the reserves at the end of 1959, partly no doubt due to the large-scale 'dollar liberalisation' and the removal of controls on imports from the dollar area as well as from Western Europe, which took place in October and November of that year. During my absence in Africa I agreed to the raising of the Bank Rate, on 21 January, from 4 to 5 per cent. I was reluctant to do so, but I could not resist the long and balanced arguments that were sent to me. In particular much importance was attached to the action of the United States and Germany in raising their discount rates and thus attracting money to these centres. Meanwhile, though I accepted the Treasury advice I could not help observing in a note to the Chancellor of the Exchequer on 20 January 1960:

> it is sad that the United States and Germany should force all this upon us by their policies. If there is now to be a competition in discount and bank rates between the great international centres I would think this would mark the beginning of a very dangerous era.

Heathcoat Amory, whose success as Chancellor of the Exchequer was only equalled by his desire to retire as soon as possible into private life, began to show signs of concern. He had been exceedingly successful in his conduct of affairs which, in his own words,

H

had resulted in a combination of 'high production, a high level of employment and stable prices'. But now a little cloud had begun to show itself on the horizon, and the combination of increased estimates of public expenditure and the undoubted investment boom which resulted from our electoral victory raised new fears. Changing the metaphor into the jargon of the day there was a risk of 'the engine becoming overheated'. Perhaps the worst sign, in the eyes of many talented, if morose, critics was the fall in unemployment and the rise in unfilled vacancies. Writers in the *Economist*, for whom I had a deep respect, had long maintained that unemployment should be kept at the rate of 3 per cent in order to preserve a reasonably stable economy. I was constantly accused by these and other somewhat cold-blooded commentators of being far too much concerned about the personal tragedy of unemployed families. This was, it was alleged, a survival from the traumatic experience of Tees-side in the years of the Great Depression. It may be, of course, that this argument was correct and will still prove to be justified; but I found difficulty in accepting it at its face value. However, this large and apparently regrettable fall of the unemployment figures in recent months as well as other symptoms were held to show that we were moving into a new period of stormy weather with all the familiar signs of a developing trade deficit, and corresponding pressure upon the reserves. Of course, it must be remembered that in the times about which I am writing we were dealing with relatively narrow margins. We had not reached the days of spectacular deficits and prodigious borrowings which were to characterise a future period. Even in the perennial problem of trying to secure that wage increases bore a proper relation to increased productivity or, in simple language, were honestly earned, we were not faced with the outrageous demands which have since been put forward. For instance, while I was on my travels urgent telegrams passed regarding the prospect of another railway dispute. It had been agreed in 1958, as part of the settlement between the Transport Commission and the unions, that an independent committee would be set up to work out a fair wage structure based on examination of rates of pay for comparable jobs in other industries. This report, under the chairmanship of Professor C. W. Guillebaud, was due in April 1960; but even the promise of the Transport Commission to backdate any awards to January seemed unlikely to satisfy the railway unions. The National Union of Railwaymen demanded an immediate 'interim' award; to this Sir Brian Robertson, the Chairman of the British Transport Commission, was disposed to agree.

On 9 February, however, Guillebaud informed the parties that his report could be out by the end of February or the first week in March. Accordingly, Sir Brian Robertson suggested that an interim award backdated to 11 January should be made within a week of the publication of the report. The N.U.R. refused this very reasonable offer, and a strike was announced. In this attitude the N.U.R. did not have support of the staff of the other unions—the Salaried Staff Association and the Associated Society for Locomotive Engineers and Firemen. The situation was as usual complicated by the varying interests of the unions concerned. The N.U.R. wanted a percentage increase throughout; while the other unions were anxious to maintain stable differentials. The necessary emergency plans were put in hand, but there seemed little purpose in a purely 'face-saving' dispute. Four per cent had been generally agreed even before the discussions opened, and it was now well known that Guillebaud would allot a higher figure. The Cabinet, therefore, with my full telegraphic approval, supported Robertson in reaching a settlement of 5 per cent. Yet this additional 1 per cent was fiercely attacked by the financial pundits.

Thus the prospect of further railway payments, the increased estimates of some £340 m. and the likelihood of other wage increases and the pressure upon sterling all began now to reappear like familiar spectres from the past. As I have already recorded, these forebodings poured in upon me during our sea voyage from Cape Town with irritating persistence. We could only seek encouragement from the words of Keble's noble hymn, appropriately chosen for the service on board, 'the hopes that soothe, the fears that brace'.

On 17 February, after my return to Downing Street, I had an hour with the Chancellor of the Exchequer and the Governor of the Bank together.

They do each other harm—for there is a sudden mood of despondency and alarm. We are spending too much. We are too rich. Wages are going up. Imports are going up. Unemployment is falling. We are in for another inflationary boom. I said, 'What about Savings?' This rather took them aback. But I am worried —not so much about the boom but the loss of nerve. (I sense that the Treasury officials are much more calm—as indeed they were during the Thorneycroft crisis.)[1]

It was the same old story; and even the grace and courtesy combined with a most delicate sense of humour which were characteristic of Heathcoat Amory could not conceal his anxieties.

Luncheon, Chancellor of the Exchequer. I foresee another row looming up. Governor of Bank and Chancellor are suddenly very pessimistic about the future.... So they want violent disinflationary measures and a fierce Budget.[2]

The next day I wrote to the Chancellor in the following terms:

The more I think about our conversation yesterday the more depressed I am.

Max Beerbohm once said that history does not repeat itself; it is the historians who repeat one another. This is certainly true of the economists and professors. They are very apt to make the same diagnosis and apply the same remedies although the circumstances may differ in character. The *Guardian* today rightly says: 'The economy is not yet working at full stretch. Many industries still have some capacity unused and there are reserves of labour in many parts of the country. At the same time sterling has not begun to come under pressure.' It is quite true that it goes on to point out some of the difficulties; railway wages, general rises in wage rates, increased expenditure, and so forth, and it concludes as follows: 'The question that may have to be answered next is how the Government can continue to exert the necessary disinflationary grip once the seasonal strain on the banks' resources is over.'

There is good sense in all this. It is probably true that when the banks' seasonal strain is over they will not be so sensitive to a mere failure to support the gilt-edged market, for they will not

[1] 17 February 1960.   [1] 26 February 1960.

have to sell so much. But the obvious conclusion is that we should use the other weapons, the impact of which they cannot very easily avoid—the Special Deposits. If you like, add Hire Purchase, to taste. All this seems capable of being done without too much confusion. Moreover, it is this which is the really effective weapon. An additional £50m.–£100 m. of taxation in the Budget will have practically no effect. It is purely marginal. After all the national income is of the order of £20,000 m. Do you mean to say that taking away 1/200th part of spending power is going to alter the result of this year's out-turn on the balance of payments and the overseas monetary position? I just do not believe it. Moreover, following the Budget of last year and the Election last autumn, a deflationary Budget would either be very foolish or very dishonest. Unless it is supposed that we would be thought very modern and up-to-date, like those young ladies who oscillate daily between the stimulant and the tranquilliser. The new Progressive Conservatism will turn out to be a policy of alternation between Benzedrine and Relaxa-tabs. I don't like it at all.

For these reasons I still think that you should consider a *stand-still* Budget. By this I mean that any minor concessions which have to be made (like Entertainments Tax, something for the widows, orphans, etc.) should be met by increased taxation to that amount. Of course, in the calculations one could give oneself a certain favourable margin. But to go out openly to collect an extra £50 m.–£100 m. seems to be both unnecessary and psychologically bad. A gentle squeeze may be right; but it cannot be sensible to cheer the economy on vigorously one moment and then push it violently back the next. And there is of course the danger that all this, partly real (e.g. the restriction of bank lending) and partly psychological (e.g. your desire for a Budget surplus), will work too well. What will happen if the motor companies cancel their plans for expansion on Merseyside, etc? What will happen if Pressed Steel decide after all not to set up in the North East? What will happen if our Scottish plans, upon which so much depends, break down? Then I suppose we will have to go back to the stimulant instead of the soporific and the alternation will become not merely politically impossible but even ridiculous.

Moreover, what is all this based upon? Not the certainty of a loss on the balance of payments; but only upon a very shadowy calculation that our overseas monetary position at the end of the year may be rather less good than it is now. My confidence in the accuracy of figures of this sort is just about as much as I have in Old Moore. The fact is that nobody can make these calculations accurately. You will remember that the shipping figure was £100 m. or more wrong. When we complain, we are just told that it is too bad. I have not much confidence in any of these figures; and certainly not enough to reverse what seems to me a sound policy of expansion and start again the whole dreary cycle of squeeze and disinflation. It is the policy of Sisyphus, and the Governor is well cast for the part.

I put these views strongly, because I have found that it is the only way to make anyone pay attention to what one says. But I would be grateful if you would have them in mind for our next talk.

I was very much struck by a paper on export promotion circulated by the Minister of State, Board of Trade. It is sensible and encouraging. But it makes it clear that it is much easier to sell exports at the right price from a buoyant home market than it is to do so from a depressed home market. For price depends on volume. One thing that stood out in this paper is the handicap we put on our exports by giving such short terms of credit. It used to be said that we did not want to lengthen credit for fear of stimulating other countries to outbid us. I think in fact they already do this, either overtly or covertly. Perhaps this credit question could be studied further.

I am sending a copy of this note to the Home Secretary [Butler] but to nobody else.

This was perhaps a rather prolix way of saying that I did not believe that violent reflationary measures were necessary and that a neutral Budget was all that was required.

Since I knew that Amory was very anxious to resign at least by the end of summer, I had to revise my plans with a view to a considerable reshuffle after the Budget and the Finance Bill were safely over.

Chancellor of the Exchequer seems oppressed by all his troubles. He would really like to resign and will certainly do so in the summer. But he will not, I feel sure, desert now.[1]

[1] 5 March 1960.

A week later he came to luncheon.

> We had a good talk and I am hopeful that we shall get through the Budget and the economic problem without a row. Heathcoat Amory is a sweet man—a really charming character. But he is tired and overdone. He feels his responsibilities almost too much.[1]

I could not help recalling Gladstone's dictum—'No man should ever lose a night's sleep over any *public* disaster'. At a talk among our colleagues on 20 March the whole situation was deployed in a full-dress argument.

> There was an excellent discussion, and my more confident approach got quite a lot of support, notably from Lord Mills. But the new import figures, and the estimated *loss* of £18 m. on the balance of payments account for the last quarter of 1959 have confirmed the Chancellor of the Exchequer in his more pessimistic view. I am *very* unhappy and *very* anxious about all this. If we do as the Treasury propose, we shall have to do it with great skill *presentationally*, if we are not to injure ourselves politically *at home* and talk ourselves into a crisis *overseas*. I got some help from Macleod, more from Maudling, more from Eccles. But the burden lies on me and the poor Chancellor; and he is such a charming, even noble, man.[2]

It is somewhat ironical to recall how alarming even small deficits in the balance of payments seemed to our primitive minds in those unregenerate days. There was, of course, none of the international structure which was afterwards built to bridge the vast gaps and there was no question of another devaluation such as that achieved in 1967. Even so, these puny figures seem ludicrously irrelevant compared to the gigantic deficits which we have enjoyed under Administrations with more enlarged views.

On 24 March the main lines of the Budget were settled.

> All the afternoon with the Chancellor of the Exchequer. The Budget is now agreed. Two pence on tobacco; two and a half per cent on Profits Tax. The first brings £40 m. this year; the second £40 m.–£50 m. *next* year. The concessions in the Budget (Entertainment Tax, etc.) will cost £20 m. [or perhaps more].

[1] 11 March 1960.   [2] 20 March 1960.

Final decision about *Bankers' deposits* (the new form of 'credit squeeze') and *Hire Purchase* to be taken later—perhaps at end of April. Increase in the Health Stamp postponed. All this is satisfactory, so far as the actual proposals are concerned. But I still feel that the whole mood and presentation may result in our talking ourselves into a crisis. . . . So I asked to see the speech, which he left with me. I have since been through it, and I must confess that it is . . . not unduly pessimistic.[1]

The Chancellor accepted all my suggested amendments but I was still a little anxious.

I think the actual text is about right now. But, since he genuinely feels lugubrious about our economy, it will be delivered in a very lugubrious voice—like the White Knight reciting to Alice—and will be in marked contrast to last year's buoyancy. I fear that the *political* repercussions must be bad and may be permanently dangerous. However, we may be able to 'get away' with the theme 'Preserving Prosperity' or 'You've got it good; keep it good.' (Anyway, prices, etc., are still pretty steady.)[2]

When we came to the Budget Cabinet, as it is called, at which the Chancellor of the Exchequer outlines for the first time his full proposals for the Budget these 'were received with relief, if not with enthusiasm, by his colleagues'.[3] I could take comfort in the reflection

after all the talk and argument, we are back to £40 m. more on tobacco, to match some £30 m. of concessions, above and below the line, ranging from end of *cinema tax* to increase of house-keeper's allowance for Income Tax purposes, and another £9 m. on Post War Credit repayments.

The important monetary restrictions (if we finally decide on them) are Bankers' deposits (to reduce lending) and some rules on Hire Purchase (to reduce pressure on Home Market for 'consumer-durables').

The Opposition will make fun of the Budget. But the Chancellor of the Exchequer has a high reputation. He is known to be honest and thought to be clever.[3]

On the next day the Chancellor of the Exchequer opened his Budget with a speech of one and a half hours.

[1] 24 March 1960.   [2] 25 March 1960.   [3] 2 April 1960.

It had one great merit and one great fault. The merit was that there was *no* note of despondency or alarm; reversal of engines; end of expansionist policies, or any of the horrors which the Chancellor and the Treasury were threatening up to a few weeks ago. I have won this battle quite definitely. I feel, therefore, that we shall not *talk* ourselves into a crisis—as we did . . . in 1957. It will depend now on what are the realities of any situation. The fault was that he dwelt too long and in too great detail on all the various 'protection of the revenue' measures. The Opposition took the opportunity and cheered each in turn, thus trying to make us out to be 'bond-washers', 'dividend-strippers', 'golden-handshakers', and all the rest.[1]

When it came to criticism

the Labour Party could find little fault with the Budget, even on 1955 lines. After all, last year they had asked for *greater* reductions of taxation than we gave. They also promised immensely increased expenditure—far above what we have been able to absorb.[1]

The Conservative back-benchers were on the whole satisfied. The Budget was even popular. But 'budgets, like babies, are always little loves when they are first born. But as their infancy passes away, they also become subject to many stripes.'[2] On this occasion, even the infant in the nurse's arms had no special charm. Accordingly some of the Conservative back-benchers were critical from the start. Eight or ten of our people abstained—the simpleton, as usual, being the prey of the artful. The Budget, I felt, should have a theme. The only Budget I introduced, that of 1956, was known as the 'Savings Budget'. I desired that this should be known as the 'Consolidating Budget', for that indeed was what it was. On this basis, our Party propaganda was duly launched.

Easter was late, and the short recess was especially welcome after a rather gruelling session. I managed to get to Sussex on Thursday in Holy Week but had to return to London on Good Friday to talk with the Foreign Secretary just returned from Washington. The chief subjects were the negotiations on Cyprus and the arrangements for the approaching Summit.

[1] 4 April 1960.   [2] Anthony Trollope, *The Prime Minister*.

H2

On Cyprus, Julian Amery has proved an excellent negotiator, patient and resourceful. The Archbishop Makarios is well matched. They have had six weeks and are progressing slowly.[1]

As regards our affairs at home I recorded:

the Chancellor of the Exchequer . . . will have . . . stormy weather for his Finance Bill. But I try to comfort him with these facts.

1. It's a *purely* Parliamentary row—the Nabarro-boys, Lord Hinchingbrooke, and Thorneycroft as far as *substance* is concerned.

2. It's also a purely Parliamentary row about the anti-tax-dodging clauses. Pundits are shocked by it, but the public approves the new powers of the Inland Revenue to deal with 'bond-washing', 'dividend stripping', and the like.

3. The country accepts—without enthusiasm, but with respect—the Budget for what it is—'consolidated success'.

4. Foreign opinion is very favourable, as is shown by the strong support given to sterling.[1]

Nevertheless, exports were not altogether satisfactory and I began to feel that it would be more difficult to resist the growing Treasury pressure.

The internal 'boom' continues to gather momentum and we shall have to take some measures to restrict Bankers' Credit and Hire Purchase. (The H.P. firms—not the most reputable, of course—are beginning to offer *no* initial payment and *four* years to pay !)[1]

By the end of the month

I . . . agreed that the Chancellor of the Exchequer shall give the economy a touch of the 'brake'. This is to be announced tomorrow. There will be 'Special Deposits' (one per cent or £70 m. to begin with) and H.P. rules (twenty per cent down as deposit, and two years—in most cases—as maximum period for repayment).[2]

When these decisions were made public, they were generally regarded as tiresome but reasonable. Since we now took the decision

[1] 17 April 1960.   [2] 27 April 1960.

to increase old age pensions in the spring of the following year, it was clear that still greater expenditure would have to be faced in the near future.

I did not wish to be pressed to any panic measures; so many things can be done if they are done quietly and without confusion or alarm. At the beginning of June I noted:

> The 'economic and financial' position causes some anxiety, although the actual out-turn for May (£15 m. up on the reserves) is better than we expected. The pound is beginning to slip a little. But perhaps the German situation will improve and their efforts to turn away foreign money (short term) may succeed. Also, the reduction in American money rates is helpful.[1]

The next day there was a high-powered meeting of a number of Ministers, together with Sir Robert Hall, economic adviser to the Treasury.

> A very useful talk. No one quite knows the extent of the disease (if any) or agrees on the cure. The instruments for control are very limited—and (if it is a question of exchange) Bank Rate operates more quickly and effectively than Special Deposits. But if there is *no* immediate risk, I would much prefer to use increased Special Deposits.[2]

The trade gap was now beginning to widen somewhat alarmingly, and eventually, after a long discussion, at which both the Governor of the Bank and Sir Robert Hall were present, the Cabinet agreed to an increase of the Bank Rate from 5 per cent to 6 per cent and the Special Deposits from 1 per cent to 2 per cent. When the announcement was made on 23 June the Opposition affected great indignation, but neither the Press nor public opinion was unfavourable. They accepted what seemed inevitable. A timely touch on the brake might avert far more painful measures later on. When it was all over I wrote to the Chancellor on 26 June:

> I had to leave London early on Friday. The Press seems to have been, on the whole, pretty reasonable—as is the general public reaction.
>
> I hope you realise that while I feel it right to subject such

[1] 2 June 1960. [2] 3 June 1960.

proposals as you have recently had to make to critical examination, yet you command absolute and loyal support once decisions have been taken. I feel sure that all our colleagues feel the same.

We are grateful to you not only for the skill and integrity with which you carry out these tasks, but for your willingness to explain your thoughts fully and frankly.

After the publication of the Guillebaud Report, I had felt that the time had come for a thorough study of the problem created by the Railway Nationalisation Act of 1947 which had, in fact, charged the British Transport Commission with a vast hotch-potch of enterprises for the management of which it was ill-devised. Not only were there the railways, there were the hotels, docks and canals, as well as a good deal of road freight transport and also road passenger transport. What was to be done with this complex? How were we to prevent the annual deficits reaching a size and scale which would prove a running sore to the economy? As soon as I returned from South Africa I set in motion some discussions and presided myself at a committee of Ministers and officials. As a result of intensive work I was able to make a statement on 10 March on the Government's decision. The Government fully accepted the objective underlying the report by the Guillebaud Committee, involving 'fair and reasonable' wages. In return the railway workers, the British Transport Commission and the public must accept corresponding obligations to make it possible for a radically reorganised railway system to operate on a reduced scale without placing an intolerable burden on the national economy. Although it was clear that any such review must result in higher fares and freight charges, the dismissal of superfluous staff and the closing of uneconomic lines, it was equally certain that the sooner this question was faced the better it would be.

I made my statement in the House of Commons about the Railways. It went very well, and the Opposition seemed rather dazed. But we must act quickly if we are to avoid further trouble.[1]

An enquiry of the kind which I proposed naturally depends for

[1] 10 March 1960.

its usefulness on the quality of the members of the Commission appointed to conduct it. I was determined that we should include some of the younger industrialists now coming to the front rather than rely upon those who might be better known to the public but not so active and alert. This was a technical and financial problem, and it needed men accustomed to dealing with such issues. I was fortunate in being able to persuade Sir Ivan Stedeford, Chairman and Managing Director of Tube Investments Limited, whom I had known in the old Ministry of Supply days, to act as Chairman. The three members were C. F. Kearton, joint Managing Director of Courtaulds, Dr. Richard Beeching, Technical Director of I.C.I., and H. A. Benson, partner in Cooper Brothers, chartered accountants.[1] By excluding representatives both of the Transport Commission and of the Railway Unions, we avoided endless discussions which would certainly have distracted the Commission from their real purpose. In looking back I confess to some satisfaction about the choice. All these men were already respected among the inner circles. They have since become recognised as among the most notable figures in the industrial and commercial life of the country. My task throughout this anxious and delicate affair was immensely lightened by Ernest Marples, Minister of Transport. With his agile mind and his thorough grasp of business principles and methods he was admirably equipped for this and indeed for any other difficult piece of work. We both relied greatly upon the mature wisdom of Lord Mills.

Owing to Derry Amory's desire to exchange the fierce conflicts of national politics for the comparative calm of business and philanthropy it now became necessary to undertake a major reconstruction of the Administration. Even a change of Ministers in less important posts, whether in or outside the Cabinet, always involves a whole series of moves, each of which reacts upon the other. But when such a key figure as the Chancellor of the Exchequer has to be replaced it presents a grave problem. I pondered much about this, and came to the conclusion that the best course would be to persuade Selwyn Lloyd to go to the Treasury. He had been Foreign Secretary for four and a half years, often under great

[1] Now Lord Kearton, Lord Beeching and Sir Henry Benson.

pressure—a gruelling experience. The Treasury would not be easier, but it would be a change. He had both the experience and the intelligence, also, I believed, the political agility to undertake a new task. Naturally I first consulted Butler; but he had no desire either to return to the Treasury or to take on the Foreign Office. After much deliberation I decided first to approach Lord Home. He came to luncheon alone with me on 3 June and

> I asked him whether, *if* I decided to ask Selwyn Lloyd to take the Exchequer (when Heathcoat Amory goes) he would take Foreign Office. He seemed rather flabbergasted but recovered slowly.[1]

A day or two later I received

> a very nice letter from Alec Home, to whom I talked on the telephone this morning before he left for Scotland. He is willing to do whatever suits me best, but he is anxious as to his qualifications, his being in the Lords, and his health. About the first, I have no doubt. He has just what a Foreign Secretary needs. About the second and the third, there is more doubt.[2]

I had now to leave for four days' visit to Norway, but on my return

> after a most frank and straightforward talk, Selwyn and I agreed that the best solution would be himself at the Treasury and Alec Home at the Foreign Office. But we have to face the two difficulties of Alec's health and the House of Lords. Selwyn believes that both these might be met by a Minister of State—or without Portfolio—*in* the Cabinet, but under the Foreign Secretary. I am not sure that this would help, although I can see that (if it did) it would help to meet both objections.[3]

Ultimately this solution was adopted, and Edward Heath became Lord Privy Seal with Foreign Office responsibilities.

With the two main positions now fixed, I had to find a new Commonwealth Secretary to replace Home. I thought it right to offer this also to Butler.

> I think he will decide to remain Home Secretary, but I should

---

[1] 3 June 1960.   [2] 5 June 1960.   [3] 11 June 1960.

really like him to take Commonwealth Secretary. He would be particularly good at dealing with Rhodesia, etc.[1]

A reconstruction of the Government necessarily spread over so long a period naturally became known, at least in political circles. The usual aspirants to office were not slow in putting forward their claims. There were some who certainly admired themselves, and some who were admired by others—generally those who knew them least. There were others whose friends saw in them qualities they were never able to disclose. In the beginning of July the reconstruction was still not complete.

> Rab does *not* want anything but his present position—so that is settled. Duncan Sandys will go to Commonwealth Office; John Hare to Labour (if he agrees) and then Christopher Soames to Agriculture. This still leaves the problem of Thorneycroft and Powell. On the whole, I am in favour of making them an offer, but I must carry the Cabinet and the Party with me.[2]

Ultimately both Thorneycroft and Powell agreed to return to the Government, the former as Minister of Aviation, the latter as Minister of Health, replacing Derek Walker-Smith who wished to go back to the Bar. Naturally these negotiations proved both delicate and protracted. It was not until 27 July that the changes were publicly announced. The choice of a peer to act as Foreign Secretary was regarded in 'progressive' circles as provocative and reactionary, in spite of many recent precedents. Even some of the younger Tories, whose knowledge of history did not go back beyond the fateful date of their selection as Parliamentary candidates, seemed surprised and even alarmed. But I felt certain, in my own mind, that Home would make an admirable Foreign Secretary with all the qualities of judgement, tact and integrity which were needed. My instinct proved thoroughly justified and was reinforced as the years passed.

> As I expected, a great row developed about a peer going to Foreign Office. There was a premature leak (which on the whole helped the Party first to get excited and then to calm down). The Opposition [asked for] a debate—and Gaitskell made the

[1] 28 June 1960.   [2] 5 July 1960.

cleverest and most effective speech I have heard him make. My reply was not too good, but the Party rallied round, and we won by a majority of 110 (our paper majority being 94). We had, in the end, as far as is known yet, no abstentions. I have not seen the analysed list. This was a great act of loyalty to me, and several of our chaps came from sick beds and even hospitals to vote.[1]

However, we were not alone in our troubles. I noted in the middle of June

the Labour row seems to grow in bitterness and intensity. One begins to wonder whether Gaitskell will be able to survive and ride the storm. I should be sorry if he went, for he has ability without charm. He does not appeal to the electorate, but he has a sense of patriotism and moderation.[2]

Fortunately, a few weeks later

Gaitskell has got a 'vote of confidence' from the Parliamentary Labour Party by a large majority. I was beginning to get anxious—for, on the whole, Gaitskell suits us pretty well.[3]

When Amory finally left I received a charming and characteristic letter, dated 26 July, including this phrase.

In writing to tell you this I would like to thank you for the patience and understanding and friendship you have invariably shown me while I have served in your Cabinet. I shall take away with me the happiest recollections. Seldom surely can a team of Ministers have worked together in greater harmony and friendship.

I need not say that I shall continue to give you and the present Government and our Party my full support in every way I can.

In the course of my reply, I wrote:

I know, of course, that you only stayed on last October at my urgent request. I am grateful to you for that. Nevertheless, it does not reduce the great sorrow that I feel that you will no longer be with us. You have said some very nice things about our work together which I entirely reciprocate, and I am equally happy to know of your promise of continued support in the future.

[1] 30 July 1960.   [2] 19 June 1960.   [3] 30 June 1960.

During this period there was one agreeable interlude. The death of Lord Halifax imposed upon Oxford University the duty to elect a new Chancellor. The first candidate to enter the field was Sir Oliver Franks, nominated by a Committee of Heads of Colleges. I had known Franks for many years and had a great admiration for him, for he had had a brilliant career, including a successful term as Ambassador in Washington. He had every possible qualification for the task except one—he was still young and active and there was a possibility that he might actually 'do' something, perhaps even do too much. In spite of many doubts and warnings I was persuaded by some old friends to allow my name to be put forward as a rival candidate. There was a good deal of risk in this. There was nothing at all to be gained in reputation if I was successful, and a good deal to be lost if I failed. But that, after all, is true of all field sports. An active Committee was formed at Oxford of which Hugh Trevor-Roper was a pivot. Balliol rallied nobly to the cause, putting college loyalty above any political bias; and a large number of my friends who had failed to qualify for the vote by not taking their M.A. degree paid up the considerable fees involved in order to become electors. Thus, unlike eighteenth-century elections where the voters often accepted bribes from the candidates, in this case the voters had to pay to exercise their privilege. Moreover, the elector must appear in person and in academic dress. On the appointed day trains were full and cars streamed down from London to Oxford. Since every college provided some entertainment for their old members, the day turned out a sort of mixture between the old hustings and a 'Gaudy'. In a word, it proved a most exciting election, where nearly half of those qualified made the journey in order to exercise the franchise. I enjoyed one unforeseen and perhaps decisive advantage. The Editor of *The Times* printed, and no doubt wrote, a somewhat pontifical leading article attacking my candidature the day before the poll. By this unexpected assistance and by the loyal help of all my friends, I was elected by a majority of two hundred and eighty. Naturally neither Franks nor I took any part in the campaign. This would be far below the dignity of a prospective Chancellor. Those who voted for me were no doubt satisfied that as a Prime Minister I should not be able to interfere, and that when I retired I should be too old to do so. In any event, apart from the high honour, I have thoroughly enjoyed my post; it has brought me again into touch with the University that I love so well and in which I spent the two happiest years of my life. I have tried to carry out such duties as properly fall to the post conscientiously but not obtrusively.

At last the Session came to an end—six hard months since the Election.

> On reflection, I feel that we have got through the first Parliamentary session reasonably well. But there are some grim problems ahead. The failure of the Summit Conference, followed by an Election in U.S. where no doubt each candidate will try to outbid the others in 'patriotic' and 'stand up to Khrushchev' sentiments, the loss of Cuba (at least temporarily), the break up of Africa, the . . . monetary policies of West Germany—collecting all the monetary chips and *not* re-lending them to the others (especially the younger and undeveloped players), all these are grounds for apprehension if not alarm. Moreover, I fear that Khrushchev may himself become a victim to 'Neo-Stalinism' or 'Communist Fundamentalism' and be forced to move away from the policy of the 'détente'—which he had made his own.
>
> At home, our chief worries are rising imports and rising Government expenditure.[1]

In the course of a long report to the Queen on 30 July, I wrote:

> We finished the Session with a very good legislative record, a fine division in the House, leaving, I think I may say, the Government and its supporters in good heart. Of course politics are like boating on a lake. Upon the calmest waters blow down the fiercest storms. Nevertheless, considering that we have been nearly nine years in office I would have expected a decline. I must be quite frank, however, and remind Your Majesty that everything is relative. Such popularity as we may have been able to obtain among the people is not of our own creation. We owe it to the strange goings-on in the Opposition Parties.
>
> Nevertheless, when we turn from politics and come to the realities there are some hard problems ahead of us. As always one

[1] 30 July 1960.

never seems to have enough money. When one was at a private school or at a public school one felt that ultimately this indigence might rectify itself with reaching manhood or middle age. On the contrary, most individuals have found that as they get older the claims upon them become more and more embarrassing. And so it is with our country. Government expenditure, that is, the demands either of the Services, or of the new scientific methods of warfare, or of the social services, education, health and all the rest, or rebuilding Britain and repairing the neglect of many years, all these things together seem to cost more and more. The public want them all, but they do not like the idea of paying for them. That is the internal problem, the perpetual public dilemma of politicians, in which indeed they merely find reflected the everlasting private dilemma of private individuals.

Then there is the problem of foreign trade, European complexities, the balance of payments, the fact that we are investing overseas more than we are earning, and that we meet this by short-term borrowing. All these questions are there for us to try to resolve or at any rate try to face.

Meanwhile, we could only 'watch and pray'.

CHAPTER IX

Aftermath of Paris

I N spite of the disastrous collapse of the Paris meeting I felt confident that Khrushchev would make no immediate move on Berlin. He would be likely to wait for the end of President Eisenhower's term of office in January 1961, and until he had had an opportunity of assessing the character and policies of his successor. Indeed, as part of his vengeful feelings against Eisenhower he repeatedly referred to the desirability of another Summit after a new President had been elected. My expectation proved to be correct. For it was not until August 1961, and after Khrushchev's unhappy meeting with the new President, that the building of the Berlin Wall brought the whole issue into dramatic prominence again.

The Three-Power Conference on the discontinuance of nuclear tests, which had adjourned on 12 May, reassembled at the end of that month and remained in session until 22 August. But the failure of the Summit had altered the atmosphere. British, Russian and American experts debated at length the technical problems of any effective supervision and control, but little was gained. The Ten-Power Disarmament Committee, which reassembled on 7 June, was less fortunate; for, on 27 June, the Russians staged a 'walk-out'. I was not altogether surprised at this somewhat melodramatic gesture, for Khrushchev had already made a personal appeal to me in connection with the new Soviet proposals, which, as usual, ignored the whole question of Russian superiority in conventional weapons and described all the Western ideas of 'control and inspection' in any sphere as 'mere intelligence and espionage'. Accordingly he called for the immediate prohibition of the means of delivery of missiles and the elimination of foreign bases, to be followed by a ban on the manufacture of all nuclear weapons. 'The liquidation of all armies' would be carried out at a later stage. When, therefore, the Russians decided to leave the Conference and appeal to the General Assembly of the United Nations, it became clear that disarmament was now to be treated as a subject for propaganda rather than for serious discussion.

> The Russians have 'walked out' of the Disarmament Conference. Mr. Khrushchev has written a long, argumentative, false and curiously boring letter to me and to the other Heads of Government. I have made a pretty good reply, published in the Press and on the whole applauded. At any rate, it is simple and sincere.[1]

All this was disappointing but not immediately alarming. Little else could be expected after the Paris débâcle. But I began to feel more and more persuaded that Khrushchev was being forced by his political situation at home into a more intransigent and even insulting mood. There now followed a new 'incident'. On 1 July an American RB 47 aircraft which had set out from a British base at Brize Norton disappeared during an electro-magnetic survey flight across the Arctic Ocean. After ten days' delay the Soviet Government announced that the plane had been shot down over Russian territorial waters. They sent a formal note to the British Government giving warning of the dangerous consequences which might follow 'the provocative acts of the American Air Force operating from British territory'. At the same time they sent protests to the American Government and for some reason to the Norwegian Government. It soon became clear from the American reply that the RB 47 was not flying over Russian territorial waters when it was chased and shot down by Russian fighters in order to stage an incident. Indeed the American reply, when it came on 13 July, proved that the whole affair was a fake. Meanwhile the expected storm arose in the House of Commons and the Press, involving the whole question of American bases in Britain. On 12 July, before the American official explanation, I had to do my best, relying on the many telegrams which had passed between London and Washington.

[1] 30 June 1960.

Question Time on Tuesday was quite an ordeal. Both wings of the Labour party joined in the hunt—although the Gaitskellites were a little conscious of their own weakness on defence matters. I had about half an hour or so of it—on a Private Notice question by Mr. Gaitskell—and got through fairly well. (Actually, it was a most difficult and anxious job—the worst since Suez. . . .) I fully expected a motion for a debate at 7.00 p.m. ; if it had been moved, I think the Speaker would have accepted it. I had a private word with Mr. Gaitskell before Questions and showed him my main reply, about seeing whether any improvements were needed in the Anglo-American agreement. On this, he said he would try to keep his people quiet. Anyway, it passed off all right, and a 'crisis' much heralded by the Press never came to a head. [The] battle was renewed in a mild form on Thursday; but the steam was out of it.[1]

Nevertheless, I felt that we ought to look carefully again at the precise terms of the agreements for the American bases in order to ensure that they were watertight. Accordingly I asked for Eisenhower to arrange for a careful re-examination, to which he agreed. On 19 July I made a further statement in the House of Commons. In addition to the formal reply to the Soviet note on behalf of the British Government 'I decided to write an "open letter" to Khrushchev—more in sorrow than in anger—and to read it out in the House of Commons.'[2] Since this was an unusual procedure, it involved some risks; but the result was all that I could have wished. The House listened in complete silence, and at the end Gaitskell made a short statment, which was very generous and helpful. The letter ran as follows:

I am sending you separately a formal reply to the Note from the Soviet Government to Her Majesty's Government which was delivered by Mr. Gromyko to Sir Patrick Reilly in Moscow on the 11th of July concerning the shooting down of a United States aircraft. This reply sets out clearly the position of our Government in this matter; but I feel that I must, in addition, write to you personally about my anxieties as to the way in which the world situation is developing.

I would like to remind you of the conversations which we

[1] 17 July 1960.   [2] 30 July 1960.

have had from time to time when we have both agreed to seek methods by which the underlying tensions in the world could be reduced. When I had the pleasure of being your guest in Moscow last year I think we succeeded in setting in motion a sequence of developments which appeared to have great promise. My visit to you and the subsequent interchange of visits and frank discussions between the members of the proposed Summit Conference made me hopeful that when we came to the Summit Meeting we would make, if not a spectacular advance, at least some forward movement.

It is not necessary now to go back upon the reasons why the Summit Conference was broken up before it really started. I still feel that it would have been better had you been willing to put other difficulties aside in order to pursue the major purpose for which we were to meet. All acts of intelligence or espionage on either side are, after all, symptoms, not causes, of the world tension which we should both seek to reduce. However, I took some comfort from your statement that when the dust had settled we might be able to take up again the task.

Since then, however, a number of events have occurred which have made me less hopeful. First, the action of the Soviet delegation in leaving the Committee of Ten on Disarmament at a moment when new United States proposals were, with your knowledge, about to be presented. As I told you at the time, I deeply regretted that you should have found it necessary to bring this Conference to an end, in my view prematurely.

Now we have the new incident regarding the United States RB 47 flight. Our formal Note, to which I referred in my opening paragraph, gives the reply to the accusations against the United Kingdom in this matter. But I feel I must add that, even if the facts had been as stated by your Government, I do not think the Soviet authorities should have taken so grave an action and one so calculated to turn the incident into a major international dispute.

Then there comes the question of the Congo. I have read the statement which you have distributed which accuses Great Britain, in concert with the United States, France, Belgium and West Germany, of organising a conspiracy to destroy the independent State of Congo. I must ask you, Mr. Khrushchev, whether you really believe such a conspiracy is likely in view of the policies which British Governments of all parties have followed not only since the last war, but for many generations.

For more than a century, it has been our purpose to guide our dependent territories towards freedom and independence. Apart from the older independent countries of the Commonwealth, since the Second World War India, Pakistan, Ceylon, Ghana, Malaya, comprising over 510 millions of people have, with our help, reached the goal of independent life and strength. We have aided this process both by our technical assistance and by generous financial contributions. All these States are completely independent members of our free Commonwealth association.

Nor is this movement at an end. In October this year, Nigeria, with its 35 million people, will be another great independent country. Sierra Leone will become independent in April 1961. The West Indies Federation is moving rapidly in the same direction. And so the process goes on.

I ask you, Sir, can you really believe that a Government and a people who have pursued these policies so consistently and so honourably are engaged in a conspiracy to destroy the new independent State of Congo?

But my purpose in sending you this personal message is not to debate in detail the individual issues which have lately arisen between us. Rather, it is to express to you my deep concern over what now appears to be a new trend in the conduct of Soviet foreign policy.

As I think you will agree, I have consistently welcomed and have given much weight to your assurances of the Soviet Government's desire for peaceful co-existence and détente in international relations. I have shown my sympathy with such purposes. It is, however, my firm opinion that these objectives cannot be successfully pursued without the exercise of patience and restraint. Much of my present anxiety derives from the fact that these elements seem to be absent from recent manifestations of Soviet Government policy.

I write to you now so plainly because I have the memory of our frank discussions with you in mind. I simply do not understand what your purpose is today.

If the present trend of events in the world continues, we may all of us one day, either by miscalculation or by mischance, find ourselves caught up in a situation from which we cannot escape.

I would ask you, therefore, to consider what I have said and to believe that I am writing to you like this because I feel it my duty to do so.

We cannot disguise, and we have never attempted to disguise, the fundamental differences on political, social and economic questions which divide your country and your associates from our country and our Allies. Nevertheless, in the nature of things we are united by the fact that both our people and yours want to live their lives in peace and to build something better for their successors. I have always hoped that if we could have followed the path which we seemed at one time to agree upon we could have made progress to this end.

Eisenhower, de Gaulle, Adenauer, Menzies and Nash to whom I had sent copies of my letter sent personal telegrams of thanks and congratulations. Khrushchev's only reply was an attack on the 'depravity of the Western Powers in their attitude towards disarmament and their sterile concentration on control'.

This proved to be the end of the RB 47 affair. I felt justified in telling Eisenhower that my impression was that the incident had increased rather than diminished the sense of solidarity between our two countries.

If the Russian reaction to the Paris failure had been peevish and sometimes brutal, it was all the more necessary that the other Powers which had been subjected to this traumatic experience should grow even closer together. I lost no time therefore in trying to press forward the plan for correlating French, American and British policies by close co-operation between their Heads of Government. Accordingly, on 25 May, I wrote identical letters to Eisenhower and de Gaulle enclosing at the same time a minute on the possible mechanism of tripartite consultation.

Since our discussion in Paris with President de Gaulle about improving co-operation between our three governments we here have been thinking about the methods to use. The United States, France and the United Kingdom have between them an overwhelming responsibility for the wise direction of Western alliances. We are also, as Powers victorious in the last War, in a special position with regard to Germany. On the other hand, we do not want unduly to offend our various other allies by seeming ostentatiously to exclude them from our deliberations.

I expect that you and President de Gaulle will have ideas on all this, and I suggest that the Foreign Ministers should discuss the problem when they meet in Washington early next week. Meanwhile I thought it might be helpful to send to you and to President de Gaulle the enclosed memorandum which attempts to explore some of the possibilities as regards mechanics for consultation between us. I feel that by moving along the lines of this memorandum we should be able to develop better between us a common attitude towards the great global problems, upon our handling of which the peace of the world and the security of the West so much depend.

MECHANICS OF TRIPARTITE CONSULTATION

(a) The main instrument of tripartite consultation, apart from personal meetings of Heads of Governments, to supplement normal diplomatic exchanges, should be meetings between the Foreign Ministers. They already meet four times a year; at the United Nations General Assembly, in May and December each year at NATO and also at the SEATO Ministerial Meeting. In the past there have been other additional meetings. The aim should be for them to meet about every two or three months, using these other occasions for the most part. When they meet adequate time should be set apart for tripartite discussion. Their agenda for such discussion should be prepared in advance with approval from the Heads of Governments and any necessary papers should be prepared and circulated before each meeting. In arranging the agenda Ministers should feel free to suggest any subject or problem with which the three Governments were concerned. This would include both concrete and immediate problems, and also long-term questions of a more general character requiring harmonisation of the future policies of the three Governments.

Each Foreign Minister would designate a member of his Foreign Office—perhaps a Counsellor—to be directly responsible for preparing the agenda, circulating papers and ensuring that the subsequent follow-up action is taken. These three officers could correspond directly with each other in the intervals between the Ministerial meetings but should not be regarded as constituting a formal Secretariat.

Should it be desirable or necessary for any preliminary work to be done on a tripartite basis before a meeting of Ministers, this should be performed in the place where the Ministerial meeting is to be held by a small working group of officials, i.e. representatives of the two Embassies and the home Ministry of Foreign Affairs, assisted where necessary by expert advisers.

The Foreign Ministers should report to the Heads of Governments the result of each meeting.

(b) The Heads of Governments might also supplement their direct correspondence by meeting either bilaterally or tripartitely in an informal way at intervals. Care will have to be taken, however, that such meetings do not upset the susceptibilities of other Governments and the aim should be to have it accepted that the Heads of Governments can meet without formality and without it becoming a State occasion, i.e. no Press conferences or communiqués or Parliamentary statements.

On 4 June the President answered at some length. His reply was more forthcoming than I had expected, since I knew there was a good deal of pressure in Washington against the idea. It certainly contained a warning with regard to the military discussions and the need to meet the susceptibilities of other NATO countries. Nevertheless, the spirit which Eisenhower adopted to de Gaulle's proposals was fair and even generous.

I want to thank you for the thoughtful memorandum on improving tripartite consultation which you sent me with your letter of 25 May. In accordance with your suggestion the three Foreign Ministers met here in Washington and had a profound and, I believe, useful discussion of ways and means to improve the consultative process.

As you pointed out, we have had a series of tripartite meetings in recent years but these have not always been as efficiently organised as they might have been. This we hope to improve in the future. During the 1 June discussions here Chris Herter suggested that Livie Merchant who has global responsibilities within the State Department, be charged with keeping in touch with his opposite numbers in the French and British Foreign

Offices. The three could prepare agenda and discussion papers for future meetings and could assure both systems and continuity in our tripartite consultations without, however, creating an official secretariat or other apparatus which might lead sensitive members of the Alliance such as Italy or Canada to believe that an 'inner directorate' had been created.

This proposal sounds eminently sensible to me. It is essentially that which you proposed in your memorandum.

I believe that our consultations should concentrate on those areas where the three powers have special responsibilities and on global questions in which the three have unique interests. I believe that we should also continue to develop consultation in NATO, paralleling progress toward more effective tripartite consultation.

I agree with you that we must be most circumspect about our tripartite meetings in order to avoid upsetting unnecessarily other Governments, both our allies and those newly emergent countries, especially in Africa, who look with suspicion on consultation among the Western powers on African matters. We cannot, on the other hand, maintain such a tight secrecy that our motives and actions are suspected. This seems especially true in NATO. We have therefore suggested that a means be worked out to keep other NATO members generally informed of our conversations.

From our talks should emerge a means by which we can have more regular and better organised consultation among the three of us on political problems facing the free world. We cannot however be sure that we have satisfied General de Gaulle's desires. This was hinted at by the French Foreign Minister when he said that the problem of military coordination is a matter for future discussion. The memorandum which General de Gaulle promised to send us should give us a further insight into his thinking and I am sure we will want to consult about how to reply to it after it is received.

In essence I believe that we have moved somewhat along the path towards a greater harmonisation of our policies. It seems to me essential to continue this effort.

A few days later, on 10 June, as Eisenhower had anticipated, de Gaulle replied expressing appreciation of the way in which the

three Foreign Ministers had got together during the recent SEATO
meeting in Washington which he regarded as most satisfactory. As
regards the machinery he made the suggestion that these meetings
would be more useful if they had been prepared by *un fonctionnaire
de rang elevé ayant une compétance générale*. This struck me as a
somewhat obscure phrase, and when I asked the French Ambassador, Chauvel, what he thought it meant, he could only suggest that
de Gaulle had in mind the official known at the Quai d'Orsay as
Directeur Politique.

But a more important proposal followed. Apart from occasional
meetings of the three Heads of State or Government there should
be political co-operation extended to military matters by meetings
either of Ministers of Defence or Chiefs of Staff. The agenda
might be prepared by the military representatives of the 'Permanent Group'—an organ of NATO, consisting of British, American
and French representatives, which was located in Washington. All
this seemed very satisfactory, and after consultation with Chauvel
I passed on de Gaulle's suggestions to Eisenhower. He replied on 30
June. As regards the political discussions he at once approved the
proposal for further meetings. These might be prepared by the
heads of the State Department and the Foreign Office with their
French colleague appointed by de Gaulle. The Foreign Ministers
could easily hold a tripartite meeting in New York while the General
Assembly was meeting. With regard to the military arrangements
Eisenhower felt doubtful as to the wisdom of using any part of the
NATO mechanism.

> It would be difficult to keep secret such consultations and the
> very fact that our representatives to the standing group were
> meeting separately to discuss global strategic matters would lead
> other members of the alliance to believe that we had, in fact,
> established some sort of inner directorate.

Nevertheless, the President felt that something must be done.

> We must find some way to cope with this aspect of General de
> Gaulle's thinking. It might be possible, for instance, to have
> talks here in Washington by appropriate military representatives.
> You and the French might delegate this responsibility to a senior

military officer assigned to Washington. The French might, in such case, select their representative to the standing group. We, on the other hand, could select an appropriate general officer who has no connection with the standing group itself. These talks, of course, would have to be conducted along previously agreed guidelines, but I am sure that we could work this out.

He followed this up with a practical suggestion.

In this connection, I would like to recall that a year ago we did hold tripartite talks on Africa under the chairmanship of Robert Murphy. At these talks military representatives were present. Both you and the French were represented by your members of the standing group. At those talks the French requested separate and continuing military talks. After a period of consideration we agreed to do this, selected an appropriate office to head up our side, and informed the French we were ready. They have never responded to this offer.

I think, nevertheless, that we could renew this offer and I would propose so doing in my reply to General de Gaulle.

On 2 August the President sent me a copy of his proposed letter. On the political side the methods were agreed; on the military side the Washington meetings of the representatives of the military staffs were acceptable. Nevertheless, and perhaps this offended the General, Eisenhower emphasised his view that close military co-operation for Europe would best be protected through NATO. But to the General NATO was a dirty word, and although the President's offer of 2 August seemed to meet the French desire on every point of practical co-operation and consultation, these final paragraphs must have seemed to destroy some of the value of the tripartite system to which the French attached so much importance. This was confirmed by the next two moves from Paris.

On 5 August, in relation to the Congo crisis which now occupied all our minds, the General could not resist underlining his point.

I am sure that you will understand the regret I experience in pointing out the lack of cohesion of the West in the Congo affair. While our two countries were able to adopt the same position, our American friends, once more, took up a separate attitude. And yet, if we all three had immediately acted in concert this would probably have been sufficient to nullify Soviet blackmail, to remove all ambiguity from what the Secretary-General of the United Nations is doing and finally to bring to reason both the Congolese and the Belgians with regard to the best way of assuring the life of this region in the centre of Africa.

A few days later he wrote to President Eisenhower and to me lamenting the paralysis of the West and proposing a meeting in September in order to get to grips with organising effective political and strategic co-operation throughout the world. NATO covered too narrow a compass to fulfil the purposes which he had in mind. This letter reached me just before I left for Germany, where Adenauer had invited me for general economic discussions, and I wrote in my diary:

> Just before we left for Germany, two rather strange things happened. Chauvel, the French Ambassador, asked Lord Home and Shuckburgh to luncheon. They found it an intimate party, and Chauvel made it quite clear that the French did not intend to make any economic proposals and did not expect their partners to do so. They are clearly nettled at the Bonn meeting. They have put about (which they know to be a lie) that I asked for it. Lord Home told Chauvel that Dr. Adenauer sent me this pressing invitation *before* he (Dr. Adenauer) set out for Rambouillet. The French Ambassador got as near blushing as diplomats ever do. However, the purpose of this was to 'warn us off the course'. It was not—for a French manoeuvre—very subtle. But it was, in any case, clear. This was the first French move. The second (which seemed very strangely timed) was a message from de Gaulle to me personally, enclosing a copy of a message which he had sent to President Eisenhower and suggested a *tripartite* meeting in September. He begged me (in almost passionate terms) to use all my influence with President Eisenhower to accept. Could we not, all three, meet in Bermuda?
>
> So first the French menace, almost insult us. Next (on the same day) they cajole us.
>
> Nevertheless, I think this situation can perhaps be turned to advantage. I have always felt that de Gaulle cares more for the glory of political leadership in Europe than he cares about the

economics of the Six. He is always rather contemptuous of money. '*L'ordonnance toujours suit.*'[1]

I thought it right when I was in Germany to tell Adenauer

about the possibility of de Gaulle organising a meeting with me and President Eisenhower. I thought it only fair to tell him. I would not like this to reach him from other sources. Dr. Adenauer was pleased at being told, but seemed not to mind.[2]

I answered de Gaulle's message on my return, on 12 August:

I was very interested in these messages and have been thinking about them when I could while I was in Bonn. I certainly feel that the meeting which you and I had with President Eisenhower at Rambouillet was valuable. Like you I was disappointed at the difficulty of translating the general understanding between us into some practical method of consultation. This is always the problem today, for if we set up regular organisations for our purposes these tend to become institutionalised and even fossilised. If we rely on purely informal methods, however, there is a danger of a breakdown in the communication, and so vital world events take place without our properly having consulted together. As I have said on several occasions I am therefore in favour of the principle of holding meetings of this kind whenever practicable.

Accordingly, I asked the President to do what he could in spite of all the difficulties in the internal situation in the United States with the Presidential election now sweeping into its full flood.

On 17 August Livie Merchant, an old friend from Algiers days and a leading member of the State Department, came for a talk. The President was uncertain how to answer de Gaulle's request for a tripartite meeting in September. Merchant informed me that

he will decline a tripartite meeting in September—on practical grounds—suggest a tripartite Foreign Secretaries' meeting during the U.N. Assembly instead—and hold out hopes of a meeting towards the end of the year. De Gaulle will be disappointed, but cannot, I think, be offended.[3]

While I did my best to support de Gaulle because I believed that the tripartite system, if it became fully effective and in spite of all

[1] 11 August 1960.   [2] 10 August 1960.   [3] 17 August 1960.

its dangers, would help de Gaulle to take a more reasonable view of other matters, I was not surprised at the President's desire to postpone this discussion until the end of the year, when at least the main meetings of the U.N. would be over and the leading world personalities had left New York. Merchant told me that

> the President is very concerned at de Gaulle's veiled attacks on NATO and his general unwillingness to co-operate. But he has agreed to the sort of line which I hoped he would take.[1]

In the event Kennedy's election at the beginning of November meant the end of Eisenhower's power. This effort, therefore, to please and attract the French could not be taken any further at this time. We had done our best, and de Gaulle must have recognised the spirit in which I had tried to overcome his deep suspicions of America and all that it implied. Bur clearly any further steps must wait on future events.

During this period I was anxious, in spite of so many pre-occupations, to bring to an issue with the Americans a number of questions so vital to the effective organisation of our new defence structure. To make the question clear it is necessary to cast a rapid glance over the events of the last few years.

The Defence White Paper of 1957 for good or ill marked a new era. Our decision to develop and maintain an effective nuclear deterrent had important consequences both internationally and nationally.[2] It involved the British Government in the problem of convincing our NATO allies both of its wisdom and its consistency with the theme of interdependence which I had agreed with President Eisenhower and preached in and out of season as a sound basis for the effective defence of the non-Communist world. Equally it engaged Britain, as one of the three nuclear powers, in the long arguments on tests and negotiations for their restriction or abolition. It may indeed be claimed that our determination, in spite of heavy expense and many technical difficulties, to remain in the nuclear club at least allowed us to play an important and perhaps decisive part in the negotiations which finally led to the abandonment by the Three Powers of all atmospheric tests.

[1] 17 August 1960.   [2] See *Riding the Storm*, chap. vii.

I

Over the following years there was a prolonged debate over both the morality and the prudence of our policy involving violent attacks from the Left of the Labour Party and considerable dissensions within its ranks. There was also widespread, and sincere, public anxiety. But these were not my only troubles. These broad decisions required detailed implementation; and the problem of maintaining our nuclear forces over the years was to prove one of increasing complexity. Our scientists found little difficulty in developing an effective warhead. After the amendment of the McMahon Act in 1958 they had the advantage of sharing their research with their American colleagues. Nor was there any problem in planning the necessary capacity for producing fissile material. So far as the means of delivery were concerned the existing bomber force would remain, at least for some years, an efficient instrument. But a long battle raged as to what was to succeed the bombers.

In all these affairs Prime Ministers, Ministers of Defence and Cabinets are under a great handicap. The technicalities and uncertainties of the sophisticated weapons which they have to authorise are out of the range of normal experience. There is today a far greater gap between their own knowledge and the expert advice which they receive than there has ever been in the history of war. I often felt jealous of my predecessors in this respect. Moreover the scientists and experts of all kinds often differed, and put forward the most conflicting recommendations. For even they were dealing in unknown or almost unknown fields of applied science and technology. In addition, these mechanisms were immensely expensive, even in the planning and development stages, and almost always outran the estimates originally provided for this part of the cost as well as for their ultimate production.

Finally, even if successful, these terrible engines of war could become rapidly obsolescent or even obsolete either for technical or for tactical reasons. I must bear the full responsibility for many costly decisions and mistakes. I can only claim that successive Ministers of Defence and their professional advisers struggled nobly with their tasks.

The first and most attractive method of prolonging the life of the bomber was a device by which a rocket of some kind could be projected from the bomber in flight, thus increasing its range and reducing the risks of the aeroplane succumbing to any enemy anti-aircraft device, whether by gunfire or by more sophisticated methods. For this purpose the so-called 'guided bomb', Blue Steel, was devised. Mark I proved successful; but there were long debates as to the wisdom of developing Mark II. It was, therefore, decided to seek an alternative which might ultimately take the place of the guided bomb, and for this purpose a ground-to-ground ballistic rocket was to be developed under the name of Blue Streak. It was to be a rocket operating from a fixed site, and able to deliver the deterrent to a great range. Duncan Sandys, as Minister of Defence, with his usual thoroughness gave special attention to this project, and the Blue Streak ballistic rocket was undoubtedly a triumph for the vigour and skill of our scientists and technicians. There is no doubt that had we persevered it would have been technically successful. Moreover, the Australian Government had assisted us generously with the Woomera rocket range, and if we were to abandon the weapon it would be a great blow. The Woomera programme could, of course, be used for the testing of shorter-ranged missiles, but to give up Blue Streak would be a disappointment at home and a cause of great concern to the Australian people. Nevertheless, it was difficult to resist the pressure which was beginning to grow in many quarters against the concept of ballistic rockets fired from a fixed—and therefore vulnerable—site.

By the end of 1959 it was clear to me that the future of Blue Streak was in doubt. By February 1960, the issue came to a head. After several days of formal debate among the Ministers specially concerned and long informal discussions, the Defence Committee decided on 24 February in principle to abandon Blue Streak as an operational weapon. This decision was not easy to make, and I am not now convinced that it was wise. Duncan Sandys, then Minister of Aviation, dissented with powerful and exhaustive argument. Nevertheless it was hard to resist the objections raised by the Chiefs of Staff, now presented with a unanimity and force which had hitherto not been achieved. It is true that we had spent £60 million in development of this weapon, and we would have to spend at least another £500 million to get the adequate supply of rockets.

But it was not the financial considerations which swayed the Defence Committee, including the new Minister of Defence, Harold Watkinson. It was the almost irresistible case put by the Chiefs of Staff in favour of replacing weapons fired from a stationary position with a missile delivered from a mobile firing point, now that such a method seemed practicable. This, in fact, meant from a submarine. Meanwhile, the life of the bomber force could be extended if in substitution of Blue Steel Mark II we could obtain a new air-to-ground missile being developed in the United States, called Skybolt. The decision to abandon Blue Streak could not of course be finally taken until some understanding could be made with the Americans. It was therefore agreed that work on Blue Streak should continue until this question could be resolved. In the course of my visit to Washington from 27–31 March 1960, which was chiefly to deal with the test ban negotiations, I was able to secure

> a very valuable exchange of notes about Skybolt and Polaris. They undertake to let us have the *vehicles* (by sale or gift), we making our own nuclear heads. This allows us to abandon Blue Streak (rocket) without damage to our prospects of maintaining—in the late 60s and early 70s—our *independent* nuclear deterrent.[1]

With regard to Polaris, although Eisenhower was very helpful, he was unwilling to enter into a definite arrangement until the outcome was known of discussions which were going on as to whether NATO should be equipped with Polaris, either by purchase from the United States of America, or production in Europe. It was certain, however, that we could obtain Polaris, although at a heavy cost, in one form or another when we might need it. Meanwhile, we could look forward to Skybolt which should serve our needs for many years.

Therefore I felt justified, on my return from Washington, in asking the Cabinet to take the final decision to abandon Blue Streak and to rest upon the firm agreement for Skybolt to prolong the life of the bombers. At a later stage the submarines, whether purchased

[1] 29 March 1960.

or built by us, seemed to be regarded by all the Chiefs of Staff as the most efficient means of deterrent. The argument was summarised in my report to the Queen on 3 April:

> I was able, while in America, to get an assurance from the President that we shall be able to obtain either Skybolt or Polaris when we need them. This will enable us without further hesitation to put an end to Blue Streak, a weapon which the Chiefs of Staff now feel to be obsolescent and unsuitable. To finish it would cost us another £600 million, and by the time it was ready it would really be out of date. Moreover, for political and morale reasons I am very anxious to get rid of these fixed rockets. This is a very small country, and to put these installations near the large centres of population—where they have to be—would cause increasing anxiety to Your Majesty's subjects. A bomber is somehow accepted on its bombing field; and a mobile weapon, either on a truck or better still in a submarine, is out of sight. It was made clear to me that no strings—to use the technical expression—will be attached. In other words, we shall be able to buy the vehicle and make our own warhead. We can thus maintain our independent deterrent, first by prolonging the life of the bomber force (if Skybolt proves satisfactory) and later by acquiring a mobile weapon in some form.

On 13 April the House of Commons was informed, and a full debate took place on 27 April. In making the announcement we had reserved the further question as to whether Blue Streak could be developed for space research either as a European or a British project. Discussions and negotiations on this aspect were destined to be prolonged. Blue Streak was thus kept alive for a time, but in the end could make only a slender contribution to the European project in comparison with the large sums involved. Fortunately for us, when the debate took place, the Opposition were more divided than the Government benches. Instead of uniting upon a concentrated attack on the Government for accepting the objective of an independent nuclear deterrent but failing to achieve it and wasting large sums of money through their incompetence, the Labour Party devoted a great part of the debate to the discussion as to whether we ought to have a nuclear force at all. So we ended with a good majority and were able to escape from what might be legitimate censure through a deep division among our opponents. I noted

> Brown was very able (for the Opposition), Watkinson solid and loyal (for us), Harold Wilson too much of a 'knockabout', Sandys very good.[1]

Nevertheless, there were some anxieties ahead. The President and I had merely interchanged a note and in return for Skybolt I had agreed, also 'in principle', to the establishment of an American submarine base in Scotland. Actual details were to be set out in a formal agreement.

> A very successful Defence Meeting, in the sense that everyone agreed!
> Watkinson leaves on Friday for Washington, with a directive which will enable him to make a definite agreement for Skybolt, if U.S. authorities will sign it. He can open up the more difficult problem of allowing U.S. submarines, armed with Polaris, to make a base . . . on the Clyde.[2]

Everything was soon arranged, and the Minister of Defence was able to conclude a formal agreement regarding Skybolt, while maintaining the understanding about our claim to Polaris, if this should at any time become necessary. It was this undertaking, entered into by President Eisenhower, that his successor was to honour, at my request, two years later. But if the Americans had met us so fairly we must do the same. I was well aware of the likely public reaction to setting up a nuclear submarine base with all the apparatus that would be required—the mother ship to which submarines reported from time to time—and above all the presence of the fearful nuclear weapons. A picture could well be drawn of some frightful accident which might devastate the whole of Scotland.

> I had agreed 'in principle' at Camp David to do what we could, more or less in return for Skybolt. But Watkinson has managed to disassociate the two 'deals'.[3]

[1] 27 April 1960.   [2] 25 May 1960.   [3] 12 June 1960.

When I brought this to the attention of the Cabinet, there was a good deal of anxiety, and I did not press for an immediate decision. They naturally wished to include as a *quid pro quo* our right to buy or build the Polaris submarine should we later decide to do so.

However, the President was still hankering after some NATO arrangement for ballistic missiles, whether static or mobile. At the same time, General Lauris Norstad, now acting as the Supreme Commander, was trying to persuade the NATO powers to have not merely small tactical atomic weapons, but medium-range ballistic missiles. On the whole the NATO powers showed little interest except as possible beneficiaries of any weapons that the United States might care to give them.

Although my colleagues were now ready to offer submarine facilities, they were still anxious to secure a definite commitment in return. In all these negotiations, of which I had now some experience, there was always a problem of how far to try to formalise legal or semi-legal contracts and how far to rest on what might be called 'gentlemen's agreement'.

Finally, on 15 September, the Cabinet formally approved the submarine base, resting on the broad assurances which Eisenhower was willing to give. There now began to be the first hints that Skybolt might prove unsatisfactory. On these rumours I sent an urgent message to Eisenhower to ask for some clearer picture. I pointed out that since we had abandoned both Blue Streak and Blue Steel on the understanding that Skybolt would be available, its cancellation would be a terrible blow. However, I was not too disturbed. Eisenhower's reassurances, on 31 October, that Skybolt was proceeding satisfactorily, were comforting. In any case I felt certain that whether it came in Eisenhower's time, or in that of any successor, the Americans were so committed to supporting the effectiveness of our nuclear weapons that, whether by Skybolt from the air or by Polaris from underneath the sea, Britain could look with certainty to the maintenance of her nuclear contribution to the deterrent.

When Parliament met on 1 November I referred to the Polaris missile submarine which would become operational before long. I went on to say:

There would be operational advantage and to that extent the deterrent would be strengthened if sheltered anchorage on this side of the Atlantic were available for a submarine depot ship and a floating dock. This Her Majesty's Government have undertaken to provide.

There were, of course, violent objections from certain sections of the community, including both those who in principle were opposed to the nuclear weapons and those whose fears had been exploited by the most fantastic stories of the dangers involved. I, at least, knew enough about these mysteries to realise that an atomic bomb is an uncommonly difficult thing to set off, since it needs a powerful explosion to detonate it. Moreover the safety devices built into the bomb are both extremely sophisticated and effective. But many of the inhabitants of Glasgow and the West Coast of Scotland were led to believe that these horrible and destructive engines might explode with the ease of a Mills bomb or a fifth of November firework. There were, therefore, in the months to come the usual demonstrations, marches and protests, standing and recumbent. On the other hand the arrival of a large number of American sailors and the permanent installation of the mother ship and all its accessories would bring not only work but quite considerable sums of money to be spent in the neighbourhood. These I believed would in due course act as compensation for either moral objections or physical alarm.

The Opposition were, at this moment, fortunately for me, still in a confused state—their animosities being directed more against one another than against the Government. As an example I noted that

Gaitskell has been re-elected Leader of the Parliamentary Party by a two-to-one vote. Nevertheless, to have eighty-one M.P.s of his own Party vote against him, cannot be said to be a comfortable position. Harold Wilson seems to have made an error. It may well be that by the time the General Election comes, Gaitskell's personal position in the country will have been much enhanced. People admire tenacity and courage—and he has shown both.[1]

[1] 5 November 1960.

'*And may I say to Hon. Members opposite me*' – by Vicky

As a result the Defence Debate on 13 December proved satisfactory from our point of view. In this

> the Official Opposition put down a motion censuring—or at least criticising—our Defence Policy. But the manoeuvre did not turn out very well for them. The debate became one between the unilateralists and the multilateralists in the Labour Party. Gaitskell wound up, but I preferred not to join in, so I got Ted Heath to do it—which he did very well. The division was curious. Over fifty of the anti-Gaitskellites sat defiantly in their seats below the gangway (including Shinwell) and refused to vote for the Opposition motion. It is thought that seventy-three 'abstained', being in the House or available. This is a very large number, and I remember nothing like it since the vote which led to Neville Chamberlain's fall from power in 1940.[1]

This event deterred the popular Press from its recent activities of making violent attacks on me personally. These had been due partly to Lord Beaverbrook being in a mischievous mood and partly to the fact that Lord Rothermere's papers, the *Daily Mail* and the *Evening News*, 'want to stick to all they can of the readers of the defunct *News Chronicle* and *Star* (which Rothermere has bought)'.[2]

From all this confusion there followed at least one advantage—the decision to allow the American Polaris base in Scotland was now generally accepted. But, among so many other troubles, these defence questions added to our burden. The decision on Blue Streak had been difficult and even heart-breaking. Doubts were being raised about Skybolt, although the Americans were still confident. As for Polaris, I was certain we could get it one way or another if we needed it, but it would cost a great deal of money. Moreover such a change of medium would involve the abandonment of static weapons operated by the Army and Air Force in favour of a mobile weapon operated by the Navy. This would mean a complete change of balance between the forces. Indeed it was one of the considerations that led me to one of my last actions before leaving office—the unification of the three Services under the reformed Ministry of Defence.

[1] 13 December 1960.   [2] 11 December 1960.

To the witches' cauldron of recrimination and suspicion between the great Powers which had been steadily brewing after the break-down of the Paris Conference there was now added a new ingredient. The Romans had a saying 'something new always comes out of Africa'. If this was true in ancient times it has been equally true in the twentieth century.

The storm which broke over the Congo was both sudden and devastating. In the past it had often been regarded as a model African colony owing to the docility of the people and their apparent lack of interest in nationalist agitation. To quote from the words of *Annual Register*:

> This reputation, never really deserved, was finally and savagely destroyed in 1960. At the beginning of the year it still seemed possible that the Belgians and Congolese might agree on a time-table for political development with self-government as its first target, to be reached in a number of years. By the middle of the year the Congo had, with Belgium's blessing, become independent. By year's end the country had virtually collapsed into civil and tribal warfare.[1]

Although the Belgian Government had agreed, at a Conference held in January 1960, to independence within six months, no understanding had been reached among the Congolese leaders about the constitutional form which should be adopted. A bitter dispute arose as to whether this immense area should become a unitary state or whether it should follow a federal structure. Patrice Lumumba was the champion of the first and Joseph Kasavubu of the second solution. In theory a provisional programme had been accepted providing for the election by universal adult male suffrage of a central body, which was to act both as a constitution-making and a legislative organ. There were to be six provincial legislatures which were to choose a Senate of eighty-four members, fourteen from each province. A 'fundamental' law, that is a law of the constitution, was to be immediately adopted, and democracy was to begin her benign reign following long years of colonialism.

Unhappily, no single party obtained a majority, and it soon

[1] *Annual Register*, *1960*, pp. 344–5.

became clear that the rifle would be used to settle a question which the ballot had left obscure. The Belgian Government, which had organised in the past a comprehensive and efficient system of administration, had agreed to leave many of its civilian officials to assist in the early stages of independence. In addition, they had placed in the hands of the Government the only effective instrument of order. This was the *Force Publique*—a well-trained and efficient body, 25,000 strong, with Belgian officers. Unhappily, on the fifth day after independence, the soldiers in this *Force* started to mutiny in one of the local garrisons. Within a few days the revolt spread to Léopoldville, and the troops started indiscriminately attacking Europeans in the main cities.

Lumumba made a gallant effort to quell the mutiny by a somewhat novel plan. All the Belgian officers were dismissed, and all other ranks were promoted by one step. The *Force* therefore became one of African officers and non-commissioned officers. But these measures, however well-meant and original, were unsuccessful. Within a few days, following terrible outrages, a great wave of refugees began to roll through the country. Administrators, technicians, doctors, businessmen—all those indeed upon whom the life of the people depended—made their escape while there was still time.

> In addition to other troubles, the Congo (which became independent only a few days ago) has fallen into chaos; murder, rape, intertribal warfare, mass flight of Europeans, etc. The Belgian Government doesn't quite know what to do. The Prime Minister (Congolese) called Lumumba ... is [said to be] a Communist and probably a Russian agent; the Premier of Katanga (where the mineral wealth is) is a moderate, and wants to be independent. Sir Roy Welensky wants Katanga to be independent and would like to send in troops.[1]

On 8 July the Belgian Government announced the despatch of reinforcements of troops, and this was followed, on 11 July, by a request by Lumumba on behalf of the Congolese Government for United Nations help as 'protection against Belgian aggression'.

[1] 10 July 1960.

He also made a direct appeal to certain African countries such as Ghana and—sinister evidence of his sympathies—to the Soviet Government. Since Belgian troops had already taken up positions in many parts of the Congo to protect their civilians and since clashes between Belgian and Congolese soldiers had already begun; since Russian technicians and equipment were said to be on the way to this unhappy territory; since Moise Tshombe, a figure afterwards to reach great notoriety and meet a sad end, proclaimed the independence of Katanga, it was clear that we were on the verge not only of a catastrophe for the people of the Congo but also of a situation which might well lead to a wider and even a world conflict. Ghana offered to respond with troops, and the Russians were already on the move. But one of the most difficult problems was that presented by the interests of the Central African Federation and the Copper Belt. Congo was limitrophe with the Federation, and chaos or communism in the former territory presented equal dangers.

On 13 July Welensky appealed to me to try to keep the United Nations out of the Congo and thus minimise opportunities for communist penetration. Could we not work for a 'buffer state' in Katanga? However superficially attractive, I could not but agree with the Foreign Secretary that this action would be dangerous, at least at this stage. Our decision to work through the United Nations had the great advantage of preventing a direct Russian intervention.

> There is still uncertainty about the Belgian attitude. Meanwhile, the Russians are making a tremendous propaganda attack on all of us—France, Belgium, U.S., U.K., etc. We are accused of destroying the independence of Congo, etc., etc.—of 'colonialism' —or 'imperialism' in the most violent and bitter attacks, by note and radio.[1]

Apart from these wider issues, we had considerable anxiety about British residents in the Congo.

> We have had tremendous telegrams and telephoning about our own people—we have managed to rescue some British from Stanleyville by airlift.[1]

[1] 17 July 1960.

When, therefore, on 14 July, a Tunisian resolution was put forward to the Security Council of the United Nations authorising the Secretary-General in consultation with the Congo Government

> to provide . . . military assistance . . . until . . . with the technical assistance of the United Nations the national security forces might be able, in the opinion of the Government, to meet fully their tasks,[1]

the British and French Governments found themselves disinclined to oppose, far less to use the veto. In the event, we abstained because we had reservations about a paragraph asking the Belgian Government to remove its troops.

Hammarskjöld acted rapidly, relying largely on African countries for help. Within a few hours units from Ghana and Tunis arrived at Léopoldville, and General von Horn, from Sweden, took command of a United Nations force on 18 July. By the end of the month these troops were stationed in all of the major towns of Congo, except in the Katanga province where Tshombe refused to receive them. Undoubtedly, they did their best to preserve order and to reduce inter-tribal or civil war.

On the political side Dr. Ralph Bunche and Rajeshwar Dayal tried to promote some kind of settlement and to secure the liberation of prisoners. It is perhaps a tribute to both these officials that they were attacked by the Russians as American imperialists and by some of the Western Powers as communist stooges. The main dispute arose about the withdrawal of Belgian troops. Neither we nor the French thought it wise to lose at this stage the only disciplined and effective forces readily available. Although the Americans took a different view on this point, yet broadly we all agreed that our main purpose must be to counteract by all possible means Russian infiltration and occupation.

At this stage a somewhat Gilbertian situation arose. The Congo Senate, on 18 July, passed a resolution forbidding Russian military intervention, and Lumumba was therefore forced to retract his invitation. He countered by undertaking a rapid tour of Britain,

---

[1] *Annual Register*, 1960, p. 146.

America and Canada, and some African countries, asking for economic and political support.

Apart from certain criticisms of some of the actions of Hammars-kjöld's officers in the Congo, which were soon to develop, the main issue was now to turn upon Katanga. The arguments were certainly balanced. Tshombe was the Premier of a province which contained the rich mining areas of the Congo and provided nearly two-thirds of its revenue. He was on good terms with the Belgian proprietors and managers of the mines. He appeared to be able to maintain order in his large area. Essential services, which had practically broken down throughout the rest of the Congo, still operated in Katanga. Welensky and his Government were naturally anxious to maintain Tshombe's rule at any rate for the time being. Overt or even covert British support might, with the help of the Federation troops, have achieved this purpose. There was strong pressure in Britain, partly from business interests and partly from the right wing of the Conservative Party, to support Tshombe in a declaration of independence and to recognise and assist Katanga as a separate African State.

Nevertheless there were powerful arguments on the other side. Menzies, for whose judgement I had the deepest respect, sent me a warning telegram on 18 July. Alarmed by the Congo situation, and especially by Russian accusations, he felt that the West must give no credence to the charge that the Western Powers were proposing to intervene for their own benefit. He did not propose to make any response to a message from Tshombe requesting recognition.

> . . . and if I am called on to comment I propose to say so, adding that we have recognised the Congo Republic and do not wish to take sides in the dispute between Mr. Tshombe and the Central Government which is no affair of ours.

This view was supported in Washington and in Paris. On the whole, in spite of the many temptations to follow a more adventurous policy, it seemed to my colleagues and myself that our long-term interests would best be served by the emergence of a Congo Government of some responsible kind, largely depending on American rather than Russian aid and support.

Accordingly, when the Security Council met on 21 July, we gave our support to the resolution requesting the Belgians to withdraw their forces. This resolution was passed unanimously. Having taken the decision to support the United Nations as an instrument for preserving the integrity and unity of the Congo and to keep out Russian infiltration, it seemed wise not to do so hesitatingly or by half measures. Khrushchev, of course, continued to attack what he called 'the crude imperialism of Belgium in the Congo'. Nkrumah seemed genuinely anxious to avoid a confrontation between Europeans and Africans, and sent me many messages making various not unhelpful proposals.

But the crunch was soon to come. All turned upon the simple question as to whether the United Nations troops were to move into Katanga. From a practical point of view there was no need for them, for Katanga was quiet. Psychologically it was, of course, of great importance to Lumumba, who had now returned to the Congo. The issue was referred by Hammarskjöld for decision to the Security Council.

> Congo still more confused. Hammarskjöld has 'called off' the entry of U.N. forces into Katanga and referred the matter to the Security Council, which is to meet tomorrow night. Now the fat is properly in the fire.

> Hammarskjöld's recommendations, or perhaps one should say report, on the Congo situation reached me about 10 p.m. The Foreign Office had drafted a telegram to Sir Pierson Dixon (in New York). After some telephoning backwards and forwards between Alec Home and myself, we agreed the text at about 11.30 p.m.

> If the Security Council can be got to follow a sensible line, there is good hope of peace. But the great danger now is that the Congolese extremists (Lumumba and company) will try to defy the U.N. forces (now that Hammarskjöld has been unwilling to enter Katanga) and call in Russian or Russian satellite troops. Hammarskjöld has himself stated that the question is now (since the Belgians have really agreed to go) an internal African dispute. This is true. It is nonetheless a very dangerous position. Civil war in Africa might be the prelude to war in the world.

> Ever since the breakdown of the Summit in Paris I have felt

uneasy about the summer of 1960. It has a terrible similarity to 1914. Now Congo may play the role of Serbia. Except for the terror of the nuclear power on both sides, we might easily slide into the 1914 situation.[1]

Before the Council met there was, as can be imagined, a continuous flow of telegrams between the capitals, especially of the Western Powers. To dispel all this confusion Alec Home brought a wonderful combination of patience and understanding. Naturally I left the detail in his hands, but he kept me daily and sometimes hourly informed of the changing moods. On 7 August

Nkrumah has now joined in the clamour. 'If U.N. troops do *not* enter Katanga, Ghana will conquer the rebels, etc., etc.' This is the impression he wants to make. But, read carefully, his statement has several reservations and lines of retreat.[2]

On the same day at a meeting at Chequers, to which the Foreign Secretary and some of his officials came,

We had a good talk about the situation. Nkrumah is going to be difficult, because he sees in all this confusion a great chance to play a leading role. Round 'secession' will be built a great controversy. (Our own left-wingers, who demand secession for Nyasaland, are, characteristically, against independence of any kind for Katanga.) After Ghana, Guinea. Next Nasser. Behind, the Russians. It is a very tricky situation. If only we can get a *date* by which all the Belgians are to be out, it will be clear that this has become a row between *blacks* and not a *colonial* or a *black* versus *white* dispute. This should help us. But I am frankly alarmed at possible developments. Moreover, as long as Cabot Lodge is at U.N., the Americans are quite unreliable.[2]

On the 8 and 9 August the Security Council debated Katanga. As usual there were a number of resolutions, and as usual there was a great confusion in the method by which they were put forward and debated. In the intervals of discussing the problems of Iceland and fishing, and before leaving for a short visit to Bonn, the question of how we should cast our vote and influence was not easy to decide.

The U.N. Security Council start their discussion tonight. The

[1] 4 August 1960.   [2] 7 August 1960.

resolution tabled by the 'neutrals' and supported by the Americans is *not* good, but might be worse. Shall we vote *for* it or abstain?

The chief objects of British policy must be—

(1) To prevent Congo turning into Korea. Therefore, however attractive in some ways the separation of Katanga may seem, the result may well be a Korean-type war, following on Russian support to the rest of the Congo.

(2) To support, through U.N., some kind of 'federalist' solution—by which Katanga can have 'Home Rule' *but* make a contribution to the rest of this immense area. (Katanga is about the size of Spain.)

(3) To stop foolish but dangerous movements by *African* countries *alone*—Ghana, Guinea, Egypt, or any other—which may, in guise of Pan-Africanism, throw the whole continent into confusion.

(4) To work as closely as we can with French and other Europeans in NATO, including Belgians.

(5) To get Americans to be temperate and intelligent.[1]

The resolution which was ultimately carried by nine votes to none, with France and Italy abstaining, required the withdrawal of Belgian troops from the province of Katanga and declared that the entry of a United Nations force was necessary. But it also declared that the United Nations was not to intervene in force in any internal conflict. It was clear therefore that Hammarskjöld and his officials had no authority to depose Tshombe or restore Katanga by force to Lumumba's rule. Seen from our end this is an account of what happened:

There was a lot of telephoning all through the night. (I had gone from London to Birch Grove.) Dixon told us that, if *we* abstained (which was quite a possibility), the French, Italians would also abstain. Then the Russians and their friends would also abstain. So the motion would fall to the ground. The Russians would then move a very disagreeable motion, which would also be defeated or fall to the ground through insufficient votes. There would then be a vacuum; Hammarskjöld would have no authority; U.N. would presumably withdraw. Then, the Ghanaians, etc.,

[1] 8 August 1960.

from one side, and Russians (or Russian inspired and supplied forces) on the other, would move in. The fat would be properly in the fire. . . .

Bob Dixon convinced us. I spoke to Foreign Secretary at midnight (7 p.m. New York time) and at about 2 a.m. (9 p.m. New York time). We authorised Dixon to vote *for*.[1]

All these decisions taken under such difficulties have afterwards to be submitted to the critical eye of the British House of Commons and defended by Ministers who have often had only a modest share in the formulation of broad policies still less of details. Nevertheless the resolution was carried, and for the moment, with the entry of a United Nations force agreed to by Tshombe, there seemed to be some hope. Although Lumumba's Government had dismissed the Belgian Ambassador and his staff, the issue between East and West influence still remained in the balance.

During August and September some alarming reports were received.

> The Congo situation is very bad. Still worse is the news from Accra. Nkrumah is playing with fire. He has now got Russians in considerable numbers and Russian aeroplanes, which are beginning to oust the R.A.F. There is talk of a 'Pan-African' army—Ghana, Guinea and now Egypt! The Ethiopians are thoroughly alarmed and supporting U.N.O. Sudan is wobbling. We are certainly not yet out of the wood.[2]

Accordingly, I asked Sandys, who was now Commonwealth Secretary, to go to Ghana and if possible bring some moderating influence to bear on Nkrumah. There was certainly nobody better suited for this purpose.

> The Congo situation is still very alarming, and there are signs of the new African states—led by Ghana—trying to encourage Lumumba in his struggle against Hammarskjöld and the U.N.[3]

It was, of course, difficult for some of the African countries to take an impartial position or to understand that the United Nations

---

[1] 9 August 1960.   [2] 14 August 1960.   [3] 18 August 1960.

forces were to maintain order, not to make a decision on the constitutional conflict between Lumumba and Tshombe. Although
there was much criticism at home of Hammarskjöld, and especially
of some of his officers, it was satisfactory to find that the Communist
countries were far more violent. For myself, I was satisfied that 'so
far at any rate, by backing U.N., we seem to have avoided a direct
or indirect intervention by the Great Powers'.[1]

On the other hand Sir Malcolm Barrow, the Minister of Power
and Home Affairs in the Central African Federation, reported an
interview with a Belgian emissary from Tshombe which gave a
quite different picture. According to him, the Russians were
infiltrating military equipment and personnel to Lumumba, and the
studied neutralism of the Western Powers might result in a complete
domination by Russia of all the Congo including the vital province
of Katanga. This was, to some extent, confirmed by the arrival of
the first Soviet Ilyushin aircraft at Léopoldville on the very day that
the United Nations announced that all Belgian troops had now
left the Congo. Nevertheless, the Foreign Secretary still continued
to advise caution. Let the Africans fight it out themselves subject to
such advice and moderation as the United Nations force could
supply.

This view was certainly strengthened by another rapid and
dramatic reversal in the fortunes of the leading actors. President
Kasavubu, on 5 September, announced the dismissal of Lumumba
as Prime Minister and the appointment, in his place, of Joseph
Ileo. In return Lumumba declared that President Kasavubu was no
longer Head of State. In this crisis Sandys reported from Accra
that Nkrumah was expressing moderate and reasonable views and
was grateful for the close co-operation that he had received from
London.

The next day, 6 September, United Nations officials in the
Congo closed all the radio stations and airfields to all but traffic
carrying their sanction. Although some of the African countries
threatened to withdraw their contingents, the effect was good.

The next act in this tragi-comedy was a resolution by the
Congolese Chamber of Representatives invalidating both Kasavubu's

[1] 27 August 1960.

and Lumumba's dismissal of each other, thus leaving the stage clear for a military coup by a certain Colonel Joseph Mobutu.

> The Congo situation changes every moment. It is more like the Crazy Gang than anything I can remember. It now seems as if a colonel . . . has seized 'power' in Léopoldville; expelled Lumumba (who is said to be (a) killed; (b) in flight, (c) in hiding in the Guinean embassy) and told the Russians to leave, lock stock and barrel. It is too good to be true ![1]

The Russians were now definitely overplaying their hand. They began to attack the United Nations command in the most violent form, and at the same time the Security Council accused Hammarskjöld of being 'a screen for colonialism'. They even vetoed a resolution proposed by Tunis and Ceylon in support of the Secretary-General. Indeed, on 17 September, the very day upon which the Emergency Meeting of the Assembly was convened in New York, Kasavubu ordered the Russian and Czech diplomatic missions to leave the Congo.

> The Russians are (nominally out). But I cannot believe that they will be content to accept this apparent defeat.[2]

On the whole, therefore, in spite of increasing anxieties about the situation in Katanga and its impact on the Central African Federation, the policy of neutrality and firm support of the United Nations seemed to be successful. For this all credit must be given to the new Foreign Secretary, Lord Home. Nevertheless, this was clearly only one act or even scene in what might prove a long drama. We must expect some counterstroke.

The question now arose as to how to handle the meeting of the Assembly. At the beginning of September Khrushchev had announced that he proposed to lead the Soviet delegation and rally, if possible, all the Communist, semi-Communist or fellow-traveller support. He would especially attempt to influence the new members, sixteen out of the seventeen coming from various African states. Two questions arose which I put to the Foreign Secretary for his advice. There had been hints that Khrushchev's plan was not

[1] 16 September 1960.   [2] 18 September 1960.

merely to defend the Russian position as regards the Congo, and to make a dramatic, if disingenuous, plea for disarmament, but was seeking under cover of this a meeting with the President and myself. We had had certain indications through diplomatic channels that this was so. On the other hand his purpose might simply be to embarrass the President in the middle of the American elections and to establish a kind of unchallenged leadership in the Assembly itself. I sent a note to the Foreign Secretary on 3 September asking for advice.

> How do we deal with it? This is the point that we and the Americans have got to face. Do we deal with it on a gentlemanly line, refusing to have anything to do with it, or, the world being what it is, will we lose face among the neutrals and the un-committed countries, etc. That is the question we have to decide, and quite a lot depends upon it. For instance, if Khrushchev makes a great speech full of clever but false statements, a sort of mixture between Mr. Gladstone and Lloyd George, both at their worst, a very large number of people in all countries will believe him unless he can be shown up. The question is what is the best way of showing him up? I believe a powerful speech on the lines of that French telegram, which I thought admirable, would be a good thing. That is to say, to take the one point where he is weak and hammer at it all the time. Genuine inspection and genuine control—no other point matters in our disarmament plan, which has often been too complicated by detail. That is his Achilles' heel. The question then arises who is to try to pierce his Achilles' heel—the Foreign Secretary, supported by [David Ormsby] Gore, [Sir Patrick] Dean and [Harold] Beeley; and Herter, supported by Cabot Lodge, etc., with the two Achilles themselves still in the tent. That is the question and it is one which needs balanced judgement. . . .
> These points might perhaps be put to the Americans so that they can think about them before we talk to them again on Tuesday or Wednesday.

When I was at Balmoral on 6 September I discussed this matter with the Queen and asked her advice. My present instinct was to go to the United Nations Assembly if there was any question of negotiation, but to avoid joining in a slanging match. On 15 September I sent messages to all the Commonwealth Prime Ministers hoping that at any rate we could present a united front. It would indeed be impressive if the multi-national, multi-racial Commonwealth could demonstrate a common purpose. I also naturally consulted both de Gaulle and Adenauer, as well as Eisenhower. Owing to the recent Russian veto at the Security Council an Emergency Assembly was to be called under the so-called 'uniting for peace' procedure. The Afro-Asian group, as it came to be known, very sensibly submitted a resolution broadly supporting the United Nations and the Secretary-General and refusing the various Russian amendments. This was rather a blow to Khrushchev's prestige and was not at all the plan that he had envisaged in August when he appealed to all Heads of Governments to come to New York to discuss a vital and ambitious plan for disarmament. At the Emergency Meeting the Russians were abandoned by all except their small team of satellite countries. Indeed the resolution in support of the Secretary-General was carried three days later by seventy votes to none. After this preliminary, a formal Assembly was to open as agreed on 20 September. Here was to be joined the great battle between East and West, and Khrushchev hoped to make a great hit. I was still uncertain whether to leave the matter in Home's hands or to go myself. Menzies was doubtful, Nash was in favour, Adenauer hoped that I could do something to counteract Communist influence, Eisenhower was on the whole favourable. The Foreign Secretary, having tested the water in New York, sent me a telegram strongly advising my attendance. Accordingly, I made the necessary arrangements and informed the Commonwealth Prime Ministers as well as the allied leaders. In accordance with Home's advice the announcement of my decision to go to New York was made *before* Khrushchev's main speech, which was delivered on 23 September. This decision, although questioned by some of my colleagues, was welcomed by the Party and the Press.

President Eisenhower addressed the Assembly on 21 September in his usual attractive and simple style. 'It seems to have been moderate, sensible, not sensational or novel, but sincere and effective.'[1] He emphasised two points—first, Africa's need for food

[1] 22 September 1960.

and education in which the United States were ready to play a full part; secondly the impossibility of any effective disarmament without some form of control. I arrived too late to hear Khrushchev's speech, or rather the first of his speeches; for he intervened more than once in the debates before his departure in the middle of October.

Khrushchev's arrival in New York had, of course, created an immense furore, as it was intended to do. With the large and mixed population of the city, the question of his security presented the authorities with serious difficulties. Of all this he took full advantage. These precautions led him to appear on the balcony of the Soviet Headquarters and complain jocularly to a friendly crowd that he was under house arrest. Indeed he pulled out every stop in his buoyant and lively character. His staff still left it uncertain what were his real motives. There was talk of his having come for serious negotiation, but all the time it seemed to be a high-class demonstration in the art of popular advertising.

If the Congo crisis was embarrassing to the Western Powers, it presented even greater difficulties to the Soviet Government and to Khrushchev himself. He had planned his visit to New York as a triumphant demonstration of Russia's peace-loving purposes. He had appealed to the Heads of Governments to come to New York for this Assembly in order to discuss disarmament and the epoch-making, if deceptive, proposals which he was putting forward. Total disarmament was the cry—without, of course, any question of how it was to be achieved and above all how it was to be policed. He had hoped by this to take his revenge upon the Western Powers, especially the United States, over the U 2 espionage which had led to the collapse of the Paris Summit. He would appeal not only to Communist but also to neutralist states, as well as to many worthy people all over the world who longed for some relief from the threat of modern weapons and the terror of possible nuclear war. However, subsequent events had somewhat overshadowed this plan, and to Khrushchev's disadvantage.

The Assembly of the United Nations, like the House of Commons, finds it difficult to think of more than one thing at a time. Disarmament was a hardy annual, and some of the members were even getting a little tired of it. The troubles of the Congo were new and exciting and highly dramatic. In this situation Khrushchev also made the mistake of attacking the decisions of the United Nations, allowing himself to be put in the minority both in the Security Council and, more important from the propaganda point of view, in the Assembly itself. He also fell into the error of attacking the Secretary-General, who commanded the respect and affection of all the members, whatever criticisms they might have of some of his actions. Khrushchev, therefore, was unlucky both in the timing and in the execution of his great propaganda plan. Nevertheless, wherever he went and whatever he did was news. Unlike so many of the dreary orators who address the United Nations his own interventions were brisk and lively. His speeches, although long, did not follow a common form. You never knew what he would say, or how he would say it. His interventions in debate and interruptions were more natural and spontaneous than was customary. In other words he permitted himself interruptions by word or gesture which would hardly have attracted notice in our more boisterous Parliamentary life, but which flouted the high standard of decorum which is traditionally maintained at international assemblies.

Khrushchev's speech—18,000 words, three hours—has certainly not disappointed his admirers. Unfortunately, Dr. Nkrumah (Ghana) played into his hands with a demagogic speech about Africa. However, Dr. Nkrumah has the sense to support U.N. and the Secretary-General.

Mr. Khrushchev's speech was directed to excite and inflame the Afro-Asians. He demanded immediate 'freedom' for *all* colonial territories; he attacked Eisenhower and America with extreme bitterness. He attacked Hammarskjöld and demanded the abolition of the office of the post of Secretary-General and the substitution of 'an executive of three'. U.N. should leave New York. He then proposed a Summit in a few months' time to 'deal primarily with Berlin'.

One Indian is supposed to have said 'Eisenhower opened the door yesterday. Today Khrushchev slammed it shut'.[1]

I was annoyed by the Foreign Office spokesman who issued to the

[1] 24 September 1960.

Press a bitter reply to Khrushchev. I had a feeling that this was not good tactics.

Khrushchev's line won (at least emotionally and temporarily) great support from the Afro-Asians. We must not under-rate his power with them if he can work them up and excite them. Dr. Nkrumah is a case in point. He wavers all the time between common sense and emotionalism. I fear that his speech must have been arranged to tune in with what Mr. Khrushchev wanted. I am still, therefore, inclined to keep my speech in reply moderate and constructive.[1]

On the morning of Sunday, 25 September, I left for New York by R.A.F. Comet, stopping at Iceland, where the plane was refuelled, for a talk with the Icelandic Prime Minister on the eternal problem of fish and the extent of territorial waters. The Prime Minister seemed

a very nice man, but rather an ineffective one. We lunched alone together, and he explained at great length why it was impossible for him to make any concessions to us over the twelve-mile fishing controversy. He had only a majority of two or three, and a coalition Government—with the Socialists. The Communists were the strong opposition, determined to use the fishing dispute as an instrument for getting rid of the American base and Iceland out of NATO. I tried to impress on him the arguments he could use.

(a) He had got us to accept twelve miles as the final settlement. All we asked for was a 'fading out' period. Norway was going to concede us ten years. We could accept five years from Iceland. Why have a bitter conflict over this. He could claim to have done *twice* as well as Norway.

(b) We could probably make some further concessions about particular areas *within* the six—twelve miles, which would help him.

(c) We could give some economic help to his fishing and merchandising of fish.

I did not feel very encouraged by our talk. The Icelandic Prime Minister was a nice old boy, but clearly a weak man in a weak position.[2]

[1] 24 September 1960.   [2] 2 October 1960, describing earlier events.

From Iceland we flew to Goose Bay, Labrador, where we had to refuel.

> A pleasant enough interlude. We had a drive round the airfield and all the American and Canadian establishments. The Americans have 6,000 men; the Canadians 1,500. Arriving in New York about 10.00 p.m. and after a talk with the Foreign Secretary went to bed.[1]

Since I decided not to speak until the Thursday, 29 September, I had three days in which to listen to the debate and hold a number of talks with various notabilities. These included, apart from the Commonwealth Prime Ministers such as Diefenbaker, Menzies and Nkrumah, a useful talk with President Tito and a purely formal meeting with Nasser. On 27 September

> I had breakfast with President Eisenhower. We had a satisfactory talk about some Anglo-American questions, especially Polaris and the use of our bases for reconnaissance flights. Then a general talk about the situation. It was not clear whether the Russians were determined to break up U.N.O. or not. I thought the President rather ill and tired.[2]

In view of the importance of the occasion I took a good deal of trouble not merely about the composition of but also in the method of delivery of my speech. The purpose of coming to New York was, if possible, to present an effective contrast to the Russian posturing by developing a theme which would be at once moderate, constructive and appealing. I had observed during the previous days that although the Assembly was generally well attended, the technique of speaking was singularly ineffective. In nearly every case the text of the speech was distributed before it was made, and this took away all its freshness and its vigour. Nor was this at all necessary, for the simultaneous translation was in general admirably done. I decided not to follow this course and only allowed the text of my speech to be distributed to the delegates after it had been delivered. I adopted the ordinary Parliamentary style, with full notes but not excluding insertions and improvisations. The Chamber was full and the galleries crowded. My plan certainly had the result of making

[1] Ibid.   [2] Ibid.

listeners more alert. I had taken the trouble to go through the notes very fully with the translators and to leave them copies. I also followed the House of Commons tradition of making references to the previous speakers in the debate. All this seemed a novel and not unwelcome procedure. One of the few constructive proposals in Khrushchev's speech had been to suggest a 'reform' in the constitution of the United Nations. He had proposed that the Secretary-General should be replaced by a triumvirate or *troika* representing the West, the Soviet bloc and the neutrals. Although at first sight some neutral countries were attracted to the idea of a change which would give them a decisive vote as a group in the inner structure of the United Nations, it was evident on reflection that such a plan would bring its work to a halt. As to the British view of this point I left my audience in no doubt.

> Whatever its difficulties and perhaps shortcomings the United Nations is the best—indeed the only—organisation which we have available. Its influence is continually growing. Like all organisations, it can no doubt be improved. The President of the United States made certain suggestions for this purpose, which I greatly welcome. Their object was to increase, not to reduce the power of the Organisation to deal with crises as they may arise.
>
> The Soviet proposal, if I may say so, seems calculated to have the opposite effect. For it would extend the veto, with all its embarrassments into the realm of the Secretariat. It would freeze into the permanent structure of the Secretariat what we must all hope will be only temporary divisions among us. I believe therefore that it will be unacceptable to the majority of members.

With regard to the Congo I defended both the United Nations and the Secretary-General:

> The present division of the world exists and in this situation the interposition of the United Nations is often the only way to prevent the spread of these rivalries into areas where they may be a source not merely of local disturbance but of world danger. For that reason the United Kingdom Government feels that what the United Nations has done in the Congo was timely and should continue. . . .
>
> As for the Secretary-General. I would like to associate myself

and my country with the wide expression of confidence in his energy, resourcefulness and, above all, integrity.

It was not possible to avoid a reference to the Summit meeting and to the failure in Paris. After mentioning the declaration of the three Western Powers in favour of continued negotiations I went on:

Similarly, Mr. Khrushchev, although he permitted himself some forcible language, has seemed anxious to regard the path as temporarily obstructed and not permanently barred. At all events, it is in this spirit that I have worked during the period that I have been Prime Minister of my country and it is in this spirit that I speak today.

I did not wish to indulge, like so many speeches, in propaganda.

Indeed, the sponge of public opinion is almost saturated with the persistent flood of propaganda. It can pick up no more. Ordinary people, all over the world, in their present mood are beginning to tire of the same conventional slogans and catch-words.

After referring to the widespread, even passionate, hopes for peace and progress, I said:

But if we are to free mankind from ignorance, poverty and fear, we must at least free ourselves from old and worn-out slogans and obsolete battle-cries. Let me take a single example. Words like 'colonialism' and 'imperialism' have been slung about here without much regard to the facts, at least of modern colonial and imperial history. Mr. Khrushchev made great play with this theme, but his exposition was demonstrably a complete distortion.

After a short review of British colonial history and a rebuttal of the old familiar accusations I stopped, pointing to the hall, and said:

Gentlemen, where are the representatives of these former British territories: here they are, sitting in this Hall. Apart from the older independent countries, Canada, Australia, New Zealand, South Africa—here are the representatives of India, Pakistan, Ceylon, Ghana, Malaya. Here, here in this Hall. In a few days' time, Nigeria will join us. Sierra Leone and then the

West Indian Federation, will follow. And in due course others. Cyprus is already represented here. The problem of Cyprus, always an international rather than a colonial problem, has now been resolved, and the island has become an independent Republic as the result of friendly agreement between all the countries concerned. Who dares to say that this is anything but a story of steady and liberal progress.

I made mention of the similar record of the French community of nations and then turned to Europe. The Federal Republic of Germany was not a member of the United Nations but I was

amazed how backward-looking and reactionary much of the Communist argument is. Both the Polish and the Czech representatives talked of the spirit of revanche, which they alleged was reviving in West Germany. I am bound respectfully to say that their own speeches were not flowing over with the spirit of reconciliation.

Similarly the attacks on NATO as the 'instrument of West German militarism' seemed to me completely unjustified. I thought it right to defend Dr. Adenauer's Germany.

I will be frank, I represent a country that has no particular reason to regard German militarism with any special favour. Twice in my lifetime the British people have suffered most grievously both in blood and treasure as the result of German militarism. But we must look forward and not backward. Nor can you, to quote a famous phrase, 'draw up an indictment against a whole people'. Germany is divided into East and West, and so the German people in spite of their great population and importance cannot be represented in this Assembly today. Eastern Germany is armed. Great Soviet forces are stationed there. That is part of the unhappy state of the world today. Yet at the same time Western Germany is condemned for rearming. We have an old proverb in our country about the pot calling the kettle black.

The rest of the speech was taken up with the problem of disarmament. Whereas the United Kingdom like the United States and Canada were prepared to allow any form of inspection or control which was accepted by the Soviet Union, yet I recognised the

Soviet feeling that the inspection could become a cover for espionage. I did not agree with this. Nevertheless we must face the facts.

Some countries partly from their historical traditions, partly from the present state of the world division, regard with suspicion—natural suspicion—and would wish to reduce to a minimum any international inspectorate. Yet, if we are to succeed, and we must be realistic about it, these doubts, however reasonable, must be overcome. Fear of espionage, fear of strangers, resentment of the fact that words are not enough, that each nation needs to be reassured by, and reinsured by, effective inspection and control. All these misgivings are very human, but they must not stand in the way. And if we succeed, if disarmament can progress step by step, keeping time with the setting up of the controls, then these fears and suspicions will begin to fade. They will wither away.

Then taking up the suggestion made by various other delegates I proposed the appointment of a purely expert committee to review the progress already made and to put forward new methods by which, in the same way as the report of the scientists had provided a basis for the Geneva Conference on the abolition of nuclear tests, a new study covering the whole field of disarmament might be the basis for genuine advance. In the course of my speech, especially in the earlier parts, Khrushchev made a number of interruptions, familiar enough to me but apparently regarded as discourteous and almost disgraceful. When Khrushchev started banging on the desk or hitting it with his shoe, which he did from time to time, these interruptions seemed in this strange body to prove far more to my advantage than to his. On one of these occasions I stopped and said in a quiet tone—'Mr. President, perhaps we could have a translation, I could not quite follow.' This for some reason was thought very witty and effective. Naturally the world Press took up this episode, and British phlegm was contrasted with Russian excitability.

The effect of the speech was good both at home, in the United States and throughout the world and fully justified my decision. But I kept the general tone calm and moderate, with its appeal to the neutrals and especially to the emerging states in Asia and Africa.

On the same evening at 6.15 p.m.

I called, with Lord Home, on Khrushchev (Gromyko and Ambassador Soldatov were with him). A long talk–one and three-quarter hours–but very little progress. He was polite enough, though clearly my speech had upset him–especially the tremendous applause which it got from neutrals and Africans.[1]

Although little was achieved, it was evident to both of us that in view of all that had happened no serious negotiation could take place during this last stage in Eisenhower's presidency. We must wait. This became clear enough when Khrushchev called on 4 October for a farewell visit. We had 'a useful talk, in a much quieter mood'.[2]

Although I was anxious to get home I had the feeling that having spoken myself I ought at least in courtesy to stay and listen to the replies. Finally, I decided to leave on 5 October. Before doing so I tried

to summarise my feeling about this extraordinary experience.

(1) *Mr. Khrushchev*, by deciding to come in person, and bringing all the satellite team with him, imparted an element of drama into U.N. Assembly which everyone has secretly enjoyed. His extraordinary behaviour in the streets and by his balcony orations; his speeches in the Assembly; the U.S. Government's foolish attempt to constrict his movements–all this has kept the limelight on him all the time. (Castro stole it for a bit, by his retreat to Harlem and his four-and-a-quarter-hour speech.)

(2) *Mr. Khrushchev's* attack on the Secretary-General (due to the firm handling of the Congo against Russian infiltration) has (so far) failed to win approval of 'neutrals' or to intimidate Hammarskjöld.

(3) His *style* of debate (which I enjoy and find amusing) has shocked the members–especially the new members, who are very dignified.

(4) If he fails to get [the] disarmament debate into Plenary session (instead of the first Committee) Mr. Khrushchev will probably soon leave. Committees are no good to him.

(5) The U.S. Government have been shown up as weak. The

[1] 2 October 1960.   [2] 4 October 1960.

Speaking at the United Nations,
29 September 1960
'When Khrushchev started banging on the desk or hitting it with his shoe . . . these interruptions seemed in this strange body to prove far more to my advantage than to his.'

Khrushchev interrupts

With Diefenbaker and Nehru

President made a good enough speech—but it had no fire in it nor was it especially adroit. Herter is a charming man—but [ineffective]. The most powerful country in the world has, at the moment, weak leadership.

(6) Khrushchev hoped to carry everything by storm. He has not done that. But if a lot of small countries are shocked, they are also frightened.

(7) In spite of all the bluster, I do *not* think Khrushchev means to precipitate a crisis—e.g. over Berlin. He will wait for the American election; hope for more 'flexibility' in a new President; and agree to negotiation in the spring.

(8) Meanwhile, he will continue strong propaganda about disarmament. He will hope that Congo will go wrong. He will exert pressure, or bribery, wherever he can hope to influence the 'neutrals'.

(9) I think my visit *was* worth while, from point of view of putting some courage into neutrals; answering Khrushchev, but courteously and constructively; giving some leadership to U.S. and Commonwealth.

(10) But Nehru and India are both *strictly* neutral. Nkrumah (Ghana) is flirting (and perhaps more than flirting) with Russia and the whole fabric of U.N.O. is perilously weak. We do *not* yet know whether the Russians mean to leave it; destroy it; or try to bully it into subservience.[1]

After a short stop at Bermuda we got home to find plenty of problems:

Welensky and Monckton; a strike in London Docks; a threatened railway strike ! It is time to get back.[1]

Meanwhile the tragi-comedy of Congo continued, with the rival claims of Colonel Mobutu and Lumumba threatening civil war. In the United Nations Assembly President Kasavubu was recognised, on 22 November, as Head of the Congo, and throughout the rest of the year the members of the United Nations, other than the Soviet bloc, supported his attempt to restore order. Later in the year Colonel Mobutu's forces arrested Lumumba, although the latter's deputy was able to set up a régime in Stanleyville. Both in

[1] 5 October 1960.

K

the Assembly and in the Security Council the sorry picture was presented of great nations using the Congo tragedy purely as part of their ideological warfare. Throughout, the British and the Americans supported the gallant efforts of Hammarskjöld and his team. If there were mistakes they were certainly pardonable, and at this period, at any rate, the only hope seemed to be to give every help to the efforts of the United Nations forces to restore and maintain some kind of order. So matters remained throughout the winter and the greater part of the following year. It was not until the end of 1961 that the Congo crisis flared up again.

So far as relations with Russia were concerned we must wait the outcome of the Presidential Election. Khrushchev's great disarmament campaign with all its flamboyance, not to say buffoonery, had proved rather a flop. The meeting of scientists on the test ban continued quietly at Geneva throughout the winter. On 8 November came the news of the American Presidential Election. By a tiny majority over the Republican candidate, Richard Nixon—just over 100,000 out of nearly 69,000,000 votes—John F. Kennedy was elected President of the United States. Thus the Eisenhower regime came to its end, and the world turned with hope and sympathy to a new and exciting prospect, where youth and enthusiasm would take the place of age and experience.

This was the end of Eisenhower's public career, and although he loyally carried out the duties of Head of his Party, which falls traditionally upon the ex-President, it was clear to me when I met him from time to time that he felt these more of a burden than an interest. We remained close and even intimate; indeed one of my main purposes of a journey to California in 1968 was to make a last visit to my old friend.

Eisenhower's achievements are well known. He commanded with success large armies both in the African and the European campaign. He was President of the United States for two terms, and if in the last part of the second term there seemed to be a loss of American authority in the international field as well as a definite recession in her economic strength, yet this is not an uncommon symptom of any period of power, whether Presidential or Parliamentary. Eisenhower's methods, whether as a commander or as a statesman, were similar. He believed in the selection of men whom he could trust and in the devolution of authority wherever possible. As a soldier he relied upon the commanders of the forces by land, sea and air and contented himself with the dual task of presiding over a broad plan of campaign and keeping the confidence of all the allied forces who served under him. When he took control into his own hands he was not always so happy. Nevertheless his sweet and simple character, his probity, his sense of fair play, combined to make him an ideal commander of such varied forces, drawn from so many nations and origins. He could not claim the profound technical knowledge of the art of war that Montgomery had achieved. Nor had he the flexibility and cool assessment of strategic and tactical situations displayed by Alexander. Nevertheless, on two great occasions when his will and his alone made the supreme decision, Eisenhower showed supreme courage. The first was the invasion of Sicily, when the conditions by sea and air were wholly unexpected and dangerously tempestuous. The second was the launching of the invasion of Europe in similar conditions. In both cases there were strong arguments powerfully presented for postponement; in both cases Eisenhower made the sole decision and the right one.

As President his first term was highly successful. His second term was unlucky. In my dealings with him I had certainly an advantage over my British colleagues, and indeed over any other European statesman, arising from my close association with him during the difficulties of the North African campaign. We had grown very fond of one another, with implicit trust if not in the other's wisdom at least in his good faith. Yet Eisenhower's attempt to introduce into the civil field methods which he had found useful in the military sphere was not altogether a success. He tried to operate a Cabinet rather like a military staff, or perhaps it might be truer to say he began to turn the position of President into that of a constitutional monarch. But in either case his trouble was that he had no real chief of staff. The result was to throw far too much authority into the hands of one or two powerful Ministers.

Under a strong President Foster Dulles might have been a good Secretary of State; under Eisenhower he was a disaster. Yet after the illness and death of Dulles Eisenhower was never able to find the right successor. At first he tried to do more of the work himself. But whether from physical or mental exhaustion he soon got tired of it. In moments of difficulty, like that of the Paris Summit meeting, he had not the flexibility of mind to adopt a course which would allow Khrushchev an easy way out. A few words of apology, some suitable formula, might at an early stage have saved the situation. But the President allowed a number of foolish statements to be made, both false and contradictory; and when the moment came he was too honourable to rely upon a diplomatic white lie and too conscious of his position as commander in chief to throw the responsibility upon a subordinate.

All these were endearing features of his character, although sometimes rather embarrassing. I cannot tell how historians of the United States will rank Eisenhower as a President either with regard to his policies at home or abroad. I can only pay tribute to him as a man of great charm, absolute integrity and deep personal loyalty. It was upon these qualities of his that our long friendship was based. To complete the record I ought to perhaps add the message I sent him on 10 November which he reprinted in full in his own memoirs, *Waging Peace*. Happily, for me, the last sentence proved not to be true.

I feel I must write a few words to you on a purely personal basis at this time. The election of a new President has brought home to me the situation which of course I knew must come, that the period of our close co-operation together in so many fields is drawing to an end. When I look back on the first time we met in the Hotel St. George, nearly twenty years ago, I realise how long this friendship has been. I know that nothing will ever impair its strength or its usefulness to our two countries.

As a soldier you had under your command the largest forces that Britain has ever put into action by air, sea or land; as President you have done everything to maintain the close friendship of our two countries. I think you must have realised when you drove from London Airport last year what the British people feel about you.

I can only assure you that I will try my best to keep our Governments and our countries on the same course. But I cannot of course ever hope to have anything to replace the sort of relations that we have had.

CHAPTER X

Commonwealth Crisis

ALTHOUGH we had survived the Commonwealth Conference of May 1960 without disaster, I knew that the struggle over South Africa and her racial policies had only been postponed. Dr. Verwoerd, who made a remarkable recovery from the wound inflicted by his would-be assassin, declared, at the beginning of July, that he was convinced that if South Africa decided to become a republic the influence of Britain, Australia, Canada and even India, would ensure that she retained her membership of the Commonwealth. In logic, of course, he had a strong case. The abandonment of a monarchical and the substitution of a republican regime had been adopted by almost all the new members of the Commonwealth without affecting their continuance in the association, provided they accepted the position of the Queen as Head of the Commonwealth. Dr. Verwoerd certainly had a powerful argument, based on sound precedents; but he altogether underestimated the feelings which had been aroused, partly by his own speeches and actions, and partly by the tragic events which seemed to accompany the strict dogma of apartheid, and had recently culminated in the Sharpeville tragedy. Both Malaya and Ghana decided to boycott South African goods, and there was strong pressure in other countries to adopt the same form of protest. Accordingly, I thought it necessary, on 13 July 1960, in order to avoid any misunderstanding to remind the Prime Minister of the Union of the discussions at the last Prime Ministers' Conference. Although I personally expressed the hope that South Africa would remain a member, it was clear, both from the communiqué issued after the Conference and from the debates which led up to it, that none of the Prime Ministers present was prepared to be committed in advance as to the decision which would have to be taken, if and when an application was made by the South African Government on becoming a republic. I added :

> You will be forming your own assessment, but my appreciation is that if and when such an application is made, and if at that time those aspects of South African policy which were criticised here in May (and I am not here concerned with the validity of those criticisms) remain unchanged, there would be more than one Commonwealth country which, despite the practice adopted hitherto, would, for reasons of policy, oppose the continued membership of South Africa.
>
> We should then be faced with a sharp divergence of view on an issue of major importance, namely membership, on which collective agreement is required. This would create a most critical situation, and I must say quite frankly that I myself do not find it easy to forecast what the outcome might be.

On 2 August, having received a message through the South African High Commissioner that Verwoerd intended to hold a referendum on the issue of a republic on 5 October, I made a further appeal :

> In my message to you of 13 July I sought to put to you the difficulties which I see looming ahead. Since then these difficulties have sharpened. It has become clear that certain Commonwealth Governments would very probably, as matters stand, feel compelled to oppose the continued membership of South Africa if and when the time comes for their consent to be sought, and there is a great risk also that all the other non-European members of the Commonwealth might be constrained to join them in this attitude. I need not stress what painful results would be likely to follow from a division of the Commonwealth on racial lines on an issue of such importance for us all.
>
> So seriously indeed do I view the prospects that I feel impelled to ask you in all friendship and with the Union interests uppermost in my mind, to reflect before proceeding with your announcement at this juncture. Taking a long-term view, would it not serve your interests better to postpone it until times in Africa are calmer? To secure a breathing space amid all these fast-flowing developments would be very valuable.

I hope that you are now fully recovered from your grievous injuries.

My communication crossed with a letter from Verwoerd saying that if the republic was unacceptable to the Commonwealth, then South Africa would have to be a republic outside. His country, of course, would wish to maintain friendly relations both with the United Kingdom and other countries who were ready to do so, but he must make it clear that pressure from other Commonwealth countries concerning the internal affairs of the Union was unacceptable in principle, and South Africa would not be prepared to doctor her policies to suit the requirements of other countries. If she were to do so it would only lead to a series of further demands. In any case the Government and people of South Africa were convinced of the moral rectitude of their policies.

When the announcement was made as to the holding of the referendum, I wrote to all the Commonwealth Prime Ministers, urging them at this stage to say as little as possible on the issue. Whatever else might happen, it was clear that the choice between a monarchy or a republic was entirely a matter for the country concerned. I myself would continue to refuse to be drawn as to the attitude of the United Kingdom Government on one hypothesis or the other. On the whole most of the Prime Ministers seemed willing to accept this policy of waiting until the issue was formally raised. Nehru added that it would not be possible to avoid all reference to 'considerations relevant to the question of South Africa's retention of its membership'. At the same time I sent personal messages to Menzies and Diefenbaker asking for their advice.

Later in the same month, I sent a further letter to Menzies asking for his help, for I had a great respect for his wisdom and experience. It seemed pretty certain that Verwoerd would win the referendum. How could South Africa's subsequent expulsion be prevented? So dramatic a scene at the next Commonwealth Conference would undoubtedly have serious consequences. It would be regarded as a move by the Asian and African members, and thus damage the multi-racial concept which we were anxious to sustain. Perhaps he and some of the other Prime Ministers of the old members of the Commonwealth could bring some pressure on Verwoerd to postpone the issue? Alternatively could they persuade the Afro-Asians that the expulsion of South Africa could bring no benefit to the non-White population of the Union?

On 7 September I was encouraged by a report from the Commonwealth Secretary who was visiting Accra. As a result of a long conference Nkrumah stated

> that he was impressed by the real threat to the future of the Commonwealth which might result from a split over the issue of South Africa's membership. Therefore despite the difficulties he would have in explaining his attitudes he felt that in all the circumstances it would probably not be wise for him to object to South Africa's application though he would have to reserve his right to raise the issue of apartheid separately.

Messages from Malaya were not so hopeful. The Tunku made no attempt to disguise his strong feelings on the racial issue. I left for my holiday with anxieties about this among other matters, but tried to forget it in happy relaxation upon those grouse moors which formed so convenient a background for the cartoonists and gossip writers. During a few days at Tillypronie, where I was the guest of Gavin Astor, my surprise was mixed with a certain feeling of displeasure that this short interval of repose was interrupted by the visit of Eric Louw. My host took it all very calmly, and the South African Minister of External Affairs was entertained lavishly and introduced to some of the pleasures of the Scottish hills. He arrived with many apologies, but he had been instructed to deliver to me personally, and into no other hands, a message from his Prime Minister. After a long conversation he left behind him an *aide-mémoire* consisting of no less than twelve foolscap pages.

> All it really amounted to was (*a*) complaint that the loyal opposition in the South African referendum campaign are arguing that if South Africa abandons the Monarchy, her request to stay in the Commonwealth will be vetoed by Ghana or Malaya; (*b*) a complaint against the 'unanimity rule'; (*c*) a complaint of the unreasonableness of the Africans and Asiatics in the Commonwealth; (*d*) an assertion of Dr. Verwoerd's sincere desire to

retain the Commonwealth connection, which he valued both for its material and spiritual values; (e) a threat to 'blackball' Cyprus if South Africa is blackballed.

I listened, and except for observing that South Africa was continually invoking the 'unanimity rule' to prevent discussions which were not to their taste, and that since the result of the referendum was not yet known, I made few but general comments.[1]

Louw argued that South Africa's continued membership should not be dependent upon unanimous approval. Although he admitted that there was no precedent, the correct procedure should be that general approval should over-ride one or even a small number of objectors. Undoubtedly the mere transference from a monarchical regime to a republican had not in the past and should not in the future be taken as an objection. To do so would be a radical departure from the precedent established in previous similar cases. If it was the wish of the Commonwealth to expel South Africa on the grounds of her racial policies, a direct motion to that effect would be more honourable. Alas, logic and the strict rules of procedure are not the sole motives which influence human action. The opportunity offered by the necessity for a further application was to be grasped by those countries who felt themselves affronted, even insulted, by the apartheid principle. However, I still felt hopeful of persuading the Commonwealth members as a whole to accept the view that we could bring more influence in the long run on the policies of the Union if she remained with us than if she left our company. Much however would depend on the tone and temper of the discussions when the time came.

Meanwhile, I received a long and valuable letter from Menzies, promising to do his best to work upon the other countries on these lines, and I knew that I could depend upon his loyalty and strength when the time came. Friendly messages now began to come both from Malaya and Ceylon and even from Pakistan, promising to withhold comment for the present.

On 5 October the referendum was held. There was a poll of 90·73 per cent. On a total vote of 1,626,336, the majority in favour of a Republic was only 74,580. These figures reflected two things—first

[1] 8 September 1960.

K2

the overweighting of the Dutch-held seats in the Parliament by the arrangement of constituencies, and second the remarkable rally in favour of Monarchy by the people of British descent. Many statesmen would have hesitated to make so drastic a constitutional change or would have thought it a poor response to the liberal policies which Britain had shown to the Dutch people after the South African war. However, Dr. Verwoerd had no such qualms; and the only concession which he was willing to make in the new constitution was to guarantee the equal status of the two official languages — English and Afrikaans. At the same time, he declared that it was the wish of South Africa to remain in the Commonwealth, but that she would not permit herself to be subjected to any humiliation or any attempt to interfere in her internal affairs.

In the same confident mood Verwoerd now addressed me a long letter on 24 October asking for an early decision :

> It is my view that there are three methods by which the approach may be made. The first is that I inform each of the Prime Ministers separately and directly of the Union Government's intention and desire, in order to ascertain their views. The second would be that you undertake to do so at the request of the Union Government. The third is, of course, a Prime Ministers' Conference to be called in order to deal with the matter. The purpose of this letter is to seek your advice as to the most effective and expeditious course to be followed.
>
> Whatever method is decided upon, I consider it necessary that the required action be undertaken as soon as possible, and it therefore seems to me preferable that the matter be finalised by correspondence, one of the courses visualised at the last Prime Ministers' Meeting. A further Conference this year would not, to my mind, be feasible, and a lengthy delay would inevitably permit of protracted speculation in the Press and elsewhere, which could render the position more difficult for all concerned and might even oblige certain Prime Ministers to commit themselves to fixed attitudes.

He went on to set out his views in some detail as to the best method.

> It is for these reasons that an early decision by correspondence appears to me to be the best course. If you agree with this view,

the question then arises whether I should communicate with the other Prime Ministers direct, or whether you would be prepared to approach them. This is a matter on which I must be guided by your views. It may be that you are already sufficiently informed as to the attitude of the other Prime Ministers to be able to undertake this without embarrassment to yourself.

If you should believe that, notwithstanding the views expressed by me, South Africa's continued membership should be decided at a Prime Ministers' Conference, I would of course raise no objection and would be prepared to attend in person.

Since Verwoerd, to do him justice, never left any doubt or loophole for negotiation or argument, he went on to restate his position.

As regards the general question of South Africa's continued membership, suggestions have come to my notice that we would experience no serious obstacles if the Union Government were to amend its racial policies. I mention these suggestions only because I must make it quite clear that we regard them as attempts to interfere in South Africa's domestic affairs. It would obviously also be quite impossible for us to bargain for continued Commonwealth membership. We regard it as fundamental that the manner in which other Commonwealth members should approach our desire to continue our membership, should be governed by the same considerations and be based upon the same concept of the Commonwealth, as motivated our decisions when we were approached with regard to the membership, or continued membership, of other member states. We have never felt justified to permit our views on the internal conditions or policies of those countries to influence our decisions; nor have we been swayed by the fact that some of them were in open economic and political conflict with us. We have chosen to base our decision on considerations which recognise the true nature of the Commonwealth, and on the existence of a community of interest, in spite of differences. Since it has been our consistent endeavour, despite provocation, to avoid attacking other members and not to interfere in their domestic affairs, the adoption of a proper attitude towards South Africa's continued co-operation and collaboration in the Commonwealth on matters of common concern should therefore be so much easier for them than it was for us in certain similar circumstances.

One could never either read or listen to the Prime Minister's arguments without being impressed by the clarity with which they were expressed. Nevertheless, he seemed to have no understanding that anyone could consider the political and social position of the vast majority of the population of South Africa was not a purely 'domestic' question, especially having regard to the present constitution of the Commonwealth. However, it is perhaps worth remembering that no such considerations as to the 'natives' ever seemed to enter the minds of those great Liberal statesmen, Campbell-Bannerman, Asquith and Grey when they handed over without any guarantee the control of the life and future of the so-called 'Kaffirs' to the tender mercies of a Dutch majority. In any event, it was clear to me that the matter could not be dealt with by correspondence, and it would be essential to have a meeting of all the Commonwealth Prime Ministers to discuss so grave an issue.

It is never easy, especially with the present size of the Commonwealth, to fix a date that suits everybody. Moreover, a new point had been raised by Dr. Verwoerd about the different treatment of the new application of Cyprus from that which was to be given to the position of South Africa. Once again in law and logic this was a good point. It was quite true that to deal with the rather special case of Cyprus, in view of her relationship with Greece and Turkey, I had agreed to canvass the various Prime Ministers as to their attitude. But here the point at issue was not the domestic policies of the island but the curious character of her situation in the international field. At one time I expected Verwoerd to continue to press this point with vigour. However, towards the end of November, Louw saw me and gave me the impression that this Cyprus objection would be withdrawn and that Verwoerd would come to a meeting that was to be held in the spring. A later message confirmed these decisions.

By the end of 1960 it was generally agreed that the meeting should take place in March. At this point, and until the end of the unhappy controversy, I was determined to make every effort to keep South Africa in the Commonwealth. In the first place it seemed to me an unfair use of the purely procedural point to refuse to a republican what we continued to accept under a monarchical system. The domestic policies of South Africa, however objection-able, would not be changed, nor was it really proper for countries which had taken advantage of the right to become republics to use this technicality as a lever for the expulsion of a member of such long standing. If such a course was thought necessary it should not be associated with the change of regime; it should be a separate proposition put forward with due solemnity at a special meeting. Moreover, I felt that by retaining the Union in the Commonwealth there might be a hope that, as the years passed, the pressure not merely of public opinion in the world but the actual necessities of living alongside their African neighbours, would lead to a gradual change in the philosophy which lay behind this racial Calvinism.

In the course of the winter of 1960, I was encouraged by the growth of this feeling, sometimes in unexpected quarters. Nkrumah had already made it clear that he would not like to force the issue now, and somewhat to my surprise the same position was taken by the Prime Minister of Malaya. On 16 November he came to see me and made his position perfectly clear.

> He is going to agree to Cyprus joining and South Africa remaining in the Commonwealth. I am much relieved.[1]

But on 16 November to my surprise I received a disturbing message from Diefenbaker, in the course of which he said:

> In view ... of developments since May which give no indication of any change of attitude by the Government of South Africa, I feel obliged to let you know that unless significant changes occur in the Union Government's racial policies, Canada cannot be counted on to support South Africa's readmission to the Commonwealth.

On this I noted:

> John Diefenbaker is going to be troublesome about South Africa. He is taking a 'holier than thou' attitude, which may cause us infinite trouble. For if the 'Whites' take an anti-South African line, how can we expect the Browns and Blacks to be more tolerant.

[1] 16 November 1960.

After consultation with the Commonwealth Secretary, I felt that
the position taken by the Prime Minister of Canada might well be
decisive if expressed when the Conference took place. I therefore
wrote to him, stating the position which I and my colleagues in the
British Government took in this affair.

I was so glad to have a word with you on the telephone
yesterday about your message on South Africa and the Commonwealth. I know that you are as concerned over this problem as I
am. While I am sure that we must do all we can to bring pressure
upon the Government of South Africa to modify their racial
policies, I am very anxious, as I know you are, to find a way of
keeping them in the Commonwealth. May I put one or two
thoughts before you?

First on the reality of the situation. We have all disliked these
policies for many years. Since the death of Smuts they have got
much worse. All the same, we have not tried to make this a reason
for ejecting South Africa from the Commonwealth. There are
bound to be, from time to time, other members of the Commonwealth whose policies are disagreeable or doubtful to one or
other of us. For instance, I suppose one could accuse the President
of Pakistan of pursuing anti-Parliamentary and anti-democratic
lines, although I think he has probably done the only thing to
save Pakistan—and ultimately to save free government there. Or
one might criticise the President of Ghana for the attitude
towards the Opposition in his country which you and I think
contrary to Parliamentary tradition. The only reason that we find
ourselves in immediate difficulty with South Africa is because of
what is really a procedural point; that is the change of status from
a monarchical to a republican system. I think we are all agreed
that that change is purely an internal matter. We have certainly
taken it as such in the case of India, Ghana and Pakistan; and, no
doubt, fairly soon it will come to us in Ceylon. Up to now we have
taken the consent of the other members as a matter almost of
form. Of course, last May the South Africans asked us to do
something which you and I both thought wrong; that was to give
prior consent before the issue had arisen and thus in some measure
to seem to be influencing the outcome of the Referendum. I am
sure we were right to resist this. But now that the change to a
Republic has been settled by the Referendum, I believe we

should consider carefully how far it is wise to use the change of status as an occasion for a protest against South Africa's racial policies.

I have found in recent discussions with some of our Commonwealth colleagues a growing sense that the expulsion of South Africa—for that is what it would amount to—on the issue of her becoming a Republic would be somewhat anomalous. In any case, I am sure that there is a strong desire to take counsel together and to weigh all the implications before coming to a decision. The Tunku, for instance, to whom I have just been talking, is very much alive to the possibly disastrous effect on the whole Commonwealth structure of the beginning of a break-up now. Much as he abhors apartheid, I think he would prefer to accept the constitutional change rather than force the issue, at any rate for the time being. Of course it would be difficult for him, as well as for Nkrumah and Nehru and some of the others, to acquiesce if it seemed in some way to condone apartheid. But I hope that when we come to consider the whole question, especially the procedural question, we may find some way out of our difficulty.

Naturally I understand your desire to make your position clear to Verwoerd. Nor have I concealed from him how difficult is the road that lies ahead of him, and that he would be very wrong to count on general agreement. Pressure on him may be all to the good; but I hope that you will be very careful not to take a decision which would bind you to come down against South Africa in any circumstances, whatever the result of our further examination of the question may prove to be. There is obviously not much hope of South Africa changing her policies in the next few months, but what I am anxious about is that none of us should take a definite position before we meet. If by chance the knowledge of anything you said to Verwoerd leaked out, it would make the position of the African and Asiatic members of our Commonwealth almost impossible. What I am therefore pleading for is that we should come to the discussion in March uncommitted, publicly or privately.

Such are the political arguments that I venture, my dear John, to put before you. But there is just another point of view that I know you would not mind me putting forward. This is really a human as well as a political problem. We all hate the racial policies of the present South African Government; but surely we must try to think of all the people who have made this great country. The expenditure of blood and treasure from Britain that has gone to create it; the long and rather splendid story behind it; and the future of all those who are there—white, coloured and black. After all, nearly half the white population are passionately loyal to the Queen and really all seem anxious to stay in the Commonwealth. Moreover there are nearly ten million who are not able to make their voice in any way felt on these matters but look to us for help—'Come over to Macedonia and help us' is their cry. It will not help them—indeed it might be a fatal thing to them—if the rest of the Commonwealth were to expel them from the community. We must all try to do what we can to help—we must not pass them by on the other side. After all, we can do more to influence the future of these people if they are within the framework of the Commonwealth than if they are outside it. And I do really feel that we should regard our responsibilities as covering all those in South Africa and not just the South African Government or the Nationalist Party caucus. There is a further and more immediate point. Now that the Republican issue has been settled the one great aim that has kept the Nationalist Party together will have been achieved. This will give an opportunity for a resurgence of liberal thought within the Party and throughout the country. But if they are turned out of the Commonwealth the process will never begin, or be much curtailed. We should in fact be doing the opposite of what all of us believe to be right, namely to try and get South Africa to change her racial policies. We should be condemning the country to further years of apartheid and ever-growing bitterness.

We ought to remember Burke's famous words:

'A partnership between those who are living, those who are dead, and those who are yet to be born.'

I hope you do not mind me writing to you at such length and so freely. I take the liberty to do so not merely as a colleague but as a friend.

Since I knew how much weight India carried both from its size and importance and the outstanding character of its leader, I wrote a similar letter on 6 January to Nehru.

In the light of these exchanges I had some basis for hoping that a way out could be found, in spite of the increasingly bitter feelings which South African policies were arousing throughout the world. At a similar conference in the previous year we had, at the last moment, been able to devise an acceptable formula.[1] There seemed a fair chance of finding a similar solution now. Nor was this confidence unreasonable. Even a small—almost a trivial—concession by Dr. Verwoerd would have been accepted with relief.

The members of the Conference gathered on 8 March 1961 at Lancaster House. It was only after a most painful series of discussions, and the vain consideration of many draft resolutions, both in full session and in smaller groups, that I was forced to the sad conclusion that no compromise could be devised which would avoid serious conflict and a probable break-up of the Commonwealth. Although the outward forms of courtesy were maintained, there were moments when feelings ran so high that I was forced to suggest repeated adjournments from the council chamber to the lobbies. It had been my plan to persuade my fellow Prime Ministers to accept the membership of the South African Republic in accordance with established precedent, but to issue, at the same time, a firm and, with one exception, unanimous reaffirmation of the principle of multi-racialism and the consequential rejection of apartheid. This would, at least, have averted the crisis for the time being. There was, of course, the danger that the interval before the next Conference would be taken up with a violent campaign of severe criticism of South Africa's policies and the demand for her expulsion. But much could happen in these twelve or eighteen months, and many other world problems could arise of greater or more immediate importance. In my attempts to urge this solution I enjoyed the most loyal co-operation throughout from Bob Menzies, both in the full sessions and in the many private discussions that took place behind the scenes.

So far as I personally was concerned the Conference could not have taken place at a worse time.

We have had three weeks of continuous crisis—the worst I remember since the days before Suez. For the same reason as then, I have not been able to keep this diary, day by day. There simply has not been time, and the nervous strain has been too

[1] See above, pp. 175–6.

great for me to make the effort. I have had little sleep—sometimes not more than two or three hours a night. . . .

There have been four separate crises going at once—

(1) Rhodesia (first stage) involving a possible break-up of the Government and/or a revolutionary movement by Sir Roy Welensky.

(2) Financial crisis, threatening collapse of sterling.

(3) Commonwealth crisis, with ultimate withdrawal of South Africa from Commonwealth.

(4) Rhodesia (second stage) with a fresh threat from Sir Roy Welensky and possible Cabinet crisis.

These all ended by 21 March. Now

(5) The Laos crisis has blown up, with possibility of war in South-East Asia.[1]

Yet there were moments when I was confident that I could achieve a compromise. I still believe it would have been possible,

except for the following difficulties, which (taken together) proved insuperable: (a) The tremendous newspaper agitation and build-up, supported by political leaders and publicists here, against what was called 're-admitting' South Africa because of apartheid. (b) The decision made by Nehru—on the day before the discussion—to urge the Afro-Asian premiers to refuse, while lying pretty low himself. (c) The extreme rigidity of Dr. Verwoerd, who never made the smallest concession to his colleagues in the Conference, even on matters strictly outside the apartheid dogma—e.g. diplomatic representation between Commonwealth countries.[1]

It was Dr. Verwoerd's attitude and method of arguing his case, as well as the inflexibility of his dogmatic position, which finally turned the balance. Had he made the slightest concession, for instance regarding the acceptance of diplomatic representatives of African states without subjecting them to the indignity of separate treatment, the mood might easily have changed. But the plan for a special hotel for the benefit of African representatives, if admitted at all, where it was presumed they would not contaminate the

[1] 24 March 1961.

superior white race, seemed just another insult, however luxurious might be the accommodation presented. Thus every proposal which Menzies and I made to get over one difficulty or another was destroyed by Verwoerd himself.

The Conference lasted from 8 to 15 March; but there were many other questions to discuss, and the debates on South Africa took up only two and a half days. It was more than enough. Finally, on the afternoon of the third day, I was forced to the conclusion that neither my plan nor any other could succeed.

> Even President Ayub [Khan] (Pakistan) usually so moderate, was deeply offended by some of Dr. Verwoerd's remarks. Ayub (who is pure Indo-European) is apparently regarded by South African Government as black. Nehru (India) and Mrs. Bandaranaike (Ceylon) would equally have forced the issue. What then I had to avoid was a *vote* (which I suppose Dr. Verwoerd might have asked for). This would have put United Kingdom Government into a great difficulty. We should only have got Australia and New Zealand (Menzies and Holyoake). Canada (Diefenbaker) would have been against.[1]

When this danger became apparent there seemed only one way of avoiding a catastrophe and a possible dissolution of the whole Commonwealth. Accordingly, I

> devised a plan by which Dr. Verwoerd should be induced to withdraw his application if it became clear that the result of forcing the question to a vote would be an almost overwhelming vote against. He, therefore, after a final talk with me on Wednesday alone, took this course.[1]

As a result a communiqué was immediately agreed and issued in the following terms:

> At their meetings this week the Commonwealth Prime Ministers have discussed questions affecting South Africa.
> On 13 March the Prime Minister of South Africa informed the Meeting that, following the plebiscite in October, 1960, the appropriate constitutional steps were now being taken to introduce a republican form of constitution in the Union, and that it

[1] 24 March 1961.

was the desire of the Union Government that South Africa should remain within the Commonwealth as a republic.

In connection with this application the meeting also discussed, with the consent of the Prime Minister of South Africa, the racial policy followed by the Union Government. The Prime Minister of South Africa informed the other Prime Ministers this evening that in the light of the views expressed on behalf of other member Governments and the indications of their future intentions regarding the racial policy of the Union Government, he had decided to withdraw his application for South Africa's continuing membership of the Commonwealth as a republic.

On the next day I made a short and formal statement in the House of Commons, which was received in a grim and painful silence. I confined myself to a few formal words.

I am sure that I speak for many of us on both sides of the House when I express our deep regret that the Commonwealth ties with South Africa, which have endured for fifty years, are shortly to be severed, and our regret, also, for the circumstances which have made this unavoidable. Remembering that the Commonwealth is an association of peoples of all races, colours and creeds, we must hope that, in the years to come, it will be possible for South Africa once more to play her part in the Commonwealth.

Exhausted by the heavy pressures of these strenuous days, and weighed down by a sense of grief and foreboding, I could not conceal from my fellow Members my deep emotion. I felt the heavy responsibility of presiding over so tragic a break, especially remembering the many loyal British people in the Union. Once more a genuine effort at pacification had failed, and the outcome of the Conference was to embitter rather than to soothe the feelings which had been aroused. Nor could I hide from myself the effect on the delicate negotiations now taking place with Sir Roy Welensky, whose close relations with the Right Wing of the Conservative Party, both in the Lords and the Commons, were notorious and dangerous. But I was concerned with the still wider consequences. I felt almost a sense of despair. Was every problem in the world to be handled by men who altogether failed to understand, still less to compromise with, any other view than their own? Added to the great division between the Communist and the Free World, were we now to be tortured by racial divisions with ever-increasing bitterness?

While our arrangements, both in the sphere of defence and economic relations, with South Africa might remain unchanged after she ceased to be a member of the Commonwealth when the Republic became effective, nevertheless the effect of the secession of the Union upon the extremist politicians in Salisbury must be considerable—and might prove fatal. There were some even at home who were beginning to wonder whether these internal disputes in the Commonwealth, which threw such a heavy burden on the Old Country, could be tolerated indefinitely, and whether the Commonwealth concept could have any permanent value in the changing circumstances of today. I need hardly say that I did not share this view.

The only personal compensation in these disastrous meetings was the kindness and consideration shown to me by all the Prime Ministers, who showed a genuine sympathy for me in my difficult position. Even Verwoerd, with his usual courtesy, expressed the deepest appreciation of what I had tried to do. This did not, of course, preclude him from organising a hero's welcome by the Nationalist Party on his return home. In spite of the isolation with which South Africa was now threatened and the general dismay of any moderate and liberal opinion in that country, Verwoerd, who was a brilliant politician, was easily able to transform a reverse into a triumph.

Apart from more distant reflections there were some immediate steps to be taken. The various departments concerned were instructed to consider all the technical aspects of the situation. It was clear that relations with South Africa must in future be conducted by the Foreign Office and not by the Commonwealth Office. There were many other questions, including those regarding citizenship and trade preferences, which must be examined with care and urgency. Remembering at this moment the friendship and loyalty shown to me throughout by our High Commissioner, Sir John Maud, I felt it right to send him a letter on 21 March in my own hand.

During these rather trying days, I have thought a great deal about you. It is sad that we have not achieved our immediate purpose—to keep South Africa in the Commonwealth in order to help the ideas in which we believe. It is particularly sad for you—after all your splendid work.

But I am persuaded that nothing which we could have done could have prevented what happened. It was anyway a better solution than a motion to expel—which must have followed next year, if not this year.

There it is—the wind of change has blown us away, for the time. But peace will come one day, although perhaps after much sorrow and tribulation.

My faith is not dimmed—nor, I know, is yours.

The unhappy outcome of the Conference formed the subject of debate on 22 and 23 March both in the Lords and in the Commons. The general mood in both Houses was that the breach had become inevitable. Nevertheless, Lord Salisbury stated the opposite view with some vigour.

I believe that it would have been wiser to stand firmly, even rigidly, on the principle that there should be no interference, either by the Commonwealth as a whole or by individual members, in the domestic affairs of member states, and that we should have refused to budge, whatever the pressure that was brought upon us and whatever the results might have been.

In regretting that the Government had not stood firm by the accepted tradition he added:

For, if once we abandon that ground, I gravely fear that the Commonwealth will be unable to survive the strains that are likely to be put upon it in the testing years that lie ahead.

This argument, for which I had great sympathy, was indeed perfectly sound both in logic and on the basis of established convention. It broke down, however, like so many similar arguments, against the march of events and the force of human feelings.

In the course of his reply defending the Government's position, Lord Hailsham made an extremely apt comparison:

It is all very well to assume that general racial or social doctrines are always internal matters alone. The bloodiest war of all time came from the doctrine of the *Herrenvolk*, which emerged in its earlier stage largely as a persecution of Jews within German territory.

In the House of Commons a number of speakers followed Lord Salisbury's line and in some cases with severe criticism. They would have been more effective had they not been individuals who continually attacked the Government on many other issues. In my own speech I made no attempt to hide my regrets.

I have never concealed, nor do I wish now to conceal, from the House or the country that in my view there were very good arguments for taking the course of allowing the application of South Africa on constitutional grounds, but at the same time expressing the strongest disapproval of her racial policies. I know that many hon. Members, and many people in the country, took a different view, but I will give my reasons frankly. No one in this House approves, indeed we all deplore, the principle which underlies the policy which is generally known as *apartheid*. That is not because many of us are unaware of our own feelings or are anxious to throw the first stone. Hardly any country at some time in its history, nor even at the present time, can stand blameless.

All kinds of discrimination—not only racial, but political, religious and cultural—in one form or another have been and are still practised, often as a survival of long tradition. But the fundamental difference between ours and the South African philosophy is that we are trying to escape from these inherited practices. We are trying, with varying degrees of success but always with a single purpose, to move away from this concept in any form. What shocked the Conference was that the policy of the present South African Government appeared to set up what we would regard as an unhappy practice, inherited from the past, perhaps, as a philosophy of action for the future. This philosophy seemed altogether remote from and, indeed, abhorrent to the ideals towards which mankind is struggling in this century, in the free world at any rate, and perhaps—who knows—sooner or later behind the Iron Curtain.

It was not, therefore, because all of us are without sin that we felt so strongly. It was because this *apartheid* theory transposes what we regard as a wrong into a right.

I went on to point out that the policy of apartheid in its new and crudely accentuated and systemised form was really something very new. Of course, there had been discrimination in the days of the great South African leaders, Smuts and Botha, but they had never pressed it so hard and had in their minds, I felt sure, a vision of gradual development. I went on to refer to the long connection between South Africa and Britain.

> Our two countries have links forged in history. We have known what it means to fight against each other. We have also known what it means to fight side by side in defence of freedom in two world wars. There are the close connections of our own countrymen, hundreds of thousands of whom will deeply regret the severance of the Commonwealth ties. But, apart from all these strong considerations of sentiment, I was not satisfied that the exclusion of South Africa from the Commonwealth would best help all those European people who do not accept the doctrine of *apartheid*, and the growing body whose opinions are in flux. Nor, as far as I could see, would it help the millions of Africans.

I felt bound to say, in addition, that

> had Dr. Verwoerd shown the smallest move towards an understanding of the views of his Commonwealth colleagues, or made any concession, had he given us anything to hold on to or any grounds for hope, I still think that the Conference would have looked beyond the immediate difficulties to the possibilities of the future. For, after all, our Commonwealth is not a treaty-made league of Governments; it is an association of peoples.

Unfortunately, the Prime Minister of South Africa,

> with an honesty which one must recognise, made it abundantly clear beyond all doubt that he would not think it right to relax in any form the extreme rigidity of his dogma, either now or in the future. And it is a dogma. To us it is strange, but it is a dogma which is held with all the force of one of those old dogmas which men fought and struggled for in the past.

At any rate let there be no undue bitterness.

I do not feel that we should regard this as the end of the story. We shall always have a special feeling for the people of South Africa, of all races. We shall watch with a continuing interest their development, and I still think that the more we are able to maintain personal and individual contacts with our friends there the greater our influence will prove to be.

The day was a day for sorrow.

Whatever one's view, this is a very sad event; sad because of what seems to us a tragically misguided and perverse philosophy which lies at the root of apartheid; sad because of the many people in South Africa who, I am certain, would like it at least tempered and made more elastic and more humane; sad because this event marks the end of an association of our countrymen for over a hundred years with colonies formed in Capetown, Natal and elsewhere; sad because it is the end of a fifty-year connection which began with a decision then hailed as an outstanding example of magnanimity after victory; sad because it makes a breach in a community which has a great part to play in the world.

I ended with these words.

I read in one of the newspapers a phrase which struck me greatly. It said that the flag of South Africa must now be flown at half mast. So be it. But let us look forward to the day, perhaps not so distant as it may seem now, when it can again be hoisted in triumph to the masthead.

CHAPTER XI

The New President

THE policies and personality of a President of the United States today are of deep importance to every Government, friendly, neutral, or hostile. To none are they more significant than to a British Administration struggling with so many problems—at home, in Europe, in the Commonwealth and, indeed, throughout the world—which are the legacy of the Second World War. With equal responsibilities and diminishing power, a British Prime Minister in a still divided Europe must inevitably look to Washington for support. Equally, it may be of value to an American President to draw upon the long British experience of great affairs throughout the centuries.

I had known President Eisenhower from the Anglo-American landings in North Africa—'Operation Torch'—in November 1942. The close friendship which we had made in war was maintained in peace. If I knew some of Eisenhower's weaknesses I was also conscious of his virtues. I had learnt to understand his character, and in spite of some difficulties and rebuffs, largely due to his loose control of the leading departments, I felt always on firm ground. Our talks and messages were frank and intimate.

The new President, Jack Kennedy, was unknown to me, although I had a distant family connection which afterwards, such is the strength of family loyalties, especially in America, was to prove of value. (One of his sisters, 'Kick', married my wife's nephew, Lord Hartington. I was in Italy when the marriage took place. By a tragic blow, the young husband was killed a few weeks later in the landings in Normandy, and the wife lost her life in an aeroplane accident in 1948.)

We met for the first time six months after his election. He was young, attractive, buoyant and above all appealing to the young throughout the world. I was an ageing politician—not yet old enough to be a statesman (which you are only called when you are dead)—and of an altogether different experience and background. To him I should inevitably appear a 'stuff-shirt' or a 'square', or whatever was the suitable phrase in the current jargon. By a strange chance I had seen the new President on television in the course of the campaign. When I was in New York for the United Nations meeting, I happened to listen to the first television confrontation between the two candidates, Kennedy and Nixon. I thought myself that it was foolish of Nixon to accept the challenge. For the attacking party—the Outs—necessarily have an advantage over the defenders—the Ins. Since the debate was mainly on home questions I was not able to follow the argument closely, but I was struck by the extraordinary charm of the young man who was soon to find himself, even though by the slenderest of majorities, the head of this vast and powerful nation. I went up later in the evening to Eisenhower's suite in the same hotel. He asked me my impression of the performance. I remember saying to him that, knowing nothing of the subject, I had only been able to compare the candidates, and in my view it would be difficult for Nixon to fight against the charisma, to use another word in popular usage, that seemed to surround Kennedy and the life and vigour of that remarkable family. Later on I mentioned this incident to the new President, and he observed that, although it suited him to have this confrontation as the challenger, he looked with apprehension at the possibility of a renewal of such a contest at his next Election. Alas, he was not spared to put the matter to the test.

On 9 November, when the Election result was known, I immediately began to ponder over the problem of the best approach. I wrote to the Foreign Secretary:

> As you know, I have been for some time thinking how we would handle the new American President if it should be Kennedy. I discussed this shortly with Harold Caccia when he was here. With President Eisenhower we have a long comradeship covering nearly twenty years of war and peace. We therefore could appeal to memories. With this new and comparatively young President we have nothing of the kind to draw on. We

must therefore, I think, make our contacts in the realm of ideas. I must somehow convince him that I am worth consulting not as an old friend (as Eisenhower felt) but as a man who, although of advancing years, has young and fresh thoughts.

I have been thinking as to how this could be done, and I am sending you a draft of a possible letter which I might send to Kennedy.

There was plenty of advice, not to say gossip, available about the character of the new President, both from the Ambassador, Jock Whitney, and from occasional visitors. For instance, on 28 November,

I entertained to dinner (before returning to Chequers) Senators Lyndon Johnson and Fulbright. The first is Vice-President Elect—a Texan, an acute and ruthless 'politician', but not (I would judge) a man of any intellectual power. The second is very able and already a powerful figure in 'foreign affairs'.[1]

Meanwhile, things at home were fairly cheerful. There were a considerable number of by-elections, always dangerous for a Government, especially after a General Election where the swing has been so favourable.

The 'little General Election' is over—with considerable success for Conservatives. We have held every [Conservative] seat. Foot has been elected [in Ebbw Vale] with an immense majority—not very pleasant for Gaitskell.[2]

Apart from a formal telegram of good wishes I decided to wait, unlike some of my European colleagues who were already pressing their claims to visit Washington. On 8 December the British Ambassador, Harold Caccia, reported that the President Elect had asked to see him. After enquiring our views on a large number of matters—relations with Russia, the United Nations, disarmament and the like—he said that

he would very much like a meeting with me in February or March. I am therefore preparing a letter to be sent to him after the weekend. This *must* interest him and put out one or two exciting

[1] 28 November 1960.   [2] 19 November 1960.

ideas—yet it must not be pompous, or lecturing, or *too* radical!
I spent the morning on trying my hand at various drafts.[1]

A few days later

Jock Whitney called for a talk. He seemed to think the new
President's appointments were 'conservative'—therefore reassur-
ing to him (but, as I did *not* say, correspondingly depressing to
me).[2]

A somewhat different note was struck just after Christmas from
Moscow.

Our new Ambassador, Roberts, had a long interview with
Khrushchev (at the latter's request). He seemed rather run down
after his recent illness, but confident and relaxed. 1961 will be a
pretty tricky year, for it is quite clear that Khrushchev means to
press the German question.[3]

Meanwhile, I had succeeded in sending off my letter to Kennedy
on 19 December. It was a result of a number of drafts and much
discussion.

I was very glad to receive from Ambassador Caccia an account
of his talk with you last Thursday. I need not tell you how glad I
would be to accept your invitation to a meeting at your convenience. As you have probably realised, I have refrained from
making any proposal to you myself because I know how heavily
you must be engaged during these weeks. Apart from anything
that Khrushchev may confront us with, I have only one fixed
period in early 1961 when I must be in London. That is in the
first half of March, when I shall either be preparing for or con-
ducting the Commonwealth Prime Ministers' Meeting which
ends on 17 March. I could therefore go to Washington at any
other time that suits you.

Now for the subjects. There is indeed plenty to talk about, and
as I have just read the collection of your speeches called *The
Strategy of Peace* I am looking forward with special pleasure to
discussion of some of these things. If I may say so, I much
sympathise with your approach and your determination to put
the immense strength of your position and of your country behind

[1] 16 December 1960.   [2] 21 December 1960.   [3] 28 December 1960.

a new effort to face the problems of the second half of this century.

I have in mind my deep conviction that the policies and institutions which have served the Free World well since the war are now inadequate if we are to meet the challenge of Communism. I believe this to be particularly true in the economic field. But there are also military and political aspects of this challenging situation which cause me great concern. It is up to us now to rethink urgently and radically. The effects and policies of the various countries making up what one might generally call the Western Alliance are, I believe, not properly adjusted to the realities of the 1960s.

I think the first and most important subject is what is going to happen to us unless we can show that our modern free society— the new form of capitalism—can run in a way that makes the fullest use of our resources and results in a steady expansion of our economic strength. Therefore the problem of money, the problem of its proper use in each of the Western countries, and of securing that there is sufficient credit available to keep all our countries working to the full extent of the potential available, is really the prime question of all. If we fail in this Communism will triumph, not by war, or even subversion, but by seeming to be a better way of bringing people material comforts. In other words, if we were to fall back into anything like the recession or crisis that we had between the wars, with large-scale unemployment of men and machines, I think we would have lost the hand. Of course, things are not as bad as that, but there are great dangers facing us. For one reason or another, I believe the total credit available is either not sufficient or improperly used and this makes it necessary to reconsider the whole basis on which it stands.

This leads on from the question of maintaining confidence in a free society in our own countries, to that of spreading it to the uncommitted countries. Of course, I am anxious that we should do all we can to give aid in a direct form. That in our case depends largely upon being able to maintain full production without falling into either inflation or a balance of payments crisis. In other words, our capacity to help is tied up to the world solution of the first problem. Secondly, important as direct aid is—the financing of public works and public health and so forth—probably the most immediate way to help the undeveloped countries is the rise in the value of world commodities following on the maximisation of production by the advanced countries. It is worth recalling that the price of commodities has fallen eight or nine per cent in recent years. Therefore despite all that we have tried to do in direct help, more producing power has been taken away from the primary producers by the fall in commodity values than we have been able to give back to them in aid. In a country like ours these so-called favourable terms of trade help us in the short but not in the long term, either in exports, or in the sense of doing our duty by the undeveloped countries and stabilising their position.

The next set of questions seems to me to be disarmament, and especially the Geneva Test Agreement. I believe that if we could bring the Geneva talks to a satisfactory and early solution we would have made a very big step forward. I hope the Russians still attach importance to this; they certainly did when we began, but of course it has dragged on and become tremendously technical and almost academic. I expect you have much the same feelings about this.

Next there is the immense problem of disarmament. I still cannot quite make out whether Khrushchev has misunderstood or misrepresented what we have been trying to say to him. Perhaps you may be able to make him realise that we do really want disarmament in the sense of reduction of conventional and unconventional weapons, and control and inspection, as a single operation. He tries to pretend that we want only control and not disarmament. We ought really to try to agree on a scheme which will hold the imagination of the world and at the same time be realistic. At the present the Russians have got much of the propaganda advantage. This must be corrected. All the same I have a feeling that our failure to agree with the Russians comes from a complex of reasons. In the first place, they are perhaps incredulous that the West will ever agree to disarm. In the second, they shrink from any form of inspection which will make inroads upon their closely controlled society. But we must force this issue into the open.

Well, this is enough, perhaps too much; and I would only add this. We all realise here that the leadership in the Western World must come today largely from the United States. But although the United Kingdom's power in the world is relatively so much less than yours, I believe that our special ties with every continent and the new relationships which we have built up since the war in transforming the old Empire into the new Commonwealth, give us the opportunity of being of real and important service to the cause of freedom. I am sure that the fundamental interests of our two countries are identical and that, when our policies are harmonised, they stand a better chance of success. I can assure you that we in this country will not shrink from sacrifice, nor I believe have we lost our power to think and act imaginatively in the great crisis of our time.

I am sorry to inflict all this on you when you have so much to think about. But I felt it would be easier to give you some of my thoughts before we met for they are matters on which I have brooded much.

I await our first meeting with great eagerness.

During the Christmas holidays and the comparatively calm days before the return of Parliament, I was led by that fatal itch for composition which is the outcome of a classical education to compose a memorandum on the 'problems of 1961'. This was partly to clear my own mind, partly for the benefit of my colleagues, but above all as a basis for the discussions with the new President and the objectives which we would try to persuade him to support. This became familiarly known in the Private Office and in the inner circles of Government as 'The Grand Design'. Since we have authority for saying it is better—or at least as good—to travel hopefully than to arrive it is perhaps worth explaining this ambitious plan.

A useful morning with Sir Norman Brook and Bishop. They read my memorandum and seemed to approve (rather to my surprise) for it is a grand design to deal with the economic, political, and defence problems of the Free World! I shall have to try to get de Gaulle, Adenauer, and Kennedy to agree. But first I must get my colleagues to agree.

The first stage is this—to work on the memorandum, with additions and amendments. Then Sir Norman Brook will take it to Foreign Secretary and Chancellor of Exchequer on Wednesday morning to read. There will be a covering letter from me, and a bit showing what work has been done and what needs to be

First meeting with the new President, Key West, 26 March 1961

To Prime Minister Harold Macmillan
who has "pointed the way" on this and
many previous occasions - in the highest
esteem and every good wish -

John Kennedy   April 5, 1961

At the White House, April 1961
Rusk, Macmillan, Kennedy, Home

done on the plan. . . . If they think it is, on the whole, worth going forward, they will show it to Sir Frederick Hoyer Millar and Sir Frank Lee. Sir Norman Brook will then discuss it with them. Then we will see.

Now for my plans. On January 28–29–visit to de Gaulle. Middle of February–visit from Adenauer. March 8–16 or so –Commonwealth Prime Ministers. End of March–visit to West Indies. . . . First week in April–visit to Washington. Back April 7 or 8 for final Budget decisions. (Most of these, Sir Frank Lee says, can be made before I leave.) It is a tremendous programme.[1]

In order to describe the European situation in the last period of the Eisenhower regime, it is necessary to recapitulate the events of 1960. There were two separate issues–the first short-term and the second long-term. It was of immediate importance to try to persuade the Six not to operate their mutual tariff cuts in such a way as to injure the remaining European countries. Accordingly, during my visit to France on 13 March, 1960, I had pleaded with de Gaulle to oppose the proposed acceleration which went far beyond the requirements of the Treaty. As usual, the General took the somewhat lofty view that since the Treaty of Rome was merely a commercial treaty without any real political significance, it should not be given undue importance. Indeed, it should be rated with that class of affairs which are looked after by the supply and commissariat departments and scarcely worth the notice of the high command.

He thinks a treaty should be possible between the Six and the Seven. I pressed him strongly *not* to accelerate the tariff reductions between the Six next July (as is now being proposed) because this would increase the discrimination and might have very serious results. Although I came back to this several times, I could get no firm promise from him.[2]

I made the same appeal in the United States a few days later.

I made an impassioned plea for American help in preventing the *economic* division of Europe, which *must* involve its *political* and *military* division. U.K. simply could not afford the discrimination against our exports, which would produce a new crisis of sterling. We should *have* to take economic measures

[1] 6 January 1961.   [2] 13 March 1960.

European problems as seen by Vicky

(import controls; non-convertibility of sterling; restrictions and measures of all kinds) which were contrary to everything which we and the American Administration had been trying to achieve in the last eight years. We could also be forced to take our troops out of Germany (to save expenditure across the exchanges). These were not threats, but facts.

The Americans seemed rather taken aback by my vehemence. They tried (unsuccessfully) to question my figures as to the degree of discrimination. But Cromer, Sir Frank Lee, etc., had given me splendid ammunition.[1]

Although Herter of the State Department, and Dillon of the Treasury, were the only Ministers at this meeting, there were of course a number of officials present, and a garbled account of this talk was published in the *Washington Post* and afterwards in the *New York Times*. This leak made something of a flurry at the time and occasioned questions in the House of Commons on my return, but it did no real harm.

Gaitskell then asked about the Washington leak on Sixes and Sevens. This gave me a most welcome opportunity of explaining our position. We wanted European unity. The Labour Government had founded the Council of Europe; Churchill had been the first to move the admission of Germany. But we wanted unity, *not* a new split. I had said nothing to the Americans that I had not said repeatedly over the last two or three years to the Germans and the French. We welcomed the Six. But somehow or other a bridge must be built, to prevent the widening of the economic and trading gap and undue discrimination. Failing that, I saw grave troubles, in the long if not in the short run. Gaitskell and the Opposition were again *most* friendly and reasonable. Gaitskell even smiled—almost laughed—at the idea of private conversations being repeated. He had suffered from this! Altogether, it was a helpful little scene, and I was grateful.[2]

During de Gaulle's State Visit in April 1960 there were many other things to discuss but I did not miss the opportunity of saying something on this question.

I argued the case against 'splitting' Europe. De Gaulle affected

[1] 28 March 1960.   [2] 1 April 1960.

not to understand the details. I said I would send him a memorandum about this . . . he said he would be glad to study it
sympathetically.[1]

Accordingly, I sent him a carefully prepared document, with
detailed figures showing how seriously the United Kingdom trade
would be affected by the proposed speed-up of discrimination by
the Six. My colleagues agreed that if the Six did decide to accelerate
the tariff reductions on 1 July we must make sure that the Seven
—EFTA—should do the same. At least my representations had the
effect of stimulating the General to produce some counter-figures
trying to prove that our assessment for future trade prospects for
countries outside the Six were too pessimistic. But our own experts
did not accept either the French arguments or the French figures.
In the event both the Six—E.E.C.—and the Seven—EFTA—introduced their tariff cuts on 1 July; but the pressure which we had
brought, especially in Paris, at least led to the decision that the cuts
should be ten per cent and not twenty per cent as had been at first
proposed. This gave us more time for consideration, and possible
action.

After the collapse of the Paris Summit I continued to argue with
de Gaulle and Eisenhower that this tragic failure might soon bring
us up against active Russian aggression. This made it all the more
essential not to divide Europe. Meanwhile, my mind was turning
more and more to the dangers of Britain remaining outside a
community which controlled a central position in what was left of
free Europe. But how was this to be done?

> Shall we be caught between a hostile (or at least less and less
> friendly) America and a boastful, powerful 'Empire of Charle-
> magne'—now under French but later bound to come under
> German control. Is this the real reason for 'joining' the Common
> Market (if we are acceptable) and for abandoning (a) the Seven
> (b) British agriculture (c) the Commonwealth? It's a grim choice.[2]

These, of course, were the somewhat exaggerated forms in which I
recorded my passing thoughts. But they serve, perhaps, to show how,
after careful deliberation, the decision taken a year later was made.

[1] 5 April 1960.   [2] 9 July 1960.

As part of the changes at the Foreign Office at the end of July, Edward Heath became Lord Privy Seal with a special responsibility for European affairs. He soon began to build up a useful team and prepare himself for the onerous task which lay ahead. Duncan Sandys, who was one of the founders of the European movement and whose remarkable gifts of energy and determination have been devoted to this cause since the beginning, had in the recent changes become Commonwealth Secretary. Accordingly I sent him a note on 1 August which, in addition to calling his attention to the growing dangers in Africa—his first major task—continued as follows:

> The second great question which I want you to study is the problem of the Commonwealth in relation to Europe. At present, as you know, very few imports from Commonwealth countries pay duty in coming into the United Kingdom. If we are in the Common Market they would be hit this way. Then of course there is the question of preference. If we went into the Common Market we should give up the preferences and all that that implies.
>
> Finally, there is the question that we would really be discriminating *against* the Commonwealth. I know how keen you are on the European Movement, as I have always been. I am not satisfied that there is not a way to be found [of] getting over the Commonwealth difficulty. If you could put your acute and active mind to the study of this you would be doing a great service. It is perhaps the most urgent problem in the Free World today.

On 10 August, accompanied by the Foreign Secretary, I left for Bonn.

> I am not at all looking forward to our visit to Bonn. Dr. Adenauer has deceived me before, over the great economic issue. He promised to support the [plan for an industrial] free trade area. But, under French pressure, he went back on his promises. Having a guilty conscience, he then accused me of defeatism vis-à-vis Soviet Russia. I think our best line will be that of Brer Fox. Always before I have been frank and expansive. But— although many Germans are very sympathetic and secretly ashamed of Dr. Adenauer's trickiness—I fear I have never

succeeded in getting anything tangible out of these talks. Nevertheless, I think it would have been wrong to refuse the invitation.[1]

However, with the new Foreign Secretary and his advisers we worked out

quite a good approach for Adenauer—to accept his pessimism about the triumphs of Khrushchev and the increased strength and danger of Russia and then to try to point the moral—why divide Europe—first economically, and now politically? But I fear we shall waste our breath. For the Germans will agree with us (or many of them will) but Adenauer has sold his soul to the French.[2]

However, we were met with unexpected warmth by the Chancellor.

I suppose this results from his delight at the failure of all my attempts towards a 'détente' with the Soviets. It is rather a bitter pill.[3]

During the long drive to Bonn Adenauer told me a good deal about his meeting with de Gaulle at Rambouillet.

1. Adenauer had asked for it—directly or indirectly. This was because of a number of incidents (including a speech by Prime Minister Debré) which wounded German pride by suggesting that Germany was now only a French satellite.
2. At the meeting both Adenauer and de Gaulle opposed the Hallstein bureaucracy in Brussels taking on too much power.
3. The *political* advance was to be on a Governmental basis. Federalism must wait. De Gaulle was against a Federal Assembly for the Six except on the Strasbourg model—i.e. not elected but delegates from national parliaments.
4. They did *not*, repeat *not*, 'discuss Sixes and Sevens' or the problem of U.K.'s relation to Europe.[3]

In the afternoon there was a full and somewhat formal meeting.

Adenauer began the meeting by a rather melancholy picture of the world today—the ever-growing strength of Russia and Communism and the relative loss of authority by the forces of the Free World. I responded—and underlined—this mood. Accord-

[1] 6 August 1960.   [2] 7 August 1960.   [3] 10 August 1960.

ing to the plan I had devised, I emphasised the seriousness of the crisis; reviewed the resources available; how they were being used; who was contributing (U.S. and U.K. enormously; France little; Germany less than nothing, for she actually has a *net* profit of £250 m. on military expenditure by her allies in the Federal Republic). What were the unifying and what the divisive movements in the Free World (anti-Americanism, etc.); the same in Europe (the fatal drift since our meeting two years ago in Bonn and our joint communiqué *in favour* of European Free Trade Area, which Germans abandoned on French orders) Sixes and Sevens? I ended up even more depressed than Dr. Adenauer. It was really a pretty hopeless situation.[1]

These tactics seemed to work successfully, and when we separated at 6.30 p.m. the Chancellor had clearly decided to act in a somewhat dramatic way.

'Give us twelve hours,' he asked. 'This problem must be resolved. We must find the way.'[1]

We heard later that Adenauer had ordered his experts to get going. There must be something ready for the next day.

Dinner (which was on the usual lines) went off well. I asked Foreign Secretary to do a lot of talking today, and they obviously liked him. I have arranged that he shall take charge tomorrow. Dr. Adenauer made a very genial speech (in the mood of the 1958 meeting). I replied, and said that this might well prove an 'historic meeting'.[1]

I had an interesting talk with Dr. Erhard at dinner.

He is rather a tragic figure. He knows what *ought* to be done but cannot get it through his Government, or the banking industrialist forces. He said the Government were the more difficult, however, of the two obstructionists. Germany *must* lend abroad and ought not to collect these huge reserves and sterilise them. I said that he should *revalue* the Mark (which is *under*-valued) one day, suddenly and soon. He agreed. But he cannot do it.

About Sixes and Sevens, his advice had not been taken. But what could he do? He had wanted the European Free Trade

[1] 10 August 1960.

Area. But Dr. Adenauer had not understood the economic dangers and only thought of the political gains of the Franco-German friendship. He seemed quite excited about the way things had gone today. (He is, I must add, *excluded* from all but social meetings with me and the Foreign Secretary.)[1]

After dinner I talked to Adenauer about different subjects—the Congo, the United Nations and so forth. Meanwhile

all the various 'experts' (together with Erhard and some other Ministers) were having a great talk with Foreign Secretary and his advisers. It was clear that Dr. Adenauer's sudden change of front had created quite a dramatic situation.

At about 10.30 p.m. I suggested to Dr. Adenauer that *we* might perhaps go to bed and leave these younger men at work. Dr. Adenauer was very pleased by this idea. So, like truant schoolboys, we stole out of a side door—crept round the garden to the front door—got into our cars and drove home.[1]

The next day at the formal meeting, after some account of what the experts had discussed the previous night,

I then asked Lord Home to recapitulate the agreed procedure over the next few weeks—informal interchange of ideas between us both—British, German; then more detailed but still informal talks in Paris when the O.E.E.C. meets—in its new form. At this point, we hope to have French experts with us. Inform our friends and allies on all sides as to what we are doing. All this was very clearly set out by the Foreign Secretary (who has made quite an impression already).[2]

Luncheon took place at the British Embassy with the Germans as our guests.

The atmosphere was good. Erhard (who had heard the accounts of the meeting this morning) was overjoyed. . . . Von Brentano was happy—but he always agrees with everyone in turn. . . . But the Germans are *all* (whichever side they are on) wondering what the French will say and in great alarm as to how firmly and brutally they will say it. For—after all—the Germans are tied up, hand and foot, by the Treaty of Rome. So we can never make progress unless we can get French goodwill.[2]

[1] 10 August 1960.   [2] 11 August 1960.

Immediately on my return I found, as so often, the imminent threat of a serious industrial dispute.

The Power strike situation was reported to me at intervals. . . . *August 13.* . . . We have completed all the immediate work arising out of Bonn. The Power strike is off. Hammarskjöld's in the Congo. All's right with the world. But alas, it isn't. The unofficial shipping strike is spreading and playing havoc with our poor economy.[1]

I completed a note to the Chancellor of the Exchequer, on 12 August, giving him a full account of our meetings in Bonn. Had there been a Cabinet meeting, Lord Home and I would have reported in the ordinary way to our colleagues. Fortunately, at this time of the year, they were mostly either on the grouse moors or at the seaside resorts. There was already a Committee under Sir Frank Lee covering the whole field of possible solutions to the European problem, but I asked that it should now consider in detail the following possibilities :

(*a*) The suggestion that the Six should join the European Free Trade Area as a unit;

(*b*) an arrangement under which the United Kingdom would join the European Customs Union but on condition that, although the Commonwealth would lose on manufactured goods, they should keep their present proportion of the United Kingdom market for non-industrial products, particularly foodstuffs. It would also be necessary to have special arrangements for supporting agriculture (this also applies to (*c*) below);

(*c*) an arrangement by which the United Kingdom would be in a special position within the common tariff by being allowed a limited form of free entry for Commonwealth agricultural goods and raw material. These goods could be selected, commodity by commodity, either on the principle of a general exclusion with some exceptions, or on the basis of the broad principles of free entry modified by exceptions in certain sensitive commodities;

(*d*) some scheme similar to the original idea of an industrial free trade area in the sense that it would exclude agricultural products, but akin to the Common Market in that it would accept a common tariff.

[1] 12–13 August 1960.

L2

The last three possibilities will naturally have to be considered with full regard to the interests of the other members of the Seven.

In sending my impressions to Eisenhower I told him that I felt that the Germans had now woken up to the seriousness of the division of Europe, and perhaps the French would do so in due course. Meanwhile, since we ourselves were not ready with any clear plan there was bound to be some anxiety in the Commonwealth, but for the moment this was confined to the somewhat technical discussions at the meeting of Commonwealth Finance Ministers in September.

On 21 October the German Chancellor wrote me a letter in which he reported to me the results of his recent discussions with M. Debré.

> With regard to the European problems France does not seem to try to question the existing treaties. In discussing this matter I have drawn M. Debré's attention above all to the fact that we must try to do everything in our power to overcome the existing differences of opinion between the Customs Union of the Six and the Free Trade Area of the Seven. I hope I have made clear to him the importance of close co-operation with the United Kingdom for preserving the determination and unanimity of the Western world in the difficult times that lie ahead of us.

At the end of November the Foreign Secretary and I made a short visit to Rome which was, as usual, a welcome change from the continuous pressure in Whitehall. The Italians are excellent hosts, and I was much struck by the Prime Minister Amintore Fanfani, who seemed to be able and effective.

> The Italians are (like the Germans) genuinely anxious to do business on Sixes and Sevens. The French are (and the Italians say so openly) the real obstacle.[1]

Before leaving, we were granted an audience at the Vatican. It was the first time that I was received by the new Pope, John XXIII.

> His Holiness was in capital form. He talked (without any pause at all) for thirty-five minutes in powerful but incorrect

[1] 22 November 1960.

French. He was quite delightful—obviously both friendly and sincere. (What will happen when the Archbishop of Canterbury sees him, I do not know, for the Archbishop never draws breath either.) The Pope's sincerity and kindness were very moving. Also his desire that we should know more of each other. 'In this great palace,' he said, 'there are many windows. They should be opened, so that [they] can look in and [we can] look out.'[1]

It was in the light of these experiences and brooding over their lessons that I completed my memorandum, half jokingly called 'The Grand Design', and circulated it to my colleagues.

Its main purpose was 'to call attention to the need to organise the great forces of the Free World—U.S.A., Britain and Europe—economically, politically and militarily in a coherent effort to withstand the Communist tide all over the world'. The opening paragraphs of this document set out the problem before us.

1. The Free World cannot, on a realistic assessment, enter on 1961 with any great degree of satisfaction.

In the struggle against Communism, there have been few successes and some losses over the past decade.

In the military sphere, the overwhelming nuclear superiority of the West has been replaced by a balance of destructive power.

In the economic field, the strength and growth of Communist production and technology have been formidable. (Indeed, it ought to be, for after all that is what Communism is for.)

In the political and propaganda field, Russian (and to a lesser extent Chinese) subversion, blackmail, seduction and threats, as well as the glamour of what seems a growing and dynamic system, have impressed hesitant and neutral countries, and are proving especially dangerous among the newly independent nations of Africa and Asia. Against this background the long predominance of European culture, civilisation, wealth and power may be drawing to its end.

2. On the other hand, we have seen a pretty firm cohesion on our side, based on the readiness of the United States to reject 'isolationism' and to play its full role, militarily and economically, as the leading nation of the Western coalition.

Western Europe (including the United Kingdom) has made

[1] 23 November 1960.

a remarkable recovery from the calamitous destruction of the
Second World War.

Nevertheless, there are great weaknesses. We are facing the
monolithic strength of the Kremlin with a number of groupings,
in Europe and in the Middle and Far East, which have nothing
like the same unity of purpose or of practice.

3. Britain—with all her experience—has neither the economic
nor the military power to take the leading role. We are harassed
with countless problems—the narrow knife-edge on which our
own economy is balanced; the difficult task of changing an
Empire into a Commonwealth (with the special problems of
colonies inhabited by European as well as native populations);
the uncertainty about our relations [with] the new economic, and
perhaps political, state which is being created by the Six countries
of continental Western Europe; and the uncertainty of American
policies towards us—treated now as just another country, now as
an ally in a special and unique category.

4. We are faced with a complex of political and economic problems, affecting our relations with many nations and groups of
nations. These problems are all intermingled. It is difficult to
deal with them separately. Yet it is a tremendous task to attack
them as a whole. So we are in danger of drift. Yet, if we are to
influence events, we must not shrink from strong, and sometimes
dramatic, action. Nor shall we achieve our ultimate aims—which
must be the strengthening of the Free World to meet the tasks of
the next generation—if we are afraid to take some risks in the
effort to make friendly and allied nations face the realities of the
situation.

5. I am an unrepentant believer in 'interdependence'.

The Communist danger—in its various forms—is so great and
so powerfully directed that it cannot be met without the maximum
achievable unity of purpose and direction.

It is no longer a question of Europe or the Commonwealth or
America—we need a united Free World. Of course we can't get it
—in the sense of a politically federal or unitary state. We cannot
altogether get it in the sense of a military alliance which can
really work as a single team. We could perhaps get nearer to it in
a monetary and economic policy.

In the light of this assessment we must urge on the new American Administration the need for the expansion of world trade including the expansion of credit by whatever means, orthodox or novel. Until the United States and other leading countries accepted the need for a much more flexible monetary system preserving the principles of Keynes's original plans, we would sooner or later find ourselves in a world shortage of credit, insufficient to finance the growing volume of trade. I had, therefore, been slightly discouraged by some of the President's appointments in this sphere which included orthodox Wall Street figures.

Next we must prevent the Six–Seven split in Europe from getting worse. This meant reaching an accommodation with de Gaulle. This was primarily a political and not an economic problem. We could woo the French more easily by backing their great power ambitions—that is, by putting real life into Tripartitism—than by any other means. We might even be able to persuade the Americans to give the French some help in their nuclear plans.

As for Germany, we needed American assistance in putting pressure on Adenauer, both as regards Sixes and Sevens, and regarding their general monetary policy. If we could obtain the expansion and liberalisation of trade, including the provision of credit, we should be able to create a degree of prosperity in the Free World which would prove our superiority to Communism, enabling us to offer a better developed market for underdeveloped countries and provide a surplus for aid. At the same time, we should be able to carry our military burdens without too much strain. We might even be able to persuade the Americans to go still further.

There is a further question which I might in any event raise with Kennedy.

Military defence, and military defence planning, is—with varying efficiency—carried out under NATO, CENTO, and SEATO.

We also have very close direct Anglo-American co-operation in many fields outside these Alliances (e.g. Strategic Air Command and the Bomber Bases—and now Polaris). If anything like 'Tripartitism' develops from a more effective use of the Standing Group, this can be extended into the politico-military sphere not only in the European but in other theatres.

But there is a gap. The *economic* power of the Free World ought to be more efficiently organised and used. There ought to be more of an overall plan and less rather 'hand-to-mouth' giving of aid in all its forms. Perhaps such a group, *not* connected with or built up on purely military alliances, could plan a useful role. It would be directed by the Heads of Governments of the states involved—and responsible to them. It might include—in addition to the United States, the United Kingdom and France—Germany, Japan and a leading country in Latin America, e.g. Brazil. Australia might also be invited to join.

Its purpose would be to maximise the wealth of the world, maximise its trade and direct its surpluses, by aid and investment, towards the raising of general standards. It would not supersede existing world agencies. But—if these Powers agreed on any policy—it could bring sufficient pressure on these existing agencies to ensure that its views were effectively translated into action.

In the next few weeks there was much discussion of the broad plan to which my colleagues had now given their complete adherence. But it is one thing to sketch an ambitious design; it is quite another and much more difficult task to reduce it to detail and convince the leaders of different countries of its value. Much work was done by officials, particularly in preparation for my meeting with de Gaulle at the end of January.

After staying the night at the British Embassy in Paris,

Saturday morning [Dorothy and I] motored to Rambouillet (M. de Courcel came with me). We were met by de Gaulle and Madame de Gaulle and shown to our rooms. We were in the same rather romantic suite in the François Premier tower. But this time the creature comforts were better. The rooms were heated; the bathwater was hot; and there were sufficient bedclothes.

Luncheon was only the de Gaulles; ourselves; Philip [de Zulueta] and the A.D.C. So was dinner. The talks took place in the grey sitting-room, downstairs. I had Philip; he had one young man, interpreter and note-taker.[1]

After dinner there was a film—a good one—of exploration in New

[1] 29 January 1961.

Guinea. It was made by a French team and of notable merit. The indigenous people of this distant territory had apparently hardly reached the Stone Age. They were enjoying the primitive happiness of mankind before the fall—'naked and unashamed'. I remember that on leaving the room where the picture was shown I asked my host what he thought should be done with these people. 'Oh,' he replied, 'they ought immediately to be elected to the United Nations.' This was typical of his mordant wit.

On Sunday, a short talk with de Gaulle alone, summarising our conclusions; another with Debré (Prime Minister) present; another (after luncheon) with Couve de Murville, Bob Dixon, Ambassador Chauvel. . . .

Broadly speaking, I think we made good progress. De Gaulle was relaxed, friendly, and seemed genuinely attracted by my themes—Europe to be united, politically and economically; but France and Great Britain to be something more than European Powers, and to be so recognised by United States. I think everything now depends on (a) whether we really can put forward a formula for Sixes and Sevens which both Commonwealth and British Agriculture will wear, (b) whether the Americans can be got to accept France's nuclear achievements and ambitions.[1]

Although occupied with many other urgent questions, of which those of Northern and Southern Rhodesia seemed at once the most complicated and the most acrimonious, I was determined to pursue these wider tasks. I had taken the precaution of sending a long message to Adenauer on my return from Paris and at his suggestion he came to see us for a short visit at the end of February.

We have had two days of Dr. Adenauer and his Germans—four hours' talk, dinner, luncheon—and little or no result. Whatever they finally give the Americans [for support costs] we shall get *pari passu*. . . . But the large economic issues which face the world they affect not to understand. In other words, they are rich and selfish.[2]

In spite of my arguments to prove that, in view of the grave and persistent imbalance in trade among the countries of the West, the

[1] 29 January 1961.   [2] 23 February 1961.

surplus countries must take action in order to avoid restrictive policies by the countries temporarily in deficit, the Chancellor affected not to grasp the point and preserved his impassiveness. At the same time he told me that some useful exploratory talks were taking place with the French about various plans for developing some greater political, as well as economic, unity in Europe.

A somewhat discouraging message now arrived from Ormsby Gore, Minister of State at the Foreign Office, describing a private talk with Kennedy. While agreeing with our views on most other questions, it was clear that the new President was no great admirer of de Gaulle's general political philosophy, as well as distrustful of French security methods. He was not likely, therefore, to accept Tripartitism in full. Against this I had already received Kennedy's confirmation of his acceptance of all the arrangements and understandings entered into between successive Presidents and the British Government on the use of British bases, on nuclear weapons and on the interchange of information. Equally, the Pentagon and the Ministry of Defence were working in close co-operation over a wide field. The abandonment of Blue Streak for military purposes had been a severe blow, but we were relying confidently on Skybolt or, if by any chance Skybolt should fail, some alternative from American resources. Nevertheless, I was determined to press my main theme—the unity of the Free World, economically, politically and militarily.

I was now ready, after a difficult session, for a short trip to the West Indies. It would enable me to see these parts of the Commonwealth which I had never visited, and then to go on to Washington for my talks with the President. Accordingly, Dorothy and I left London with a small staff, including Norman Brook and Tim Bligh, on 24 March. While the visit to the West Indian islands would be an agreeable, but not particularly testing time, I knew that when I got to Washington my real task would begin. In asking the Queen's permission for this visit on 31 January, I had observed:

I am sure that the sooner I can meet Mr. Kennedy and discuss our affairs frankly with him, the better. I cannot hope to re-establish at once the same close personal relations as I had with

President Eisenhower, but it is difficult to form any very strong impression about the new Administration until I have established some personal contact with the President.

In the event, our first meeting was to take a more dramatic form. We reached Trinidad on 24 March. At 4 a.m. there arrived a telegram from Kennedy saying he was very anxious to see me without delay to talk about Laos, a crisis which was now causing the deepest anxiety. He suggested Key West air and naval base in Florida. Could I come the next day—Sunday?

In a similar Laotian crisis in 1954, Eden, as Foreign Secretary, had succeeded by almost a miracle of patience and diplomatic skill in reaching agreement in Geneva. Under this compact the Communist (Pathet Lao) forces were to retain their arms but to concentrate in the two Northern provinces pending a political settlement. Although they were supposed to be subject to the Royal Government of Laos, in practice they prevented Government officials from entering their territory and thus established an effective partition. The Pathet Lao received aid and encouragement from the Communists of North Vietnam, and this unsatisfactory, if typically Oriental, situation was prolonged throughout 1955 and 1956.

The Geneva agreement had set up an International Commission consisting of representatives of India, Poland and Canada. During the course of 1956 the Commission reported the position to the United Kingdom and the U.S.S.R., who were the co-Chairmen appointed at the same time. Discussions were held without result between the two co-Chairmen. However, by the end of the year, the Laotian Premier, Prince Phouma, and the Pathet Lao leader had reached an agreement, under which representatives of the Pathet Lao should be included within the Government, the two provinces return to the authority of the Government, and the Pathet Lao forces become incorporated in the Royal Army. This was encouraging; but in 1957 there was an almost complete breakdown, since the Pathet Lao went back on this understanding. Nevertheless, after a year of fresh negotiations with additional concessions to the Pathet Lao, the result was a coalition Government of National Unity led by Prince Phouma. Elections followed in 1958. Their result, which showed a considerable swing to the Left, alarmed the Right-wing parties. Phouma's coalition fell and was replaced by a purely Right-wing Government without any Pathet Lao representatives.

Meanwhile, the International Commission, satisfied that national reunification had been effected, adjourned *sine die*. Early in 1959 the Laotian Government complained about the pressure on the border by the North Vietnamese. One of the Pathet Lao's battalions now mutinied and moved to the border. There followed charges and countercharges by all the parties concerned, and in the latter part of 1959 frontier warfare broke out, allegedly provoked and supplied from North Vietnam. At this point the United States Government agreed to supply civilian technicians to assist the French military mission in training Laotian forces. A state of emergency was declared, and the Laotian Government asked the Secretary-General of the United Nations to inform all member states of the situation.

At the same time Nehru wrote to me of his concern and of his appeal to the two co-Chairmen representing Britain and Russia. But discussions between Lloyd and Gromyko proved inconclusive. I therefore suggested that the co-Chairmen might be asked to propose that the Secretary-General send out a fact-finding mediator. Since the Americans had, under Foster Dulles, treated the Geneva agreements of 1954 with a good deal of aloofness and even suspicion, I felt the best chance was to deal with the matter in the United Nations. President Eisenhower agreed, and on 8 September 1959 the Secretary-General, undeterred by a Russian veto, appointed a sub-committee of Italy, Argentine and Tunisia to report on the facts. So the matter dragged on until, in 1960, further elections were held with the usual protests on both sides about 'irregularities'. Distressing as the condition might be to the people of Laos, my chief anxiety was not to allow the great Powers to be dragged in if this could by any means be avoided.

The Ministry which resulted from the elections included General Phoumi as Defence Minister. In August 1960 the Assembly, supported by the greater part of the Army, approved the appointment of the former Premier Phouma, who seemed more likely to come to terms with the neutralists and even with the Pathet Lao.

General Phoumi did not recognise the new Administration and set up an independent command. There were now, in effect, two Governments, and Phouma was recognised by the U.S.S.R., whose own planes began to bring in petrol and supplies through North Vietnam. The Laotian Assembly, alarmed at the extent to which Phouma leaned to the Left, now deserted him and joined Phoumi. A state of something like collapse, at any rate on the governmental basis, now followed, although there was not yet serious fighting, and the life of the people continued with its normal resignation.

> The situation in Laos is bad—the Americans are anxious to intervene overtly as well as covertly. They back a certain Phoumi —we, I do not know why, prefer Phouma. Outside this foolish internecine war, the Communists are waiting hopefully for their chance. The Thais want intervention by the SEATO powers. It is easy to see the dangers. China must react and perhaps Russia. Yet if Laos goes, what chance is there for South East Asia?[1]

A few days later we heard of the advance of General Phoumi's forces and the flight of Phouma and his Ministers to Cambodia. His neutralist supporters continued fighting against Phoumi until the middle of December when they withdrew northwards and began to co-operate with the Pathet Lao. A certain Prince Boun Oum, who had joined Phoumi, now headed a new Ministry with Assembly support. In this situation we transmitted to Moscow Nehru's proposal that the International Commission should be reactivated.

Just before Christmas 1960, the Russians agreed to this, but demanded that it should be accredited to Phouma. In these circumstances, on 30 December, I suggested to Eisenhower, who was now in the last few months of his office, that the best tactics would be to persuade Phouma, now in exile, to resign and at the same time to induce Boun Oum to get himself constitutionally recognised by a proper vote of the Assembly. On the next day Eisenhower replied. According to his information the North Vietnamese and possibly Chinese groups were beginning to invade Laos to assist the Pathet Lao. In his view all of us should make clear our

[1] 8 December 1960.

intentions to oppose this move and each take rapid steps to play his part.

The first day of the New Year therefore began with an alarming situation.

> The President has sent a strangely hysterical reply to my message about Laos. It looks as if Allen Dulles's policy has been accepted altogether by the State Department and the President. This is a most dangerous situation for us. If SEATO intervenes (Thais, U.S. and ourselves) it will cause trouble in India, Malaya and Singapore. If we keep out and let U.S. do a 'Suez' on their own, we split the alliance. But what is much worse, our Chiefs of Staff do not think that military intervention is really feasible, or likely to be successful. Of course, they may be wrong — but we have General Templer's experience to draw on.[1]

Prince Sihanouk of Cambodia now sent an appeal urging the immediate convening of a conference on Laos. In his view this should include all the signatories of the 1954 Geneva Agreement, together with the members of the International Commission, and the States having a common frontier with Laos, plus the U.S.A. He was naturally concerned with the effects of the trouble in Laos on his own country, Cambodia. The influx of refugees, both from Laos and from Vietnam, was a source of increasing disturbance. He added, somewhat pathetically, that this might upset Cambodia's five-year plan.

In these first weeks of 1961 and the last few weeks of Eisenhower's power, I could not feel that the American Government, in spite of their decision to increase the readiness of their forces in the Pacific, would really launch military action. At my request the Foreign Secretary sent a message to Herter emphasising the difficulties and the dangers, but

> I decided not to reply to President Eisenhower's message till we have Herter's answer to our memorandum. We all felt that we should try to get the International Commission back. Khrushchev apparently supports this; it has the advantage of working under the terms of reference of the Geneva agreements which

[1] 1 January 1961.

means a united, *not* a divided country, under the legal Government. Of course, Khrushchev will argue that this means Phouma's Government, although the King has dismissed Phouma and he has fled the country. So we must all concentrate on getting the new Government legitimised, which requires the Parliament to meet. As the Parliament is said to be quite amenable, there seems no possible reason why this should not be done at once. We all agreed that we could *not*, repeat *not*, support a military intervention by SEATO unless and until all other methods—the Commission, a United Nations 'fact-finding' body, or perhaps an appeal to Khrushchev for a meeting of Great Powers—had all been tried. The French share our view. I don't think we could agree to this, in the last weeks of Eisenhower's Government, without grave risk to the Commonwealth and even to our own Parliamentary position at home. At the same time, we must not let the Communists take over Laos. This would be a terrible blow, and Thailand, Burma, Malaya, and Singapore would all be in a very dangerous—if not hopeless—position. We must be firm, but not rash.[1]

The next day it seemed that the Americans were calming down, and coming round to the idea of political action. For several weeks the telegraphic battle raged. The Indians would now agree to the Commission, but the Canadian position was not so certain. In effect 'Everyone is really stalling—including the Russians—because no one seems to know which side is winning the civil war.'[2] Russia, together with China, Indonesia and North Vietnam, now demanded a conference; but even if this could be set up, which would take much longer than the reactivation of the Commission, a more important issue had now become that of a cease-fire.

The Russians, etc., are stalling and Khrushchev sends me long and offensive letters, because he doesn't now want a cease-fire. The Pathet Lao (Communists) are winning.[3]

President Kennedy had now taken office. Before leaving for the West Indies I heard from Washington that Kennedy would be likely to accept a conference without conditions if it seemed the only way out of the mess. Nevertheless, I was disturbed to get a message on

[1] 2 January 1961.   [2] 10 January 1961.   [3] 27 January 1961.

22 March that in the American view the Royal Laotian forces were now definitely being beaten by the Communists and that some intervention would be necessary to save at least part of the country. Accordingly, after full discussions with my colleagues, we decided to call for an immediate cease-fire, the reconvening of the Commission, and the holding of a full conference as soon as the Commission reported that the cease-fire was effective. As for intervention, whether by SEATO or by America on her own, we decided to put all the difficulties and the objections frankly to the Americans. It was not an easy choice; there was a grave danger of provoking Russian or Chinese intervention, and from both the strategic and the logistic point of view, the advantage lay with the Communists. On the other hand, it would be tragic to separate ourselves from the Americans. We had suffered enough in a previous crisis from an Anglo-American schism. At all costs, we must try to work with the new President and the new Administration. I was therefore not altogether surprised, in view of our last message, when the invitation to Key West reached me in Trinidad. Fortunately, we could work quickly, and with the help of my small staff,

> we got off a telegram at once to try to get London's views and to collect what we could from Butler, Heath (Lord Privy Seal and Foreign Office Minister), Foreign Secretary (at Karachi on his way to Bangkok), Sandys (to sound Tunku again, and also other Commonwealth countries). I did not wish to *accept* meeting with President without general approval, for I fear it may cause a scare in the world and trouble in Parliament. However, by 11 a.m. everybody seemed in favour of accepting, and we telephoned Washington accordingly.[1]

By midnight we had a very full telegram from my Private Office summarising the general view, together with long messages from Heath and the Foreign Secretary on the substance of the problem and the various possibilities. At any rate it was clear

> that I must not commit any military support (even more or less symbolic) without specific Cabinet approval. I have asked Cabinet to meet on Monday morning, as early as possible.[1]

[1] 25 March 1961.

In the afternoon we had an agreeable change from all these distractions. Churchill, who was on a yacht in the harbour, came up to Government House 'to pay his respects'. After he left, I asked his secretary what was meant by this phrase and was told that he 'wanted to make a "demonstration of his support". . . . This was very kind and touching.'[1]

The next day, 26 March, was at the same time one of the strangest and one of the most interesting among my experiences. I left early in the morning accompanied only by Tim Bligh, a detective and two of the 'young ladies', part of our splendid Downing Street staff of secretary-typists. The President, in his telephone message, had been very insistent and seemed to think it was quite a normal expedition since I was so near. Actually, it was a five-hour flight in our plane, and I had never before been 1,800 miles to luncheon, 3,600 miles in all. There was little to do during the journey except speculate on what would be the outcome of our meeting.

> We touched down at Key West—the great naval station and airport—at 11.30 a.m. (Trinidad time) having gained a little on the flight. The President's plane came in just before us. There were guards of honour; (Navy and Marine) band (playing the British National Anthem); salute of nineteen guns—and a very large number of spectators. After the usual ceremonies, [the] President and I drove in [an] open car to the Naval Administrative Headquarters—along the causeway road and through the town of Key West. A large number of spectators, in a great variety of costume or no costume, lined the route and applauded enthusiastically.[2]

Harold Caccia, who had come in the President's plane, and I had time for a few words before the Conference opened. The actual proceedings were limited to a detailed exposition by the American generals, admirals and airmen, of whom there seemed to be a great number, which included all their aides and attendants. There were excellent maps and a large blackboard. Neither the President nor I spoke—we listened. There was a strange contrast between the two participants. On the one side was the President of the United States and Commander in Chief of all American forces surrounded

[1] 25 March 1961.   [2] 26 March 1961.

by officers of every rank and degree in a great naval fortress and receiving all the honour due to a Head of State; on the other, Tim Bligh and I, with Harold Caccia in support.

After the exposition of the proposed plan had finished, Kennedy only asked one or two questions and I continued silent. The Conference then adjourned for luncheon. The President and I went into another room where we remained alone.

Before our conversation had gone on for many minutes I felt a deep sense of relief. Although we had never met and belonged to such different generations, he was just forty and I was nearly seventy, we seemed immediately to talk as old friends. From all the accounts I heard I was not surprised that I should take a vast liking to him. It was encouraging to find that he seemed to feel something of the same. We had hardly begun to eat the meat sandwiches provided when he turned to me and said, 'What do you think of that?' I replied, 'Not much. It is not on.' This referred to an ambitious plan prepared by the military involving, as I thought, very large-scale and dangerous operations. During the Conference I could get no indication of the President's reactions. He listened politely while bridges were flung across rivers, troops deployed on a great scale, and all the rest. But his silence was chacteristic. Nevertheless, it was evident that he was

> in control of the Pentagon, not the other way round. He was clear and decisive. He was not at all anxious to undertake a military operation in Laos. If it had to be done (as a sort of political gesture) he definitely wanted it to be a SEATO exercise. He did *not* want to 'go it alone'. I rather objected to anything on the scale of the present SEATO plans. They were, to my mind, unrealistic. United Kingdom did not wish to get involved in a big way—only, if at all, in a 'symbolic' physical solidarity. President pressed me very hard on this. But I could not recommend any of the large SEATO plans to the Cabinet. Our Chiefs of Staff thought them unrealistic.[1]

We then discussed an alternative proposal which the American experts had put before us in general terms.

[1] 26 March 1961.

Even this, as I understood it, was to involve 31,000 troops in the end—to be supplied by air, or largely by air—a ruinous undertaking.[1]

Although he did not say so, the President seemed to me to share my doubts. He then

explained that he had in mind as a possibility a much modified plan—involving about four or five battalions—to hold Vientiane and some other bridgeheads on the river. This would (a) preserve some Laotian territory, however small, and the authority of the King in an enclave; (b) it would allow advance, if thought possible at a later date; (c) it would free 7,000 Laotian troops to fight Pathet Lao, should they be inclined to do so; (d) it would encourage the Thais to hold firm.[1]

Even this more modest plan must be carefully guarded against the danger of sliding into unlimited commitments. Nevertheless, I did agree

that it might be *politically* necessary to do something, in order not to be 'pushed out' by the Russians. This I thought might well be their intent at the beginning of his Presidency. . . . I would certainly join in the *appearance* of resistance and in the necessary military planning. But I must reserve to Cabinet the ultimate decision. President quite understood this.[1]

While planning might go ahead, we must make every effort to persuade the Russians to accept the British proposal for a cease-fire and conference. There was still a chance that they wished to limit the danger. No doubt they would wait to see what would happen at the SEATO meeting, and it was still possible that they would prefer some kind of settlement. Both the President and I felt one of the main difficulties was

that the SEATO countries have very inflated ideas. Any planning done with *all* of them together must be on an ambitious scale. . . . But what the President and I have discussed is something more modest. I thought that Admiral [Harry] Felt (United States) and General [Sir Richard] Hull (United Kingdom) who are at Bangkok, might be able to have some private talks.[1]

[1] 26 March 1961.

There had been some fears expressed in London that if a military operation, however limited, became necessary, there would be danger in allowing America to act alone. Our influence would be reduced, and the scale of the operation might be correspondingly enlarged. After my talk with the President I felt largely reassured. At the same time, it was clear that he was already under strong pressure from his own advisers. When our talks ended, during a short interval before we were to leave,

> owing to the efficiency of our little staff, I was able to dictate and get back in ten minutes, records of our talks, which (with some minor amendments) [the] President accepted. They also accepted our communiqué (which we had done in the plane on the way). It is always more important at these international conferences to have good shorthand girls than to have Generals and Admirals.[1]

In the course of the discussion the President had made it very clear

> that it would be very difficult for the United States to take military action alone even as an agent, or under the aegis of SEATO. He thought there would be a large body of opinion in the United States who would regard active, if limited, British support in this matter as the determining factor. If this were to be withheld he was not sure he could get his people to accept unilateral action by the United States.[2]

On his return journey he reiterated to Caccia his desire for a peaceful solution if possible. He would accept anything short of the whole of Laos being overrun.

> If the Russians made this impossible, that he had no intention of any military operations beyond what was essential to keep bridgeheads in Laotian territory for a non-Communist Laotian Government. He had no intention of being involved in a 'Malayan operation'.[3]

Among the other things which I discussed with Kennedy was the question of the successor to Harold Caccia.

[1] 26 March 1961.   [2] From my note to Home Secretary, 26 March 1961.
[3] Caccia to Prime Minister, 27 March 1961.

He was emphatic for David Gore. 'He is my brother's most intimate friend' (and, of course, 'my brother' is thought by many to be the Grey Eminence).[1]

When the time came, I was happy to make this appointment, and no Ambassador has ever served us so well in Washington. He enjoyed the intimate friendship of Kennedy and his family. He had access to the White House such as no Ambassador has had before or since. In the somewhat unusual conditions of the Presidential system as operated by Kennedy, David Ormsby Gore was to play a unique role of immense value to both countries. Fortunately, there is a long tradition that the Embassy in Washington should, from time to time, be held by amateur diplomatists. In any case, I have always considered the appointment should be based solely on the most effective way of doing the Queen's business—it should never be a case of 'Buggins's Turn'.

We got back to Government House, Trinidad, very late, but managed to send off all our telegrams before going to bed.

> But with London five hours ahead and Bangkok twelve hours ahead, this triangular affair is getting very confusing.[2]

Although all these anxieties naturally filled my mind, nothing could prevent us enjoying to the full the short visit which we had planned. The Governor-General, Lord Hailes, who as Patrick Buchan-Hepburn had been our Chief Whip in the House of Commons, was a wonderful host, and from his long political experience a wise counsellor. But, it was already beginning to be clear that, in spite of his efforts, the new Federation was likely to meet many difficulties. The Federal plan had been proposed at the London Conference of 1953 and was supported by all the British Caribbean Islands, although British Guiana and British Honduras had not committed themselves. Accordingly, the Federation of the West Indies was launched on 3 January 1958, to include Antigua, Barbados, Dominica, Grenada, Jamaica, Montserrat, St. Kitts–Nevis, Anguilla, St. Lucia, St. Vincent, and Trinidad and Tobago. The capital was in Trinidad; the Legislature consisted of a Senate nominated by the Governor-General from the various territories,

[1] 26 March 1961.   [2] 27 March 1961.

and a House of Representatives elected by adult suffrage. Defence, external affairs, and financial stability remained the responsibility of the United Kingdom.

But there were two major difficulties which were already becoming apparent. The immense distances which separated Jamaica from most of the other islands and the differences in economic development and interest were beginning to create trouble. The natural tendency of Trinidad and the smaller islands was to press towards complete economic federation. But Jamaica, with its strength both in population and wealth, was hesitant. In spite of generous support from the British Treasury, one of the main problems was that the economies of the various islands were competitive rather than complementary. Moreover, Jamaica and Trinidad, which between them contained 77 per cent of the people and 83 per cent of the land, continued to differ fundamentally on the economic policy for the Federation.

Although we arrived in Trinidad after midnight on 24 March the next day was well occupied.

A full day, with both Federal and Trinidad Ministers. A very cheery luncheon with the Trinidad Legislative Council at a very colourful restaurant—'The Tavern on the Green'. We had nothing but local food. As I have already got my inside upset, I ate as little of each dish as I could. A curious game animal called 'lappe' was rather good—a sort of hare. A long tour of Chaguaramas Base. The Trinidad Government are very pleased with the outcome of the recent negotiations with the Americans. The length of the lease has been reduced (from original ninety to seventeen years) and Americans have surrendered 1,000 acres (out of 11,000).

An immense dinner; then 1,250 guests with whom Dorothy and I shook hands. Then bed (at midnight).[1]

26 March was spent at Key West, but the next day was again a full one in Trinidad.

10 a.m. Speech at Federal House. 11 a.m. Party for Senators and M.P.s. 12–12.30 Chief Ministers of St. Vincent and Dominica. 1–3 Imperial College of Tropical Agriculture—lunch

[1] 25 March 1961.

and speech. 3–4 Drive with Premier Williams. 5.30 Press Conference (British). 6.30 Press Conference (all). 8.15 Dinner – Governor of Trinidad.

My speech at the meeting of the Federal Party had been very carefully compiled – with Commonwealth Office, Colonial Office and my staff. I worked on it during the long air journeys yesterday. . . . I am not too happy about the prospects, and I tried to bring some pressure on the island politicians to take a wider view.[1]

Although my stay in each of these island places was very short, it was still possible to get some impressions.

Trinidad is an interesting place – rich (with oil) and lively. Incidentally, we did the island a good turn when we allowed Trinidad Oil to be sold to a really go-ahead American company. There does not seem excessive poverty; there is an impossibly large middle class; there is as near 'multi-racialism' as we can hope to get anywhere. I have no doubt that when the last piece of British help is withdrawn, administration will get worse. . . . But they are certainly more advanced than many independent countries in the world today.[2]

The 28th we spent at Barbados.

We got to Barbados . . . at 11 a.m. The Governor and Lady Stow and all the notabilities. A guard of honour of Police – very smart – and a good band in the picturesque uniform of the old Barbados Regiment. 12–1 was taken up with talks with Ministers ; Party delegations, etc. A large and cheerful luncheon at Government House. [Sir John] Stow is a good man, and seems to have the confidence of the Premier. At 4 p.m., after a drive through the town (Bridgetown) to a very old, and rather pretty Town Hall. The Mayor in his robes; the Town Clerk in wig and gown; the Aldermen and Councillors (of all colours and races) and about three hundred to four hundred people packed into a room that could comfortably hold one hundred to two hundred – the speech of welcome – the Freedom of the City – the stifling heat – a crowd of 14,000 outside (mostly children) – and it was quite a scene. The streets were crowded. We had an open car, in which

[1] 27 March 1961.   [2] 28 March 1961.

I stood up during the drive to wave to the people. Everyone seemed very friendly.

Then to the new Deep Water Harbour, with a magnificent shed—one hundred feet long or more—full of sugar. (This has just been built by Richard Costain.) At 6.00, on return to Government House, a Press Conference. At 6.30–7.30, a reception given by the Government, at the Government House, but happily in the open air. It was very hot in the afternoon, but cooled off in the evening.[1]

By a piece of good luck, the Edens were able to come to luncheon just before leaving for home. I was very glad of this chance of a talk, and to see that four months in the West Indies had done him good.

By this time, telegrams were flowing in from the Foreign Secretary in Bangkok, from Caccia in Washington and from Butler and Watkinson, Minister of Defence, on the Laos problem.

The next day, 29 March, we spent at Antigua. This is indeed

a lovely island—much more beautiful than the other two which we have seen. The colours of the sea are wonderful and the island is not so flat as Barbados or so mountainous as Trinidad. They arranged a very lazy programme for us, of [which] the chief feature was a visit to English Harbor and the old naval dockyard —now being restored. The house built for the Duke of Clarence is a gem and in good condition. The little harbour (where Nelson first served as a Lieutenant and which played a great role in his chase after Villeneuve and the French fleet in 1804–5) is very beautiful.[2]

There were the usual receptions in a very happy and relaxed atmosphere.

Our day in Antigua has been the nicest so far. Dorothy has had two bathes (I have not ventured). The programme has not been too heavy. We ended with a capital performance after dinner in the garden—a carnival parade (taken from what was actually done at Mi-carême): 'Limbo' dancers; an excellent village choir; a 'steel drum' band; tumblers; ghosts, long (on stilts) and short— altogether a very merry show, such as might have been performed by Elizabethan 'mummers' or 'morris dancers'. Puritanism certainly changed the face of England.[2]

[1] 28 March 1961.   [2] 29 March 1961.

Before leaving for Jamaica I had an interesting talk with the Administrator and Chief Minister of St. Kitts and Monserrat.

> The smaller islands are rather afraid of Federation. At present they draw large 'grants in aid' from U.K. Independence and freedom are all very well. But where is the money coming from? They have more confidence in the Colonial Office than in the politicians from Jamaica and Trinidad, who will dominate [the] Federal Government. This is colonialism reversed![1]

In the afternoon we flew to Jamaica, where there were the usual receptions and guards of honour, followed by a formal dinner in the evening. From the political point of view, far the most interesting experience was my hour's talk with Norman Manley. I had heard much about him from Stafford Cripps, who had a great admiration for him, but I was hardly prepared to meet such a remarkable figure.

Manley, who had won the first General Election in 1959 when Jamaica achieved full self-government, was forced by Sir Alexander Bustamante's opposition to agree to a referendum on secession from the Federation, to be held in 1961. This appeal was to take place in a few months' time.

> He is head and shoulders above any other politician in the West Indies. Federation really depends on his power (a) to persuade the other islands to be sensible at the Trinidad and London Conference; (b) to persuade Jamaica—which has to have a referendum—to vote for Federation. . . . Bustamante, old and ruthless, the most attractive demagogue in the area, has come out strongly against Federation. He has refused to dine at Government House to meet me. He has withdrawn his acceptance of a private talk with me. He has written a letter to the local Press, explaining these actions by reference to my speech in Trinidad to the Federal Party, which he calls an 'intervention by H.M.G. in local affairs'.
>
> Manley talked about immigrants—in all he is sensible and understanding. If we could only get U.S. to accept a reasonable number of Jamaicans, the problem would be solved. In the long run, he hopes that the birth rate will fall, if economic progress continues. . . . On financial aid *after* Federation, he recognises

[1] 30 March 1961.

they may call on us, but hopes we will do our best. (The Colonial Welfare and Development Fund must be replaced by some other assistance. It has done wonders in Jamaica.) He would be willing to become Prime Minister of Federation, since he has good men in his Jamaican Cabinet, one of whom could take his place.[1]

My little team had included on this occasion my doctor, Sir John Richardson. This was indeed fortunate, because with these long days and exceptional heat, I began to suffer in various ways. A sharp attack of gout struck me after church on Good Friday, 31 March, and I rested all that day. The next day was devoted largely to formalities, although a meeting with the Cabinet and Parliament in the morning was valuable. Since most of the other ceremonies were out of doors and in shaded places, I found the heat more tolerable.

This rapid journey prepared me for what seemed to be the inevitable development in the short life of the Federation. Conferences in Trinidad in May and in London in May/June were acrimonious. The Jamaican idea of a weak Central Government prevailed. But in September 1961, Jamaica nevertheless voted to secede. This destroyed the Federation, which was formally dissolved by the United Kingdom Parliament in April 1962. Jamaica was granted full independence on 6 August 1962, and Trinidad and Tobago on 31 August 1962. The other islands remained a British colonial responsibility. Plans for them to set up a new Federation (the so-called 'Little Eight', with its capital in Barbados) were produced at a conference in London in May 1962; but in the event never came to anything.

While I was in the West Indies, there was some development in the Laos crisis. The SEATO meeting took place in Bangkok, attended by the Foreign Secretary. Unhappily the restraining effect of my talks with the President at Key West had not yet been reflected, and the American authorities still seemed to be pressing forward an ambitious plan. Home rightly expressed his fears lest the United States and their allies should be dragged into far deeper military involvement than they really intended.

[1] 30 March 1961.

Rusk (in spite of my proposal to the President) has refused to allow any talks between Admiral Felt and General Hull. He says he has received no instructions. So the full plan . . . holds the field—a ridiculously ambitious plan, which the President and I in fact discarded. But I think the President's reason for not sending instructions is the one he frankly gave me. 'Everything leaks from the State Department.' If this very modified plan leaks, SEATO members will be discouraged, and Russian intransigence encouraged. I have telegraphed this view to Foreign Secretary.[1]

The Chancellor of the Exchequer, whose views I had sought, was naturally anxious about any action in the Far East which might affect dollar and sterling currencies. Nevertheless I felt it best to stick to the line I had agreed with the President.

Meanwhile, I

have just got telegram containing the Russian reply to our note on Laos. It is encouraging. If the Americans do not suddenly run amok, it looks as if negotiations can begin. The cease-fire will be difficult to get at once *de jure*. But we may get it *de facto*. It will certainly be a great relief if this crisis can be overcome without military intervention. It will also be a great triumph for British diplomacy and especially for the Foreign Secretary.[1]

The Russian acceptance much simplified my problem in Washington and allowed our discussions to range over a wide field, especially on the matters which I had outlined in the paper called 'The Grand Design'.

The British and Russian Governments made a joint declaration on 24 April appealing for a cease-fire and requesting the Indian Government to reconvene the International Control Commission and summon the Fourteen-Power Conference to meet in Geneva. When I was Lord Beaverbrook's Parliamentary under-secretary at the Ministry of Supply, I used to observe with admiration a large poster in his room which ran as follows: 'Committees take the punch out of war.' I felt some hope that conferences might do the same; and in effect the Geneva Conference, which sat until the end of the year, although it accomplished nothing, did, at least, prevent

[1] 1 April 1961.

M

anything happening which would endanger the peace of the world. But there were plenty of anxieties.

The position in Laos was clearly deteriorating. In the early hours of 26 April, I sat up with Butler, and with the new American Ambassador, Bruce, for two hours in my bedroom while telephone calls were coming through from Washington on the situation.

> I spoke myself to the President—who seemed fairly calm. Unfortunately, there has been no effective cease-fire. The Royal Laotian Army are (so far as the wet weather and boggy roads allow) on the run. The Pathet Lao forces may occupy practically the whole of the country, including the capital, Vientiane, before the cease-fire or the arrival of the International Commission. What then happens to the International Conference in Geneva? So there is great American pressure to put in military forces. . . . We are rather sceptical about this news, which comes from the American 'Stratford de Redcliffe' on the spot—Ambassador Johnston, not Ambassador Bruce. It's a very tricky situation.[1]

A cease-fire in these kinds of situation is an elastic term. What we had to do was to prevent full-scale operations. I pressed Nehru to see that the Commission should at least get out and do its best to arrange some terms in spite of Russian hesitation.

The Prime Ministers of Australia and New Zealand considered that their own interests were closely involved. Menzies felt that if the United States took action Australia would be placed in a real dilemma. A typical example of the difficulty of these discussions by telegram is perhaps what happened on the evening of 1 May.

> 6 p.m. Meeting on Laos. . . . The Americans, supported . . . by Australia and New Zealand, now want to take the preliminary troop movements for a military intervention. . . . They want to declare the alert at the SEATO meeting tomorrow. Their reason is that the two sides have not yet managed to meet to discuss the cease-fire; that the Pathet Lao are obviously stalling till the whole country has fallen; that they are advancing all the time; that the Thais are getting very restless; that only United Kingdom and France are out of step, etc., etc.
> I am not persuaded that the delay in the two sides meeting to

<hr />

[1] 27 April 1961.

discuss the cease-fire is due to anything but incompetence, torrential rain, bad communications, etc. I am also not at all clear what the military objectives now are, or what forces will be necessary to achieve them.

I dictated a draft telegram to President Kennedy, setting out the problem and posing certain questions. This was agreed, and it was sent off about 9 p.m. (after some redrafting in Foreign Office). Telegrams also prepared for Menzies, Holyoake, etc. I asked the President in my message to telephone to me tonight.

About midnight we rang Caccia in Washington. He told us that news had just come through that the two sides (Royal Laotian Government and Pathet Lao) *had* made contact and would continue their talks tomorrow. The Americans are therefore willing to postpone the SEATO meeting and not raise the question of the 'alert'–at least for a day or two. Accordingly a new set of telegrams were drafted (Lord Privy Seal with me) and sent chasing each other round the world. Bed at 1.30 a.m.[1]

The next day I informed the whole Cabinet of the situation.

If the cease-fire talks break down (as they may well do) the question of intervention will arise immediately. So the Cabinet must be fully informed and prepared.[2]

However, by 4 May I was able to record:

the last two days have been rather hectic–with good and bad mixed up. Laos cease-fire seems now definitely agreed. The Control Commission should be able to return and the Fourteen-Power Conference start in Geneva. The Foreign Secretary and Lord Privy Seal have handled this crisis very well indeed.[3]

There was at least now some lull in Laos, in spite of a long argument before the Conference opened about the status of the Pathet Lao at the Conference table, and the usual difficulties of supervising the cease-fire. Yet, at the end of the summer and even at the end of the year, the Russians seemed to be losing interest; and although Communist pressure in Laos, and later in Vietnam, was beginning to grow, I could feel at least some hope that no general flare-up would follow. These people would continue to live for a bit longer

[1] 1 May 1961.   [2] 2 May 1961.   [3] 4 May 1961.

in their normal state of tribal and ideological warfare and incompetent government.

To resume the main story, we reached Washington from the West Indies on the evening of 4 April. The talks began the following morning.

> Our team consisted of Secretary of State [Home]; Sir Frederick Hoyer Millar; Sir Norman Brook; (Philip de Zulueta, behind); Sir Harold Caccia. In the morning, we had Sir Robert Hall and [David] Pitblado (trade, money, economics generally). We also had Sir Patrick Dean (United Nations) in afternoon. They fielded, in addition to President and his assistant (Bundy), Secretary Rusk; Chester Bowles; Dean Acheson (for NATO and Germany) and lots of others, coming and going.[1]

The President impressed us all, not only by his quiet confidence but by his great courtesy. He listened well, did not talk too much, and encouraged others on both sides to speak.

> I opened on the general theme—the Soviet advance in recent years and the need to organise the unity of the Free World. I emphasised the strength of the Six in Europe and the dangers of France—under de Gaulle—of Europe moving into a 'Third Force'—still more dangerous, perhaps, after de Gaulle's death and the rise of a post-Adenauer Germany. All the economic arguments—money, trade, etc.—were well received by the Americans.[1]

At the luncheon interval the President took me upstairs to introduce his wife and to drink some very strong cocktails. This was the first time that I met Mrs. Kennedy, with whom I was afterwards to form a warm friendship. My wife arrived and lunched with Mrs. Kennedy upstairs; downstairs there was a 'working lunch' including all those on both sides who were present at the Conference.

> The President made a charming little speech—I replied.
> After luncheon, the talks went on till nearly 6 p.m. A really good day.[1]

I was particularly glad that Lord Home, the Foreign Secretary, had been able to meet me in Washington, for he contributed greatly to the success of this first and somewhat anxious meeting with the

[1] 5 April 1961.

new Administration. The next day there was a luncheon at the Senate with Senator Fulbright in the chair. This was a useful occasion, and the Foreign Secretary spoke with great force and charm, which pleased them all. In the afternoon, I had an hour with the President alone.

> It was really *most* satisfactory—far better than I could have hoped. He seemed to understand and sympathise with most of the plans which form what I call 'The Grand Design'. How far he will be able to go with de Gaulle to help me, I do not know. But he will try. It was left that I should compile a . . . memorandum and send it to him, setting out my plan.[1]

His visit to Paris at the end of May had already been announced, and he proposed to come to London before returning to America. His excuse for doing so

> will be a private visit for the christening of his sister-in-law's baby (Princess Radziwill). He will then be able to discuss the whole situation with me.[2]

After this talk we went on a cruise on the Potomac as far as the point opposite Mount Vernon. This was a combination of pleasure and work for a conference was continued on board. 'About six a side—subjects, Berlin, the Nuclear Tests, and more Laos.'[2]

Dorothy and I left for Boston the next day, where I delivered a speech at the Centenary celebrations at the Massachusetts Institute of Technology. There was an immense audience, but I was slightly disconcerted by a brass band, which separated me by a considerable distance from the front rows. However, the speech seemed to go reasonably well, although the subject was rather heavy.

> The main theme 'Unity' came out well—military and economic unity in the Western Alliance. The Economic part was divided into *Trade* (European groupings; Sixes and Sevens; Commonwealth; U.S.A. as Free Trade Area), *Aid*, and *Credit* policy (in balance and total volume of credit). This was all good and clear. The Defence part was, in reality, a modified form of what I had been saying to the President—find a way of sharing the nuclear with France (and thus, in theory, at least with Europe).[3]

[1] 5 April 1961.   [2] 6 April 1961.   [3] 7 April 1961.

The next day, having returned to Washington, Lord Home and I went to say goodbye to the President. Dean Rusk was present. Kennedy

> gave me a photograph with a most generous inscription. . . . Some more and quite intimate talk. The President seemed to think he would be engrossed with the *Foreign* front this year, but would get his essential measures through Congress. Next year would be the time for more radical things at home.[1]

This visit, to which I had looked forward with some apprehension, was made much easier by the unexpected meeting at Key West. The ice was broken and another stage taken in that close and intimate friendship between us which lasted to the end of Kennedy's life, and was maintained by his brother, Robert, until the second tragedy befell that unhappy family. Although the full discussions in plenary session were of great value, it was in the private talks with the President alone that the foundations of this intimacy were laid. He spoke to me very frankly about the internal situation, his lack of a majority in Congress, the many pressures upon him. Nevertheless, he felt that he would be able to carry through most of his plans— housing, education, etc. He was more nervous about the Foreign Aid programme, against which a good deal of opposition was building up. He also spoke about the problem of the 1,200 Cuban exiles who were at Miami. What did I think about it? I said I thought they were more nuisance in America than they would be in Cuba. What would he do with them if he kept them? He said that was just the point that worried him. He thought it would be better to let them go to Cuba and become guerillas. This was the origin of the unhappy story of the Bay of Pigs. It would have been better if Kennedy had stuck to his original plan of letting these men drift over and form a resistance group of their own. After all, this was the way in which Castro started.

As regards Europe, Kennedy repeated how anxious the Americans were for us to get into the Six. This for two reasons. Economically they thought it would be better for them to deal with one large group than with two groups; bargaining on tariffs and trade would

[1] 8 April 1961.

be easier. Politically they hoped that if we were in the Six we should be able to steer them and influence them, whatever might be the political personalities.

With regard to the vital question of the French, he surprised but pleased me by saying that he did not think Tripartitism would present great difficulties. He thought we three might have six-monthly meetings. He had read the records of the Rambouillet discussions held by President Eisenhower, and gathered that de Gaulle was more anxious for the appearance than the reality. When it came to practical discussions, the French were very negative. However, he realised that things could not go on as they were. If the French army returned to France from North Africa, de Gaulle would certainly disorganise NATO. In this connection, the President thought it might be a good idea to have a French Commander-in-Chief as SACEUR. I mentioned to him that de Gaulle disliked SHAPE sitting on his doorstep and—with some justification—thought it was grossly overstaffed.

We then turned to the really difficult problem, 'the nuclear question'. I remarked that if we could somehow or other get de Gaulle an independent nuclear force, however small, we should be able to persuade him to put it back into 'trusteeship', as we could probably do with the British, and as perhaps the Americans might also do for some part of their forces. He thought this not impossible, although difficult for the Americans. I said perhaps we could study whether he had the power, as President, to allow the British to give either warheads or nuclear information to the French. He agreed. All this was satisfactory, and yet I could not help feeling that

> he spoke about all these things in a rather detached way. Perhaps because it is his character to be ready to listen to anything. What he decides, is another matter.[1]

The communiqué was long, but impressive and certainly showed that we intended to maintain close co-operation. Since it had been a common jibe of the Socialists that the old reactionary and Tory Prime Minister would not be able to get on with the young radical and progressive President, the success of this visit was of special

[1] 6 April 1961.

importance. I felt that Kennedy, perhaps conscious of these rumours, had put himself out to correct them.

In my long letter to the Queen, sent on 12 April on my return, I tried, in addition to reporting the details of our talks, to give a general impression as to the character of the new President and his Administration.

> He has surrounded himself with a large retinue of highly intelligent men—young and old. He has satisfied the older men, like Harriman, Stevenson, Dean Acheson and the like, by re-calling them into the inner circle of power, and giving them various tasks to perform—mainly advisory. He has kept one or two of the old Administration, like Dillon, in order to reassure conservative opinion, particularly in the financial world. He has collected from the universities, foundations and other similar institutions in which this country abounds, a number of highly intelligent men, of all shades of opinion, representative chiefly of 'progressive' thought. He has given appointments to the representatives of the 'underprivileged', including several of Negro race.
>
> All this great army of advisers are engaged on studying all the more or less insoluble problems which the modern world presents to its baffled inhabitants. There is a saying in Washington that 'all the egg-heads are in one basket'.
>
> So far, apart from various messages to Congress, and some excellent Press Conferences, nothing much has happened. The American business recession has deepened. The number of unemployed continues to grow. All the same, there is a sense of intellectual expectation and even excitement in the air.
>
> The honeymoon with the American people is still continuing —indeed the affection felt for the President grows in every quarter, including Republican sympathisers. The contrast between the declining years of the last President (now openly accused of senility) and the opening months of the new one is thus dramatic.

In describing the Conference, I added:

> The President seemed responsive. He listened well, both to our side and to his own. He was very quick to take every point, and extremely fair in his appreciation of each argument. . . .

The President, apart from his intelligence, has great charm. He is gay and has a light touch. Since so many Americans are so ponderous, this is a welcome change.

On leaving Washington, we made a short visit to Ottawa, with the usual ceremonies. It was a great pleasure for my wife to be back in Government House, where she had spent several years as a child; the Governor-General and Mrs. Vanier were, as usual, gracious hosts. He and I were old friends from North Africa days.

The usual talks with Prime Minister, alone; talk with the Cabinet; reception by Senate and House of Commons; reception by High Commissioner; dinner with Prime Minister; dinner with High Commissioner; luncheon and speech to Canadian Club. Dorothy and I saw some of the old friends who survive.

The political business done was rather perfunctory—but I think they like me to go to Ottawa after Washington. It may help if, and when, we have to undertake a serious negotiation over Europe.[1]

A few days later, after I had returned, I heard the news of the Cuban fiasco, which was undoubtedly a great blow to the young President. Only his courage enabled him to survive the violent attacks to which he was subjected. My only anxiety was lest the failure of the covert action in Cuba might lead to the Americans insisting upon overt action in Laos. Much has been written about this affair. It may be worth recording a contemporary view.

Foreign Secretary—back from Bangkok; Ankara; Rome. He seemed in very good form and pleased at the way Laos was working out. He said that Rusk seemed very shaken by Cuba. It seems to have been a complete muddle, and a compromise between different plans. The simple one (which from what President said to me was what I believed they were considering) was to put two to three hundred men unobtrusively ashore, to go to the mountains, and start a centre of resistance. This is what Castro himself did. Then there was a plan for a big invasion, to include American troops. It seems that the President vetoed this and gave his approval to the simple landing of some partisans. But the 'agencies' operated the full invasion plan, but without

[1] 12 April 1961.

American troops, hoping, no doubt, to force the President's hand. He stood firm—hence the fiasco.[1]

However, the President, although naturally shaken, was by nature brave and resilient. His visits to Europe were now due, and on 22 April he sought my advice about his proposed meeting both with Khrushchev in Vienna, and de Gaulle in Paris. I could only tell him that, so far as Khrushchev was concerned, although it was made clear that there was not to be a formal negotiation, as in the case of my visit to Russia, yet they would have to talk about something. It seemed to me that the most important thing would be Disarmament, especially the Test Ban Treaty, Berlin, and the Far East—particularly as to how to play our hand at Geneva.

The successful explosion of France's fourth atomic bomb, coupled with the collapse of the revolt by the French Army in Algeria, resulted in

a complete and overwhelming triumph [for de Gaulle]. He is now supreme. The revolt broke (largely due to his moral influence with the ordinary Army) in four days.

I decided, unlike President Kennedy, that it would be best to send—and not publish the text of—a purely personal message. This was in these words: 'My dear Friend, I would like you to know how much you are in my thoughts and prayers.' This seemed to please the General, rather than the published messages of support and readiness to help, which de Gaulle thought rather patronising. I have now had (in his own hand) a charming letter from him. Is this a good augury for the Grand Design?[2]

There was a moment when the chances of de Gaulle's survival in power seemed evenly balanced. But, as had happened so often before, his calm and cool determination carried the day.

At Kennedy's request, and with the approval of my colleagues, I began to prepare a memorandum for his guidance before his meeting with de Gaulle. This document set out again the broad principles of our plan, but it was specially directed to try to persuade the President to deal sympathetically with de Gaulle's ambitions. For this it was necessary to accept in principle, and to operate in

[1] 5 May 1961.   [2] 29 April 1961.

practice, what we had called 'Tripartitism'; but, in addition, it would be of immense value if the Americans could give some assistance towards France's ambitions to develop a nuclear deterrent. The future of NATO, of Europe and, perhaps, even of the effective operation of the whole Western Alliance, now depended on France. In his reply, of 5 May, Kennedy made it clear to me that on Europe and on 'Tripartitism' he was in perfect agreement, but it would not be easy to help with France's nuclear aims. It would be necessary to get the approval of Congress in order to communicate nuclear technical 'know-how'. How could this then be refused to other allies? Might not Germany, at any rate Germany after Adenauer, ask for the same privilege? On 8 May he wrote his views in greater detail. Although I continued to press the President, I was not able to make much progress. Nevertheless, I felt that there would be some possibility of the Americans allowing us to assist the French in this field (which of course we could not do without their permission or condonation) if, and this might be the decisive point, the French would agree to put any of their nuclear capacity into NATO, reserving only the final right to use it independently in dire emergency. It was this thought which ultimately I worked out in respect of British Polaris, and I continued to urge that something of the same kind might be arranged for France. Meanwhile, of course, it was of great importance that neither of us should raise any false hopes in de Gaulle's mind until we had worked out an agreed plan.

Kennedy visited France for three days at the end of May and the beginning of June and carried out loyally his undertaking to support our desire for the reunification of Europe, at least on the economic field, but it was clear from the reports that de Gaulle maintained an attitude of dignified reserve. From Paris, Kennedy went for a meeting with Khrushchev in Vienna, on which I knew from our talks in Washington he laid great hopes.

The arrival of the Kennedys in London on 4 June was a cause of widespread interest and even excitement. The young President with his lovely wife and the whole glamour which surrounded them both, caused something of a sensation. Normally, the visits of foreign statesmen do not arouse much enthusiasm. These elderly men come and go, and apart from some exceptional figures, the mass of the people take little interest. But the Kennedys were news on every level, political and personal.

Dorothy and I went to meet them at London Airport in the evening.

> The President and I drove in an open car; Mrs. Kennedy and Dorothy behind us, in a closed one. There was a *very* large crowd, almost—but not quite—as big as for President Eisenhower last year. It was as enthusiastic, I thought. There were a number of POLARIS and NO BOMB placards—but these did not amount to more than five hundred people, obviously arranged at intervals on an organised plan. We drove to Princess Radziwill's home in Buckingham Place, where the Kennedys are to stay. A large and very cheerful crowd in the neighbouring streets. Dorothy and I went in, and stayed about twenty minutes. The President was in good form, and talked all the way up on his experiences. These had certainly had the effect, not of reducing his ardour and courage, but of making him realise how much more difficult the problems of the world are in reality than he had imagined before he assumed some responsibility for dealing with them.[1]

For the next day a formal meeting had been arranged with the usual advisers, Ambassadors and experts. But it was clear, as soon as the President arrived, that he wanted nothing of this kind. He wanted a private talk, and this lasted from 10.30 a.m. to 1 p.m.

> The greater part of our talk consisted of the President giving us his impressions of de Gaulle and of Khrushchev—what they said or did not say. Naturally, he was full of Khrushchev (having just left Vienna) and he was obviously much concerned and even surprised by the almost brutal frankness and confidence of the Soviet leader. The Russians are (or affect to be) 'on the top of the world'. They are now no longer frightened of aggression. They have at least as powerful nuclear forces as the West. They have interior lines. They have a buoyant economy and will soon out-match Capitalist society in the race for materialist wealth. It follows that they will make no concessions (unless these suit them), and will not be afraid of our reaction to what they may choose to do—in Germany or elsewhere.

[1] 4 June 1961.

Of course, part of this was an act—as always with Khrushchev. It is not as simple as all that. All the same, the President was impressed and shocked. It was rather like somebody meeting Napoleon (at the height of his power) for the first time. In effect, *no progress was made on any issue*. It is true that some soothing words were put into the agreed communiqué about Laos. But they were pretty weak, and so far, nothing has been done by the Russians to get the cease-fire working. The Conference only goes on—or staggers on—by constant adjournments. The Geneva Test Conference is dying. Disarmament seems hopeless. In South-East Asia, the Communists will get Laos—by one means or another—and it is hard to see where we are to make a successful stand. (It may even be better to accept—at some point—all the military dangers and difficulties of intervention now. Certainly if the Conference breaks down altogether, it is hard to see what else we can do.) On Berlin, Khrushchev delivered to the President a long *aide-mémoire*—which was pretty plausible and will be difficult to answer effectively. Khrushchev is determined to bring the issue to a head in the autumn—probably *after* the German elections.

Faced with all this, and by no means encouraged by the reality (apart from the superficial success) of his visit to Paris, the President seemed rather stunned—baffled, would perhaps be fairer. This was the real reason for his wish for a *private* talk— the presence of even the leading experts and trusted civil servants on both sides prevents talk from being absolutely frank. I welcomed this. For I did not wish, if I called attention to some of the underlying realities of the Berlin problem, to be reported verbally and then misrepresented by hearsay, so that Americans would think we were 'yellow' and French and Germans (who *talk* 'tough' but have no intention of *doing* anything about Berlin) could ride out on us. (This has happened before, and I was determined not to let it happen again.)[1]

I felt myself that Khrushchev had decided to take this offensive and even brutal line partly from a tactical point of view. Moreover, he no doubt wished to test the character of this new figure in the political world. Could he be intimidated, or would he stand up boldly? On Kennedy's side, he had clearly been disappointed

[1] 11 June 1961.

because he had hoped for something more reasonable and constructive. He had made the mistake of being drawn into an argument about Marxism. Khrushchev was well equipped in dialectics, and it was wiser to avoid a direct clash on theory. It was better to try and reach some practical arrangements.

The French visit had not been very productive.

> Mrs. Kennedy was admired and fêted. There were luncheons and dinners, and all the rest of the official entertainments which the French do so well (including, of course, Versailles). But (having regard to the fact that all the talks involved translation) the time given to serious discussion was not very considerable.[1]

Nevertheless, it was clear that the President had played up loyally. He had

> with the exception of the actual delivery of nuclear information or nuclear weapons, carried out most loyally our arrangement, and really did do everything I had asked him to do, both in Washington and in the memorandum which we sent him recently. De Gaulle was very avuncular, very gracious, very oracular, and very unyielding. He would take all the plums—Tripartitism, new arrangements in NATO, and help with the technique of missiles and bombs (other than the actual nuclear content). . . . But when it came to *giving* anything in return—e.g. Britain's desire to enter Europe on reasonable terms, having regard to Commonwealth and British agricultural structures—then the General was in his most austere mood.[1]

I could not help feeling a certain disappointment at all this. My great plan seemed to have failed; at least, little progress with the French, and none with the Russians had been achieved. Nevertheless, we must soldier on, and I was encouraged by the President's buoyancy.

Meanwhile,

> the social side of the President's visit was delightful. We had a very gay luncheon at 1.30 p.m. at Admiralty House—two round tables (ten each)—and lots of nice men and pretty women. Both families were in strength—Kennedys and their allies, Macmillans

[1] 11 June 1961.

and their allies. Dowager Duchess of Devonshire; Duke and Duchess; David and Sissy Ormsby Gore played for the home side. Prince and Princess Radziwill for the visitors. Added, the Homes (Foreign Secretary), Harold Caccia, Ambassador and Mrs. Bruce, the Chancellor of the Exchequer.[1]

After further talks in the afternoon, the day ended with a small but very enjoyable dinner at Buckingham Palace.

This was now the third time that I had met Kennedy. Our friendship seemed confirmed and strengthened.

> The President's visit was a success from the point of view of our personal relations. He was kind, intelligent and *very* friendly. I find my friendship beginning to grow into something like that which I got with Eisenhower after a few months at Algiers. *Intellectual* relationship (to put it rather pompously) is, of course, much easier. Eisenhower was an American soldier, trained as a soldier and talking that language. He had no other experience at that time. He did not find it easy to *discuss* a problem, although his instincts about how to handle it were generally right. Kennedy, with an entirely different mental background, is quick, well-informed, subtle; but proceeds more by asking questions than by answering them.[1]

So ended the story of East–West relations in the first six months of 1961. It was one of wild oscillation; the high hopes before the Paris Summit meeting, the despair that followed it; the dangerous crises both in Berlin and in Laos; and a growing sense of Soviet pride and intransigence facing a Western structure that had still not achieved any real unity of direction. But at least it could not be held against the British Government that they had not done their best.

[1] 11 June 1961.

CHAPTER XII

Squaring the Circle

FULL employment, stable prices, a favourable trade balance, growth; these form the circle which successive Governments since the war have had to try to square. In all their difficulties they have certainly not lacked advisers, professional and amateur. During the fifteen months from July 1960 to October 1961, economic fluctuations were of a minor character, and a solution of the major problems seemed to be within our grasp. Even when fresh storms began to threaten, some of our wounds as so often were self-inflicted. The desire to consume started to outrun the willingness to produce. It is true that some of our critics seemed to take a malicious delight in prophesying every form of mischief, especially when employed upon promoting it themselves. Even the undeniable prosperity of the nation as a whole caused them either chagrin or disappointment. How far it is possible for any Government of whatever complexion effectively to guide the varying movements and pressures which affect us remains to be seen. They can devise the strategy of the battle; but, like a general of an army in the field, they must rely largely upon the loyalty and discipline of the troops to achieve success. Nor should it be forgotten that in addition to the task of trying to achieve all these four objectives at the same time we, in this country, must pay regard to the additional complication, with all its advantages and disadvantages, resulting from sterling being not merely a means of exchange but an international currency forming part of the world reserve system.

At the end of July 1960 the new Chancellor of the Exchequer, Selwyn Lloyd, came with a fresh mind to his responsibilities after a long period of heavy work as Foreign Secretary. He was at once confronted with a somewhat depressing appreciation by his advisers.

Rather bad papers from Treasury on balance of payments and future Government expenditure have alarmed the Cabinet. Once again, admirable diagnosis, no remedies ![1]

Although every authority seemed to agree that we had reached a point where the brake had to be applied rather than the accelerator (always a less pleasant process since—to change the metaphor—it is more agreeable to turn the tap on than to turn it off) and some steps had already been taken, I was happy to find the Chancellor of the Exchequer 'in capital form, full of confidence, buoyant, and with many practical ideas'.[2]

There was however one urgent matter upon which I thought it right to send my views to the Chancellor of the Exchequer. It was necessary to impress upon the Clearing Banks and the City as a whole that they must take a broad view of their functions in the national interest. They must accept co-operation with the Treasury even at the cost of reduction of profits. As I wrote to Lloyd on 1 August

> It is because, broadly speaking, the owners of property have not taken [a narrow] view, have accommodated themselves to changing conditions, and have begun to regard themselves not merely as trustees for their beneficiaries but for the whole nation, that we are in such a politically healthy position today.

Nevertheless, there was one difficulty which had come to my notice :

> Whether the Bankers like the Special Deposit Scheme or not, they promised to adhere to it and to make their deposits as the Chancellor asked. But to do this with any sense of fairness means that they should make their deposits honestly and not merely by selling Gilt Edged securities. I was told that [one] bank had gone into the market and offered £15 m. one morning some days ago. I think the Government Broker was wrong to be intimidated by this. He should have let the sales take place and the price fall, with a handsome loss to the [bank]. However, he was frightened into buying. What does this mean ? It means that on the one hand so many millions are being put into the Special Deposit to reduce the power of the bank to make [advances to] its customers. At

[1] 30 July 1960.   [2] 15 September 1960.

the same time they are selling £15 m. of Gilt Edged in order to increase their power to do this very thing.

It should be possible for the Chancellor of the Exchequer, the Governor and the leading members of the City to work together as a team. If the Chancellor says that he wants the base of credit restricted, he ought to be able to have a meeting with them, tell them what he wants, and rely on them to carry it out, or *vice versa*. At present it is all kept as a sort of mystery, very much on an 'old boy' basis. This is all very well, but it needs some new look at it all.

At this time, with such a daily complexity of troubles, I was beginning to feel that

the strain is too great . . . year after year. After all, we shall soon have had *ten* years of it—or rather the survivors of Churchill's 1951 Government will have had this long experience.[1]

August had not been a very happy month on the labour front; but the threatened Power strike was settled on terms which are perhaps worth recalling.

The Unions asked 6*d*. per hour (the sum calculated to bring the lowest paid workers to £10 a week). The 'nationalised employers' offered 2½*d*. After some thought and consultation with the Ministries of Power and Labour I authorised 3*d*.—on which a settlement was reached late tonight.[2]

But an unofficial shipping strike began on 12 August and threatened considerable losses of exports, visible and invisible. Happily, on 18 August

the *Queen Elizabeth* managed to sail today. This was generally regarded as the real test of whether the unofficial strike would grow or collapse. I hope this prognostication may prove true.[3]

In effect the strike ended on 24 August, and there was a general sense of relief.

Equities are rising again—quite a boom. But I fear the base is not really sound—unless we can, by hook or crook, increase exports. I have sent Reggie Maudling a minute about this, and

[1] 15 September 1960.   [2] 12 August 1960.   [3] 18 August 1960.

hope to arrange a meeting with him next week. The Treasury
—or rather the Inland Revenue—are rather sticky about any
relaxation of their strict rules. But I feel we must *encourage* instead
of discourage people to go abroad on business—and even to take
their wives! (This is specially frowned on by I.R. It is easier to
charge a mistress than a wife to 'business expenses'.)[1]

Accordingly I circulated a directive on exports to all my colleagues
asking them to make sure that all departmental and domestic
interests in conflict with our main objective—a substantial and sus-
tained improvement in overseas earnings—should be set aside. There
now began a determined effort to ensure that all our posts abroad
were made fully aware of the creative part that they could play. This
proved highly successful. Undoubtedly businessmen today receive
assistance and support from the Foreign Service which would have
been unthinkable in the past.

The labour situation remained relatively calm. A threatened strike
in the railways was called off, and with the exception of a strike of
tally-clerks in the London Docks in September, we were remarkably free of troubles during all this period. It was not until the
increasing pressure upon the economy forced the Government to
recommend further measures of restraint that we began to face
serious difficulties. The Minister of Labour, John Hare, showed
great skill in managing some of the most ticklish aspects of these
disputes. He had every quality for this post—intelligence and
integrity. He was both liked and trusted by the trade union leaders.

At the end of October there were some minor changes in the
Administration, though not in the Cabinet.

The new appointments to the Government include Julian
Amery (to succeed Geordie Ward as Secretary of State for Air)
and Andrew Devonshire (to Under-Secretary, Commonwealth).
At the same time, Maurice has been chosen to *move* the address.
So there has been a little mild fun in the newspapers about
'nepotism' and 'happy families'—but all in a very good tone. I
think everyone recognises that Maurice has suffered, rather than
gained, by being my son. A Duke, of course, is always fair game.[2]

[1] 24 August 1960.   [2] 30 October 1960.

When my son moved the address at the opening of Parliament he did so in an admirable speech.

> After all the talk in the newspapers about my 'family' appointments . . . he delighted the House by his opening sentence 'as the only back bench member of the family'. Gaitskell was . . . generous and even gracious.[1]

By this time (27 October) the situation seemed sufficiently improved for the Bank Rate to be reduced on the proposal of the Chancellor, supported by the Governor, from 6 per cent to 5½ per cent. Yet the trend in the balance of trade was discouraging, and by the middle of November it seemed that, although the reserves were being increased by the arrival of 'hot' money, the underlying situation was not satisfactory. On 30 November a full-dress 'debate', lasting two and a half hours, took place in a full Cabinet.

> It was an extremely interesting discussion, in which everyone took part. The situation is really baffling. We are borrowing short and lending long; exports are stable or falling; imports leaping up—yet the £. is strong and money—some 'hot', some genuine investment . . . keeps flowing in. 'Everyone believes in Britain—except the British.'[2]

After the Cabinet meeting I worked on the results.

> I have asked for a number of enquiries on different aspects of the Balance of Payments problem, to see what steps we can take to reduce Imports. I will [preside over] a committee on increasing Exports myself.[2]

By the middle of December, so uncertain were the fluctuations, the balance of trade seemed to be improving.

> Trade figures not so bad as I had feared. The gap is £60 m. (£100 m. last month) and exports have gone up well. Imports are still too high. But if it is for 'stock', it is not too bad.[3]

Accordingly, when he called to see me on 16 December,

> the Governor of the Bank . . . did not seem too much alarmed

[1] 1 November 1960.   [2] 30 November 1960.   [3] 15 December 1960.

about the immediate future. But he is apprehensive about the pressure on sterling when the dollar recovers.[1]

At this period one of the major problems, towards the solution of which some progress has been made in later years, was that of the provision of a sufficient base for international credit to finance a greatly increased international trade, both in volume and value. On this I received from my friend Lady Rhys-Williams some interesting thoughts, which were, as usual, both far-seeing and imaginative. Although on a modified scale compared with the great inter-war depression, there seemed to be a general deflationary movement in the Free World. How was that to be countered? In reply I wrote to her on 29 November:

> Naturally it is absurd if the Free World gets itself into a deflationary spiral because of a lack of credit, and it would, of course, be best if the Americans would raise the price of gold. How we can get them to do this is almost an insoluble problem, for they all seem to be possessed by a sort of moral and spiritual attitude towards the dollar, a kind of modern fetish.
>
> On this subject there is one point on which I would be grateful for your views. In the old days the availability of gold of course was the only ultimate basis of credit. I know this is true to a certain extent today, but is it wholly true? In other words, how far can the International Monetary Fund and similar organisations create sufficient credit to do the trick without actually raising the price of gold? The other problem is of course that whatever the price of gold, if the Germans insist upon holding these great quantities of counters out of the round game we are all trying to play, how can we force them? You say, devalue the dollar and the pound, and thus upvalue the mark. But cannot the Germans follow the same course and not allow the mark to be upvalued? In other words, devalue it to the same extent as the dollar and the pound.

Strangely enough, the difficulty seems still to be recurrent and baffling. Meanwhile, it was clear that we must take some short-term action. Since various proposals, however useful, were likely to be either long-term or minor in their effect, the only immediate action

[1] 16 December 1960.

seemed to require reductions in Government expenditure, either by economies or by increases in various forms of contribution from the public. Just before Christmas the estimates for the following year became available.

> A long and difficult Cabinet. The Minister of Health wants to make what he calls 'economies' in the Service. As usual, they are not real economies—they are the old stagers—welfare milk, prescription charges, and all the rest. I do not like this 'regressive' taxation very much—nor do some of my colleagues. . . . But the enormous increase in the Estimates makes one feel that something must be done. We compromised on a scheme to produce £25 m. or thereabouts.[1]

I rather moodily felt that unless there was some startling improvement we were now going to enter one of those disagreeable periods of which I had all too vivid memories. At the same time I was determined to resist any precipitate or unconsidered action. I remembered Talleyrand's warning to his coachman—'Not so fast; not so fast; we are in a hurry.'

Two other matters with immediate impacts on the economy came before us during these autumn months. The first was the desire of the United States Ford company to buy up all shares of the British company in the hands of the public. In the short term the large sum involved would be of benefit to the reserves. But there were wider issues to be considered. I felt strongly that in the light of our long-term problems it would be unwise for the Government to interfere with the American bid.

> A great row is developing about the offer of Ford U.S. to buy all the shares (about thirty per cent of the whole) of Ford U.K. The usual anti-Americanism is developing on the Opposition side of the House, with the usual aberration of the usual people on our side. Of course, it is absurd for us, who have such immense overseas investments and are adding to them all the time, to take this 'nationalistic' stand! Lord Beaverbrook's papers—the *Express* and the *Evening Standard*—are fanning the flames. I must admit that I would have been very upset if Ford U.S. had [wanted] to *sell* their holdings in Ford U.K. But if they want to

[1] 21 December 1960.

buy (to the tune of £130 m.) they must feel confident about the future of Britain and their British business. The argument that they will close down or reduce the output of Ford U.K. is rather difficult to sustain, since they can do this already, without any new investment, because they own fifty-five per cent of the Ford U.K. shares and control in U.S. about seventy per cent. The Chancellor of the Exchequer and the President of the Board of Trade seem quite confident that they ought to allow the bid to be made. It is, of course, for the shareholders to decide whether they think the price high enough or not.[1]

Perhaps encouraged by a successful series of by-elections, or perhaps basing themselves on sound principles, the Cabinet agreed 'to the Ford sale (subject to certain guarantees). No one seemed in any doubt as to what it was right to do.'[2] In spite of considerable pressure, both inside and outside the House, my colleagues remained staunch.

> The Cabinet have re-affirmed their decision to approve the Ford share transaction. It is the only course which reason or interest could recommend. Of course, the American Government may well object, but (I think) have no power to stop it.[3]

A much heralded debate in the House of Commons duly took place and duly fizzled out. I was in Rome at the time, and was glad to receive a message from Rab Butler on 21 November as follows: 'Ford. A good day ended with a majority of ninety-six.'

A more important issue was how to deal with nationalised transport in the light of the report of the Committee which I had appointed under Sir Ivan Stedeford.

> Although they (the four of them) are not themselves agreed on all questions, yet their reports have proved most helpful. Marples (helped by Lord Mills) has now produced a plan, and the object of this meeting (at which the Chancellor of the Exchequer was present) was to get it into final shape for Cabinet. The chief point of discussion was whether the Transport Commission is to survive at all. In the end, we all came down in favour of *autonomous* group. . . .

[1] 15 November 1960.   [2] 17 November 1960.   [3] 29 November 1960.

The financial proposals are drastic but sensible and will mean writing off £1,200 m. or so as lost.[1]

By the beginning of December we were able to agree upon a White Paper[2] setting out the plan, but as usual personalities were more important than paper schemes. It will be perhaps convenient to continue the story up to the end of my Premiership. We were fortunate in being able to persuade Dr. Beeching, one of the most able and fertile brains in the industrial and commercial world, not only to sit upon the Committee which drew up the scheme, but to become Chairman of the Transport Commission in succession to Sir Brian Robertson in order to preside over the changes. The new plan provided for replacing the British Transport Commission by four separate boards to administer Railways, Docks, Inland Waterways and London Transport. All of these tasks were difficult enough; but to try and combine them all under one head (as provided in the Transport Act of 1947) had been clearly proved unworkable. Accordingly the Cabinet agreed upon legislation to carry out the recommendations, and the Bill to make the necessary changes received the Royal Assent in August 1962. The vesting date for the transfer of assets and liabilities to the new boards was fixed for 1 January 1963. Dr. Beeching, who had conducted the transition period, became head of British Railways, and set about his task with remarkable energy. During 1962 he and his team were carrying out the most detailed studies of freight and passenger traffic on a scale and by methods quite unknown in railway history.

The publication, in September 1962, of his report on the railway workshops led to a battle with the National Union of Railwaymen who wanted to

continue to build wagons which are not wanted and steam locomotives which are not required. . . . This is fantastic and everyone knows it.[3]

Although the threatened strikes came to little, I was anxious that the changes, although justified on technical grounds, should be

[1] 14 November 1960.

[2] *Reorganization of the Nationalized Transport Undertakings,* Cmnd. 1248 (H.M.S.O., December 1960).

[3] 27 September 1962.

combined with the same care for the human aspects as Lord Robens was already showing in the coal mines. In a note to the Minister of Transport, Ernest Marples, on 30 September 1962, I wrote:

> It must also be made clear what steps the Ministry of Labour and the Board of Trade are taking to consider how new industries could be brought in at special places ... or employment made available nearby. In other words, while we must not hesitate from the slogan 'Growth means change—innovation and change are all the time necessary', yet we must not let it be thought that so far as men and women are concerned they are to be treated in the Victorian happy-go-lucky way when they thought of humans almost less than they thought of machines.

I was also concerned about what would be the public reaction to the expected recommendations on the closing of uneconomic lines.

> It is very important that you should also make clear again the procedure that is to be followed about the railways. You explained it to me very clearly, and you should do so to the public. What really interests them is the procedure as regards closures. If the Government decides that on social grounds a railway from Inverness to Wick is necessary then, as I understand it, Dr. Beeching will quote a price to the Government for keeping the line open and running a number of trains. The Government will pay this, if it decides to do so, as a social service, but the management of the railway will not be accused of inefficiency or an increase in their deficit made a subject of attack upon them on this account.

The financial situation of the railways was certainly deplorable. The capital liabilities in 1960 stood at £1,600 million; the deficits in the three years 1960, 1961 and 1962 were £113 million, £136 million, and £159 million respectively. Nevertheless, when Dr. Beeching's report was published at the end of March 1963, it proved something of a shock. He pointed out that half the passenger stations contributed only two per cent of the revenue; the freight stations were equally wasteful. The new Chairman therefore recommended closing half the stations altogether and abandoning one-third of the route mileage, concentrating goods traffic at one hundred modernised depots and

introducing 'liner trains' to carry containers which could be transferred from road to rail. There should be fast inter-city passenger
and freight services; the number of employees would eventually
be reduced by some 70,000. There was, naturally, a tremendous
outcry, especially from the lightly populated areas of Scotland and
Wales. There was talk of a strike but

> the railway union (N.U.R.) are 'on the hook' and trying to get
> H.M.G. and Dr. Beeching to get them off. It is not easy to find
> the middle way between being too weak or too provocative.
> Cabinet drafted a memorandum which Dr. B. accepted. Later in
> the day the strike was called off.[1]

Members of Parliament naturally objected to the closures, and
while retaining his main purpose Beeching was able to make a
number of concessions and ameliorations. The labour which he had
undertaken was indeed Herculean. The nation owes him a deep
debt of gratitude.

Another distraction was the general concern over the newspaper
mergers—the *Daily Herald* had been bought up by Odhams, and
the *News Chronicle* had already been swallowed by the *Daily Mail*.
The anxiety was on two accounts—first, the dangers of a monopoly
as regards policy (a free Press must be one expressing many different
points of view). Secondly, the threat to employment. I was not
much impressed by the first, for it seemed to me that radio and
television had long undermined the power of the Press; newspapers
were becoming more and more regarded as magazines. Moreover
we had too bitter an experience of the harm done by the proprietors
and editors of the national Press in the inter-war years, and above
all in the supreme disgrace of Munich, to take them too seriously
now. On the question of employment of the staffs and workmen I
felt more concerned. Yet I was well aware of the over-staffing and
restrictive practices in the metropolitan offices. However, since the
Labour Party seemed very anxious for an enquiry, and no one else
seemed to object, I agreed. But I insisted that it must cover the
wider issues involved and not be confined to these particular trans-

[1] 9 May 1963.

actions. Accordingly, on 9 February 1961 I announced the setting up of a Royal Commission on the economic and financial factors affecting the Press. Fortunately I was able to persuade Lord Shawcross to act as Chairman. The Commission made an admirable report; everyone concerned praised but did not follow its recommendations.

To resume the main theme; in the search for 'economies' the Cabinet had with some reluctance agreed to an increase in pension stamps and various health charges. Prescription charges—melancholy legacy of Attlee's Government—were doubled from 1s. to 2s.; the charge for dentures was increased, and the subsidies were removed from orange juice and cod-liver oil. Not a very inspiring but, I was assured, a salutary programme.

> The Health charges have been announced by Minister of Health (Powell) and the usual Socialist storm. At least we have given them something on which they can agree—a vote of censure on us.[1]

If the economic situation in the spring of 1961 was subject to unexpected fluctuations, so was the advice given to me by Ministers, officials and friends. For instance, a few weeks before the Budget I had a visit from an old and trusted adviser, Roy Harrod, on this occasion a

> prophet of woe. He says the £. will crash in the summer. We *must* restrict imports. Treasury and Board of Trade say the opposite. What is a poor Prime Minister to do?[2]

These doubts and anxieties followed a serious alarm at the beginning of March.

> There has been, and continues still, a tremendous 'bear' attack on sterling. No doubt the weakness of our balance of payments prospects has come into it. But it has been set off by the sudden revaluation of the Deutschemark—*up*-valued by five per cent. This has caused wild speculation in London, New York, Paris, Amsterdam, Zurich, and all the rest ever since. (*a*) The

[1] 4 February 1961.   [2] 5 March 1961.

fact of revaluation reminded all speculators and owners of hot money that fixed exchanges can, after all, be changed. If once, why not again? (*b*) The fact that the up-valuation is far too small to correspond to realities has led everyone to think the first move in this direction may be followed by a second. Since this could only be upwards, it's an absolutely safe bet to sell dollars and sterling in order to buy Deutschemarks. This has been done on an absolutely unprecedented scale. We lost £67 m. *one day* (£26 m. was the worst post-Suez day). Altogether we have lost about £187 m. of *hot* money from the reserves. America has had the same experience.[1]

The careful reader will recognise these symptoms of the troubles of a previous decade with a certain ironical amusement. *Plus ça change....*

We decided to fight and spend all this money defending the *rate*. We have no doubt caught out some speculators, who were borrowing at eight per cent and more to 'bear' the £. All the same, it's the worst patch I have been through.

Selwyn Lloyd (Chancellor of Exchequer) has been splendid all through. He has been calm and confident. The Governor (Cobbold) was in America at the start and made a very useful visit to Basle.

The fact that this started at the *beginning* of the month was lucky. We need not publish the figures of the reserves till the end of March. We have had very good support from Central Banks—German and Swiss—which have put immense credits at our disposal—thereby cancelling out collectively what speculators have done individually.[1]

Unfortunately the balance of payments figures published on 1 April were discouraging. In the circumstances it was not easy to frame a Budget, certainly not a popular Budget. Nevertheless, it proved to be by no means unimaginative. There were some novel features. By raising the starting point of surtax on earned income from £2,000 to £4,000 and applying the earned income tax allowance of two-ninths up to £4,000, the exemption of earned income from surtax was, roughly speaking, extended up to an income of £5,000. I had long pressed this on the Chancellor of the Exchequer in my talks.

[1] 24 March 1961.

It is not going to be easy to have a 'popular' Budget, but I feel we must do something now for the relief of direct taxation. After the health stamp and the prescription charges, it will not be easy to do the surtax changes—but I think we should do them *now*, before the Parliament gets too advanced.[1]

This concession, owing to the system of assessing surtax, would not become effective for nearly two years. Perhaps it was this thought that comforted the authorities. Meanwhile £80 million would be raised in new taxation by various well-tried means—the only novelty being a 10 per cent tax on television advertising, which was generally regarded as overdue. The outstanding innovations were the two so-called 'regulators'. Powers were taken to add up to 4s. per employee per week to the National Insurance stamp. This was commonly known as the 'payroll' tax. Powers were also taken to vary by 10 per cent, up or down, purchase tax and certain duties, including those on tobacco, alcohol and petrol. These medicines were to be given to the patient public as the economic doctor might prescribe, without all the complications of a summoning of Parliament, an additional Budget and a finance bill. We thus introduced into the management of the economy the now popular concept of the stimulant and the tranquilliser.

[The Budget] has been very well received by the Party. I believe it will be understood and accepted by the public and respected by the foreign bankers.[2]

It was believed to show a 'determination to defend sterling and stability by all means in our power'.[2] Alas, the summer months were to show little improvement. Indeed each week brought its tale of gloom.

This has been a bad week in the market; partly because of our bad balance of payments position; partly because of widespread rumours that the Swiss franc is to be upvalued; partly because of [a] sense of the worsening foreign situation—there has been a great loss (£100 m. or more) in the reserves. Of course, this is just the 'hot' money going back. Still it's a bad sign, and if it goes too far, a critical situation may well occur. I have had long talks with

[1] 22 February 1961.   [2] 17 April 1961.

the Chancellor of the Exchequer, who expects to put a comprehensive plan before me next week. Meanwhile, the Governor of the Bank is at Basle this weekend, and may be able to arrange more help from the other Central Banks.[1]

In June the trade figures announced were bad—the gap up to £80 million. Being under some pressure, I took two days' rest at home. I lay in bed counting my blessings:

1. *Economic problem* (probably insoluble)
Trade balance.
Loss of invisibles.
Overstrain in economy.

2. *Europe—Sixes and Sevens* (obviously insoluble)

3. *Laos*
No settlement in sight.
Communists now breaking cease-fire.

4. *Central Africa* (Welensky, etc.)
Political crisis certain—at home and in Federation.

5. *Berlin*
No solution possible; if anyone tries to talk sense, he is at once called a coward and a traitor.

6. *Security*
Troublesome, but I think manageable—Opposition will try to get a Ministerial resignation.

7. *Recruiting Regular Forces*
Target will *not* be reached. So what to do? 'Selected Service', or what?

However, I suppose the obvious retort is '*tu l'as voulu, Georges Dandin*'. I can resign any day, if I wish to.[2]

Selwyn Lloyd now warned the Cabinet that further measures might soon be needed. Our real need was to cut down expenditure for defence and overseas aid in the light of the serious fall in invisible earnings. But how to achieve this, without betrayal of our duty to the Commonwealth and the Free World, was not easy. The Party in the House was solid and indeed urged drastic action, how-

[1] 11 June 1961.   [2] 15 June 1961.

ever unpopular, to halt the deterioration in the economic situation. I was by now feeling very exhausted and seriously contemplating resignation.

All this concentration of work on special problems, combined with the usual Parliamentary routine (Parliamentary Questions, etc.), speeches, as well as the calls of hospitality, have tired me greatly. It is quite an effort now to make an effort. But I cannot leave the ship now. I must try to get her into calmer waters before I do so.[1]

Towards the end of the Session, at the Chief Whip's suggestion, I addressed the 1922 Committee.

I was rather nervous about it, having heard talk about great discontent in the Party. But in fact it went off very well. I made a serious and carefully prepared speech. . . . One piece of good news came out yesterday, in the shape of the trade figures, showing a much reduced gap—down to £20 m. Of course, it may be a flash in the pan—but it may be a beginning of better things.[2]

We had two internal difficulties to face:

the *utter irresponsibility* of labour in some of the *new* industries (motor-cars, aviation and the like) and the *hopeless conservatism* of labour in some of the *old* industries (shipbuilding, etc.). So what with 'wildcat' strikes in one and 'restrictive practices' in the other group, our poor economy suffers grievously.[2]

I was comforted by the good mood of the back-benchers. Of course, as usual, the most empty made the greatest noise.

I had already begun to feel that we needed some more imaginative approach to the wages question. At the end of July money was still flowing out of the reserves and naturally

the House of Commons has become rather restless. . . . There was a stiff little debate on Tuesday, which gave the Opposition a good chance. Gaitskell was very good, I thought, and both his professional exposition and his waspish attack on me were in good style. Harold Wilson was also very good. Maudling and

[1] 8 July 1961.　　　　[2] 15 July 1961.

Selwyn Lloyd spoke—the former very effectively, the latter not so good. But he was hampered by the circumstances of the debate. In view of his statement next week, he could really say nothing.[1]

Although I could not but agree with the Chancellor of the Exchequer and the new Governor of the Bank of England, Lord Cromer, that some steps must be taken, I felt unhappy at the demands which were being made upon us.

> If we are to get our 'drawings' from the International Monetary Fund, we shall have to make—or pretend to make—large savings on Government expenditure. This is (in the short as well as in the long run) more difficult than extra taxation. It is also very hard to achieve quickly, whether on Current or on Capital Account. But if the package is not good enough, the international usurers—bankers—will turn us down. Then sterling will go. (Whether this matters as much as we all think or not, I am not sure. It matters politically, because sterling has become a symbol. What really matters is that we should *not* add to demand by wage increases.)[2]

On the next day, 24 July, the Chancellor's packet was almost ready, but there were still two points to be settled.

> The Governor is anxious to alter Hire Purchase terms . . . to the stiffest on record. Two years and 30 per cent or perhaps more 'down'. (This is, of course, to make the monetary measures less unattractive to the Clearing Banks.) He also wants the Chancellor to use the 'second regulator'—the so-called 'payroll' tax. Lord Cromer's argument here is that people will not understand why the Government has chosen to arm itself with this weapon and forced the House of Commons to agree, and then decided not to use it. Will it seem as if the crisis was less severe than we are saying? The Chancellor of the Exchequer has doubts on both these. Hire Purchase will hit too hard the same industries as are hit by the first regulator. The 'payroll' tax is so unpopular with both employers and trade unionists that we shall get them against [us] in the next great struggle that awaits us—and the most important—the Battle of Wages.
>
> The argument ended, inconclusively, at 4.30. It must go to tomorrow's Cabinet for resolution.[2]

[1] 22 July 1961.   [2] 23 July 1961.

When the Cabinet met the next day, all the Chancellor's proposals were agreed, but

> there was general support for not using the second regulator (payroll tax) and for not altering Hire Purchase terms. We must now 'wait and see' the result on sterling.[1]

On 25 July Selwyn Lloyd made his statement to the House with admirable clarity and firmness. The facts spoke for themselves. Balance of payments in deficit for third successive year; rising personal demand and investment demand not being met by rising productivity. In 1960–1, wages and salaries increased by 8 per cent, national production by 3 per cent. We were becoming uncompetitive. A pause was essential. Government expenditure had to be cut —and that meant among other things that the provisional agreement on teachers' salaries would have to revised downwards. To safeguard the balance of payments it would be necessary to review with NATO our expenditure for defence in Germany; to prevent further rises in overseas aid; to cut overseas administrative expenditure; to restrict overseas non-sterling investment to cases which would clearly benefit the balance of payments and encourage the repatriation of overseas earnings. Further special deposits would be required from the Clearing Banks, and they would be asked not to lend for personal consumption. Bank Rate would need to be raised from 5 per cent to 7 per cent. Indirect taxation must be increased by 10 per cent of the existing rate. A substantial drawing from the I.M.F. would be arranged.

On the evening of the Chancellor's speech I noted that

> our side took it well. The Opposition seemed rather stunned. Everything (in the first round) now depends on what happens to sterling. Everything (in the second round) depends on what happens to wages.[2]

This was the first intimation of what came to be described in a famous phrase as the 'Pay Pause'. Although it was to lead us into great difficulties in detail, it certainly was not unsuccessful in general.

There followed a two-day debate, and while it was in progress I saw all Ministers not in the Cabinet, including those in the House

[1] 24 July 1961.   [2] 25 July 1961.

N

of Lords; all seemed in good heart and confident. The debate was quite an unusual experience.

> Yesterday Chancellor of Exchequer was competent and firm. Harold Wilson tried to be serious, and as a result rather bored the House. The debate produced some good speeches from the back-benches, sincere and constructive. Brown (Deputy Leader) started with a terribly bad speech—over an hour of pompous and irrelevant declaration. Edward Boyle (Financial Secretary to the Treasury) replied in an admirable effort. Gaitskell wound up with a good speech, ending in a fierce (and rather witty) attack on me personally, and demanding my disappearance from the stage, where an old actor had outstayed his welcome. I had prepared (with immense trouble) a good reply. But, obviously as the result of a plan organised by the Opposition Whips, I was hardly able to speak two consecutive sentences audibly. However, I struggled on, and curiously enough, after about twenty minutes, I got the mastery. The last ten minutes were pretty quiet. Our people were rather taken aback. They did not want to add to the row by cheering me and this may have caused an impression of uncertainty. However, they made up for it later. The division was a triumph—*one hundred and ten majority* and after the division I was given a tremendous ovation by the Conservatives, who all stood up and cheered.[1]

The immediate reaction in the exchange market was good. Sterling recovered, with considerable foreign buying. I felt strongly that one of the disadvantages of a fixed currency exchange rate was the time lag and complexity of all the calculations. The rate now had become merely a measure. A floating rate would be a barometer and any weakness of the economy much more quickly detected by the market than by the Government statisticians. But this question, so often discussed, seemed to be beyond our power to decide unilaterally and still remains unresolved. Meanwhile, it was clear, by the beginning of August, that the immediate attack on sterling had been met and held. The July figures showed that the trade gap was much narrowed, and broadly the economic situation was improving. We had thus won the first round.

[1] 27 July 1961.

But, of course, all this is preliminary to the *second round*—that is, whether we can restrain personal incomes to a level justified by productivity. If we can do that, exports should begin to rise and imports fall. The short-term measures, including the use of the first regulator, the Bank 'squeeze', etc. should have some impact on demand—perhaps, as months pass, to the tune of several hundred millions. But this will all be nullified if we put up personal incomes by £1,000 m. in the next twelve months, as we have in the last twelve months.[1]

On the wages front we were faced with

the very difficult question of the Government's *own* employees —civil servants, industrial and non-industrial; health service employees; police, etc. Here we have *compulsory arbitration* agreements, binding on both sides, and going back to 1925. Are we to honour them? If we do, in one or two 'disputes' outstanding, the arbitrator will be sure to give anything between six per cent and eight per cent. Then private industry will despise the Government and throw up the sponge. This means devaluation next spring. . . . Are we to 'suspend' them—as an Act of State? . . . Or are we to give notice that while the machinery of negotiation, including arbitration, is to go on, we must reserve the right of when and in what stages to implement any decision. This is really the 'pause'.[1]

It was finally agreed to follow the last course. The awards would be honoured, but there would be a period of delay. Naturally the trade union leaders were forced to resist, and there was talk of strikes. Nevertheless, I felt that they knew very well in their hearts that wage claims must lead to inflation unless accompanied by an increase in productivity. They dare not say so openly; but if this was their real feeling I felt that our relations had been so friendly that it should not be impossible to get through the next period without excessive bitterness.

Public opinion was also beginning to move to our support, and even the teachers' organisations felt that an increase of £43 million amounting to 14 per cent, although spread over a period, was not an unfair settlement.

[1] 5 August 1961.

With so many other difficulties facing us at this time in every part of the world I was persuaded to deliver a broadcast on all the urgent problems which confronted the nation. For several weeks there had been a Press campaign against me

> carried on in almost every paper—as being tired, failing, losing grip, etc., culminating in a report in the luncheon editions of the *Evening Standard* and the *Evening News* that I had had a 'heart attack'. Harold Evans was rung up all the day by every conceivable paper, news agency, etc., in every country in the world.[1]

At my Tuesday audience in this week

> the Queen expressed concern at these reports of my health. I could only remind her of what Mark Twain said of the reports of his death—'they are much exaggerated'.[1]

I found the broadcast a troublesome task. I had learnt to do

> the interviews or discussions adequately. But the 'solo' (which is thought [suitable] when one speaks as Prime Minister to the nation—and other nations) is much more difficult.[1]

Fortunately, this was well received.

> The Press today is quite good about the broadcast, and prints the text—which is rather unusual. I spoke on three subjects —Economic situation at home—Common Market—Germany and Berlin.[1]

This broadcast took place on 4 August, the forty-seventh anniversary of the outbreak of the First World War. In writing the diary of this week, I could not help meditating on this

> fatal date from which spring all our troubles—the beginning of the end of Europe's supremacy [and of] the predominance of the white man in the world. From this date began the end of the old British Empire and the capture of the greatest Euro-Asian country—Russia—by the strange doctrines of a German Jew intellectual—Karl Marx. Happily, we did not realise all this when we were young.[1]

[1] 5 August 1961.

CHAPTER XIII

A Squall in the Gulf

THE events of 1956 in the Middle East had undoubtedly left Nasser in an improved if not a commanding position. To have successfully challenged all the maritime nations of Europe; to have outwitted the subtle and devious Dulles; to have seen a brutal and apparently final breach between the Old World and the New; to have watched the strange episode of the American and Russian delegates walking arm-in-arm from the lobbies of the United Nations Assembly and planning the discomfiture of Britain and France; to have seen the Anglo-French forces withdraw and to have been left finally with the possession of the stolen property of many nations—the Canal; all this must have done much to enhance the reputation and strengthen the power of the Egyptian Nationalist leader. Against this, all the 'face' that had been won against the West had been lost in the East. Nasser's army had suffered an inglorious, indeed a devastating, defeat at the hands of Israel. Moreover, the sudden reversal of American policy leading to the promulgation of the Eisenhower doctrine and to the American and British military operations in Lebanon and Jordan in 1958 had to some extent restored the balance, although the tragic events in Iraq, culminating in the murder of the King and his uncle, as well as that of the old and well-tried statesman, Nuri Pasha, were all grist to Nasser's mill. These events, together with the violent agitation carried on from Cairo by every means of propaganda, kept the Western Powers in a state of uncertainty and apprehension. It was clear that Nasser, now the Mussolini of Egypt, was determined to foster discontent and promote trouble in every Arab state. Those which had already thrown off their traditional leaders he would try to 'merge' or annex under his own authority. Those who were still ruled by Kings and Sheikhs he would try to subvert. With considerable skill he harped upon both strings—Communism to excite the discontented, pan-Arabism to inflame the faithful. Wherever one looked in the Middle East there were traces of Nasser's baneful operations. Against all this we could only strive to maintain our traditional spheres of influence. We fully realised the vital importance to British interests of the Gulf and of Aden. This was not only a question of upholding our authority, but of denying these strategic areas to the new imperialism masquerading under the cloak of Communism. The firm line that the British had taken on their own to defend the rights of the Sultan of Oman and to defeat the rebel forces (a decision taken only a few months after the Suez episode), as well as the strong position we had maintained over Buraimi in 1955, amounted to a substantial gain on the other side of the account. Then, as now, any sign of weakness was welcomed by our enemies; any exhibition of strength gave corresponding gratification to our friends. The majority waited to see which way the balance would tip.

The Sheikhdoms of the Gulf had long looked to Britain for protection. Before the First World War this function had been carried out throughout the area, as well as in the Horn of Africa, by the Government of India. These duties were later transferred, in due course, from Delhi to London. In the old days our task had been the traditional one of keeping peace and promoting trade in these still undeveloped parts of the world. Since the coming of the oil age these areas, like many others in the Middle East, sprang into an unexpected prosperity with all its benefits and all its dangers. Naturally, they became the target for every form of pressure from the 'progressive' elements. In 1959 there were serious disorders in Kuwait fomented from the U.A.R. This propaganda was directed against the Government of the Sheikh on the usual Jacobin lines— pro-Nasser, pan-Arab and in general subversive. A number of Left-wing Iraqis resident in Kuwait were drawn into the game and some Kuwaitis fell victims to these ideas. But the Sheikh's Government was firm and, somewhat to the astonishment of Nasser and his friends, deported a number of trouble-makers.

In June 1961, in conjunction with the Government of Kuwait, now one of the richest territories in the whole area, the British

Government agreed that the old 1899 Treaty, which was suitable enough in the conditions of that date, could no longer be applied. The Kuwait Emirate was now too rich, and in a sense too powerful, to continue under the old Treaty of protection suitable to its character sixty years before. In its new position it rightly claimed to be regarded as a purely independent state, and it was now aspiring to become a member of the Arab League, as well as of the United Nations. The Kuwait Government had shown considerable foresight in this move, to which the British Government willingly agreed, and the Treaty was replaced by an exchange of letters embodying 'a close friendship between our two countries'. Moreover, Britain undertook to stand 'ready to assist' Kuwait if called upon.

We had not long to wait. A few days after the announcement of our guarantee a peremptory demand was issued to Kuwait by General Abdul Karim Kassem, the revolutionary leader of Iraq. He called upon the Government and people of Kuwait to surrender immediately to his rule since they were 'a long lost but integral part of Iraq'. Irredentism is always a popular cry for revolutionary leaders; but when the patriotic hook is baited by many millions of tons of oil and many millions of money it becomes almost irresistible. General Kassem was perhaps only following in the footsteps of greater men. The Kuwait Government, however, was not to be brow-beaten into surrender, especially by Arabs who appeared to the Sheikh in the role of revolutionaries and murderers. This wholly unacceptable claim and its accompanying menaces were therefore immediately rejected by Sheikh Abdullah. The demand was made on 25 June; on the 26th it was rejected with contempt. I therefore sent telegrams to the heads of the leading Commonwealth Governments on 30 June:

> I feel I should let you know that the situation in Kuwait looks increasingly serious. There are indications that Kassem is preparing to send a substantial force from Baghdad to Basra. From there he could of course, should he decide to do so, invade and seize Kuwait territory in a very few hours. We are making all the necessary preliminary preparations that we can short of actually entering Kuwait territory, but it is more than likely that the

Ruler will make an appeal to us for help. We are doing all we can in various Arab countries to stimulate protest against this aggressive action by the Iraqi Government, but of course protests alone may not be sufficient. We hope to get further information in the next day or two but things may move very quickly and I thought it right to let you know the position. As you know, our new Treaty, substituted for our old system of protection, puts us under an obligation to help the Ruler and in the nature of the case we may have to act at very short notice. I will keep you informed all the time.

On 30 June Kuwait formally requested British assistance. At the same time they made an appeal to members of the Arab League to which they had applied for membership on the abrogation of the old Treaty with Britain. The matter was immediately brought before the British Cabinet, and there was general acceptance of the view that our honour as well as our interest was involved. I accordingly informed the Commonwealth leaders as well as General de Gaulle of our intention to send troops into Kuwait as soon as possible. The response from all was friendly, although Ayub Khan, the President of Pakistan, expressed his doubts as to whether Kassem really meant to force the issue. I could not help feeling that Kassem's irresolution would be removed by our strong reaction to his threats. De Gaulle's reply of 7 July, acknowledging the courtesy, added a more serious note.

> As the Iraqi threat has arisen and you have recently concluded a treaty of assistance with the Sheikh of Kuwait, I realise that you are obliged to give him help. Let me add that I fully appreciate that you will take into account the position in which our common interests in Iraq might be placed. If things should turn out badly in this respect, I think we should make our plans immediately.[1]

All the rest promised support at the United Nations, to which the Ruler of Kuwait had now made his appeal. Although not yet a

[1] La menace irakienne se manifestant et étant donné que vous avez récemment conclu avec l'Emir de Koweit un traité d'assistance, je comprends que vous vous trouviez dans la necessité de lui apporter votre aide. Laissez-moi ajouter que j'apprécie pleinement que vous considériez la situation ou pourraient être placés nos intérêts communs en Irak. Si les choses devaient tourner mal à cet égard, je crois que nous aurions à nous concerter aussitôt.

member, he felt it proper to advise this august body of the threatened aggression and seek its aid.

Meanwhile, the British acted rapidly.

> The Cabinet left the whole management of this affair to me. I got the Foreign Secretary and the Minister of Defence to work side by side with me, which they did with admirable loyalty and skill. But ... I was careful throughout to have meetings of Ministers (including Chancellor of Exchequer, Lord Chancellor and Home Secretary) and also—before the final decision to launch the forces—of the whole Cabinet.[1]

The first troops landed on 1 July, and by 2 July a brigade group had moved into its position in the desert. Within ten days the build-up was complete, with naval and air forces in support. As yet there was no visible enemy save the torrid heat of the blazing sands.

> We had good support from Chief of the Defence Staff (Lord Mountbatten) and the Chiefs of Staff. The plan (in spite of inescapable difficulties, chiefly due to 'overflying' problems) worked out pretty well. We worked through some long and anxious nights, especially when we thought Kassem would seize Kuwait city and territory virtually unopposed. Now our worry is the opposite. Since the Iraqi attack has *not* in fact developed, all the pressure will be turned on us. It is going to be difficult, and expensive, to stay; hard to get out. The Opposition in Parliament have behaved pretty well—so far. But this will not last.[1]

The Minister of Defence was thinking of building up the Kuwait force with tanks and even aeroplanes. I doubted the wisdom of this, since these weapons might just as easily be used against us or the Ruler. I had not forgotten that the tanks which we had sold to Iraq were soon used to overthrow the Hashemites. The Security Council, with America and Russia divided, proved ineffective. Kuwait's application for membership on 30 June was to be vetoed by the U.S.S.R. on 30 November, while Soviet opposition to any plan of international action in support of Kuwait was declared on 5 July. Fortunately, action had already been taken by the loyal allies and traditional protectors of the Sheikhdom.

[1] 8 July 1961.

N2

When, on 20 July, the Arab League accepted Kuwait as a member, although the Iraq delegate walked out in a temper, it was clear that many Arab states were having second thoughts about the wisdom of Kassem's intemperance. The rapid move of a small number of British troops had averted the immediate threat. Partly from shame, partly perhaps from jealousy, the Arab League, largely under the influence of the conservative forces led by Saudi Arabia, now took up the Kuwaiti suggestion that they themselves should take over the protection of their new member.

> I have hopes that we shall soon be able to get our troops out of Kuwait. The majority of the Arab League States have agreed (in principle) to send a force to defend Kuwait against Iraq and thus relieve us. There are, of course, dangers in this in the long run. In the short run, we have achieved our immediate purpose.[1]

This new move recommended itself to the Sheikh; and on 13 August he made a formal request that we should accept a proposal with which we were only too anxious to comply. The first Arab League units began to move in during the second week of September, and on the 19th the British withdrawal began. It was completed on 10 October. The Egyptians, who had contributed a small unit to the mixed force, announced on 14 October that their force would be withdrawn. They did not, in fact, complete the move until the end of the year. I was somewhat concerned by Nasser's devious policies, for I feared they might be the prelude to some new attack upon Kuwait. However, the military coup in Syria, on 28 September, which resulted in the separation of Syria from Egypt, was a severe blow to his prestige and perhaps accounted for his vacillations.

> The Syrian coup looks as if it had been (for the moment, at any rate) successful. No one seems to know, however, whether they are Right-wing or Communist. By a strange turn of the wheel, the Foreign Office have become rather pro-Nasser and seem to feel that the break-up of the United Arab Republic will cause still more trouble in the Middle East, help Kassem to be still more troublesome in Iraq, and put Kuwait in jeopardy.[2]

[1] 19 August 1961.   [2] 1 October 1961.

In a few days it became clear that

> Nasser has lost Syria, which has revolted from Egyptian rule. He is 'too proud to fight', but no doubt hopes to get Syria back by propaganda and subversion. The Middle East is getting more and more difficult. Kassem (Iraq) is mad and very dangerous.[1]

Since most countries decided, at this time, to recognise the new Syrian Government, we thought it wise to follow suit. The position in Kuwait remained stable throughout the year, although threatening noises were made at the end of December.

Since the Arab League forces were by now very weak, Kassem once more started to threaten Kuwait. On Christmas Eve I gave the necessary alert to our troops in case the Kuwait Government should once more ask for our support. On Christmas Day I heard that 'the expedition is all ready to start, as soon as I give the sign. I pray it may not be needed.'[2] Happily, the threat petered out, and the Kuwait incident seemed to be definitely closed. It afforded an admirable example of the effective use of a small British force if its deployment was rapid and timely.

[1] 8 October 1961.   [2] 25 December 1961.

CHAPTER XIV

Khrushchev in Action

THE last half of 1961 brought a marked deterioration in East–West relations. For whatever reasons—internal pressure or continued resentment over the collapse of the Summit Conference in Paris in the previous year—Khrushchev now began to force the pace. The issues were only too familiar. The first was the continued failure to reach any arrangement for a ban on nuclear tests, even in the atmosphere; the second, the problem of East Germany and Berlin. The second was more dangerous to the peace of the world; yet the first seemed to arouse deeper feelings at home, largely due to increasing anxiety concerning the effect of 'fall-out', especially resulting from so-called 'dirty' bombs used by the Russians at this stage. Already, in the middle of June, I had noted that the Nuclear Test Conference in Geneva

> is really now a farce. Yet how are we to throw the blame on the Soviet Government? Or (more hopefully) is there any chance, if we keep the Conference alive, of some change for the better? We had a Ministers' meeting this morning and sent our advice to Foreign Secretary, who is in Washington.[2]

In his new tactics, Khrushchev, so long accustomed to push, had forgotten how to parry. His methods were still crude. On 15 June he announced that a Peace Treaty would, if necessary, be concluded by the end of the year between Russia and East Germany. Even with many other distractions and anxieties, of which the most distressing was the growing crisis in Rhodesia, I felt deeply concerned at the lack of unity now developing among the Western Powers. The West German Government, faced with an election in the autumn, issued an appeal for a Peace Treaty based upon 'the right

[1] 14 June 1961.

of self-determination for the whole German people'. But however desirable or justifiable this might be in principle, in practice it was inconceivable that the Russians would accept. Meanwhile public opinion both in France and in the United States was moving not towards negotiation but towards intransigence; 'anyone who talks sense is called a coward and a traitor'.

> We may drift to disaster over Berlin—[either] a terrible diplomatic defeat or (out of sheer incompetence) a nuclear war.[1]

Yet it seemed essential, if there was to be any hope of persuading the Western Allies to propose a private negotiation on the Berlin issue, to range ourselves alongside them, at least in public. Accordingly, I took the opportunity at a rally at Bowood on 1 July to strike a note of gravity and warning:

> In Europe . . . the situation is threatening and sombre. I do not propose today to speak in detail about the Berlin situation. It is certainly a grave one. We have no desire to provoke a quarrel with the Soviet Union on this issue. But it is quite clear that we in this country, and our allies, cannot countenance interference with allied rights in Berlin. It is the freedom of the two million West Berliners which is threatened. I hope that Mr. Khrushchev will reconsider this matter. We in the West have always been willing to talk about the future of Germany; of which Berlin is, of course, a part. But the fact of our right to be in Berlin cannot be in question. We have not forgotten the lessons learned so painfully in the thirties and we are not prepared to accept acts of force. . . . This is an issue on which the peoples of the Western World are resolute. It is a principle which they will defend.

A week later, I noted that,

> by agreeing to all that the Americans propose, even the absurd 'contingency planning', we have, I think, rather turned the tables on the *Washington Post, Chicago Tribune,* and other anti-British forces in and outside the Administration and Congress. They have been accusing us of 'dragging our feet'—but Lord Home and I have been making such firm statements in Parliament and outside that we have foiled this scheme. Who thought of it in

[1] 25 June 1961.

[the] United States, I don't know. . . . Anyway, after some weeks of this manoeuvring, the President has changed his tune, and has let it be known that he favours 'negotiation'. The regular methods of attuning public opinion to this change are being applied. Even the columnists have to change their tune.[1]

In spite of Khrushchev's announcement on 8 July of a halt in the planned reduction of Soviet forces and an increase in military expenditure, the Western Powers, while rejecting the actual Soviet proposals, stated their willingness to enter into negotiations. On 20 July, in a long and somewhat formal message which was repeated in similar terms both to de Gaulle and to Adenauer, Kennedy, although accepting the need for negotiation, expressed his strong view that

> a peaceful solution of the present controversy depends on the ability of the alliance to convince the Soviet leaders that we are prepared to meet this challenge.

In addition to joint planning in private, we must all publicly demonstrate our determination. The President would himself ask Congress for a supplementary defence budget, increase the numbers conscripted and take other measures to advance military preparations. All other NATO countries should make a comparable effort. In five closely-typed pages he developed this theme at length. In my reply of 23 July, although I did not feel called upon to criticise his own military precautions, I did ask for one important modification:

> As regards the content of your statement the only comment I would make is to ask if you could avoid emphasising too much the need for air-raid shelters. In our little island they would be impossible and useless.

For the rest I contented myself with raising the question as to how and when negotiations should be begun. Whatever might be the wider effects of the President's message to Congress, it was clear that the British economy would have to take the strain.

The pound sterling, being at the moment the weakest

[1] 8 July 1961.

currency, will take the strain of the panic into which the international usurers will fall. Already this has been a bad month, and
I do not feel that the pressure on our reserves is all directed
against our economic misdemeanours. It reflects, in part, the
world's fears. In the same way, I should expect to see the price of
gold rise soon. (It showed small signs last week.) These intrepid
speculators and bankers, who have survived two wars, will start
to take themselves to Switzerland or Bermuda, having first
changed their money into gold. Then they at least—and their
gold—may survive the nuclear war.[1]

At a time when we were having to take some distasteful internal
measures of a mildly deflationary kind the prospect was not attractive. For Britain seemed always to be the main sufferer of the West's
self-inflicted wounds.

At this point I was pleased to get a message from Kennedy that
he thought it worth while to make one more effort to persuade the
Soviet Government to agree to a Test Ban Treaty with proper
control provisions. He would therefore send his representatives
back to Geneva with instructions to give a new impetus to the work
of the Conference still formally in session.

In a television broadcast the next day I restated our position on
Berlin in carefully studied terms, which while firm were in no way
provocative. Since the House of Commons had just held a debate
on our decision to enter into negotiations regarding the Common
Market, I naturally emphasised the importance of political as well
as of economic unity.

The development in American policy was marked. Although
retaining some emphasis on military moves, they now clearly
favoured negotiation. In the discussions between the Western
Foreign Ministers in Paris there was a good deal of manoeuvring
for position, but Lord Home was able to play an important and
mediating role. I summed up my position, on 5 August, in a letter
to the Queen, who had now left London.

On the question of Berlin, the third great issue which is our
concern, Your Majesty will have seen from recent telegrams that
the Americans are, as I expected, getting off their high horse.

[1] 23 July 1961.

They would, of course, like to put the blame for this upon us, but I think the Foreign Secretary has with great skill protected himself and our country from this accusation. In spite of the efforts of journalists known to be very close to the White House, the vigour of the attack upon us has much decreased, and I think they will find it difficult to pretend that the President's desire for negotiation is due to the weakness of his Allies. I think they are more likely to claim it as a mark of his pre-eminent statesmanship. However, I have always thought about American Presidents that the great thing is to get them to do what we want. Praise or blame we can leave to history.

In spite of all these manœuvres

the main problem left unresolved is when and how to open negotiation with the Soviet Government. The Americans are too pressing; the French and Germans too unwilling.[1]

On 13 August, following a record number of refugees leaving the Marxist Heaven of East Germany for the Capitalist Hell (or at least Purgatory) of West Berlin—2,400 in a single day—the East German authorities sealed the border between East and West Berlin, including the surrounding East German territory. Elections were now taking place in West Germany, and naturally the Russian action was tempting, if not forcing, Dr. Adenauer to use strong language. To me the lesson was to speed up negotiations. Unhappily, the building of the Wall—a massive structure of concrete topped by barbed wire—crossing the Potsdamerplatz brought the matter to a crisis. The three Western Powers quickly sent a protest to Moscow, which was immediately rejected by the Soviet Government. But I did not see any reason to abandon my short holiday to the North of England. With our excellent communications, there seemed to me no need to make a spectacular return to London. Indeed it might do more harm than good. These days can best be summed up in my own diary.

A lot of telephoning, morning and evening, to Alec Home about the 'Berlin Crisis'. The East German authorities have shut down on all movement from East to West Berlin. The flood of

[1] 11 August 1961.

refugees had reached such proportions . . . that they were prob-ably almost compelled to take this course. Partly because the West German elections are going on, and partly because the Americans have got very excited, the situation is tense and may become dangerous. The Foreign Secretary has behaved with admirable sang-froid, and continues to urge the importance of taking at least the preliminary steps to a negotiation. Although this cannot take place effectively till after 18 September (the German elec-tions), yet if the preliminary moves are made now, it should have a quietening effect. The Americans wanted to issue a great and rather bombastic 'declaration', but this has now been shot down, partly by de Gaulle's irony and detachment, partly by our insis-tence on combining a willingness to negotiate with any declara-tory reaffirmation of Allied rights and obligations.

The President sent me a message about sending more troops into Berlin. Militarily, this is nonsense. But I have agreed to send in a few armoured cars, etc., as a gesture.

I still feel that from Khrushchev's point of view, the East German internal situation was beginning to crumble, and some-thing had to be done. But I also believe that he does not want to produce a situation which may lead to war. The danger is, of course, that with both sides bluffing, disaster may come by mistake.[1]

I spoke on the telephone

each morning and evening to London and to the Foreign Secre-tary (who was in Scotland). This worked very well. All the rele-vant telegrams are dictated to my secretary during the day; Philip de Zulueta was at the other end, between Admiralty House and Foreign Office. Alec Home spoke to me every evening. I suppose the newspapers will criticise us for being on holiday during the Berlin crisis, but actually this is nonsense.[2]

Unhappily, the situation grew worse during the week. The story continues in my own words.

The Russian and East German pressure on Berlin is growing apace. East Berliners are literally 'sealed off', and the crossing-places are few and well guarded. There is, actually, nothing illegal in the East Germans stopping the flow of refugees and

[1] 19 August 1961.   [2] 25 August 1961.

putting themselves behind a still more rigid iron curtain. It certainly is not a very good advertisement for the benefits of Communism—but it is not (I believe) a breach of any of our agreements.

However, there is now a new note, attacking us for our misuse (as they call it) of our military air route to West Berlin. The Russians accuse us of using this route—intended for Western military purposes—for taking 'revanchists and saboteurs' (that means Adenauer and Co.) in and out of West Berlin and of taking East German refugees out. The legal issue is rather obscure.

The Americans have been very active (sending more troops and their Vice-President to Berlin) but have kept their heads. The French (which means de Gaulle) . . . seem to contemplate war with equanimity. The West Germans have behaved pretty sensibly, in spite of the elections. (I sent a private message of encouragement to Adenauer, which he published—for which I was sorry. He told our Ambassador that he was deeply moved by it. He may also have hoped to win some votes !)

The position now is as follows. The U.K. and U.S. Governments wish to send a reply to the Russian note of 3 August, which will be pretty stiff in tone, but *will propose negotiations*. The French refuse to agree to this. U.K. and U.S. wish also to send a note answering this week's Russian note about the air access to West Berlin, in stiff but correct tones. The French wish this to be couched in words which almost amount to an ultimatum. However, they are at last prepared to suggest 'a general détente'. But we are in a real difficulty. The newspapers are getting wind of the situation and the rift in the alliance. However 'stiff' de Gaulle's attitude may be in theory (he talks gaily of ground-to-air missiles, nuclear weapons, etc.) in fact the French have *none* of these weapons, and are merely 'shooting a line'. But British opinion demands (rightly, I think) that we should take some steps now—before it is too late—towards an ultimate negotiation. The Americans will wish us to send a joint note with them. Yet, in view of European Community and Common Market, I do not want an open rupture with the French if it can be avoided.[1]

At the end of a week in Yorkshire, Dorothy and I went for a few days to Gleneagles. I had agreed to the Western notes of protest

[1] 25 August 1961.

regarding the use of the air corridor, and there seemed to be no need
to return. However, at the end of a round of golf, when my wife
and I were leaving the eighteenth green, we fell into a serious trap
—a more dangerous bunker than those we had so far negotiated.

> The Press have been very tiresome, pestering us all the time.
> At every tee or green some new ones came up and asked for my
> views on the Berlin crisis. Would Lord Home and I be returning
> to London after our conference tomorrow? Was not the situation
> dangerously critical? Was war imminent, etc., etc.? The inter-
> viewers plus the photographers made our game on Saturday
> almost impossible. I'm afraid I rather lost my temper with them
> and made some impromptu remarks which were given full
> front-page treatment in all the Sunday papers. It was undoubtedly
> a 'gaffe'.[1]

Fortunately, I had already arranged for a meeting at Gleneagles
with Home, Hoyer Millar and Shuckburgh, on the Sunday. As a
result Home and I

> did our best to put things in proper perspective with a formal
> statement and Press Conference today. I also sent a telegram to
> President Kennedy.[1]

Of course, the widespread indignation at the sufferings created
by the Russian action in Berlin stirred deep feelings. The division of
families in the two parts of the city was already a hardship; anything
that added to the troubles of individuals was properly resented. But
there was little that the Western Powers could do except by formal
protest. Indeed, since we continually asserted and reasserted our
legal rights in West Berlin it was, perhaps, dangerous to go too far
in challenging what seemed an inhuman but not an illegal action
by the Soviet authorities in their part of the city. In any case it was
important that the emotions roused should not be allowed to take
the form of threats or hysterical prophecies of impending war.

> As a matter of fact, when I said that the Press were trying to
> work up an atmosphere of crisis, it was true. But it has naturally
> annoyed the Press! However, what I said about the need to

[1] 27 August 1961.

settle the problems of Germany and Berlin by negotiation and not by war, is exactly in tune with the mood of the British people.[1]

The next day my anxieties were relieved.

> This morning's Press is good. I am much relieved. They have taken the statement well, and the golf course impromptu has been put in its proper place—an outburst, not altogether wise but perhaps pardonable.[2]

Throughout this strange conflict, with each side trying to bluff the other, there were many dangers. Nor could one do more than speculate upon the next stage.

> Khrushchev wants negotiation. (This is the French reason for being against it.) He can take a number of further offensive steps in Berlin which would force us either to dangerous counter-measures or to proposing negotiation.[2]

At this point the Russians turned from Berlin to the second of the two critical issues which faced the world. After issuing a note at the beginning of September, denying our unrestricted right of access to West Berlin, they announced their decision to resume H-bomb tests; and the first of what was clearly a series was immediately exploded. I had now returned to London and immediately consulted the President on the telephone. On 3 September we accordingly sent a joint appeal to Khrushchev proposing that the three Powers should cease all atmospheric tests.

> This agreement to be without control or supervision. The World Press has received this declaration very well indeed. Even the Conference of Neutral Countries in Belgrade has been impressed.[3]

Unhappily, in defiance of world opinion the only reply of the Russians was to explode another bomb. Naturally,

> this caused the Americans to get very excited, and much pressure to be exerted from the Pentagon and from the Hill on the White House. The President gave in and has announced his decision to resume underground tests, *not*, repeat *not*, atmospheric tests.

[1] 27 August 1961.   [2] 28 August 1961.   [3] 4 September 1961.

Although the British Press has not been altogether unsympathetic, this hurried decision, of which we were given only one and a half hours' notice, has taken the gilt off the gingerbread, and relieved the Russians of some part of their presentational difficulties. It is interesting that the President's [and] Prime Minister's offer has been censored from all Russian *Press* and *radio*.[1]

Although I received an immediate assurance from Kennedy that the Americans would not resume atmospheric testing without full consultation with us, and was encouraged by his definite statement that there would not be any urgent need for such tests, I could not see the purpose in this sudden move except to meet the pressure of American public opinion. Although the President might declare that in his judgement 'the gravest of our dangers is that we may seem less determined than Khrushchev' it seemed to me that we had unnecessarily helped to get the Russians 'off the hook'. Meanwhile, I summed up the situation in my own mind as follows:

> Khrushchev is trying to frighten us and to divide us. For this purpose he is using speeches, television appearances, and interviews with foreign journalists. Unfortunately, the Americans get 'mad' at these tactics. Even President Kennedy, with all his political experience, behaves like a bull being teased by the darts of the picadors.[2]

In pursuance of his usual tactics

> Khrushchev seems to have told Sulzberger (*New York Times*) that Britain, France, and Italy are nothing but hostages in Russian hands. They will never dare to fight. The Foreign Office seemed to think that this much publicised interview might do us harm in United States. So I authorised a form of words for the Minister of Defence to use in a speech tonight, reminding Khrushchev that this was just the mistake which had been made about Britain twice in my lifetime.[2]

At this point I received a revealing message from Nehru about his visit to Moscow. His ostensible purpose had been to deliver formal letters from the Heads of the countries represented at the Belgrade Conference of Neutrals, an identical copy of which was

[1] 6 September 1961.   [2] 8 September 1961.

taken, of course, to Kennedy. This *démarche* did not amount to much, but Nehru took the opportunity to have several long and frank talks with Khrushchev. As regards his refusal to accept the Anglo-American proposal for at least a partial ban on tests, Khrushchev, while adhering to his position, seemed to be somewhat reserved and on the defensive. However, as Nehru wrote in his letter of 13 September, when he turned to the general problem of Germany and disarmament, Khrushchev insisted that Adenauer's rigid attitude was the root of the trouble, and he also criticised de Gaulle. He said that though the Western Powers laid much stress on the reunification of Germany, they did not really believe that this was feasible at present, and even that de Gaulle had told him that he was entirely opposed to it.

'It seemed to me evident,' Nehru went on,

> that the basic factor influencing Khrushchev was the growing power of West Germany and [fear of] its gradually developing again on the lines of Hitler's Germany. He could not tolerate this menace. He hinted at Adenauer's present attitude being partly conditioned by the coming German elections. Probably after that he would be in a more reasonable frame of mind.

> Khrushchev thought that some kind of acceptance of the present two German States was essential.

> I put to him especially the question of access to West Berlin from the Western countries. He stated repeatedly that full access would be provided but naturally the Western countries would have to deal with the East German Government in order to conform to the various formalities. Indeed, to some extent, though in a roundabout way, this had been the practice.

Khrushchev had then turned to a discussion of personalities.

> In referring to President Kennedy, [he] said that it appeared that the President could not have his own way easily and that the opposition to his policies in the U.S. was fairly strong. In fact the President had told him when he met him [in Vienna] that he had inherited most of his problems and he had to deal with them as he found them and not entirely as he might otherwise have done. Khrushchev also said that perhaps the very small

majority in the Presidential election was also a weakening factor for President Kennedy.

Nehru thought that Khrushchev would welcome negotiations but would insist on the acceptance of the two German States, though not necessarily formal diplomatic recognition,

it would mean dealing with the East German authorities in regard to movements, etc., across East German territory into West Berlin. I do not myself see why this should involve any insuperable obstacle. It would only be slight extension of the practice hitherto followed, and it would be in keeping with reality. If this point was agreed to, the free city idea could be developed fully.

Nehru added that West German statements about the Oder–Neisse Line were a great source of irritation to the Soviets and even more to Poland and the other East European countries.

All this becomes a symbol of Germany seeking revenge and recovering the losses she suffered in the last war. It is the reminder of expansionist aims of German Governments in the past.

Nehru ended with his general impressions:

Although I found Khrushchev very firm in regard to some matters and particularly resentful of Adenauer's attitude and statements, the impression he gave me was that there was room for successful negotiations with him. Indeed, the basic issues in regard to Germany and Berlin are limited, and there is probably already a measure of agreement about some of them.

I felt grateful for this account, and in thanking the Prime Minister of India I told him I had taken the liberty of asking Alec Home to pass these impressions on to our Western colleagues.

On 14 September the President rang up to tell me that the underground tests would start the next day. As regards the question of negotiations on Berlin, although he was clearly moving towards my position he felt that we must await the results of the German elections. I now thought that it might be best for Rusk to have a talk with Gromyko alone. The ambivalence of American policy was clearly caused by the distribution of power between the White House, the State Department and the Pentagon. Much as I admired

Kennedy, I felt that he was still suffering from the effect of his unlucky interview with Khrushchev in Vienna. Although Kennedy did not suffer under the delusion which afflicted Roosevelt in his relations with Stalin and caused such terrible harm to the world, yet it had no doubt been an unhappy experience. For the first time in his life he met a man wholly impervious to his charm.

The next day the United States resumed their H-bomb underground tests, but the Foreign Secretary reported from Washington that the Americans were definitely moving in the direction of negotiation. 15 September was a day which I could not readily forget.

> Forty-five years ago, today, I was taking part in the 15 September attack by the Brigade of Guards in the Battle of the Somme. This was the first time that tanks were used. I was severely wounded—for the third time—and spent most [of] the last two years of the war in hospital.
>
> Last night I went to dine with my oldest friend—Harry Crookshank—who was wounded in the same battle. He—alas—is very ill. We talked of old times mostly. He is wonderfully brave, but I fear he is a dying man.[1]

While we were waiting for the next stage in the Russian crisis there were other harassing problems. The Prime Minister and Foreign Minister of Turkey, with whom we had successfully negotiated the Cyprus solution, were thrown out of office and prosecuted as traitors.

> The Turkish trials are over, and poor M. Menderes and M. Zorlu are condemned to death. This is really a brutal sentence. These men no doubt did some very rough things, but they certainly behaved well to us over the Cyprus settlement.
>
> *September 16.* I decided last night to send a message to the Head of the Turkish Government pleading for mercy for Menderes and Zorlu. Sir Winston Churchill has also sent a message. But it's no good, I fear.[2]

The two Turkish Ministers were publicly hanged.

Meanwhile, the Congo situation was moving to a new crisis

[1] 15 September 1961.   [2] 15–16 September 1961.

and on 17 September we heard the tragic news of the death of Hammarskjöld in somewhat mysterious circumstances. But the British people, or at least a small section of them, seemed to be more concerned with the danger of H-bomb testing. Stimulated by a violent letter in *The Times* from Bertrand Russell, writing on behalf of the Committee of One Hundred, demonstrations began to take place in Trafalgar Square—many of the protesters lying down wherever they could cause most nuisance. On the night of 17 and 18 September over 1,300 of these misguided, but no doubt sincere, enthusiasts had to be arrested by the police.

The result of the German elections did nothing to clarify the situation.

The German results introduce a new complication in our affairs. Although Christian Democrat Union have much the largest party, they have just lost their *absolute* majority. It seems doubtful whether Adenauer will be acceptable as Chancellor in a coalition.[1]

While I was awaiting news from Washington

Gaitskell asked to see me, and as I could not refuse, he came to Chequers at 4 p.m. and stayed till 5.30. Of course his 'Shadow Cabinet' is urging him on, and he wants to *appear* energetic. We had a useful talk, and he seemed (as always) very understanding of all our difficulties. What he will say is quite another thing, when he speaks in public! The Opposition are pressing (but I think rather formally, for the record) for the immediate recall of Parliament. Nothing could be more foolish. It would create a panic. We might perhaps agree to come back a few days earlier in October than had been settled, for a general debate. I told him I would consider this tomorrow, with my colleagues. The Chief Whip must be sure of getting our chaps back, in case the Opposition try some 'funny business'.[2]

In the event

The Cabinet agreed ... that Parliament should meet on 17 October (instead of the 24th). We will have three days' general

[1] 19 September 1961.   [2] 20 September 1961.

debate; two days clearing up business; and then prorogue. The Press seems to think this reasonable. It is certainly *not* an *emergency* meeting.[1]

The Rusk–Gromyko talks continued on in Washington with a certain amount of success; but the President's speech to the United Nations Assembly, although admirably delivered, took matters little further. At this point Harold Caccia, who had served us so well, returned home and was succeeded in Washington by David Ormsby Gore. Admirable as Caccia had been, especially during the Eisenhower regime, he had not the close association and deep friendship with the President and his family which made Ormsby Gore a quite exceptional Ambassador in these difficult times.

On 6 October I had a further discussion with the President by telephone at his suggestion. He was now strongly urging a negotiation and felt that some progress could be made. It was the French and Germans who were obstructive. Yet, as I told him, I thought the French only 'talked tough'; they relied on American and British diplomacy not to push things too far. We had now installed a new telephonic link with the White House, of British design, the security of which was said to be unbreakable; but it had the disadvantage that you had to push a button after you had said anything before you could hear the reply. This made conversation somewhat jerky, and, although at the moments of great danger it was invaluable, as was later to be proved during the Cuba crisis, yet I much preferred written messages. Indeed I sometimes looked with horror at the records of our conversations, which seemed intolerably disconnected and often futile. However, since the President liked this method, it was not for me to discourage him. On this occasion he seemed somewhat baffled and asked me to send him ideas. This I did. At the same time a message from Home to Rusk enlarged on the problems about which the Americans seemed at last to be seriously worried.

> The Americans must bring pressure on the Germans. We will support them—but of course the Germans attach chief weight to what the Americans, so long their patrons and protectors, say.

[1] 22 September 1961.

President Kennedy seemed thoroughly 'fed up' with both Adenauer and de Gaulle.

It is curious how all American statesmen begin by trying to treat Britain as just one of many foreign or NATO countries. They soon find themselves relying on our advice and experience. President Kennedy and Secretary Rusk have found this out very quickly.

Time is getting short, for Khrushchev has to speak to his Party Conference on 17 October. We ought to be in a position to continue in Moscow the sort of 'negotiations' which we have been having in New York recently with Gromyko. But this needs French and German approval (if we and the Americans are to speak on behalf of the Alliance).[1]

I saw Gromyko at his request on his way through London. He came with Ambassador Soldatov.

> The conversation was friendly but added nothing to what had [been] said in New York and Washington. I suppose Gromyko's purpose in stopping off in London and seeking this interview with me is to try to drive a wedge between us and our allies. Foreign Secretary was, of course, present. I think the Russians are looking for a way out (as we are) if they can do so without too much loss of 'face'.[2]

I wrote a full report to Menzies, Diefenbaker and Holyoake, on 13 October, in which I said:

> Although the conversation cannot be said to have been very encouraging as to substance and we are obviously a long way from any agreement, I was, on the whole, not discouraged. Gromyko did not act as if he was about to join in some warlike move. I tried to be very firm with him, while of course emphasising our desire for a negotiated settlement. I do not, of course, know what impression he formed but it was noticeable that his remarks in London were more optimistic about a settlement than one might have expected.

When the House met there was a two-day debate on Foreign Affairs.

[1] 8 October 1961.   [2] 10 October 1961.

The Opposition did not divide. The only result of the debate from the point of view of *internal* politics has been to reveal again the deep rift in the Labour Party, which was nominally healed in their Blackpool Conference. When Gaitskell spoke, he was loudly applauded by his own side *above* the gangway. *Below* the gangway, they sat in stony silence. His speech was good and very helpful.[1]

During the rest of the debate the Labour front bench speakers spent most of their time trying to restore the balance in their own Party and I had little difficulty in my final speech. I spoke

> only from a few notes, and with *no* prepared speech. This seemed to please the House. I spoke very quietly, soberly, and avoided any Party points or even retorts. This seemed to suit the occasion.[1]

However, the House of Commons was not the main arena of contention.

> Although the debate went well, the situation is very obscure. Khrushchev, in the course of a six-hour speech at the Communist Party Congress, threatened to blow up a fifty megaton and even a hundred megaton bomb. *But*, he said there was no fixed date for the unilateral treaty with D.D.R. He was ready for negotiation. But the French and Germans are still unwilling to take part. So the allies are split, and this (which I have so far tried to conceal or at least to minimise) will soon become apparent.[1]

The Russian series of tests now began to spread serious alarm; beginning on 1 September they achieved by 23 October a thirty-megaton explosion, and one of fifty megatons now seemed more than likely. On 24 October I held a meeting of experts to discuss plans to meet the threat of contamination.

> We have a complete scheme for dried milk for infants, if the iodine contamination from fall-out should become serious.[2]

The Minister of Defence made a full statement in the House about the possible risk and the Government's provisions to meet them; this had a calming effect.

[1] 19 October 1961.   [2] 24 October 1961.

I asked our new Ambassador whether Kennedy would agree to a statement condemning the Russians for these atmospheric tests on a gigantic scale and at the same time undertaking that neither Britain nor America would resume atmospheric testing for the next six months, and after that only if military necessity obliged them to do so. After a good deal of discussion the President expressed his unwillingness to 'go along with' the proposed declaration. We might easily find that the Russians had concluded their series, and this had put them ahead of us. Our hands would be tied. I was sceptical about this argument and sensed that Kennedy had been forced, very unwillingly, to yield to pressure from the Pentagon. It soon became clear that we should have to have a personal meeting; but to do so immediately would seem somewhat panicky in view of the Berlin situation, which was becoming daily more perilous. British and American tanks in battle order were brought up to the Berlin sector border. The next day the Russian tanks moved into the centre of East Berlin, but withdrew three days later. All that we could hope for was to bring pressure on our allies to agree a negotiating position. Kennedy would speak strongly to Adenauer when he visited Berlin if and when a German Government was formed, and I would try to do the same with de Gaulle when he paid his proposed visit to Sussex at the end of November. This was agreed in another telephone conversation on 27 October, when we decided to meet together at the first convenient opportunity.

The threatened fifty-megaton explosion took place on 30 October. In the course of a discussion in the House of Commons on the next day, while condemning the Russian tests, I declared that we would not restart our own tests for terroristic or retaliatory purposes. We must, however, reserve our right to do so if our security would otherwise be at risk. They would be underground, if possible. Nevertheless, if we were convinced that a particular atmospheric test was necessary in order to maintain the balance of the deterrent and to preserve freedom in the world, Britain would be bound either to co-operate in or support this decision. This speech was delivered on the opening day of the new Parliamentary session, and I found myself confronted with new Opposition tactics.

[They] have now decided to counter the command of the House which I have had up to now, by 'barracking'. This makes a serious speech very difficult. They listened well enough to the first half (on Russia, Berlin, nuclear tests, etc.). When I got to the Home Front they started (obviously organised and led by Brown—Deputy Leader) jeers, shouts, catcalls, etc. I got them round a bit at the end. But I must clearly think out a new tactic to deal with this.[1]

All through this period the Cabinet gave full support, and at the meeting on 2 November there was a long discussion of the German crisis.

> I thought it wise to put all the Cabinet in the picture. They don't know what to do—nor do I. But I feel sure that they will support me if and when I decide to take a prominent part in the drama.[2]

The House of Commons, as always in moments of international crisis, was in a somewhat restive mood.

> Michael Foot made a bitter attack on me yesterday in House of Commons—calling me a 'petulant and pathetic old man'. He attacks everyone else with equal violence, so perhaps it could be said of him, 'Everybody out of step, except my Foot.' There are three brothers, 'One Foot is enough for me,' is my motto, and I have sent Sir Hugh to serve us in the United Nations.[3]

There seemed now to be a lull.

> There is still no German Government and a strange pause in the Berlin crisis. Perhaps the Russians will wait a bit longer—indeed, Khrushchev's recent speeches indicate that his timetable is elastic. The Americans seem rather subdued—the President being taken up with resisting the pressure to resume nuclear tests. He has issued a very good statement, on the lines of my declaration in House of Commons last Tuesday.[3]

On 4 November there was a report of some conciliatory noises from Khrushchev.

> He has told a travelling Italian Parliamentarian that 'The Soviet Union wants negotiations. The international situation is

[1] 31 October 1961.   [2] 2 November 1961.   [3] 3 November 1961.

very bad now and the only thing to do is to negotiate. And negotiation means not only to receive but to make concessions.' These rather obscure words are seized upon by British Press, especially *Daily Express* and other 'popular' papers. On the whole, if these words mean anything, the conclusion which General de Gaulle will draw will be that his policy of procrastination is proving successful. Khrushchev is now running after us.[1]

At last there was a German Government, since on 7 November Dr. Adenauer was re-elected Chancellor, with a Coalition Government, to be sworn in on 14 November. There now arose a somewhat delicate problem. Our experts were very anxious to get the Americans to do an underground test on our behalf or to allow us to use their facilities. In return the President, not unnaturally, asked for some *quid pro quo*. He was anxious to use Christmas Island if and when atmospheric tests had to be resumed. I had of course to consult both Menzies and Holyoake. Menzies was perfectly happy to accept the conditions which I had laid down on 31 October; but Holyoake was more concerned, largely because the islands administered by the New Zealand Government were in the vicinity. Fall-out must be minimised.

It now became clear to me that on this issue as well as others there must be a discussion with the President. He telephoned to me on 9 November asking for advice as to what line to take with Adenauer —what precisely he should attempt to persuade him to. He wanted to know

whether we should for example get him to agree now that there will be a Prime Ministers' Conference in December; or whether we should talk to him in precise terms about the various negotiating positions he might take on Berlin and Germany. In other words, I want to be sure that we accomplish something more than a rather generalised exchange by this visit and I wanted to be sure that I came out with something that you and I both thought represented an advance.

I replied:

[1] 4 November 1961.

Well, I agree with you Mr. President. I think from the latest advices that the Russians will wait a bit, certainly till after your meeting with Adenauer, and understand that real negotiations can't start till after that. But when that is over, and after de Gaulle has been to see me on the 24th, I think they will expect that it would be reasonable that something begins. Therefore, I would suggest that you brought as much pressure as you can on Adenauer and made him understand that there is the possibility of a deal, but of course he will have to give as well as receive. The things which, since you ask me, I feel they ought to be prepared to accept, are first the Oder–Neisse Line, which is generally agreed; secondly, some formula which amounts to a considerable degree of *de facto* recognition of the D.D.R., and I think the Ambassadors had got very nearly to some kind of formula, even the German Ambassador suggested a phrase, on 30 October I think, which ran something like 'respect the rules and regulations of the authorities which exercise functions in that area'—so it's some form of degree of *de facto* recognition for practical purposes; thirdly, I think, [Adenauer] must recognise that political ties between West Berlin and the Federal Republic ought to be given up, but that economic and financial ties could be even strengthened and increased; and fourthly, I think a declaration by the German Federal Government that they do not intend or wish to manufacture nuclear weapons and are prepared to stand on your declaration about the 'key of the cupboard' procedure being maintained. Now those are all things that he could give. I don't mean give them right away, but things we would be prepared to give in the negotiations—if in return we get a really reasonable settlement about proper access and all the things that we want to defend West Berlin's reality. But unless we can get him to move, I think it is going to be very difficult to start the negotiations without knowing that we have something—that your Ambassador and ours have something—of that kind to discuss.

When the President asked what benefit there was for Adenauer in all this, I could only say that we must receive in return total satisfaction on the Western position in Berlin as well as unrestricted access. Once again I found it difficult to deal with this by telephone and within a few days I sent a long message setting out the whole argument.

With de Gaulle in the garden at Birch Grove
'The visit was intended to be a simple family affair.'

Freedom of the City of London, 15 December 1961
'A most moving and dramatic ceremony.'

A few days later I asked the President to agree to a meeting of Anglo-American experts to prepare a report on what the proposed American tests were designed to achieve, so that we could consider the matter jointly when we met and decide whether it was really necessary to affront public opinion so violently. The West's morally superior stand was the one factor that might finally defeat the Communists—it should not be discarded so lightly. All this the President accepted, only asking in return that preliminary arrangements should be made to reactivate Christmas Island if new tests should ultimately be required.

About the same time the Soviet Government made a step forward by declaring their willingness to resume negotiations on nuclear tests. A few days later they issued the draft of a proposed agreement. Unhappily, it was wholly unsatisfactory as far as the vital question of inspection and control was concerned. Fortunately, the British and Americans had already presented, on 13 November, an identical note suggesting the resumption of negotiations. Our public position was at any rate secure.

All through this dangerous period, with many other difficult problems crowding in upon us, I could at least take satisfaction in the knowledge that my personal relations with Kennedy seemed to become daily closer and more intimate. We did not always agree on the best tactics or the best methods of presentation; but we understood each other and made full allowances for our differing political positions. Yet, although the Americans had now accepted the need for reaching some negotiated agreement with Moscow, both Adenauer and de Gaulle were sceptical. At least they had on their side of the argument the fact that, although the military confrontation between East and West was growing daily more alarming, the Russians seemed still to hesitate before forcing the issue. The old problem remained—how to present a position of united strength and yet to be flexible as regards possible solutions. The French and the Germans, perhaps logically, felt that these two positions were irreconcilable. The British and the Americans instinctively believed in the value of such an approach. Meanwhile we must await the result of the President's talks with Adenauer and of de Gaulle's forthcoming visit.

o

CHAPTER XV

A Country House Party

AMONG the many sobriquets or code-names for de Gaulle in common use at Allied Force Headquarters during the war, perhaps the most popular was 'Ramrod'. This nickname recalled the famous definition of a man who was alleged to have all the rigidity of a poker without its occasional warmth. Nevertheless, although, like Godolphin Horne in Belloc's rhyme, de Gaulle 'was nobly born' and 'held the human race in scorn', yet in the strange character of this remarkable man pity for mankind was as strong an element as contempt.

I had got to know him as intimately as was possible for a foreigner or even indeed for a fellow-countryman during the hectic months of Algerian politics in 1943–4.[1] Since a sense of personal gratitude was by no means excluded from his nature as long as it was never allowed to conflict with a still stronger sense of national duty, he had retained for me from the war years an unusual degree of friendship. Although I was one of the worst possible examples of 'Anglo-American', being half British and half American by birth, yet I felt somehow exempt from the sweeping condemnation with which he regarded all those unlucky enough to be classed as what he called 'Anglo-Saxons'. Perhaps he recalled sometimes the traditional ties between France and Scotland.

Accordingly, I was not unduly alarmed, when, in December 1958, de Gaulle, after a dramatic series of events during the course of the summer, succeeded in being elected President of France. Although I knew that France under his leadership would become an uneasy partner in any European collaboration, I felt hopeful that in the long run one could appeal to the General's high conception of the world drama as well as to his sense of honour. He might thus

---

1 See *The Blast of War*, chapters x–xiv and xv.

be persuaded to allow, and even to promote, the emergence of a Western Europe in which Britain could play an equal part in every sphere of endeavour. Alas, I was to find, in due course, that his sense of history only worked backwards. The France of which he dreamed was the France of Le Grand Monarque or better still of Charlemagne, who for these purposes ranked as a Frenchman. He did not seem to be able to look forward into an age in which the countries of Europe, which had dominated civilised life for more than two thousand years, were now falling as a result of centuries of internecine war followed by a cruel partition into relative weakness in the face of the rising strength of their great rivals, both in the East and in the West.

In the first years of the new régime, occupied no doubt by so many conflicting difficulties, French diplomacy, although always sceptical, was not unduly hostile. I kept in as close touch as possible by letters, personal messages and occasional meetings, with my wartime friend, and received from him, in spite of his many pre-occupations, many marks both of courtesy and confidence. For, in spite of his remoteness and the almost Delphic obscurity of his pronouncements, he had a very human side—and was a charming host, a pleasant guest and an agreeable companion.

Both 1959 and 1960 were years of trial. The *coup d'état* of May 1958 which brought de Gaulle to power had been based upon the concept of a real integration of Algeria and France. But the rebellion continued, with little progress by the French forces. A referendum was next proposed offering Algeria a choice between secession and closer links with France—a referendum to be held within four years of the ending of the rebellion and the restoration of peace. This was defined as a year in which not more than two hundred deaths occurred as a result of terrorist activity. But such an offer proved almost farcical. The civil war raged with renewed ferocity. By the end of 1959 there were plots and rumours of plots to assassinate de Gaulle. A purge of the army became necessary in Algeria and in metropolitan France. Many notable figures, including Bidault, a former Prime Minister and Leader of the war-time Resistance, were accused of moving from political opposition into conspiracy.

1960 was a year of mounting tension and terrorism in France as well as in Algeria. The extremes on both sides became more violent. An attempted *coup* by the more reactionary French settlers was suppressed in January, and among the arrests were a number of deputies. Meanwhile the Arab revolutionaries grew in strength and claimed to be receiving both Russian and Chinese aid. Total disorder now threatened. There seemed little or no hope of any moderate or conciliatory policy being effective.

1961 began with the trial of the *Algérie Française* rebels. This was barely finished in March, when in April further insurrection broke out, led by five leading Generals. De Gaulle at once assumed full powers. Paris nerved itself to face an airborne attack, but the insurrection was dealt with in Algeria, and in the trials that followed three Generals and five Colonels were condemned to death *in absentia*. Yet the O.A.S. (Organisation de l'Armée Secrète) increased its bloody activities. Plastic bombs were thrown freely in Paris, and murder and counter-murder became commonplace in French and Algerian life. Nor did these conspiracies spare the person of the President, whose life was daily at risk. On 8 September an attempt was made to assassinate him with a bomb, which happily failed to explode. A year later an assassin's bullet was to pass only a few inches from his head.

Yet amidst all these trials this intrepid man preserved his superb and splendid dignity. I have seen many brave men in the course of two wars; but I have seen few who had such outstanding physical and moral courage as Charles de Gaulle. He showed this on many occasions and under the most trying conditions. Some moralists have urged that physical courage is only a matter of vanity. It may be so. In any event, in de Gaulle high courage, in the widest sense, and intense pride were bound inextricably together.

Our interchange of letters after the April crisis had clearly pleased him, and I was delighted to hear from the French Ambassador before the summer was over that the General would welcome the possibility of a meeting and would be ready to come to England for the purpose. Somewhat to my surprise he was unwilling to come to Chequers. But I soon realised that both the date and the place were chosen in such a way as to make it clear that his visit was purely personal from one friend to another. The Queen would be out of London; since he had already paid a State Visit to England no problem of protocol would arise. Chequers had a semi-political flavour. Only in the privacy of Sussex could we meet merely as 'old buddies'. Although all this was flattering, it was somewhat unreal. It was also very inconvenient. However, on 14 August I sent the following letter.

I was very touched a little time ago to receive a message through Monsieur Chauvel about the possibility of our meeting in September. I have delayed answering this until after the Foreign Ministers' Meeting in Paris because I wanted to have a clearer idea about the autumn timetable before making any definite proposal to you.

It now seems that we cannot yet be sure whether there will be a meeting of Western Heads of Government, because it is not possible at present to foresee the timing of such a meeting in view of the developing situation in Berlin. But whatever happens I should very much value some private talk with you in the autumn. There are many matters on which it is really of great importance that we should exchange views.

As I have now been your guest on two occasions at Rambouillet, my wife and I would be particularly pleased if you and Madame de Gaulle would do us the honour of staying with us in the country. I fear that our private house in Sussex is simple, but I recognise that for you to come there might emphasise the private character of any visit. As Gatwick Airport is very close you could perhaps fly there and there would be no need to go to London at all.

I imagine that you would prefer a date after the German Elections, and so I had in mind that a suitable date might be Wednesday, 20 September. This would be just after the German Elections and at a time, incidentally, when the Queen would still be taking a holiday in Scotland. But of course I should be very happy to meet earlier in September if this would suit you better.

My wife and I hope very much that you and Madame de Gaulle will feel able to accept our invitation for 20 September or an earlier date. It would be a great pleasure for us to make a small return of your hospitality in the past.

His reply of 29 August ran as follows:

> Yes, I very much hope to have the opportunity of paying you a visit, and I thank you kindly, as well as Madame Macmillan, for having thought of inviting my wife and me to Sussex.
>
> As for the date, will you allow me to fix it definitely for a little later than September. That month will be very full for me, and no doubt for you too, with duties at home. Moreover, it seems to me that our conversations could be more complete when we can see more clearly exactly what the Soviets intend over Germany and how the next negotiations about the Common Market turn out. Would not the middle of November seem to you the best time?
>
> I would ask you, my dear Friend to convey my respects and my wife's best wishes to Madame Macmillan. Please accept my kindest regards and sincere good wishes.[1]

I immediately replied.

> Thank you very much for your letter. I am delighted that you and Madame de Gaulle feel that you may be able to pay us a visit in Sussex.
>
> While I feel that the sooner we can meet the better, I of course entirely understand the difficulties which you feel about the month of September. For my part the middle of November would be perfectly suitable. Parliament will be sitting at that time, but this should not make our meeting more difficult, particularly if it proves possible to hold it at a weekend.
>
> With all the international complications at the moment it would perhaps be rash to fix definitely now on a precise date in

[1] Oui! Je souhaite beaucoup avoir l'occasion de vous rendre visite et je vous remercie vivement, ainsi que Madame Macmillan, d'avoir pensé à nous recevoir, ma femme et moi, dans le Sussex.

Pour la date, accepteriez-vous de me la fixer décidément un peu plus tard que septembre? Ce mois-là sera très chargé pour moi et, sans doute aussi, pour vous d'obligations intérieures. D'autre part, nos entretiens pourraient être, me semble-t-il, plus complets quand nous aurons vu plus clairement ce que veulent, en définitive, les Soviétiques au sujet de l'Allemagne et aussi comment vont se présenter les négociations prochaines au sujet du Marché commun. Le milieu de novembre ne vous paraitrait-il pas la meilleure époque?

Je vous demande, cher Ami, de transmettre à Madame Macmillan, avec mes respectueux hommages, le meilleur souvenir de ma femme. Pour vous-même, si vous voulez bien, l'assurance de mes sentiments de très haute et cordiale considération.

November, but if I may I would like to get in touch with you again about the beginning of October with a view to suggesting a possible date between 10 November and 20 November. If you see any difficulties in this plan please do not hesitate to let me know.

I need not tell you with what pleasure my wife and I look forward to your visit.

Please convey my respects and those of my wife to Madame de Gaulle.

In due course the visit was definitely fixed for Friday, 24 November.

Birch Grove House is, naturally enough, not so well equipped as Chequers for the reception of a party of this kind. During the six years of war it had been a nursery school, and during the following six years it had been let as a preparatory school. Although my wife and I had moved back in 1952, the ravages of war had left their mark. Nor had we the accommodation for the various guests, secretaries, detectives and servants that would be necessary. However, from one point of view the visit proved an advantage. Dorothy was a natural hoarder, and many rooms encumbered with children's toys, old numbers of *Country Life* and garden catalogues among other paraphernalia had to be cleared of their treasured accumulations. All these adjustments were overcome with the help of the Conference Department of the Foreign Office. My son lived in a neighbouring house, where there was accommodation for some of the followers of the court. Nevertheless, the degree of security which it was necessary to preserve in view of the danger to my guest's life led to some strange incidents, partly sad and partly comic.

The General was to arrive at Gatwick Airport at 3.30 p.m. on the Friday. I thought it best to go home on the previous night, and while I was working in my study Dorothy came in with an air of uneasy concern and even anger. 'I have been rung up,' she declared, 'by a young man from the Foreign Office with a short black coat and fancy pants.' 'How on earth can you tell what he wore?' I asked. 'Oh,' she said, 'he spoke like it.' 'Well, what did he say?' My wife explained that what he said, in a high plaintive voice, was this: 'Lady Dorothy, what are we going to do about the General's blood?' Faced with this unexpected problem, I said, 'I think you had better tell him we will ring him back'—always a safe argumentative position. Further enquiries showed that fear of attempted assassination made it necessary that everything should be ready for a blood transfusion. The General had, it seemed, an unusual category of blood, and therefore provision must be made, and a store must be kept in a refrigerator or deep freeze. Even this brought new embarrassments. Mrs. Bell, our devoted cook, protested that these were needed for more appetising contents. However, a solution was found, and an additional apparatus was made available in an appropriate outhouse.

The second incident was even more macabre. I met de Gaulle as arranged at Gatwick Airport. Apart from a military guard of honour, the airport was swarming with police equipped with black marias, motor-bicycles and walkie-talkies as well as with detectives in plain clothes. When the procession left, I led with the General in my car, and Dorothy and Madame de Gaulle brought up the rear; between our two cars there were included, against all emergencies, an ambulance and one or more cars containing surgeons and physicians. Additional doctors and nurses were ready in some of the neighbouring villages in case of need. Yet amidst all these dangers General de Gaulle remained completely unmoved. Nor did he seem to notice, or deign to notice, all these elaborate precautions.

The third incident was characteristically English. On the morning after the General's arrival, I was sitting in the large library at Birch Grove House talking, or rather, listening, to my guest. Apart from de Gaulle and myself there were present Alec Home, Couve de Murville, two Ambassadors and two Private Secretaries. In the course of one of the General's lengthy but enthralling pontifications on the world situation and the American influence I heard loud knocks on the door. I sent Philip de Zulueta to see what it was, and to deal with it.

'As I was saying when I was interrupted,' said the General somewhat nettled, 'we must take great precautions to preserve Europe from this dangerous predominance.'

Now came more knocks, more and more insistent. Thinking the house might well be on fire, or some murderous attack about to take place, I went out to find our head keeper, Mr. Blake, calm, respectful but indignant. 'What has happened?' I asked. 'Why, sir, these police, French, Sussex, London, they are all over the place with Alsatian dogs, walking through the woods and park and into the coverts. They have been all through Gitlands, Binghams, Wickens, and they are now into Wheelers. We are going to shoot on Monday, and there won't be a bird in any of them. This has got to stop, sir.' I remonstrated, 'This is a great international occasion.' 'I don't know what it is, sir, but it has got to stop.' Happily it stopped the next day. With that true sense of the value of things that is the mark of a countryman, the keeper was right. The meeting led to nothing; and it would have been a good shoot. I told the story to my guest in the evening, but he did not seem amused.

Meanwhile,

> the local interest is, of course, intense, mixed with a certain pride. The house is looking lovely, and the servants are reinforced by three Government 'butlers'. Carol's cook is here to help Mrs. Bell, all sorts of other women, old and retired servants, etc., seem to have appeared. Every room in the house is full. Baron de Courcel (Chef de Cabinet) and a Naval A.D.C. with him; Philip de Zulueta and two typists for me; and valets, ladysmaids, etc. I cleared out of my bedroom (which I gave to de Gaulle—it has its own little suite) and went to the day nursery. Maurice and Katie (Macmillan) came to dinner. We have taken five rooms at the Roebuck, for his doctors, etc. Blood plasma is in a special refrigerator in the coach house. Outside the gates, the Press swarm. The Red Lion is selling beer in hogsheads. Police (with and without Alsatian dogs) are in the garden and the woods. (One Alsatian happily bit the *Daily Mail* man in the behind.) Altogether a most enjoyable show.[1]

On Friday, the talks began at 5.30 in the Library and lasted for two hours. There was nobody present except Philip de Zulueta and, on de Gaulle's side, Courcel. Dinner was kept studiously informal. Apart from the de Gaulles and their aide, Capitaine de Corvette Flohic, there were Ted Heath (Lord Privy Seal) and my son Maurice and his wife Katie.

[1] 25 November 1961.

The next day, Saturday, 25 November,

> we had photographs, and presentation of all the old employees on the place. Then all the available grandchildren. Then talks from 10.30–12 [with the Blake interlude]. Walk in woods. Luncheon (with Lord Home, M. and Mme. Chauvel, Sir Pierson Dixon, Carol, Catherine). Talks with [two] Foreign [Ministers] and two Ambassadors 2.45–6.30 (with tea interval). Dinner (to which Lord and Lady Kilmuir came) at 8.15. Bed at 10.30.[1]

There were therefore three formal sessions. Two of these were mainly concerned with Germany and Berlin; in the third the chief subject was Europe and Britain's proposed entry into the Common Market. Although the visit was in a sense fruitless, it was full of highlights and delightful moments both in the discussions and in the informality of this English version of *la vie de château*. Although Madame de Gaulle was suffering from the shock of her husband's perilous life, she was as always friendly and anxious to be agreeable. On the Saturday morning my wife took her out to a meet of a neighbouring hunt, as well as to a number of farms where she seemed chiefly interested in the cultivation of poultry of all kinds. After lunch, accompanied by Elizabeth Home, they went on a visit to Chailey Heritage Craft School, which she seemed to enjoy. But her thoughts as well as her anxieties seemed always fixed upon the great man on whom all her devotion was concentrated.

The visit was intended to be a simple family affair with some useful talks thrown in. Since this was what my friend required I did my best to conform to his wishes. He certainly behaved throughout with exquisite good manners and exerted to the full his remarkable powers of charm. De Gaulle was a man who was never rude by mistake. Now, in spite of all the internal troubles and threats with which he was faced, he was about to reach the apogee of his second period of power. Determined, calm and immovable, he represented a tradition soon to become a myth.

Before the General arrived, President Kennedy had reported to me on 23 November on Adenauer's visit to Washington. According

[1] 26 November 1961.

to the President he was willing to negotiate and seemed realistic about the concessions which might have to be made. Although naturally anxious about his own public opinion he professed to be in favour of discussions with the Russians, especially if our rights of access to Berlin could be restated in even stronger terms. He was ready to do his best to bring de Gaulle into line. Some phrases in the President's message were interesting if too optimistic.

> The general tone of the meeting was good, and I believe we are now in a good position to work on General de Gaulle. My general impression is that the German Government is now more flexible than it has been in the past.
>
> The Chancellor was very open and friendly, and his associates made a favourable impression on us. It was a much better meeting than my first encounter with him last April.

But the President added that both he and Adenauer agreed on the importance of an impressive allied military build-up and hoped that we would play our part. All this, however encouraging, was remote from what seemed to be the French view. For de Gaulle was to prove much more inflexible. He

> explained that France was concerned above all, and perhaps even more than her British and American allies, to ensure that Germany was tied in to the West. France looked on Berlin as one part of this problem, and not in itself of capital importance. Chancellor Adenauer might now be ready to contemplate negotiations with the Russians about Berlin, although President de Gaulle wished to see Dr. Adenauer first before he could be sure of this, but it was doubtful whether the maximum concessions to which the Germans would agree would be enough to satisfy the Russians. In fact once negotiations with the Russians began the Allied position would inevitably be eroded. In the circumstances he saw no advantage in embarking on negotiations at the present time. Even if the Federal German Government of the day accepted the concessions which would be asked of them, the German people would be left with a sense of betrayal. Whatever the United States and the United Kingdom might do, France, although not proposing to fight a war with the Russians on her own, would not

be party to such an arrangement. The Germans would then in the future feel that at least they had one friend left in the West.[1]

When the question was raised of some formula which would cover dealings with East Germany and the frontier, after some hesitation de Gaulle

> agreed that the division of Germany and the Oder–Neisse frontier were facts which could not be altered at least for the time being and about which an agreement could perhaps one day be reached with the Russians. But these facts were all more or less favourable to the Russians and there was no need to accept them unless at the same time the Russians would accept the situation in Berlin as it had existed since the war; this was a fact favourable to the West. However to raise all these questions would mean embarking on a very wide negotiation in the present situation when the Russians were building their wall in Berlin, threatening to sign a peace treaty with East Germany, menacing Finland and generally behaving in an aggressive way. It was quite arguable that the West might offer the Russians a wide negotiation on condition that they first changed their aggressive attitude, but the West should at the same time make clear that if the Russians refused, they would not negotiate at all. In the French view the Russians had made no concessions of substance to the Western point of view in recent months, and the time to negotiate had therefore not yet come.[1]

At this point it was not unnatural to ask the question as to how we could be sure of what the Soviet attitude would be if we were not prepared to discuss the matter with them. De Gaulle replied

> that he would not object to further soundings of the Soviet position being carried out by British or American officials in order to verify the basis on which negotiations could begin. He accepted that such soundings would now soon get into [matters of] substance. He would *not* be prepared for French representatives to take part in such exploratory exchanges nor would he agree publicly that these could gradually take on the character of a negotiation. He added that this procedure should not be too inconvenient for the Americans and ourselves since we were

[1] 29 November 1961.

already negotiating with the Russians about nuclear tests and disarmament without French participation.[1]

Of course, the General

agreed that the Russians could always squeeze West Berlin, but he added that life in Berlin was always hazardous and was becoming more so. He did not accept the view that an agreement with the Russians would give renewed confidence to the West Berliners. He had no objection to the introduction of United Nations agencies into Berlin, but then United Nations would not really affect the realities.[1]

In view of this negative attitude neither Home nor I thought it worth while to have any detailed discussion about the possible elements in an arrangement. In view, however, of subsequent developments of French policy towards Russia this unbending line taken by de Gaulle is worth recording. In the course of a considerable harangue he made

the following points. First, the D.D.R. should not be recognised in any way. All that could be recognised was the fact that one part of Germany was under the control of the Soviet Union, but this was not something which the West should regard as permanent.

Secondly, although the occupying Powers were on record as stating that Berlin was not a part of the Federal Republic, nevertheless it had in fact been regarded as such. For example, Dr. Adenauer was greeted in Berlin as Chancellor, and Herr Brandt was leader of the German Socialist party.

Thirdly the idea of an agreement about nuclear weapons for Germany was a gratuitous present to the Russians. It was United States policy not to supply nuclear arms to other countries. But although France had no present intention of sharing nuclear knowledge with the Germans, the French could *not* say that this would always be the case. The Russian menace was too great and the Rhine was too close to the Elbe for France to give any such binding assurance.[1]

On the Sunday morning after the

[1] 29 November 1961.

presentation of all indoor staff, signing of books, etc, left Birch Grove 9.15. De Gaulle left Gatwick at 10 a.m. (Fog nearly held him up, but happily it cleared enough for him to get off.)

11.15. Foreign Secretary and Sir Frederick Hoyer Millar who stayed to luncheon.[1]

We then began to work on our records, which we completed by the early afternoon. On Berlin, reported above, I sent a telegram to Kennedy setting out the facts. In view of the fact that de Gaulle remained adamant and unco-operative, what were we now to do? I therefore dictated a message which I succeeded in finishing on the Sunday evening after de Gaulle left and was finally despatched on the Monday morning.

My comments on my conversations with General de Gaulle on Berlin are as follows :

On Berlin the French have not moved at all. Their position is that at present they see no basis on which a satisfactory negotiation could be conducted; in other words, the minimum Soviet demands are greater than the maximum Western concessions. De Gaulle does not object to further explorations by the British and American Ambassadors in Moscow formally 'to verify the basis on which a negotiation might be possible', and has no objection to the explorations being taken well into questions of substance. The French Ambassador, however, would *not* be allowed to join in this.

De Gaulle's object is in fact to keep his fingers clean. This is bad, and makes it indispensable for us to try to make sure that the German Government fully share the responsibility for our explorations; otherwise there will be the beginning of a myth about an Anglo-American sell-out.

The French did not give the impression that Adenauer's letter sent via Castens had been as encouraging about negotiations as you had expected. They implied that Adenauer had *not* confirmed to them the position he had taken in Washington, especially as regards the vital Paragraph 1 of your message to me of 23 November, when you said that Adenauer 'is clearly in favour of negotiation' and 'agrees with the plan for an effort to concert an agreed position at a meeting of Western Foreign Ministers in

[1] 26 November 1961.

December in Paris, in preparation for talks with the Soviets early in the New Year, probably at Foreign Ministers level'.

With regard to substance, the French feel, not without some truth in my opinion, that what the Germans seem now ready to accept omits some of the essential components which would give us a successful deal with the Russians, the two main points being:

(a) the degree of *de facto* recognition of the D.D.R. and
(b) the Oder–Neisse line.

They argue from this that negotiations would be useless.

The meeting between de Gaulle and Adenauer is due for Thursday, 30 November, but it may be postponed if Adenauer's health does not allow the journey. De Gaulle will certainly not urge Adenauer to stick to what he agreed with you. He will try, either directly or indirectly, to achieve a German retreat. So the Germans may go backwards. Even if they do not, I doubt whether de Gaulle will willingly move from his position.

What then do we do? There are only two ways of playing it. One is to carry on with the procedure we have in mind, that is—

(a) A meeting of officials of the Four Western Governments in Paris very soon. At this probably the French representative will reserve his position.

(b) A meeting of Four Western Foreign Ministers in Paris about 10 December. Couve [de Murville] will probably continue with a negative line. It might, however, be possible to agree at these two meetings on the outlines of what should be the Western negotiating position, if and when it was subsequently agreed that such negotiation should take place.

(c) Putting the position as it then stands to the NATO meeting on 13–15 December. The other NATO Powers will be in favour of negotiation and will bring considerable pressure on the French and even the Germans. The NATO Powers should not go into the detail of the negotiating position, but they will want to be given some general indication of what it will be. It is conceivable, though unlikely, that in face of all this pressure, de Gaulle might change his mind.

The other plan would be to follow something like your original idea which we discussed in our telephone conversation, and have a meeting in Paris of you, de Gaulle and myself, which Adenauer would be asked to attend at some stage. At this we could confront Adenauer with de Gaulle and try to persuade de Gaulle to accept our point of view. But I do not think we shall succeed, for de Gaulle's policy is based not on the immediate needs of the present situation but on a picture of the future of Franco-German relations. But at least having Adenauer confronted with de Gaulle will force the former to take a definite line and prevent him softening it down as he can do in bilateral talks. And if de Gaulle is still obstinate, we shall then be in a position to consider whether or not to go ahead without him.

It may be that a combination of these two plans is the right way. That is to say, first to let pressure build up in NATO and then if that does not succeed in moving de Gaulle to have a top-level meeting of the Four Western Heads of Government afterwards.

The objections to the first plan are that public opinion in the world will build up if nothing definite emerges from the meetings in Paris of the Four Western Foreign Ministers and of NATO. There would be great impatience as to why negotiations are not agreed upon, and the division of the allies will become clear. We might possibly hold this position if, when we saw that we were getting nowhere in Paris, we could at once announce the second plan for an early meeting of Western Heads of Government. On the other hand, the holding of the Four-Power Heads of Government meeting would indicate a crisis and obvious disagreement and play into the Russians' hands. We are in a jam either way. But on the whole it might be better to start by playing things from the bottom up—i.e. through the meetings already planned in Paris of Western officials and Foreign Ministers and then NATO. It might emerge from this process that we could go ahead without the French but without having to force them into open disagreement.

I ought to add that we here do *not* feel (and I think Rusk will agree) that a negotiation will prove successful on the rather restrictive basis now outlined in your message to me of 23 November and in Kohler's[1] briefing to the Ambassadorial group on 24 November. It will only be possible if either at the beginning

---

[1] Foy D. Kohler was U.S. Assistant Secretary of State, European Affairs.

or at the end of the negotiations we are prepared to go rather further on both Oder–Neisse and a formula covering practical dealings with the D.D.R.

I ought also to tell you a new and rather significant point. While the Germans are precluded by the Brussels Treaty from manufacturing nuclear weapons and while you are precluded by the McMahon Act from giving them to them (and anyway have no intention of doing so) de Gaulle made it quite clear that he could *not* bind himself never to give nuclear weapons to the Germans. It will, therefore, be necessary, if this is a vital point in any agreement, for the Germans to make a unilateral declaration that they will not accept nuclear weapons from anyone (except of course under the agreed key of the cupboard procedure).

I should be very grateful to know how you feel we should now proceed.

The President sent me an immediate reply thanking me for my message as well as for the detailed information which we had given him. He seemed angry but puzzled. He could only propose to continue to put pressure on Adenauer to maintain, when faced with de Gaulle, the convictions of the need for negotiation with Moscow which he had freely and firmly expressed in Washington.

So ended one of the most curious episodes in Anglo-French relations. The Press and public, as a whole, were not generally aware of the strains which lay behind the apparent cordiality of our relations. Nor indeed could I find myself able to resent the characteristic egotism of my old friend. He had developed but not changed since the old days in Algiers. Although, in fact, his political position was not by any means inflexible (indeed his whole attitude underwent several drastic changes), he was able to conceal these sudden alterations of front by a wonderful outward assumption of inflexibility. Thus, elected to preserve North Africa for France, within a few months he followed the British example, which he had so much derided, of handing over French colonies and even French metropolitan territories to the Arab inhabitants, regardless of the interest of the large numbers of French settlers. Yet he executed this right-about turn with courage and determination once he formed the opinion that it was necessary. His policy towards Soviet Russia was to undergo a similar transformation. In the days following his visit, I recorded the following reflections:

> Of course, de Gaulle's policy is clear and has never changed. He does not want war. He does not believe there will be war. But he wants to pretend to the French and the Germans that *he* (de Gaulle) is the strong, loyal man. He will not 'do a Munich'. But he only dares take this line, devoutly praying that the British and Americans will get him out. He really admitted this to me. He said it was not perhaps anything but a rather *cynical* policy. Yet it was justified, for we must at all costs prevent another German 'myth', such as had made Hitler's rise to power possible. But naturally his main purpose is to see that France gets the credit for loyalty, and that the Anglo-Americans are made responsible for the betrayal of Germany.
>
> He went so far as to say that even if the present weak and incapable German Government accepted our view, he still felt it his duty to be the protector of German interests. I said, 'You would be *plus royaliste que le roi?*' He said, 'Certainly. Then the Germany of the future will know that France was true.' It would be, of course, a complete collapse of de Gaulle's plan if the Americans suddenly turned tough—which they might easily do and would have done already but for Kennedy, Rusk, and Alec Home's extraordinary success with Rusk. If de Gaulle thought there was real danger of war, he would be in a panic.[1]

Turning from the problems of Germany and Berlin to those of Europe and especially of the Common Market my private talks alone with de Gaulle were equally unproductive.

> Charming, affable, mellow as the General now is, his little pin-head is still as small as ever. His views are inward, not out-ward looking. I fear he has decided to oppose us—yet, in a way, he wants us in Europe.[1]

From the social point of view the visit was very successful. The weather was glorious, two still and sunny days with many leaves with all their colouring still on the oaks and beeches. The attraction of this remarkable figure, as well as the mystery surrounding him, led me to a further attempt to summarise the picture as I saw it

[1] 29 November 1961.

then. I quote these records because, although they make no attempt at a final appreciation, they reflect the mood of the time.

> The Emperor of the French (for he is now an almost complete autocrat, taking no notice of any advice and indeed receiving little of independent value) is older, more isolated, more sententious, and far more *royal*. . . . He is well informed, yet remote. His hatred of the 'Anglo-Americans' is as great as ever. While he has extraordinary dignity and charm, 'unbends' delightfully, is nice to servants and children and so forth, he does not apparently listen to argument. I mean this almost literally. Not only is he not convinced, he actually does not listen. He merely repeats over and over again what he has said before. And the doctrine—almost dogma—is based on intuition, not ratiocination. He talks of Europe, and means France. The France of Louis XIV (as regards its religion, boundaries, and power), of Napoleon (as regards the fanatical loyalty of its Army). He allows a little of Napoleon III, as regards the management of a so-called Parliament.
>
> Germany of today he does *not* fear. But he is a little more apprehensive than a year or two ago of Germany of tomorrow. Adenauer he knows he can dominate. What about Strauss? What about the next generation? This, of course, is his excuse for being '*plus royaliste que le roi*'—more intransigent than the *present* Germans, with his eye on the future Germans. But in all this he overlooks the danger of a real clash or a fatal diplomatic defeat over Berlin—or rather, he does not fear disorder (may even welcome it) so long as France's hands are clean. In a curious way, it is just as immoral as Bonnet trusting to Chamberlain to get him out of the war.[1]

I also could not help feeling more and more the complete isolation in which de Gaulle lived. He

> now hears nothing and listens to nothing. Couve de Murville, a functionary, not a politician, . . . sees him but rarely. Debré is a *good* man, and in many ways a sensible man. But he is loyalty personified. His Minister of Finance is the former Governor of the Bank of France (Baumgartner)—a good man, but without influence. Joxe is about the only one who dares speak to him. De Courcel . . . is to be sent to us in the spring as Ambassador. . . .

[1] 29 November 1961.

The tragedy of it all is that we agree with de Gaulle on almost everything. We like the political Europe (*union des patries* or *union d'états*) that de Gaulle likes. We are anti-federalists; so is he. We are pragmatists in our economic planning; so is he. . . . We agree; but his pride, his inherited hatred of England (since Joan of Arc), his bitter memories of the last war; above all, his intense 'vanity' for France—she must dominate—make him half welcome, half repel us, with a strange 'love-hate' complex. Sometimes, when I am with him, I feel I have overcome it. But he goes back to his distrust and dislike, like a dog to his vomit. I still feel that he has *not* absolutely decided about our admission to the Economic Community. I am inclined to think he will be more likely to yield to pressure than persuasion.[1]

There was now a new complication. Adenauer, who was a very old man, was suffering from a bad chill. His visit to Paris was consequently postponed. At the beginning of December President Kennedy wrote again to assure me that he was continuing his pressure on Adenauer and had received a favourable reply. On 4 December we agreed to meet in Bermuda before the end of the year. The actual date fixed was 21 December. It was decided that we would consider extending the invitation both to de Gaulle and to Adenauer in the light of the forthcoming NATO meeting.

Meanwhile, on 12 December, I received a long and friendly message from de Gaulle regarding his talks with Adenauer, but although he admitted that the German Chancellor was now in favour of negotiation he attributed this change of opinion as mainly due to a desire to meet the wishes of the President and myself. He repeated his own conviction that the time for discussion with the Russians was inopportune.

When the NATO meeting took place Home could make little progress,

> engaged (with his American and German colleagues and later in the week with NATO Council) in laborious and utterly fruitless negotiations with the French. De Gaulle has not moved an inch from the intransigent position which he took at Birch Grove House. So Berlin, etc., seems more difficult than ever.[2]

[1] 29 November 1961.   [2] 18 December 1961.

Meanwhile my wife and I were able to enjoy

a most moving and dramatic ceremony on Friday, 15 December, when I was given the Freedom of the City of London. As far as I know, no Prime Minister in office has received this honour, except Sir Winston Churchill, for a long time. (Of course Pitt— Lord Chatham—when 'it rained gold boxes'.) It was a wonderful day and [the ceremony was] admirably arranged. In addition to the usual people invited to a show of this kind, there were all the family. Then there were (in the Guildhall) representatives of Macmillan and Company; twelve from Birch Grove Estate (Blake, the Keeper; the Head Gardener; the Head Forester (Lucas); Stevenson (the Maintenance man); Nannie West; etc.). Then our own servants—Mrs. Bell, Miss Baker (Housemaid), etc. Mayors of Stockton and Bromley, and various Conservative notabilities from each place. Altogether a fine show.

Dorothy and I motored to Temple Bar. We were taken into a room in the Law Courts, where we were given champagne. Then we drove in an open landau (with outriders and officer from Household Cavalry) to Guildhall. Guard of Honour from 2nd Battalion, Grenadier Guards.

The ceremony of the Freedom was very impressive. The Chamberlain made a speech. I followed.

After the ceremony, we left for Mansion House, where there was a noble luncheon—speech by Lord Mayor, reply by me (in a more relaxed vein than the morning's oration) and finally away by 3.45.[1]

This honour—next to that of the Chancellorship of my own University, Oxford—I prize above any which I have ever received.

[1] 18 December 1961.

CHAPTER XVI

African Cockpit

IF the Soviet Government's threats in Eastern Europe were a cause of constant anxiety to the Western Allies, the struggle between East and West, between the Communist and the Free World, found a ready-made arena in another continent where civil war had already broken out and the great Powers were in danger of being drawn into the conflict. In the vast territory of the Congo, covering an area equal to two-thirds of the whole of Western Europe (or nearly four times the size of France) with its primitive populations and tribal and regional jealousies, the apparatus of constitutional government remained nominally in existence, although the country was breaking up into chaos. Had it not been for the machinery of the United Nations it would have been impossible to prevent a complete collapse of organised life, accompanied by famine and disease. The departure of the old Belgian officials—administrators, technicians, doctors—left a gap that the native Congolese could not fill. In spite of all the baffling perplexities, the Secretary-General, Hammarskjöld, succeeded at least in averting the worst perils, although the administrators and troops at his command had no real unity of training or structure, being hastily collected from neutral countries such as Sweden or Ireland, or from African countries such as Ghana and Tunisia. He succeeded in maintaining some kind of order and in preserving a modest system of transport by which relief could reach the unhappy inhabitants now for the first time experiencing the delights of liberty and democracy. By the end of the meeting of the United Nations in September 1960, the situation was partly stabilised. Tshombe was in control in Katanga; Mobutu, in Léopoldville with his strange cabinet of students, represented legitimate government, having been appointed by President Kasavubu. Lumumba, dismissed by the President but still claiming to be Prime Minister, although under some vague supervision, was at large and trying to drum up support for a return to power.

One of the chief anxieties of the Western Governments was to prevent the Congo from falling into Communist hands or under Communist control. The addition of this vast population to the Communist camp and the effect upon limitrophe countries, once this disease became planted and rampant, might be catastrophic. Moreover, it must be admitted that the great natural resources in the mining areas would be especially tempting to the growing imperialism of Soviet policy. Yet I was convinced from the beginning of this tortuous story, which it would be fatiguing now to recall in detail, that the best hope we had of excluding Communist influence was to rely upon the United Nations, and by their authority seek to preserve the unity of the country under some kind of federal structure. On the other hand, in the execution of this policy there were many difficulties. Although the old *Force Publique*, with its Belgian officers, had been disbanded and most of the Belgian troops withdrawn to places where they could defend their compatriots, many African elements of this once powerful army were forming themselves into bandit and guerrilla units.

The Congolese troops, now largely out of hand, were rampaging throughout the country, and, except in those areas where United Nations forces could provide some protection, the people were crushed and terrorised. If it was the object of the Soviet Government to increase its influence it could only do so by choosing one of the leading figures and giving him all their support. Curiously enough it was in Lumumba that the Communist and other 'progressive' elements put their faith. With that respect for constitutional niceties which former revolutionaries so often show, they argued that the President had no right to dismiss the Prime Minister, and that legitimacy must be the principle by which order could be re-established. A kind of Holy Alliance now came into being of which Metternich himself might have been proud:

The Congo gets worse and worse. Lumumba (who is a Communist stooge as well as a witch-doctor) has escaped from

Léopoldville and is obviously making for Stanleyville. There he has his own clansmen. He will doubtless set up his standard there and get Russian help.[1]

However, a few days later I learnt that

Lumumba has been caught by Col. Mobutu's troops and brought back to Léopoldville. This is good news; but I fear that they will kill him ... which will bring discredit on the Congo Government.[2]

On 7 December 1960 Nkrumah appealed to me, urging with passionate emotion the recognition of Lumumba and his supporters. He declared that while it was all right for Lumumba to throw his opponents into jail while he was Prime Minister, it was quite wrong for other people to incarcerate 'a legal Prime Minister'. Although this argument naturally had some appeal for me on general grounds, I was not persuaded that a man who had been Prime Minister for only a short time, had not been confirmed by Parliament, could not in the circumstances convoke a Parliament, and had been dismissed by the Head of State, should be regarded as the only, or indeed as a possible, centre for rallying the forces of law and order throughout the country. In fact the President, Kasavubu, who had remained remarkably calm throughout, seemed more likely to emerge as the best foundation on which the United Nations mission could build.

As we feared, Lumumba's partisans set up a rival régime in Stanleyville.

The Russians are trying to set up a supporter of Lumumba in Stanleyville, and we may soon find U.N. impotent and a sort of African Korea developing.[3]

Our fears were soon realised; and although Mobutu, with the help of some remaining Belgian forces, began to move troops against Lumumba's forces, he was unable to establish his authority.

Congo is worse again. Belgians are in disgrace with Hammarskjöld (for helping Mobutu) and Lumumba's strength seems to be coming up again. We have [learnt of] quite large Russian deliveries to Lumumba's deputy in Stanleyville, both of arms and

[1] 1 December 1960.   [2] 3 December 1960.   [3] 14 December 1960.

other military supplies. We have told H., who will try to get the airfields blocked.[1]

The situation was now developing on the lines which we had for some time foreseen. The Russians would back the representative of Lumumba, whoever he might be or whatever might be Lumumba's own fate. They would claim to be supporting legitimacy in the shape of a Prime Minister who had not yet lost the confidence of a Parliament which could not meet. The Belgians would, not unnaturally, favour Tshombe in the Katanga where the Union Minière had large interests. But so long as the central Government at Léopoldville remained under Mobutu or any other non-Communist nominee of President Kasavubu, the Belgians could probably be persuaded to conform to the policy which Britain and America were trying to pursue of using the United Nations to exclude Communist infiltration and intervention. This seemed to me a wise policy, since, while the Russians were inhibited by no kind of democratic or parliamentary restraints, it was clearly inconceivable that Britain, either alone or with American assistance, could embroil itself independently in this African 'cockpit'. President Kennedy broadly accepted this view; but there were many at home, powerful both in Parliament and among the public Press, who resented the weaknesses of the United Nations and were distressed by the mistakes of some of the men to whom Hammarskjöld had been forced to entrust these delicate tasks. While some of them were fine characters others were little better than adventurers; still worse, a few seemed to be working in the Communist interest.

If the Congo threatened serious differences at home, the effect upon the Commonwealth might well be disastrous. Nkrumah and all the emerging African countries seemed to be devoted 'Lumumbists'. Early in January 1961, the Conference of African States, held in Casablanca, announced their support for the Stanleyville régime, and some countries (such as Morocco, Guinea, Egypt and later Indonesia and Sudan) withdrew their contingents from the United Nations force. On the other hand Welensky favoured Tshombe's régime in Katanga. This important area with its great copper output

[1] 1 January 1961.

and proved deposits was limitrophe with Northern Rhodesia. An independent Katanga could easily be persuaded to come more and more under the influence of the Government of the Federation. To some extent this view was shared by some other members of the Commonwealth. But Nehru took the Lumumbist line and sent me sad messages declaring that Tshombe, Mobutu and even President Kasavubu were nothing but puppets of the Belgians. There was therefore a growing danger of a split in the Commonwealth on racial or ideological lines.

In a message on 23 January, Welensky pointed out that Katanga would be lost and the Russians take control if Tshombe were prevented by the inept United Nations policy from taking proper steps to defend his own province—the northern parts of which had been invaded by Stanleyville troops. Two days later Nkrumah declared that if any harm came to Lumumba it 'would have a most serious effect upon the relations of Ghana with the Commonwealth . . . the failure to help Lumumba would never be forgotten by the people of Africa'.

It can be seen therefore that during the early part of 1961 I was thrown back upon my familiar role of trying to reconcile conflicting views. Fortunately, the difficulty of movement and the bad organisation of the rival armies prevented the extension of civil war in its worst form. But the increasing hostility of the Communists against the Secretary-General made me feel it all the more necessary to prevent the greater danger of his losing heart.

To add to all our troubles Lumumba, who had been transferred to Katanga at President Kasavubu's request, was now reported dead after an attempt to escape. It was alleged, and subsequently proved to be true, that he and two of his colleagues had been put to death by the Katanga authorities. At the same time the Soviet Government and the so-called 'Casablanca Powers' formally recognised the Stanleyville régime under Gizenga as the only legitimate Government in the area. This Gizenga was to prove an increasingly important figure, as the accepted representative of 'Lumumbist' traditions.

Meanwhile, Kasavubu had replaced Mobutu and his cabinet of students in Léopoldville with a cabinet of politicians under a trusted collaborator of his own, Joseph Ileo. We had therefore at this point a central Government at Léopoldville under the President, first with Mobutu, now with Ileo; a Government at Élisabethville under Tshombe controlling Katanga; and a Government claiming legitimacy at Stanleyville under Gizenga. These are familiar conditions of a conflict of forces whether political or tribal over a large area. They have been repeated over and over again in ancient and modern history and would have caused little anxiety to us except as the arena in which the rival concepts of life and politics nurtured by the Communist and the Free World were being fought out, and in which there was a growing danger that the great Powers representing these rival principles might be drawn into direct intervention and perhaps open war. For the British Government, unlike the American, this complex situation added the additional disadvantage of involving the countries of the Commonwealth in a divergence of policy which might lead to dispute and perhaps even to disruption.

I now thought it right to send a personal message to Nehru, on 17 February, warning him of the extreme danger of Russian intervention in the Congo and the need to support the efforts of the United Nations.

Thank you for your message of 12 February about the Congo. Events have moved so quickly in the past few days that I hardly feel that I can now answer your letter point by point.

Clearly a situation has now arisen of the utmost danger and difficulty for us all. The murder of Lumumba has not only shocked the whole world but has created a highly charged atmosphere which is bound to add to the difficulties of reaching wise decisions. At the same time the Soviet Union is seeking to exploit this situation in a wild and dangerous manner. There is a threat that the Russians will intervene in the Congo outside the United Nations; and the resolution they have put up for the Security Council is clearly destructive. It seems designed not only to produce chaos in the Congo, but to attack the basic structure of the United Nations itself.

There is a grave danger that unless we can get a sensible and concerted approach to the problem and take some of the heat out of it, the whole United Nations operation in the Congo may be jeopardised. You so rightly said in your statement to the Lok

Sabha on Wednesday that, if the United Nations withdraw, it will mean disaster, and the field would be left open to civil war and large-scale foreign intervention. We must do everything we can to prevent this happening and to secure the future of the Congo as a united and independent state.

Although Lumumba's death symbolises the whole tragedy of the Congo and may greatly add to the difficulties, it does not alter the basic need to uphold and reinvigorate the United Nations effort. This is the only way to keep the Congo free from outside intervention to maintain law and order, and to help the Congolese people to get a political settlement and proper representative government.

However, it is no good looking to the United Nations force to do more than it is physically capable of doing. Nor is it possible or desirable for the United Nations to take over the job of governing the country and to assume a colonial function there. These two considerations seem to rule out imposing any political solution on the Congolese by force. This does not mean that the United Nations cannot get a lot done through moral pressure and through the presence of its troops. It could effectively interdict outside intervention. It could help to bring the Congolese forces under better control and to turn them into a more reliable instrument for keeping the peace. It could use its good offices to bring about an agreed settlement between the various factions in the Congo, and to prevent the spread of violence.

Any foreign military or para-military personnel in the Congo outside the United Nations ought naturally to be withdrawn and the Belgian Government should as far as lies within their power call back any Belgian mercenaries or military advisers in the employ of the Congolese authorities. I was glad to see M. Wigny's statement that the Belgian Government strongly disapprove of mercenaries being recruited.[1]

The immediate and vital need seems to be to keep the United Nations effort; and I hope that any foreign countries who may be contemplating withdrawing their support or their troops from the United Nations force or intervening independently of the United Nations, will stop to think of the disastrous consequences which might follow from this.

[1] Wigny was Minister of Foreign Affairs in the Belgian Government.

Messages on similar lines were also sent by the Commonwealth Secretary to all the leading Commonwealth countries.

Although Nehru sent a friendly reply he was naturally especially concerned to hold in check those centrifugal forces which already in India and now in Africa seemed to threaten the unity of a great area hitherto guaranteed by its European rulers. He attributed special importance to the removal of the remaining Belgian troops. His reply of 17 February was, however, satisfactory to the extent that he joined with me in supporting the United Nations. He shared my view of the danger of the situation, and did not agree with some of the Soviet proposals. But he added :

> we have to remember that the situation that has arisen in the Congo resulting in the murder of Lumumba is the direct result of the policies pursued by the Léopoldville and Katanga authorities and support given to them by other countries. Both Tshombe and Mobutu have been functioning not only with Belgian help but under Belgian advisers who must be held responsible for all these developments.

He felt that these advisers had been supported from without and that, in spite of the Security Council resolutions, no attempt had been made to stop them. The Congo situation was almost beyond recall, but it might just be saved if previous policies were reversed, all Belgian forces withdrawn and the armies other than the United Nations force were all immobilised.

> I think that if necessary U.N. should use force to give effect to its policies. We have been dealing with régimes which have little legal or constitutional backing and which follow gangster methods and are guilty of brutal murder for any reasons and in defiance of U.N. and world opinion.
>
> It is clear that those countries who have sent their armed forces to Congo to help U.N. will be unable to keep them there unless effective policies are pursued.

The Soviet Government now determined to make a direct attack upon Hammarskjöld and the whole United Nations policy. They charged the Secretary-General with the direct responsibility for Lumumba's murder and demanded both his dismissal and the abandonment of the United Nations' Congo operation. However, at a critical meeting of the Security Council on 21 February, no other Council member supported the Russian resolution. On the contrary, a resolution was adopted which was of the utmost significance since it gave the signal for more determined United Nations action. Its twofold aim was to avert the threatened calamity of civil war and to facilitate the restoration of Parliamentary and constitutional methods. Both these were difficult burdens to place upon so fragile a foundation as that available to the Secretary-General. The use and conduct of the United Nations forces was destined to become, in the next few months, a matter of continual criticism and debate between all the various parties concerned inside and outside the Congo.

The task of re-establishing any confidence in a constitution with such slender traditions was, in the end, largely achieved by the determination and resourcefulness of the President, Kasavubu. On 28 February he summoned a conference which was attended by all the major political figures except Gizenga, who remained at Stanleyville claiming to be the sole legitimate heir and supported with increasing Russian aid. A constitutional scheme was agreed giving considerable regional autonomy, and when on 17 April Kasavubu's Government accepted the resolution of the Security Council including the offer of assistance in the reorganisation of the army, the general situation began to improve. Yet so swiftly did events change in this distracted country that although at one moment there seemed to be a chance of comparative peace, within a few days there were new and dramatic turns of the wheel which seemed to threaten fresh disasters.

Not without reason, towards the end of April, Kasavubu decided to court Gizenga and seek some method of agreement between Léopoldville and Stanleyville. Tshombe at once reacted by declaring his total opposition to the President's decision to work loyally with the United Nations mission. Accordingly, on 28 April, he was arrested. This caused a new flurry at home where from different motives Tshombe's independent stand had evoked much sympathy. This was specially strong in the centres that had the closest connection with Welensky and the Government of the Federation. It seemed best to make a personal appeal to Welensky, to whom I wrote on 9 May:

> I have no doubt that you are as worried about the developments in the Congo as I am. We are watching them very closely. The situation seems, however, to change from hour to hour. I know how much importance you attach to this problem and I am therefore venturing to send you the best appreciation we can make of the current situation.
>
> The Congo still presents a scene of confusion, but I do not think that the possibilities of an eventual political settlement covering the whole territory are as distant as they once seemed. I am convinced we must go on hoping and working for this and that in the meantime we must look to the U.N. to hold the ring, bring the Provinces in closer relation with the centre and keep foreign interference out. Any other course would only lead to worse trouble.
>
> It is most regrettable that Tshombe is to be put on trial, but no doubt Kasavubu considers that he is an insuperable obstacle to Congolese unity; he had done his best to see that the Coquilhatville Conference could not succeed by trying to assert the virtual independence of the Katanga, by seeking publicly to upset the better relations between the U.N. and Léopoldville, and by working against the U.N. presence in the Congo. We have tried, as you know, to get the U.N. to have him released. But the truth is we cannot really expect Mr. Hammarskjöld to do more for him than he did for Lumumba. When Lumumba left U.N. protection the U.N. authorities did not feel able either to prevent his arrest by the Congolese or to secure his release; and we thought this was right. Tshombe has, I understand, never even asked for U.N. protection. . . .
>
> As I see it, we now have Kasavubu, who has strengthened his position and has been mending his fences with the U.N.; we have some tentative contacts between Léopoldville and Stanleyville on the political and military levels; we have the Katanga authorities, in Tshombe's absence apparently making some overtures to the U.N. about carrying out the February 21st Resolution.
>
> We certainly do not want to see anything done to upset the present stability of the Katanga, and I fully realise your interest

in this. We shall do our best to ensure that there is no question of the U.N. using force there, except in pursuit of their mandate to prevent armed clashes between Congolese, and this seems to be the principle upon which Mr. Hammarskjöld is proceeding. I do not think we can possibly try to treat the Katanga in isolation, or encourage it to assert its independence, or work against the U.N. An independent Katanga, and its friends, would have to face the hostility, both on the ground and in the U.N., of most of the rest of Africa. This would provide the Russians with just the kind of opportunity they are looking for to enable them to line up the Africans against the West, and then come in with material support. The remainder of the Congo would be bankrupt and a sitting target to Communist influence. I am sure that we must work to bring Élisabethville and Léopoldville together in co-operation with the U.N. If the Katanga goes on refusing to come to terms this will only tend to make Kasavubu lean more towards Gizenga, and thus to suit the purposes of the Communists; whereas a Katanga/Léopoldville axis would enable Kasavubu to negotiate with Gizenga from strength. I wonder whether you might be able to help in this, by using your influence in Elisabethville to get the Katangans to see the situation realistically and to join Kasavubu in reaching an accommodation with the U.N.

On 22 June Tshombe was freed, and two days later he signed an agreement to reunite Katanga with the rest of the Congo. Once again no sooner had this satisfactory news reached us, than we were confronted by another change. Four days later Tshombe returned to Katanga and repudiated the settlement which he had just approved. Nevertheless, the general situation was undoubtedly calmer, and Hammarskjöld felt able to report that the danger of civil war seemed now over. The Congolese Parliament met on 26 July although without the Katanga contingent. A new figure now came upon the scene, and at the request of the President on 2 August, Adoula formed a Government which included Gizenga as Vice-Premier. Léopoldville and Stanleyville were thus at least formally reunited. This Government was recognised by the United Nations as the sole legal Government of the Congo, and the main danger of Gizenga, with Russian assistance, seizing control seemed

The Queen at a Durbar in Ghana
'The genial and warm-hearted people gave her an unprecedented reception.'

The Queen at a market in Ghana
'The Queen has been absolutely determined all through.'

to be averted. Nevertheless, with Katanga still outside, grave dangers and difficulties lay ahead.

At the end of August the United Nations command decided to move against Katanga in order to compel the dismissal of foreign personnel and at the same time they broke off relations with the Katanga Government. Unhappily, the task was entrusted to individuals whose experience and capacity for such a delicate affair was at least unproved. Naturally we understood and sympathised with their difficulties; the United Nations forces were recruited from a number of countries without much political or military experience. The duty that now lay ahead of their representative would have tried even the most eminent of the great Indian or colonial governors or administrators. I was not surprised therefore when I received, on 6 September, a strongly-worded complaint from Welensky. He declared that the United Nations forces were bringing chaos into the country which up to now had remained properous and peaceful. They seemed to think that any measures were justified in order to bring about the fall of the independent Government.

Reports were now reaching us of heavy fighting in Katanga. Although it was certainly right to try to re-integrate Katanga into the Congo, since without the wealth of Katanga the Congo economy could not survive, yet there were now two serious causes for alarm. First, a sense of disapproval and even disgust at the reports coming through as to the measures taken by the United Nations forces to impose their will; secondly, which was not so generally known, the suspicion that in the new Government Gizenga and his Communist friends were strengthening their control. We might therefore find ourselves in the fantastic position that after all our efforts to eliminate Soviet influence and to reunite the Congo in peace we were in fact in danger of allowing United Nations forces, almost entirely paid for by Britain and America, to hand over the whole Congo including Katanga to Russian influence and even control.

The United Nations authorities have tried to conquer Katanga province on behalf of the Central Government by brute force. Tshombe has resisted. There have been a good many casualties and grave atrocities. Hammarskjöld has either blundered, or his agents have acted without his authority. . . . On Monday he

P

tells Sir Patrick Dean that he will not use force. On Tuesday or
Wednesday, full-scale operations begin.

What is more dangerous, Gizenga is getting powerful in the
Central Government. A Communist African has been sent as
'agent' to 'govern' the Katanga province. Unless we and the
Americans act quickly and resolutely, we shall have undone in
a week all we have done—at huge expense—in a year. Congo will
be handed to Russia on a plate. The Union Minière properties
will be 'nationalised' and run by Russian Communists, and a
most dangerous situation created in Africa—as well as [a] great
financial and moral blow to the West and especially to European
civilisation.[1]

On the evening of 14 September I had a conversation with
President Kennedy in which I expressed to him all my fears. I felt
that we must press Hammarskjöld to get a settlement on a federal
or semi-federal basis. When the President asked if we wanted
Tshombe back, I replied 'either Tshombe or someone else'. Fortunately, the Foreign Secretary was in New York and was able to
have an immediate discussion with Secretary Rusk. But difficult as
it no doubt was for Hammarskjöld to control these complicated
movements from Washington, it was still more difficult for the
British Government, responsible not only for its own interests but
for those of all the Commonwealth countries, to exercise a decisive
influence even with the goodwill and understanding of the President.

Press reports began to pour in, giving details of the struggle
in Katanga. Critical letters were being published, and complaints
reached me from many quarters. Old friends and some of my present colleagues were equally disturbed. Apart from all other dangers,
there were signs of serious political reactions at home. Fortunately,
the Americans were as much concerned as we were. Home reported
to me on 16 September that

> both the President and Rusk are very worried about the Congo.
> Their politicians, like ours, are asking what all our expenditure
> of energy and treasure has been for.

Fortunately, I could look forward to a full report from Lord Lans-

[1] 15 September 1961.

downe, Under-Secretary at the Foreign Office, who had been sent to the Congo to find out what he could on the spot.

I felt confident that Lansdowne had the necessary qualities for so delicate a task. His experience in the war, when he had been attached to the Free French Forces, and his inherited diplomatic instinct, coupled with a happy combination of courtesy and prudence, made him especially fitted for this assignment. In his first report, on 17 September, he stated clearly that in his opinion the action of the United Nations officials had been the result rather of folly and inexperience than of malice. Meanwhile, he had taken every opportunity to impress upon all those concerned the deplorable effect upon the British Government and British public opinion of the events in Katanga and of the violent and even brutal attempt by the United Nations forces to arrest some of the Ministers of the Katanga Government, with heavy and destructive fighting both at Elisabethville and Jadotville. He reported to me on 17 September:

I have also made clear in appropriate terms to the Secretary-General our preoccupation lest the United Nations action should hand the Katanga on a plate to the Gizengists. More generally with Congolese Ministers I have expressed our anxiety lest the economy of Katanga, which is so important to the Congo and to the Free World as a whole, should be damaged. Ministers expressed their determination to avoid this.

I noted at the time that

the Congo news is better. Lord Lansdowne has done very well and I hope his talks with Hammarskjöld will be helpful. What is needed is a cease-fire.[1]

On Sunday, 17 September, I was at Chequers and welcome news reached me in the morning.

Hammarskjöld has agreed—indeed has himself proposed—a meeting with Tshombe to try to arrange a cease-fire and then a negotiation for some settlement. This is *very* good news. Lansdowne has done well. The meeting is to be this evening, or more

[1] 16 September 1961.

probably tomorrow, at a place called Ndola, just inside Northern Rhodesia. Both Welensky and the Governor have agreed. Lord Alport will go up and meet Hammarskjöld and Lansdowne.[1]

The scene was now set for what we might hope to be a happy solution. The problem, never fully understood by the British public and Press, was indeed complicated. My colleagues and I wanted to support the United Nations to bring peace and relief to the peoples of the Congo and to prevent the collapse of the structure of society. We wanted to prevent the dismembering of the Congo because we believed that without Katanga the Congo was not viable and would fall an easy prey to Communism. We therefore supported any solution along federal or provincial lines which could be reached. At the same time we were apprehensive lest by restoring the politicians of Léopoldville, with the help of the United Nations largely financed by Britain and America, we should find in the meantime that Léopoldville had come under Russian control through the sinister activities of Gizenga. Naturally the Communist and left-wing propaganda both at home and abroad accused us of wishing either to annex Katanga or to set it up as a separate province under 'colonialist' and 'imperialist' control. On the contrary we wanted a united Congo, but not a Communist Congo.

The crude methods which Hammarskjöld's officers had used to try to reconquer the Katanga had caused much natural resentment. But when the Secretary-General undertook to hold the discussions himself with Tshombe I had every reason to believe that a solution would be found. The next day came shattering news. Hammarskjöld's plane had crashed outside Ndola, and with it all our hopes.

A very confused day, beginning with uncertainty and ending with tragedy. Although Lord Lansdowne's plane arrived safely at Ndola, Hammarskjöld's crashed.

News of this was confirmed about 3 p.m. today.

It is not known *how* this happened. The crash was (as it turned out) only four miles from the airfield. For some reason—I suppose the difficulty of the bush country, etc.—it was not discovered for more than twelve hours. I think it was hoped that they had gone back to Léopoldville or gone to some other airfield.

[1] 17 September 1961.

Even now, it's a mystery what happened. There were five crew and about seven passengers. One man (a United Nations Security Officer) is alive, but in a very bad way.

There are rumours that it was 'shot down'—but this seems incredible. [The pilot] was talking to the airfield authorities up till just before the crash.[1]

Not unnaturally, the air was full of the wildest rumours and the most fantastic charges. A few days later the Foreign Secretary reported to me that one of the Ghana Ministers more or less accused the 'colonialists' (presumably the United Kingdom or the Federation) of murdering both Lumumba and Hammarskjöld. What I was more anxious about was the story that there were two fighters with the Katanga forces, and it was just possible

that one of these 'pirate' planes attacked Hammarskjöld on his peaceful mission. But it seems impossible, and does not fit with their safe arrival and circling round the airfield about midnight last night. It is more probable that, for safety reasons, they decided not to land at Ndola (which is not much of an airfield) but to go on to Salisbury. However the inquiry which the Rhodesian Government will open will no doubt find the true explanation, especially if this man survives.[1]

In fact, it became clear from the official inquiry that the accident was due to an error of the pilot and to no sinister plot. Nevertheless, it can readily be imagined by what an atmosphere of charge and counter-charge the whole problem of the Congo was now poisoned.

The Press all around the world joined, quite rightly, in a tribute to the work of a truly great man. For a little over eight years his strong and dedicated leadership had transformed the office of Secretary-General of the United Nations from one of international administration to one of world statesmanship. He was a man of great personal integrity and considerable intellectual capacity and vision. Above all he was endowed with patience and courage. It is true that many British people regarded him with some suspicion. The position of neutrality which he had to assume in order to fulfil his functions seemed almost like taking an impartial position

[1] 18 September 1961.

between the principles of good and evil. Moreover, he was a Swede; and although we admired the Swedish people we could not forget their long history of skilful abstention from the great causes which had torn the world apart. Yet, whatever may have been the criticisms of his conduct by some Conservative and right-wing politicians and critics, Hammarskjöld had lately come under most violent attacks from the Russians. He had survived many crises and always with dignity and firmness. If his position was sometimes almost impossible this was due to the inherent faults of the organisation which he was called upon to serve. In this Congo expedition, as in others, the purposes of his masters were wholly contradictory and the instructions given to him to carry out the resolutions of the Council were inadequate and unsuitable. It is a tribute to the character of this man that he achieved so much with so little. He was indeed a martyr to a great cause.

Under the shock of Hammarskjöld's death there was at least one thing to be thankful for.

It now seems clear that Hammarskjöld's plane was destroyed by an accident and *not* by an attack or by sabotage. It was only four miles from the airfield and *in a direct line* with the runway. The pilot must have miscalculated and hit the trees.[1]

Moreover, a provisional agreement for a cease-fire in Katanga was concluded. This was to come into force on 21 September. The fact that Gizenga retired in high dudgeon to Stanleyville was an encouraging sign.

Lansdowne had now returned and gave me an admirable account of his visit.

He impressed me greatly. This has been his first great opportunity, and he has risen to it. He speaks excellent French. His judgements seemed clear and often rather unexpected. There is a storm of attack (Nehru and Nkrumah leading) against British policy. Foreign Secretary made a statement in New York yesterday, which has had a good Press here. But I fear much damage is being done in the 'neutral' world. Heath is to speak tonight. His draft is *excellent*.

[1] 19 September 1961.

I am sending a personal message to Adoula (Prime Minister of Congo) who is said by George [Lansdowne] to be reasonable and *non*-Communist, but seems to have got it into his head that we are working for a *secession* of Katanga under Tshombe, for colonialist and materialist reasons. Lansdowne has done some good in trying to show him that we want a united and peaceful Congo and are doing all we can to get Tshombe to a negotiation with Adoula. At least a *cease-fire* between United Nations and Katanga troops has been arranged. But I fear that the Central Government may try to take over Katanga with its own forces. Adoula is, of course, under a good deal of pressure from the Communist members of his Government, especially Gizenga.[1]

One of our difficulties was to preserve the middle position between the extremes. On the one hand Nehru, who came to see me early in November, seemed persuaded that we were pursuing a dangerous if not sinister policy. Although he had some justification for his suspicions in the speeches made by the extremists at home and in Central Africa, nevertheless the fundamental obstacle to peace was Tshombe's character.

Congo temporarily better. But I think we must now bring pressure on Belgian, American, and perhaps French Governments to join with us in urging Tshombe to negotiate now. If not, civil war is certain and in the end Communists will gain. Perhaps Sir Roy Welensky will help us over this.[2]

Yet the truce was only temporary.

Tshombe does not yet see the need to do a deal with the Central Government while Adoula (moderate) is still able to control Gizenga.[3]

As the weeks passed the state of tension rose. By the end of October,

the situation is again deteriorating. Tshombe is not amenable to advice. Adoula is losing patience. It is a bad prospect. We are to make another attempt to persuade Tshombe (who has gone to Geneva for medical treatment) to meet Adoula.[4]

[1] 22 September 1961.
[2] 23 September 1961.
[3] 11 October 1961.
[4] 30 October 1961.

Welensky was now in England, and I felt that the opportunity might be taken to make some kind of plan. I reminded the Foreign Secretary on 8 November that

> the difficulties are certainly formidable but the dangers of in-action are also great. The more I think of it the more I believe that we must use all our effort now to get Tshombe and Adoula to meet. If they cannot agree to meet outside the Congo, could we not construct some neutral place inside the Congo—a sort of raft of Tilsit? The more the situation drags on the more difficult it will be for us.
>
> I should be very interested to hear how you get on preparing a scheme with Sir Roy. I would willingly send a message to the President if you think this would help with the Americans.

Unhappily, time was running out; disorder was growing through-out the country, troops from Stanleyville went on the rampage and killed thirteen Italian pilots of the United Nations force. In other parts of the country foreigners, mercenaries, and African soldiers were creating disorder, and in spite of the truce the United Nations forces seemed to be preparing a fresh attempt to take over Katanga. On 13 November I had a long talk with Welensky, who took a sensible line. He seemed fully to understand 'that Tshombe ought to negotiate with Adoula and that it's "now or never".'[1] But Tshombe, so far from making any real effort to come to terms with Adoula, contented himself with an appeal to the British Government to take a stand against further intervention.

When the Security Council met on 24 November a resolution was proposed condemning the secessionist tendencies of Katanga and giving U Thant (acting Secretary-General) greater latitude in removing foreign mercenaries. Since the Russians vetoed amend-ments designed to make these two points clearer and more accept-able, France and Britain abstained and the resolution was carried by nine votes to none. However, the acting Secretary-General made a good speech in which he stressed that he would use con-ciliation rather than coercion. Unhappily, Tshombe was becoming more and more recalcitrant. His threats were followed by a number

[1] 13 November 1961.

of violent actions and attacks upon the United Nations officials. It even seemed that Tshombe himself had lost control; open hostilities appeared inevitable. Dr. O'Brien, having resigned from his United Nations post, appeared to accuse Britain and France of obstructing his work in the Congo. Nkrumah joined in with protests and Nehru with appeals. The Cabinet still felt determined that there should be a political solution by conciliation and not by reconquest. Tshombe's position was weakening, and there seemed every chance of obtaining the purpose of unifying the Congo without the horrors of open war.

At this point a sudden storm blew up with considerable repercussions at home. This was wholly unexpected and proved exceedingly troublesome.

There has been an internal political crisis, which has been both acute and dangerous. It arose out of a decision of the Cabinet, taken at 10.30 p.m. on Thursday 7 December, to supply twenty-four 1,000 lb. bombs to United Nations for their operation in the Congo, against the attacks of the Katanga forces. The Foreign Secretary—and Foreign Office—had been resisting this demand for some weeks, but it came to a head because of the damage which (it was claimed) the 'pirate' aircraft working for Tshombe were doing to United Nations troops. These, of course, comprise troops from our Commonwealth countries. Eventually, after grave doubts expressed by many Ministers . . . the Cabinet agreed to supply the bombs, with the clear restriction that they would only be used against aircraft on the ground or airstrips and airfields. The next day, I heard (with some relief) that United Nations Headquarters had refused the restrictions and asked us to reconsider [them]. We refused. Then (unhappily) United Nations agreed [to the restrictions].

This was on the Friday (8 December). . . . By the evening, and during Sunday, there was a lot of telephoning, and I realised that we were in for a row. The official announcement that we were supplying the bombs came out on Friday night. By Monday morning both Conservative M.P.s and Conservative Press were in full cry. Meanwhile (perhaps luckily) the United Nations officials on the spot were giving some very indiscreet interviews to the Press, suggesting an interpretation of their objectives as

P2

something amounting to 'imposing a political settlement' by conquering the Katanga forces, even if this involved the collapse of any administration in Katanga.

After a meeting of all the Ministers who could be got together, Heath (Lord Privy Seal) made a statement saying that in view of all the uncertainty, we would hold up delivery of the bombs. It was a long statement, very well done, but led to a tremendous pressure of questioning from both sides of the House.[1]

There was much discussion as to what action should now be taken. In the end we decided

to make a direct appeal to the [Acting] Secretary-General, asking for a cease-fire and for negotiations between the various Congo personalities. This we did on Tuesday night, and also put a motion down, for debate on Thursday (14th) on a Government motion 'approving' our actions.[1]

In reporting to the Queen on 13 December on this affair I wrote:

Your Majesty will have seen the trouble we got into over the Congo. I will be quite frank, and say that I think we were put into an impossible position by the United Nations Secretariat last week. We were given the impression that their troops were in a rather desperate condition and unless these bombs could be made available we would become responsible for their being in a perilous, and perhaps a fatal situation. Very reluctantly therefore, all the more reluctantly because we knew these were not the instruments which any skilful Air Force would use, but subject to the conditions which we obtained in writing, we agreed to send them. The 1,000 lb. bomb however became the detonator of a kiloton row, which threatened yesterday to become almost a megaton row in the House of Commons. The absence of the Foreign Secretary in Paris has made things a little more difficult, but we have now put down a Motion on which I hope it will be possible to rally the Conservative Party and maintain Your Majesty's present Ministers in office. It has been an anxious period and we shall not be through until the Division is taken tomorrow night.

[1] 18 December 1961.

I had a useful talk with Kennedy on the telephone on this and other matters and I was glad to hear from him that the Secretary of State and other members of his staff were now definitely on record as favouring reconciliation rather than conquest. Meanwhile,

the position in the Party was very tense on Monday and Tuesday. My 'supplementaries' at Question Time on Tuesday helped —this was a tactical error of Gaitskell and Wilson. They should have let a formal question and reply go without further ado. But they asked a lot of supplementaries which gave me the chance of a little speech—or series of speeches—comforting to my own side. On Wednesday I saw the Executive Committee, and on Thursday the debate. For some reason (I suppose, age and infirmity) I have felt this 'crisis' far more than I should have done—have worried, and slept badly, and so on. All the same forces are being mobilised as were at Suez.[1]

As so often in these storms the actual occasion for the trouble is not the same as its ultimate cause. Accustomed to criticism from a few extremists I could usually tell when there was real danger.

The trouble in the Party is that in addition to the small group of people who really hate me . . . the anxiety about United Nations performance in the Congo had spread to the whole *centre* of the Party. Nor do I blame them. For U Thant, under Afro-Asian pressure, and through the incredible folly and weakness (mixed with vanity) of Adlai Stevenson (United States Representative at United Nations), has gone on relentlessly (or, rather, allowed the United Nations military command in Congo to go on) with an attack on Élisabethville, regardless of civilian lives or material danger. They do not seem to realise that if they 'win' the battle, they will be in the same position as Britain and other Colonial Powers have often had to face—they will be forced to 'take over' and administer Katanga. At the same time Adoula . . . will fall, and Gizenga ([who is] Communist-trained . . .) will take over.[1]

The much advertised debate took place on 14 December. As so commonly in these confused situations, there were really three separate views. The Opposition, urged on by their more extreme

[1] 18 December 1961.

friends, seemed to have adopted the thesis that it was the duty of the United Nations forces to destroy the Katanga Government by hook or crook, regardless of loss of life and property, and having brought about its fall, after a long or a short campaign, to hand over the province to the Central Government. This plan necessarily involved the risk of a repetition of the tragic scenes of destruction which had already taken place at Élisabethville, where hospitals, railway stations and national buildings had been destroyed and heavy civilian casualties incurred. The right wing of the Conservative Party, supported by much of the Press, believed that the only way to solve the problem was by an independent Katanga, managing its own affairs under Tshombe, or some other leader, in friendly co-operation with its neighbours, especially the Central African Federation.

The Government took a middle course. We wished to see the mercenaries removed, as they had already been over a great part of the country, with the minimum of force. We believed that the United Nations troops were insufficient and unsuitable to a reconquest, which would, even if achieved, leave the real problem unresolved. In our view the United Nations troops should try to keep open the routes of communication; they should defend themselves if attacked—hence the tangled story of the bombs which we had been told were to be used only to attack airstrips and airfields from which the United Nations forces were threatened; but, above all, the United Nations representative should only intervene to prevent civil war and to maintain order. Apart from such operations, their purpose should be to negotiate a truce and ultimately a peace. It will be seen that the British Government's policy was harder to support in logic than perhaps to carry out in fact. Nevertheless, it represented the true interests both of the peoples of the Congo and of the outside world.

Fortunately the Opposition leaders made a fundamental error of tactics. When a Government is in trouble with its own side (there was talk of a large number of hostile votes and abstentions), a skilful manager will leave most of the debate to the Government's own critics. He will adopt a sympathetic even unctuous attitude towards the rebellious forces. Above all he should not attack them for being actuated by selfish or improper motives. In other words if he sees a gaping wound opening in his enemy's side he should not try to staunch the blood or apply a tourniquet—he should let the opponent whom he wishes to supplant bleed slowly to death.

On this occasion Wilson, leading for the Opposition, did exactly the opposite. The end of his speech—his first effort as shadow Foreign Secretary instead of shadow Chancellor of the Exchequer —was so violent as to make many even of his own side feel somewhat ashamed. Although brilliant and witty, his jibes and insinuations failed in their purpose. The moment he sat down I felt comforted.

Heath had opened the debate 'with a quiet, well-constructed, and effective speech'.[1] At the very beginning he fastened upon the Labour Party's weak point; for they, to use modern terminology, were the 'hawks' and we were the 'doves'. He said:

> I have moved a Motion asking the House for support in the formal application that we have made to the Secretary-General of the United Nations for an immediate cease-fire in these circumstances. The right hon. Gentleman the Leader of the Opposition and his right hon. and hon. Friends have put down an Amendment censuring the Government, and rejecting any appeal for a cease-fire. It must be the first time in our history that the British Labour Party has openly rejected an appeal for a cease-fire.

The debate was full of interest, and through the day turned steadily in our favour. 'Gaitskell wound up well—the first part academic, the second part rhetorical—both good.'[1] When I came to reply I confined myself to a few simple points; but by then my Party was well in hand. I was able to rebuke

> the usual smears in which the right hon. Gentleman the Member for Huyton (Mr. H. Wilson) engages. That right hon. Gentleman tried all that stuff about big business with Lord Poole, but it did not go over very well.

After setting out the story of our support—moral and material —throughout the whole sad episode, I continued:

> I come to the question of conciliation. . . . We were in favour,

[1] 18 December 1961.

of course, of removing the mercenaries. We did all we could to help. We wondered in September whether the methods used, leading to so much destruction and so many deaths, were really tolerable. It was for that reason that we appealed to the former Secretary-General and for that reason, after discussion with Lord Lansdowne, that it was the Secretary-General who decided that a cease-fire was necessary. It was he who did it.

We tried all we could for a negotiation between Tshombe and Adoula. Reference to this has already been made by my hon. Friends below the Gangway. We tried to establish a basis on which a unified Congo could function in peace and work out its destiny. We did not succeed. Unhappily, all those countries working with us—owing to conflicts which are only too well known—[Interruption]. In any case we tried to establish a meeting between Adoula and Tshombe, and so did our American friends along with us.

We tried with our Ambassador at Léopoldville and our Consul at Élisabethville, and it would be right for me now to pay tribute to the remarkable men we have had to represent our country during this crisis. Early in the year hopes were high. September put them back. We tried again. Then Adoula, as Premier of the whole of the Congo, suggested that Tshombe should go to Léopoldville. Tshombe refused, partly from fear as well as from dignity. . . .

We then suggested, and I think the Americans had the same idea, that Tshombe and Adoula might meet on neutral ground—perhaps in a boat or on a raft in the river and I think that the Americans even suggested an aeroplane. We have had no success so far. That is more likely to come when the fighting has stopped and a period of recovery has been allowed. Of course it is possible that Tshombe, obviously a very difficult man—(Hon. Members: 'Oh'.)—yes, they are all very difficult characters; all fairly tough characters. It is possible that he may fall. He may be destroyed. . . . His administration may collapse. What worries me is . . . that the United Nations will find itself with a province as large as France on its hands and no means at all of governing it.

It was then necessary to tell again the story of the bombs with all its complications. But by this time interest had passed from this incident which undoubtedly we had handled clumsily. One passage about the actual financial support received by the United Nations for the Congo operation amused the House.

> There is the question of the monetary subscription. I believe that we are one of the—is it?—nine Powers which have paid up as against eighty-seven which have not. The curious thing is—and I want to deal with this point because it is important—that there are two forms of subscription to the Congo. There is the compulsory subscription and the voluntary subscription. The only difference between them is this. The compulsory is the one that you do not pay if you do not want to, and the voluntary is the one that you need not pay unless you wish to. At present, Russia, which solemnly votes on and vetoes resolutions on this matter, has not paid a penny either by way of compulsory or voluntary subscription.

Before I sat down I was able to announce that U Thant had, within the last hour or two, reaffirmed his decision to achieve reconciliation by peaceful means and was sending two of his most trusted colleagues to Léopoldville with instructions to this end. When the vote was taken

> the majority for us was *ninety-four*. It ought to have been ninety-six—but two chaps were 'locked out'. We had ten or so 'abstentions'—and the Socialists had about the same number absent unpaired. A good result.[1]

I had the most charming letter on 15 December from Home regretting the unhappy episode of the bomb, but thanking me for my support throughout. He wisely observed that

> perhaps in the end it will be all for the best that the underlying trouble burst through to the surface. The Party's frustration with the U.N. had been on the boil for a long time.

My own reflections were as follows:

> This whole episode has been instructive and difficult. I was determined *not* to yield to the right-wing who are against United Nations in principle, and yet to maintain our right and duty to criticise United Nations when we think their Secretariat is committing follies from ignorance and inexperience.[1]

[1] 18 December 1961.

But the vote in the House of Commons although satisfactory did not solve our problems. The President, while ready to make every effort to get Tshombe and Adoula to agree, regarded this as a last chance. Happily, a meeting was soon arranged and a 'sort of cease-fire' followed. This with the prospective adjournment of the House of Commons for the Christmas holidays at least offered some relief. My own thoughts were no doubt unduly pessimistic:

> The United Nations army consists (with the exception of the Swedes, who have not fought anybody for two hundred years, and of the Irish, who will fight anybody) of a queer lot. The chances of being a survivor if you are wounded in this war are said to be slender. You are likely to be killed . . . either by the backward races of Congolese or by the advance guard of civilisation represented in the United Nations army. Yesterday, an Ethiopian soldier shot a Swiss banker in Élisabethville with a bazooka. No one knows why, and no one cares. But even Swiss bankers ought to have some rights.[1]

On 20 December Tshombe and Adoula met in Kitona, and signed an agreement to end the secession. Whether it would last or not was a very different thing, but at least there was some chance of a pause. I was now due to meet the President at Bermuda before Christmas. While awaiting his arrival I summarised my impressions of the internal political situation.

> The recent political crisis in House of Commons has been interesting. The Conservative Party in Parliament has been much shaken. The real reason is that Members (who have up to now shut their eyes to the realities of the modern world) have been rudely awakened. Britain (or France, or Germany, or any European Power) can no longer exert a decisive influence on these world events. United Nations, driven on by the Afro-Asians and the 'unaligned', with their bitter 'anti-colonial' complex, and supported spiritually and financially by the United States can do what they like. Of course, Britain can resign (as many Conservatives would prefer). But then we lose *all* influence. What we *can* do (and did very successfully in the last few days) is to try to get the President and the Secretary of State to exert themselves,

[1] 19 December 1961.

instead of leaving the direction to the Adlai Stevensons and other half-baked 'liberals', whom they commonly employ (for internal political reasons) at United Nations. But it's a laborious process.

The public, as opposed to Parliament, were puzzled. The left-wing Press (*Guardian*, etc.) was very hostile to Government, for having 'betrayed' United Nations by refusing the 1,000 lb. bomb and asking for a cease-fire. But the *Mirror* (which started on this line with tremendous gusto–'Traitor Macmillan' in immense letters) soon changed its tune. I think the public was rather shocked by the indiscriminate shooting [by forces] of United Nations–hospitals, women, children–and this affected even the Socialist Party in House of Commons. After all, to call for a cease-fire is not something in itself disgraceful or reprehensible.

Fortunately, we got a kind of cease-fire and a meeting of the two leaders before I left [for Bermuda].

But apart from the actual occasion for this revolt (which at one time seemed to be likely to destroy the Government) there was revealed a hard core–ten to twenty M.P.s on our side who are so bitter against me and my 'progressive' colleagues that they will use every difficulty or every critical situation to work up a large-scale revolt. They cannot normally attract the 'respectable' or 'middle' opinion in the Party. But they can get some of them in on a special issue–e.g. Queen's visit to Ghana, Congo, breach of Pay Pause by Electricity Settlement, Immigration Bill, Loans to Coal Industry, etc. Whether the recent 'shock' to the mass of ordinary Members will have a salutary effect, I don't know. But I think few want a dissolution or a break-up of the Government.

Meanwhile . . . the Cabinet and the Government as a whole seem in good heart.[1]

Although the troubles of the Congo were to continue with varying degrees of acuteness for another two years, they became more of an irritant than a serious danger. As with a fever the crisis had been reached and passed–although the period of convalescence was long and fitful, with many setbacks. Indeed the austere editor of the *Annual Register* for 1961 writes of the Congo:

The year had seen an increase in political stability and a return, over much of the country, to something like normal conditions,

[1] 20 December 1961.

thanks to the unobtrusive work of United Nations troops and technical experts.[1]

He might perhaps have added a modest tribute to the conciliatory influence of the British Government.

[1] *Annual Register*, *1961*, p. 318.

CHAPTER XVII

A Royal Enterprise

IN the task of strengthening the links which still bind together all the countries of the Commonwealth, old and new, no role has been more important than that played by the Crown. Nearly all the new members of non-British descent and traditions have not unnaturally abandoned their monarchical constitution; but they have all been glad to accept the concept of the Monarch as Head of the Commonwealth. Yet the maintenance of this vital connection would hardly be possible on purely theoretical grounds. We owe it to the character and personality of the Queen herself and of the other members of her family, who by their constant visits and outstanding charm have carried the Commonwealth through this hazardous period.

The Queen's visit to West Africa unavoidably postponed two years before had been provisionally arranged for November 1961. But this proved a difficult year for the new Republic of Ghana. Nkrumah—now President—and his Party had been in power since independence. In the absence of an effective Opposition, the political situation was beginning to show signs of strain. The financial position, in spite of the substantial surplus which the new Government inherited at the time of independence, had deteriorated, largely as a result of extravagance and over-hasty and ambitious plans for development in every field. Consequently an unpopular budget in the summer (framed on the advice of distinguished economists) led to widespread strikes and unrest. A growing sense of uncertainty was beginning to tarnish the high hopes with which Ghana's independence had been launched. A one-Party Government—and something like a police state—was emerging. It was in this atmosphere, as well as against a background of the confusion and disorder now raging in the Congo, that the question of the Queen's proposed visit must now be reviewed.

My own relations with Nkrumah continued to be friendly. Although I resented some of his speeches and actions, yet we always maintained an amicable dialogue. In the course of September the new President, who had become addicted to foreign travel, made an extended tour of Eastern Europe; in addition, he visited both the Soviet Union and China. In the course of his journeys he delivered a number of speeches attacking 'Western colonialism' on familiar lines. On 22 September, after his return to Accra, he took the serious step of dismissing Major-General H. T. Alexander, the British officer commanding the Army who had done so much to bring the local troops into a high state of training and efficiency.

> The situation in Ghana is bad. Nkrumah has come back from Russia in a dangerous mood. He is throwing out General Alexander, and the British officers. All British officials (except [Geoffrey] Bing . . . and perhaps [Nicholas] Kaldor) . . . will probably be ejected also. I agreed (by telephone) a message which Commonwealth Secretary should send. I think he will have to go out himself and see what he can do.[1]

A day or two later I received a long letter dated 26 September from Nkrumah defending his actions. He said that he was distressed by the acrimony which had developed in the newspapers of our two countries, and which, if unchecked, might jeopardise 'the friendliness, frankness and the mutual confidence and trust which characterised our relations in the past'. Admittedly there were important and fundamental differences in the attitude of Ghana and the United Kingdom—Ghana was non-aligned so far as the two great power blocs were concerned, and this led to some conflict of views with the United Kingdom. But several other countries in the Commonwealth were in a similar situation, and such differences should not disturb the friendly relations which had always existed between the different politically independent member States.

> Recently, however, a new element has been brought into the picture—the suggestion, or rather the insinuation (for it is never overtly expressed) that Ghana, under my leadership, is veering more and more towards the Eastern bloc, and that there has been

[1] 23 September 1961.

some implicit or secret understanding with the U.S.S.R. or associated countries, which compromises Ghana's fundamental position of neutrality, or her freedom to pursue her own foreign policy according to her inclinations or interests.

Let me assure you that this is entirely without foundation. My visit to the U.S.S.R. and to other Eastern countries has been undoubtedly very fruitful—we have much to learn from them, for they have a unique experience on the particular problem of how to accelerate the industrialisation, and how to overcome the trained manpower shortage of undeveloped countries like Ghana. We are hoping to receive from the Russians increased technical assistance in regard to some of our problems, just as we are also expecting increased technical assistance from Britain, the United States and Canada; and the fact that we are free, and are anxious to receive help from all quarters must not be taken as an indication that we are leaning on some countries more than others.

Nkrumah went on to defend various economic measures that Ghana had taken, and then raised the point which had caused us particular misgiving:

Another factor which may contribute to misunderstanding is my recent decision to terminate the arrangement by which General Alexander served as Chief of the Defence Staff of all the Armed Forces of Ghana. This was a political decision which had nothing whatever to do with my assessment of General Alexander's character and abilities, or the very high regard I hold for the admirable and exceptional manner in which he carried out his duties, and his unique services in developing the defence forces of the country. The reason was simply that I felt that the stage had been reached—just as it had been reached earlier in the case of other former members of the old colonial Empire—when the command of the armed forces could be entrusted to the country's own nationals.

Time was to show that the removal of the British commander was, by a strange nemesis, to lead to Nkrumah's ultimate fall. Meanwhile, this letter was at least frank, if in parts a little disingenuous. I replied on 28 September in a friendly tone:

Thank you for your letter, which I have just received. As

you say, there has been a regrettable deterioration in public feelings between our countries in recent months. I fully share your desire to see this put right.

I am most grateful to you for the explanation and assurances in your letter about Ghana's policy of non-alignment. After all, it is the policy of several important Commonwealth countries. We have never criticised your 'unaligned' attitude, or sought to influence you to change it. I am very glad to know that there are no grounds for the anxieties which have been felt that a shift of policy was taking place.

Whilst I greatly value personal correspondence with you and other Commonwealth Prime Ministers, there is nothing like a frank talk for clearing up misunderstandings. I had hoped that you might perhaps have been passing through London on your way home from Russia; but maybe another opportunity for a meeting between us will occur before long. In the meantime I think there would be much value in a talk between yourself and Duncan Sandys. I am glad therefore that you agree with the suggestion put to you by our High Commissioner that Sandys should pay an early visit to Accra for this purpose.

The next day I received a message from Home who was in New York expressing considerable alarm. His talks with the Ghanaian officials had not encouraged him, while the line taken by Ghana's representative in the Assembly had been wholly destructive. He added:

I fear the evidence is mounting that they are very unfriendly and are much too well in with the Communist bloc. One cannot help being anxious in these circumstances about the Queen's visit. I would value an early word with you after I return.

In reply I informed the Foreign Secretary that I had already arranged for Sandys to go to Accra and said that the best plan would be to wait until his return to discuss the whole question. In my letter of 30 September to the Queen, who was by now in Scotland, after dealing with a number of other pressing questions, I wrote:

With regard to Ghana, I think Your Majesty agreed that we should wait for a final decision about your visit until Mr.

Sandys returns, but I was glad to feel that Your Majesty's inclination, if security and similar considerations allow, was to continue with the visit. To cancel it would be a great act of policy on our side, and almost a declaration that we did not want Ghana in the Commonwealth. That would be a very grave step and not one to be lightly entertained.

Unhappily, by 3 October, the local situation was clearly deteriorating. Some of Nkrumah's leading colleagues including Mr. K. A. Gbedemah and Mr. Kojo Botsio were dismissed and a few days later some fifty persons who were Nkrumah's political opponents were arrested and imprisoned. These included Dr. Danquah, the veteran Opposition leader; Mr. J. E. Appiah, the son-in-law of Sir Stafford Cripps; and a number of other figures, some well known as parliamentarians and others as trade unionists. The setting up of a special court to deal with 'crimes against the state' was another ominous development. Nevertheless the talks between the Commonwealth Secretary and Nkrumah seemed satisfactory and the issue of a communiqué professing goodwill and mutual understanding did something to clear the air. On 10 October a full discussion took place with all my colleagues; as a result of which I was authorised 'to advise the Queen to go on with the Ghana visit, unless the situation gets worse there'.[1]

In communicating this formal advice to the Queen I repeated our strong view that although planning for the visit to Ghana and the rest of West Africa should continue, the position must be looked at continuously, the main consideration being Her Majesty's personal safety. One step I took immediately. I sent a long message to President Kennedy on 18 October informing him confidentially about our hesitations and fears.

I have discussed this with Her Majesty. She is of course a person of great courage, and is determined to carry out the visit and to complete the programme unless she is specifically advised by the Government that she should not do so. We are keeping the position under constant review, and if there appears to be a further deterioration in Ghana we may be compelled to advise the Queen not to go. But this would probably have the effect of

[1] 10 October 1961.

driving Ghana out of the Commonwealth, and might even push them into Russian hands. I am sure you will agree with me that this is something we ought to do all we can to prevent.

I know that at present the American Government has under consideration their financial contribution to the Volta Dam project and that an American Mission is paying a visit to Ghana next week to look at the general political situation there. It may be therefore that the American Government will reach a final decision during the early part of November.

I should be very grateful for your help on the timing of any announcement you may make. If you were to decide to go ahead with your contribution it would be a great help if this could be announced before the Queen's visit, which is due to start on 9 November. It would have a calming effect throughout Ghana and would go a long way towards reducing the general temperature. If on the other hand you decide that you cannot go ahead then I would earnestly ask you not to let this be known until after the Queen has left Ghana, which will be on 20 November. Were such an announcement to be made whilst the Queen was actually in Ghana it would almost certainly exacerbate a situation which is already tense and difficult, and might seriously increase the risk to her safety and well-being.

The President sent an immediate reply promising to do his best. At any rate he would avoid a negative answer at an inconvenient moment.

On 19 October there was a debate in the House of Commons on Africa and African problems. There was naturally some reference to recent developments in Ghana and demands by some members for the cancellation of the Queen's visit as a mark of disapproval. More serious was the advice reaching me from statesmen for whom I had the deepest personal respect.

> Both Churchill and Eden are concerned about the Queen's visit to Ghana. Churchill has written a long letter, to which I have replied. I have sent copies to the Queen. In the debate last night, the question was raised on both sides. I am sure that this question ought *not* to be decided on political grounds. The only real question is the safety of the Queen.[1]

[1] 19 October 1961.

It was clear to me that to cancel the visit as a political gesture would be wrong. It would be contrary to British tradition and injurious to the personal position of the Queen. Moreover the only result would be to help the Russians, who were already about to send a military mission, to move in permanently. If at the last moment we felt the risks were too great, I was determined to avoid cancellation but to persuade Nkrumah to seek a postponement on some plausible grounds.

At the beginning of November I was still hesitating.

> I have heard no more about Ghana. The Queen is due to leave on [the 9th]. I don't know whether to let her go or to cancel it. There is danger either way. On the whole, my inclination is to have faith. My colleagues have, in effect, left it to me to decide.[1]

I naturally kept the leading figures in the Commonwealth fully informed. Bob Menzies in a most friendly message of 1 November remarked with truth that

> the best that can be done in such matters is to strike a realistic balance of risks and advantages making sure that the factor of safety is given special weight. This, I know, is the way in which you have approached it and I respect your judgement.

However, this, although an admirable statement of the case, did not get us much further.

On 3 November I wrote a long memorandum to the Queen setting out the situation. I stated frankly that many of my colleagues were very unhappy about the decision to go forward, and of course there would be a large section of public opinion which, apart from the question of the Queen's safety, wished for the visit to be postponed because of Nkrumah's recent actions and speeches. On political grounds I had no hesitation in giving my advice. The question of safety was the only one at issue.

> The decisive argument therefore must be Your Majesty's personal security. We have had a number of consultations about the security situation in Ghana. Our contacts have included the British community in Ghana, among them Sir Robert Jackson,

[1] 3 November 1961.

who has been there for many years and who knows the Ghanaians extremely well; and the many British business firms with contacts spread throughout the whole territory. We have talked to a considerable number of British and Irish members of the Ghanaian Police Force who, though loyal to their Corps, are ready to speak freely about the security position as it might affect Your Majesty. The Commonwealth Secretary paid a visit to Ghana. There has been a visit by a senior member of Scotland Yard's Special Branch and we have had an assessment prepared of the situation by the Security Services. . . . All these people are agreed that there is no foreseen risk of any violence to Your Majesty or any expression of hostility being directed against Your Majesty at any time during the visit.

There remains the possibility of some attempt being made to kill or harm Dr. Nkrumah whilst he is in Your Majesty's company. This is perhaps a remote risk, but Dr. Nkrumah seems less ready than he used to be to appear in public, and it is therefore a question which must be considered. But our assessment is that the Ghana populace has respect and affection for Your Majesty; that the people are cowed by the Government's repressive measures, and the scale of protection to be provided by the Ghana Government will be massive. Moreover, during my Audience of Your Majesty last night I was told that it would be possible for Your Majesty personally to reduce to a minimum the number of occasions for driving about in a motor car with Dr. Nkrumah. If there were any risk here it would be less likely to arise in the crowded cities than on empty roads in between the villages.

Unhappily, on 4 November, there came through the news of a serious bomb explosion in Accra which brought further doubts.

We were on the telephone all the morning—to Commonwealth Secretary; to Foreign Secretary; Sir Norman Brook; Sir Michael Adeane (at Windsor) and others.

We decided just before luncheon that (if Nkrumah agreed) Sandys should leave tonight—Sunday—for Accra to report to us. The Queen is by way of leaving on Thursday morning. At 6 p.m. I heard that everything (including the Press Statements) had been arranged. So I motored to London to see and talk with Sandys for half an hour before he left. I am terribly worried about all this. There is so much to lose and so little (except rather impalpable) to be gained.[1]

I was enormously indebted to Duncan Sandys for his persistence and courage throughout this difficult time. Before he went out I sent him a note on 5 November in the following terms:

I am most grateful to you for your willingness to fly out to Accra for a discussion with President Nkrumah about the Queen's Visit. I am sure that this is a wise move and will enable us to keep opinion steady both in the House and in the country. I have spoken to the Palace and know that the Queen feels reassured by your proposed visit.

I think it would be right to say, in explaining to the Press here the reasons for your visit, that you felt it right to discuss the position personally with Nkrumah since you felt it would be wrong to expect the High Commissioner to make the final recommendation. We are dealing with the life of the Queen . . . and it would be reasonable for the final recommendation to Cabinet to be made by a Cabinet Minister and not by an official.

In your talks with President Nkrumah you should say that Ministers here feel an extremely heavy weight of responsibility for the Queen's position. You naturally wish to satisfy the Cabinet as a result of personal conversations with him that the security position is completely under control and that all precautions for the Queen's safety that can be taken have been taken.

In the course of discussion on this point the question may be raised whether you should stay in Ghana during at any rate part of the Queen's Visit. I am rather against this as it touches on difficult constitutional points and would not add to the Queen's safety. Unless, therefore, you are pressed by Dr. Nkrumah to stay I think you should return to this country before the Queen leaves on 9 November.

You should take the opportunity of your talks with Dr. Nkrumah to refer to other matters—in particular the position of General Alexander and the future of the constitutional position of Ghana. On this latter point you could ask him for his assessment of future constitutional developments in Ghana referring to the recent rumours which have been circulating about the

[1] 5 November 1961.

possibility of Ghana leaving the Commonwealth. You could say that if this were to happen so soon after the Queen's Visit as to connect the two events in people's minds, this would be a great affront to the Queen and that there would be wide repercussions; in particular, the United States might well wish to review their whole attitude towards Ghana and this might have serious effects upon the economic future of Ghana, and in particular on the Volta Dam project.

The plan which Duncan Sandys adopted has been explained by the compiler of the *Annual Register* in vivid terms. It was

> that often described by the formula 'try it on the dog'. Mr. Sandys, flying out to Ghana a second time within a few weeks and bravely assuming the role of the dog, drove with stately deliberation, accompanied by President Nkrumah, along the royal route in accordance with the projected royal timetable. He emerged to tell the tale.[1]

But, of course, as Sandys would have been the first to recognise, the real dog was not the Commonwealth Secretary but the President of Ghana. Accounts had reached us of Nkrumah's unwillingness to appear in public during recent months, and the rigorous internal measures that he was taking to defend his power increased the danger of an attempt on his life. Sandys, a man absolutely without fear, devised a plan to invite Nkrumah to join him in a tour of the whole Royal route, ostensibly to test efficiency of the timetable and the measures for control of the crowds. With his iron determination he cajoled or forced the reluctant President to drive with him in an open car, hoping by this experiment to reduce the danger to the Queen when the day came. For we were now becoming more and more confident that there would be no direct attempt upon the Queen. But there was undoubtedly a risk that she might become the victim of a bomb or bullet aimed at her host.

On 6 November there were a number of questions in the House of Commons asked by members anxious about the Queen's safety. I could only give an assurance that we would make no final decision until the Commonwealth Secretary returned. The same night

[1] *Annual Register, 1961*, p. 48.

The Chief Whip warned me ... that there was a growing feeling in the Conservative Party against the Queen going to Ghana. Although on Tuesday afternoon (when the first Press reports began to come through about the drive in an open car which Duncan Sandys had persuaded Nkrumah to make with him over the royal route) there was some amelioration, the Chief Whip was not sure what would result. If (after my statement, which must be on *Wednesday*, since the Queen was to leave *Thursday* morning) the Cabinet decide to advise the Queen to go, there would certainly be a motion for the adjournment. If the Labour Party saw their chance and voted *against* us (on the grounds of the Queen's security) at least eighty to one hundred Conservatives would be in the same lobby and the Government would be beaten.

This naturally worried me, although I felt the danger exaggerated. However, I thought it my duty to warn the Queen. For (if we were beaten) I would *not* repeat *not* alter my advice. I would resign—at (say) 11 p.m. The Queen (who was to leave at 9 a.m. [the next day] for London Airport) would no doubt have retired early. But she would no doubt see me. She could refuse my resignation, and ask me to carry on. I could agree, but I could not alter my advice. So the Queen would leave, with a *hostile* vote from House of Commons, and flouting *their* advice. I should no doubt be impeached. What would happen to her?

All this we discussed, at considerable length, during these anxious days, with a sort of mock seriousness. It all seemed too absurd to be true.[1]

In the event, after further consultation with the Queen and after hearing the Commonwealth Secretary's full report, I decided to advise her to adhere to the programme as arranged. I was encouraged by the fact that all the security authorities regarded the risks as no greater than in India, Pakistan, or even Belfast.

Fortunately, the instigators of this revolt in the Conservative ranks were very *good* men—worthy men, and only caring about the Queen's safety. It was led by John Morrison, Spencer Summers, and others of the same kind. John Morrison is, of course, *very* influential as Chairman of 1922. None of these are of

[1] 13 November 1961.

the self-advertising or embittered type. . . . So *nothing at all* got into the Press up to the end. . . .

I kept in close touch with Gaitskell throughout, who was most co-operative. Naturally on *political* grounds the Opposition favoured the visit. But they *could* have declared themselves unsatisfied on *security* grounds.[1]

By the time that I had to speak I had heard that those who had taken the lead in advising caution 'would *not* raise a demand for Debate but would yield to the Queen's wishes'.[1] Before making the statement in Parliament I sent appropriate messages to all the Commonwealth Prime Ministers. My announcement was in the following terms.

I told the House on Monday that I thought it right that my right hon. Friend the Commonwealth Secretary should pay a second visit to Ghana. This he has done and he returned to this country this morning. My colleagues and I have now had from him a full appreciation of the position based on his personal inquiries on the spot.

As I told the House on Monday, Her Majesty's safety is and must be our first consideration. Of course, no Royal tour is without risk. Her Majesty knows this as well as any Member of the House. She has never been deterred in undertaking previous tours because of the personal risk to herself, which is inevitable, especially when great crowds are assembled. Happily, she has come triumphantly through these trials with the enhanced affection and admiration of all.

After considering carefully and anxiously all the information before us, collected and assessed by those best qualified to do so, the Government have reached the conclusion that the degree of risk attached to this tour is no greater than that which has been present in many of her previous journeys.

There are those who will ask how this conclusion can be reconciled with the explosions which have taken place in Accra during the last few days. That was one of the questions which was in the forefront of my mind when I decided that it would be right for my right hon. Friend to visit Ghana again. He has given us his first-hand assessment of the significance of these incidents. While he was in Accra he took the opportunity to tour the Royal

[1] 13 November 1961.

route in company with President Nkrumah and he saw for himself the unmistakable friendliness of the crowds. We have also had throughout, as I have said, the expert advice, based on thorough investigation on the spot, of those in this country best qualified to do this sort of work. We have had the ready co-operation of the Ghanaian authorities.

I can assure the House that on the information and advice available to them the Government have formed the view that the explosions do not indicate any intention by those concerned to perpetrate acts of violence during the Queen's visit which would endanger Her Majesty's safety. We have, therefore, no reason to fear that this journey will involve any special and additional risk to Her Majesty's safety.

On the other hand, there can be no doubt the cancellation of this visit, so long promised and so eagerly awaited by the people of Ghana, would seriously impair the invaluable contribution made by Her Majesty's journeys towards the strengthening of the ties which bind together the many peoples of the Commonwealth.

Her Majesty's Government have therefore advised the Queen that she should proceed with her visit to Ghana. We are, of course, at once informing other Commonwealth Governments, with whom we have been in touch throughout.

May I, therefore, Mr. Speaker, on behalf of the whole House, send Her Majesty our warmest good wishes for the success of her West African tour and a safe return.

Gaitskell said a few words in admirable style and taste, and, in reply to further questions expressing the loyalty and affection of members for Her Majesty, I said:

I am sure that what the House has said will give the greatest pleasure to the Queen. Of course, we have all been anxious, as the right hon. Gentleman properly said, and the risks have to be weighed as best we can. All the life of royalty and the tours of Her Majesty involve considerable risks. She accepts them proudly. I am sure that the House will give her the greatest sense of strength in her task.

In my diary I recorded:

The Queen has been absolutely determined all through. She is grateful for M.P.s and Press concern about her safety, but she is impatient of the attitude towards her to treat her as a *woman*, and a film star or mascot. She has indeed 'the heart and stomach of a man'. She has great faith in the work she can do in the Commonwealth especially. If she were pressed too hard, and if Government and people here are determined to restrict her activities (including taking reasonably acceptable risks) I think she might be tempted to throw in her hand. She does *not* enjoy 'society'. She likes her horses. But she loves her duty and means to be a Queen and not a puppet.[1]

Although the decision when taken seemed to meet general approval in Parliament and among the public, yet it threw a terrible responsibility upon my shoulders. If anything went wrong I would be the guilty man. Sir Michael Adeane, the Queen's Private Secretary, who had been an admirable adviser throughout this whole affair, undertook to send me a telegram once if not twice a day as to the Queen's reception. It can be understood with what trepidation I received these messages during the next eight days—from the time the Queen arrived until she left Ghana. In the event the visit proved an outstanding success. The genial and warm-hearted people gave her an unprecedented reception. The whole tour was a continuous triumph. Journalists, who had covered many such trips, thought never had the people been so enthusiastic nor the Queen looked happier or more charming. A few morose voices were raised in some of the Press at home pointing out sourly that these demonstrations had no deep significance. Nevertheless, though this week was for me one of the most trying in my life, for the Queen it was proof of courage and devotion to duty which won the admiration of the world. When, a month later, President Kennedy decided in favour of supporting the Volta Dam project I could not help feeling that his decision was partly due to his chivalrous recognition of the resolution with which this Royal Enterprise had been undertaken and carried through to its triumphant end.

[1] 13 November 1961.

Appendix One

Address by Harold Macmillan to Members of both Houses of the Parliament of the Union of South Africa, Cape Town, 3 February 1960

It is a great privilege to be invited to address the members of both Houses of Parliament in the Union of South Africa. It is a unique privilege to do so in 1960, just half a century after the Parliament of the Union came to birth. I am most grateful to you all for giving me this opportunity, and I am especially grateful to your Prime Minister who invited me to visit this country and arranged for me to address you here today. My tour of Africa—parts of Africa—the first ever made by a British Prime Minister in office, is now, alas, nearing its end, but it is fitting that it should culminate in the Union Parliament here in Cape Town, in this historic city so long Europe's gateway to the Indian Ocean, and to the East.

As in all the other countries that I have visited, my stay has been all too short. I wish it had been possible for me to spend a longer time here, to see more of your beautiful country and to get to know more of your people, but in the past week I have travelled many hundreds of miles and met many people in all walks of life. I have been able to get at least some idea of the great beauty of your countryside, with its farms and its forests, mountains and rivers, and the clear skies and wide horizons of the veldt. I have also seen some of your great and thriving cities, and I am most grateful to your Government for all the trouble they have taken in making the arrangements which have enabled me to see so much in so short a time. Some of the younger members of my staff have told me that it has been a heavy programme, but I can assure you that my wife and I have enjoyed every moment of it. Moreover, we have been deeply moved by the warmth of our welcome. Wherever we have been, in town or in country, we have been received in a spirit of friendship and affection which has warmed our hearts, and we value this the more because we know it is an expression of your goodwill, not just to ourselves but to all the people of Britain.

It is, as I have said, a special privilege for me to be here in 1960 when you are celebrating what I might call the golden wedding of the Union. At such a

Q

time it is natural and right that you should pause to take stock of your position, to look back at what you have achieved, to look forward to what lies ahead.

In the fifty years of their nationhood the people of South Africa have built a strong economy founded upon a healthy agriculture and thriving and resilient industries. During my visit I have been able to see something of your mining industry, on which the prosperity of the country is so firmly based. I have seen your Iron and Steel Corporation and visited your Council of Scientific and Industrial Research at Pretoria. These two bodies, in their different ways, are symbols of a lively, forward-looking and expanding economy. I have seen the great city of Durban, with its wonderful port, and the skyscrapers of Johannesburg, standing where seventy years ago there was nothing but the open veldt. I have seen, too, the fine cities of Pretoria and Bloemfontein. This afternoon I hope to see something of your wine-growing industry, which so far I have only admired as a consumer.

No one could fail to be impressed with the immense material progress which has been achieved. That all this has been accomplished in so short a time is a striking testimony to the skill, energy and initiative of your people. We in Britain are proud of the contribution we have made to this remarkable achievement. Much of it has been financed by British capital. According to the recent survey made by the Union Government, nearly two-thirds of the oversea investment outstanding in the Union at the end of 1956 was British. That is after two staggering wars which have bled our economy white.

But that is not all. We have developed trade between us to our common advantage, and our economies are now largely interdependent. You export to us raw materials, food and gold. We in return send you consumer goods or capital equipment. We take a third of all your exports and we supply a third of all your imports. This broad traditional pattern of investment and trade has been maintained in spite of the changes brought by the development of our two economies, and it gives me great encouragement to reflect that the economies of both our countries, while expanding rapidly, have yet remained interdependent and capable of sustaining one another. If you travel round this country by train you will travel on South African rails made by Iscor. If you prefer to fly you can go in a British Viscount. Here is a true partnership, living proof of the interdependence between nations. Britain has always been your best customer and, as your new industries develop, we believe that we can be your best partners too.

In addition to building this strong economy within your own borders, you have also played your part as an independent nation in the world.

As a soldier in the First World War, and as a Minister in Sir Winston Churchill's Government in the Second, I know personally the value of the contribution which your forces made to victory in the cause of freedom. I know something, too, of the inspiration which General Smuts brought to us in Britain in our darkest hours. Again in the Korean crisis you played your full part. Thus in the testing times of war or aggression your statesmen and your soldiers have made their influence felt far beyond the African continent.

In the period of reconstruction, when Dr. Malan was your Prime Minister, your resources greatly assisted the recovery of the sterling area. In the post-war world now, in the no less difficult tasks of peace, your leaders in industry, commerce and finance continue to be prominent in world affairs today. Your readiness to provide technical assistance to the less well-developed parts of Africa is of immense help to the countries that receive it. It is also a source of strength to your friends in the Commonwealth and elsewhere in the Western World. You are collaborating in the work of the Commission for Technical Co-operation in Africa South of the Sahara, and now in the United Nations Economic Commission for Africa. Your Minister for External Affairs intends to visit Ghana later this year. All this proves your determination, as the most advanced industrial country of the continent, to play your part in the new Africa of today.

Sir, as I have travelled round the Union I have found everywhere, as I expected, a deep preoccupation with what is happening in the rest of the African continent. I understand and sympathise with your interest in these events, and your anxiety about them. Ever since the break-up of the Roman Empire one of the constant facts of political life in Europe has been the emergence of independent nations. They have come into existence over the centuries in different forms, with different kinds of Government, but all have been inspired by a deep, keen feeling of nationalism, which has grown as the nations have grown.

In the twentieth century, and especially since the end of the war, the processes which gave birth to the nation states of Europe have been repeated all over the world. We have seen the awakening of national consciousness in peoples who have for centuries lived in dependence upon some other power. Fifteen years ago this movement spread through Asia. Many countries there of different races and civilisations pressed their claim to an independent national life. Today the same thing is happening in Africa, and the most striking of all the impressions I have formed since I left London a month ago is of the strength of this African national consciousness. In different places it takes different forms, but it is happening everywhere. The wind of change is blowing through this continent, and, whether we like it or not, this growth of national consciousness is a political fact. We must all accept it as a fact, and our national policies must take account of it.

Of course, you understand this better than anyone. You are sprung from Europe, the home of nationalism, and here in Africa you have yourselves created a new nation. Indeed, in the history of our times yours will be recorded as the first of the African nationalisms, and this tide of national consciousness which is now rising in Africa is a fact for which you and we and the other nations of the Western World are ultimately responsible. For its causes are to be found in the achievements of Western civilisation, in the pushing forward of the frontiers of knowledge, in the applying of science in the service of human needs, in the expanding of food production, in the speeding and multiplying of the means of communication, and perhaps, above all, the spread of education.

As I have said, the growth of national consciousness in Africa is a political fact, and we must accept it as such. That means, I would judge, that we must come to terms with it. I sincerely believe that if we cannot do so we may imperil the precarious balance between the East and West on which the peace of the world depends. The world today is divided into three main groups. First there are what we call the Western Powers. You in South Africa and we in Britain belong to this group, together with our friends and allies in other parts of the Commonwealth. In the United States of America and in Europe we call it the Free World. Secondly there are the Communists—Russia and her satellites in Europe and China whose population will rise by the end of the next ten years to the staggering total of 800,000,000. Thirdly, there are those parts of the world whose people are at present uncommitted either to Communism or to our Western ideas.

In this context we think first of Asia and then of Africa. As I see it the great issue in this second half of the twentieth century is whether the uncommitted peoples of Asia and Africa will swing to the East or to the West. Will they be drawn into the Communist camp? Or will the great experiments in self-government that are now being made in Asia and Africa, especially within the Commonwealth, prove so successful, and by their example so compelling, that the balance will come down in favour of freedom and order and justice?

The struggle is joined, and it is a struggle for the minds of men. What is now on trial is much more than our military strength or our diplomatic and administrative skill. It is our way of life. The uncommitted nations want to see before they choose.

What can we show them to help them choose right? Each of the independent members of the Commonwealth must answer that question for itself. It is a basic principle of our modern Commonwealth that we respect each other's sovereignty in matters of internal policy. At the same time we must recognise that in this shrinking world in which we live today the internal policies of one nation may have effects outside it. We may sometimes be tempted to say to each other, 'Mind your own business,' but in these days I would myself expand the old saying so that it runs: 'Mind your own business, but mind how it affects my business, too.'

Let me be very frank with you, my friends. What Governments and Parliaments in the United Kingdom have done since the war in according independence to India, Pakistan, Ceylon, Malaya and Ghana, and what they will do for Nigeria and other countries now nearing independence, all this, though we take full and sole responsibility for it, we do in the belief that it is the only way to establish the future of the Commonwealth and of the Free World on sound foundations. All this of course is also of deep and close concern to you for nothing we do in this small world can be done in a corner or remain hidden. What we do today in West, Central and East Africa becomes known tomorrow to everyone in the Union, whatever his language, colour or traditions. Let me assure you, in all friendliness, that we are well aware of this and that we have acted and will act with full knowledge of the responsibility we have to all our friends.

Nevertheless I am sure you will agree that in our own areas of responsibility we must each do what we think right. What we think right derives from a long experience both of failure and success in the management of our own affairs. We have tried to learn and apply the lessons of our judgement of right and wrong. Our justice is rooted in the same soil as yours—in Christianity and in the rule of law as the basis of a free society. This experience of our own explains why it has been our aim in the countries for which we have borne responsibility, not only to raise the material standards of living, but also to create a society which respects the rights of individuals, a society in which men are given the opportunity to grow to their full stature—and that must in our view include the opportunity to have an increasing share in political power and responsibility, a society in which individual merit and individual merit alone is the criterion for a man's advancement, whether political or economic.

Finally in countries inhabited by several different races it has been our aim to find means by which the community can become more of a community, and fellowship can be fostered between its various parts. This problem is by no means confined to Africa. Nor is it always a problem of a European minority. In Malaya, for instance, though there are Indian and European minorities, Malays and Chinese make up the great bulk of the population, and the Chinese are not much fewer in numbers than the Malays. Yet these two peoples must learn to live together in harmony and unity and the strength of Malaya as a nation will depend on the different contributions which the two races can make.

The attitude of the United Kingdom towards this problem was clearly expressed by the Foreign Secretary, Mr. Selwyn Lloyd, speaking at the United Nations General Assembly on 17 September 1959. These were his words:

> In those territories where different races or tribes live side by side the task is to ensure that all the people may enjoy security and freedom and the chance to contribute as individuals to the progress and well being of these countries. We reject the idea of any inherent superiority of one race over another. Our policy therefore is non-racial. It offers a future in which Africans, Europeans, Asians, the peoples of the Pacific and others with whom we are concerned, will all play their full part as citizens in the countries where they live, and in which feelings of race will be submerged in loyalty to new nations.

I have thought you would wish me to state plainly and with full candour the policy for which we in Britain stand. It may well be that in trying to do our duty as we see it we shall sometimes make difficulties for you. If this proves to be so we shall regret it. But I know that even so you would not ask us to flinch from doing our duty.

You, too, will do your duty as you see it. I am well aware of the peculiar nature of the problems with which you are faced here in the Union of South Africa. I know the differences between your situation and that of most of the other states in Africa. You have here some three million people of European origin. This country is their home. It has been their home for many generations. They have no other. The same is true of Europeans in Central and East Africa. In most other African states those who have come from Europe have come to work, to contribute their skills, perhaps to teach, but not to make a home.

The problems to which you as members of the Union Parliament have to address yourselves are very different from those which face the Parliaments of countries with homogenous populations. These are complicated and baffling problems. It would be surprising if your interpretation of your duty did not sometimes produce very different results from ours in terms of Government policies and actions.

As a fellow member of the Commonwealth it is our earnest desire to give South Africa our support and encouragement, but I hope you won't mind my saying frankly that there are some aspects of your policies which make it impossible for us to do this without being false to our own deep convictions about the political destinies of free men to which in our own territories we are trying to give effect. I think we ought, as friends, to face together, without seeking to apportion credit or blame, the fact that in the world of today this difference of outlook lies between us.

I said that I was speaking as a friend. I can also claim to be speaking as a relation, for we Scots can claim family connections with both the great European sections of your population, not only with the English-speaking people but with the Afrikaans-speaking as well. This is a point which hardly needs emphasis in Cape Town where you can see every day the statue of that great Scotsman, Andrew Murray. His work in the Dutch Reformed Church in the Cape, and the work of his son in the Orange Free State, was among Afrikaans-speaking people. There has always been a very close connection between the Church of Scotland and the Church of the Netherlands. The Synod of Dort plays the same great part in the history of both. Many aspirants to the Ministry of Scotland, especially in the seventeenth and eighteenth centuries, went to pursue their theological studies in the Netherlands. Scotland can claim to have repaid the debt in South Africa. I am thinking particularly of the Scots in the Orange Free State. Not only the younger Andrew Murray, but also the Robertsons, the Frasers, the McDonalds—families which have been called the Free State clans, who became burghers of the old Free State and whose descendants still play their part there.

But though I count myself a Scot, my mother was an American, and the United States provides a valuable illustration of one of the main points which I have been trying to make in my remarks today. Its population, like yours, is of different strains, and over the years most of those who have gone to North America have gone there in order to escape conditions in Europe which they found intolerable. The Pilgrim Fathers were fleeing from persecution as Puritans and the Marylanders from persecution as Roman Catholics. Throughout the nineteenth century a stream of immigrants flowed across the Atlantic to escape from the poverty in their homelands, and in the twentieth century the United States have provided asylum for the victims of political oppression in Europe.

Thus for the majority of its inhabitants America has been a place of refuge, or place to which people went because they wanted to get away from Europe. It is not surprising, therefore, that for many years a main objective of American statesmen, supported by the American public, was to isolate themselves from Europe, and with their great material strength, and the vast resources open to them, this might have seemed an attractive and practicable course. Nevertheless in the two world wars of this century they have found themselves unable to stand aside. Twice their manpower in arms has streamed back across the Atlantic to shed blood in those European struggles from which their ancestors thought they would escape by emigrating to the New World; and when the second war was over they were forced to recognise that in the small world of today isolationism is out of date and offers no assurance of security.

The fact is that in this modern world no country, not even the greatest, can live for itself alone. Nearly two thousand years ago, when the whole of the civilised world was comprised within the confines of the Roman Empire, St. Paul proclaimed one of the great truths of history—we are all members one of another. During this twentieth century that eternal truth has taken on a new and exciting significance. It has always been impossible for the individual man to live in isolation from his fellows, in the home, the tribe, the village, or the city. Today it is impossible for nations to live in isolation from one another. What Dr. John Donne said of individual men three hundred years ago is true today of my country, your country, and all the countries of the world:

> Any man's death diminishes me, because I am involved in Mankind. And therefore never send to know for whom the bell tolls; it tolls for thee.

All nations now are interdependent one upon another, and this is generally realised throughout the Western World. I hope in due course the countries of Communism will recognise it too.

It was certainly with that thought in mind that I took the decision to visit Moscow about this time last year. Russia has been isolationist in her time and still has tendencies that way, but the fact remains that we must live in the same world with Russia, and we must find a way of doing so. I believe that the initiative which we took last year has had some success, although grave difficulties may arise. Nevertheless I think nothing but good can come out of its extending contacts between individuals, contacts in trade and from the exchange of visitors.

I certainly do not believe in refusing to trade with people because you may happen to dislike the way they manage their internal affairs at home. Boycotts will never get you anywhere, and may I say in parenthesis that I deprecate the attempts that are being made today in Britain to organise the consumer boycott of South African goods. It has never been the practice, as far as I know, of any Government of the United Kingdom of whatever complexion to undertake or support campaigns of this kind designed to influence the internal politics of another Commonwealth country, and my colleagues in the United Kingdom deplore this proposed boycott and regard it as undesirable from every point of view. It can only have serious effects on Commonwealth relations, on trade, and lead to the ultimate detriment of others than those against whom it is aimed.

I said I was speaking of the interdependence of nations. The members of the Commonwealth feel particularly strongly the value of interdependence. They are as independent as any nation in this shrinking world can be, but they have voluntarily agreed to work together. They recognise that there may be and must be differences in their institutions; in their internal policies, and their membership does not imply the wish to express a judgement on these matters, or the need to impose a stifling uniformity. It is, I think, a help that there has never been question of any rigid constitution for the Commonwealth. Perhaps this is because we have got on well enough in the United Kingdom without a written constitution and tend to look suspiciously at them. Whether that is so or not, it is quite clear that a rigid constitutional framework for the Commonwealth would not work. At the first of the stresses and strains which are inevitable in this period of history, cracks would appear in the framework and the whole structure would crumble. It is the flexibility of our Commonwealth institutions which gives them their strength.

Mr. President, Mr. Speaker, Honourable Ministers, Ladies and Gentlemen, I fear I have kept you a long time. I much welcome the opportunity to speak to this great audience. In conclusion may I say this? I have spoken frankly about the differences between our two countries in their approach to one of the great current problems with which each has to deal within its own sphere of responsibility. These differences are well-known. They are matters of public knowledge, indeed of public controversy, and I should have been less than honest if by remaining silent on them I had seemed to imply that they did not exist. But differences on one subject, important though it is, need not and should not impair our capacity to co-operate with one another in furthering the many practical interests which we share in common.

The independent members of the Commonwealth do not always agree on every subject. It is not a condition of their association that they should do so. On the contrary, the strength of our Commonwealth lies largely in the fact that it is a free association of independent sovereign states, each responsible for ordering its own affairs but co-operating in the pursuit of common aims and purposes in world affairs. Moreover these differences may be transitory. In time they may be resolved. Our duty is to see them in perspective against the background of our long association. Of this at any rate I am certain—those of us who by grace of the electorate are temporarily in charge of affairs in your country and in mine, we fleeting transient phantoms on the great stage of history, we have no right to sweep aside on this account the friendship that exists between our countries, for that is the legacy of history. It is not ours alone to deal with as we wish. To adapt a famous phrase, it belongs to those who are living, but it also belongs to those who are dead and to those who are yet unborn. We must face the differences, but let us try to see beyond them down the long vista of the future.

I hope—indeed, I am confident—that in another fifty years we shall look back on the differences that exist between us now as matters of historical interest, for as time passes and one generation yields to another, human problems change and fade. Let us remember these truths. Let us resolve to build, not to destroy, and let us remember always that weakness comes from division, strength from unity.

Appendix Two

Letters from Harold Macmillan to the Queen during his African Tour, 1960

1   18 January 1960

Madam:

Mr. Macmillan with his humble duty to The Queen.

I am sending this letter by bag from Salisbury which we reached tonight, having completed the first two parts of our tour. I must express my regret for not having written previously to Your Majesty; but you will know from experience that these tours are arranged to be very exhausting and to fill up most of the available time.

Our reception in Ghana, contrary to some newspaper stories, was warm and friendly. As Prince Philip will know from his recent tour, the people are most warm-hearted and good-natured. I have no doubt that they are also mercurial and could be easily raised to a high pitch of excitement by suitable demagogues. Dr. Nkrumah continued to speak most loyally of his devotion to Your Majesty's person and Crown. This will however not prevent him from showing an equal if not greater interest in his own position. I fear, therefore, that the steps towards a new constitution and a President will undoubtedly be taken. Nevertheless, the Republic will as a whole be loyal to Your Majesty and there should be no difficulty about their acceptance of Your Majesty as Head of the Commonwealth. Naturally I am a little concerned at the tendency towards personal Government which Dr. Nkrumah shows; and we do not yet know the precise form of the new constitution. It will, however, so he tells me, be submitted to a referendum of the people. Dr. Nkrumah did not object to my seeing members of the Opposition, after I had made it clear that it was my wish to do so, and that it was the common practice in the Commonwealth. We must not exaggerate the tendencies towards an authoritarian régime. There are a great number of checks which operate both politically and economically. Nor must we be surprised if in the first few years of Independence these new Commonwealth States are subjected to some of the pressures and difficulties which we have undergone through many centuries of our history. Meanwhile, the economic progress in Ghana is quite remarkable; as no doubt Prince Philip will have told Your Majesty. The opportunities for British trade seem to me to be excellent, and the relationship between our traders and the bulk of the people is well established upon a sound foundation of respect and understanding. This especially applies to the older companies, but many new firms are making a start. Your Majesty's Governor-General, Lord Listowel, and his wife entertained us very hospitably and made us very comfortable. I think his tenure of this post in a position of some delicacy has been very successful. It could have been easy to quarrel with Dr. Nkrumah. But on the contrary he has the Prime Minister's confidence and respect.

The second week we have spent in Nigeria, a large country with a large population. All the ceremonial part of the visit went off very well. Your Majesty has in Sir James Robertson a man of outstanding character who has steered the Nigerian people through these difficult and formative years with marked success.

Nigeria, with its population of thirty-five million people and its area four times the size of Great Britain, naturally looks at Ghana with a mixture of jealousy and contempt—jealousy at their having reached the goal a little earlier, but contempt for what they regard as their unwarranted attempt to lead the continent of Africa. The Eastern and Western Regions of Nigeria struck me as not dissimilar to the coast people of the old Gold Coast Colony. When, of course, you get to the North there is an entirely different people and civilisation. It is more like Arabia, and dominated by the Moslem tradition. The Premier is a great character—a local swell—who entertained Their Royal Highnesses The Duke and Duchess of Gloucester on their visit a short time ago. Perhaps Your Majesty may have seen a film of the Durbar at Kaduna. The Sardauna of Sokoto (who struck me as not unlike Trollope's Duke of Omnium) combines being a great noble and a skilful politician. He specially asked that his loyal duty be sent to Your Majesty.

In all the extraordinary and rapid changes which have taken place in these two countries, Ghana and Nigeria, the outstanding feature is the devotion of many men and women from the highest to the humblest ranks of Your Majesty's British Dominions serving in the Civil Service, in Missions and in trade, who have done so much to make possible the great progress of the last fifty years. Certainly what I saw is a tribute, not a condemnation, of Colonial administration.

I trust Your Majesty remains in good health. I will try to send Your Majesty some further thoughts after our visit to the Federation. Here we expect to find a good many difficulties, but I am not without hope that our visit can be of use.

> With my humble duty,
> I remain,
> Your Majesty's faithful
> and devoted servant,
> Harold Macmillan

2   31 January 1960

Madam:

Mr. Macmillan with his humble duty to The Queen.

I was very grateful for the letter which I received from Sir Michael Adeane expressing Your Majesty's thoughts about my letter describing the situation in Ghana and Nigeria. Since then we have completed our visit to the Federation and are now in Pretoria.

As I expected, the visit to the Federation was both trying physically and involved a good many political difficulties. So far as the immediate situation is concerned, I am happy to say that I was able to get on good terms with Sir Roy Welensky, who is always much easier to deal with face to face than by telegram. I also found Sir Edgar Whitehead very reasonable. The night before I left I dined alone with these two, with Lord Malvern as the additional guest.

I am bound to tell Your Majesty that I was impressed by the extreme difficulty presented by the Federation. To combine countries in wholly different states of advance is not an easy thing—and indeed is rather an unnatural thing. The founders gave great weight to the economic advantages, which are of course overwhelming. But in the present emotional state of African opinion these arguments do not carry great weight.

In spite of all the difficulties I think the Monckton Commission will be allowed to get on with its job, and no doubt the advice which they give us will be of great help. Without such preparatory work I do not see how we could have faced the negotiation between the five Governments at the end of this year. On the other hand, there is a danger that the visit of Monckton and his team will inflame again all sorts of arguments which it would be better to allow to die down.

I am particularly anxious about the situation in Nyasaland. There the white population is small and anxious, and the Administration struck me as tired—from the Governor downwards. To govern a modern Colonial territory while looking over your shoulder every morning and evening at the Questions in the House of Commons must be an almost impossible burden upon our officials. It takes a very great man to overcome these difficulties.

If I am able to keep to my plan of returning some of the way home by boat I hope to spend a few days of leisure in trying to collect my impressions into some coherent form. At present, I must frankly tell Your Majesty, I find myself with a great deal of evidence but still a long way from disentangling the plot.

I hope that Your Majesty is in good health and I venture to send my most loyal good wishes.

> With my humble duty,
> I remain,
> Your Majesty's faithful
> and devoted servant,
> Harold Macmillan

3 *Extract*   3 April 1960

In my absence, although not without frequent communication with me by telegram, my colleagues had to make a decision about the question of the discussion of South African affairs in the Security Council of the United Nations. The dilemma is easy to state, but difficult to escape. If we rest too much upon the legal and constitutional position, we shall certainly please the old Commonwealth countries like Australia and of course South Africa itself, but we risk gravely offending the Asian and African members. I was rather alarmed to see Sir James Robertson's report of the feeling in Nigeria.

It seemed to us best, therefore, while pointing out that discussion, and still more the passing of Resolutions, was contrary to the Charter, not to vote against either inscription of the item or the Resolution which ultimately came out of the discussion. . . . I hope therefore that the South African Government, in spite of their strong feelings in this matter, may feel that on the whole we have done the best thing, even from their point of view.

However, more important than resolutions in New York is the reality of the situation in South Africa. The rigidity, and even fanaticism, with which the Nationalist Government in South Africa have pursued the apartheid policy have brought about—as I feared when I was there—a dangerous, even ominous, situation in that country. How it will all end we cannot tell.

Meanwhile, I fear that I must warn Your Majesty that I see a very difficult period facing the Commonwealth.

I am not anxious about the pressure of public opinion at home, whether in or outside Parliament. We have the strength, I think, to hold to whatever course we think right. I feel my supreme task is to try to steer the Commonwealth through this crisis and to avoid anything in the nature of disintegration. After all, the South African Government will not last for ever, and if we can only keep everybody in the team time will perhaps prove a healing factor.

The negotiations on Cyprus are dragging on, but I am still hopeful that after all his bargaining and his bluff the Archbishop will agree to a reasonable settlement. The Defence authorities have been most helpful in all this and I must pay them a great tribute.

Your Majesty will have seen that Dr. Banda was released in accordance with the plan agreed between Lord Home and Sir Roy Welensky. It is very satisfactory that he should come to this country and perhaps this may mean that the fears of violence and disorder in Nyasaland will prove exaggerated, at any rate for the present. The trouble will come when the extremists fail to obtain their demands. Although the public in the Federation, and especially in Southern Rhodesia, are certainly alarmed, both by the constitutional advance in Kenya and by the disorders in the Union, it is just possible that the European population in Rhodesia will learn the lesson in time.

Index